Art and History of Pompeii

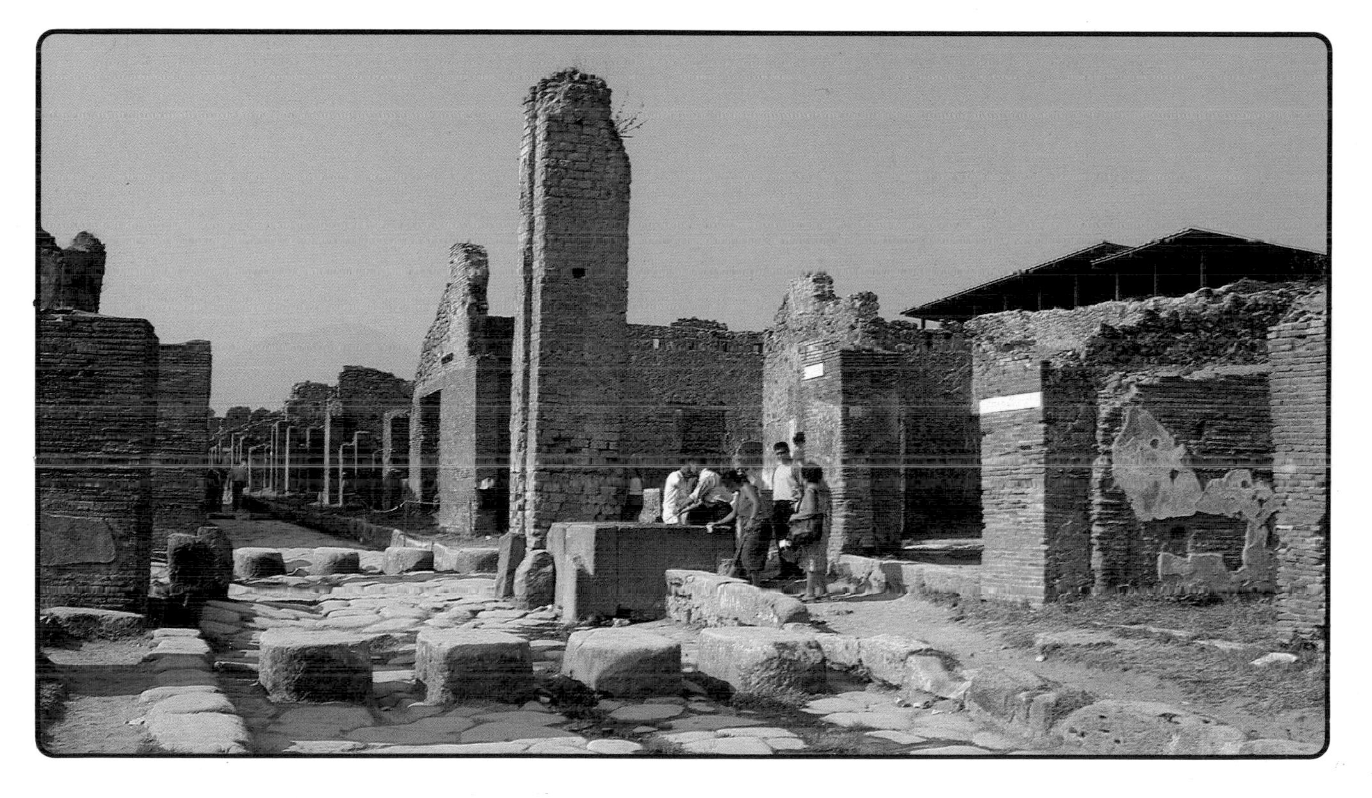

170 COLOR PHOTOGRAPHS
20 RECONSTRUCTIONS OF THE CITY
AS IT WAS 2000 YEARS AGO

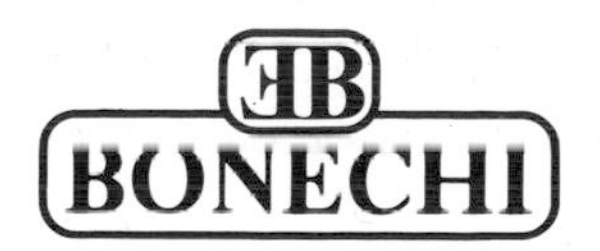

VISIT OF THE EXCAVATIONS

Entrance to the archaeological area of Pompeii is from Porta Marina or Piazza Anfiteatro. To help the visitor, this booklet has divided the city into four zones, beginning at Porta Marina (zone I) which is the usual entrance. However, visitors who enter from Piazza Anfiteatro can begin with zone II.

The visit of the entire complex requires at least one day. For those whose time is limited, three itineraries are indicated below, all starting at Porta Marina and with numbers that refer to the buildings to be visited.

This publication, off the press in March of 1989, also includes various monuments and houses which were damaged in the earthquake of 1980 and cannot be visited inside, but even a glance at the exterior is enough to stimulate our fantasy. We hope that in the meantime some of these structures will once more have been opened to the public.

2 hours: 1 - 4 - 5 - 6 - 7 - 8 - 9 - 10 - 11 - 36 - 46 - 48 - 49 - 51.

3 hours: 1 - 4 - 5 - 6 - 7 - 8 - 9 - 10 - 11 - 15 - 16 - 18 - 19 - 36 - 46 - 48 - 49 - 50 - 51 - 52 - 53.

4 hours: 1 - 4 - 5 - 6 - 7 - 8 - 9 - 10 - 11 - 15 - 16 - 18 - 19 - 30 - 31 - 32 - 33 - 34 - 35 - 36 - 46 - 48 - 49 - 50 - 51 - 52 - 53.

Printed in Italy by
Centro Stampa Editoriale Bonechi.

ISBN 88-7009-454-5

Text: Stefano Giuntoli.
Translation: Erika Pauli for Studio Comunicare, Florence
Cartography: Studio Bellandi — Giovannini — Mariani
Reconstruction: Stefano Benini
Editing: Maurizio Martinelli
Layout: Susanna Cagnacci

The photographs are the property of the Archives of the Casa Editrice Bonechi and were taken by:
Archivio Fotografico dell'Osservatorio Vesuviano - Foto Antonio Biasucci, Gianni Dagli Orti, Paolo Giambone, Cesare Tonini.

* * *

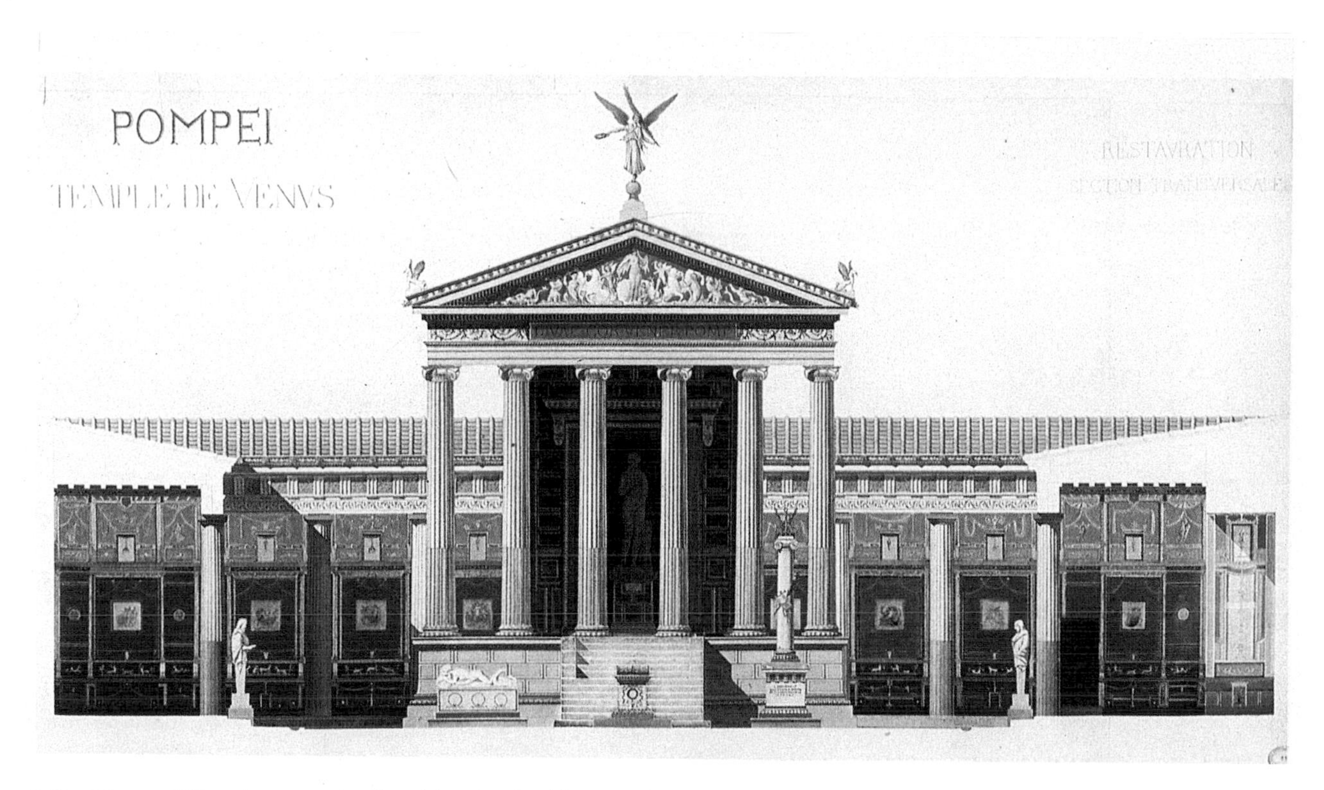

In the picture, a 19th-century reconstruction of the Temple of Venus in Pompeii.

INTRODUCTION

HISTORICAL SURVEY

*It is difficult to say just how large any protohistoric settlement on the ridge of lava where Pompeii was to rise may have been. Not enough has been found in the way of pottery that can be referred to the inhumation culture of the Iron age pit tombs (*a fossa, *9th-7th cent. B.C.), but in any case the lack of water here makes it unlikely that an inhabited center of any size existed before the middle of the 7th cent. B.C.*

In the course of the 8th cent. B.C. Greek (Ischia and Cumae) and Etruscan colonization (Capua) in the territory of Campania stimulated the development of Pompeii as a city around the area of the Forum. A point of encounter for important trade routes, it became a clearing station for traffic towards the hinterland. Up until about the middle of the 5th cent. B.C. the city was dominated politically by the Etruscans, whose presence is verified by the finds of bucchero with Etruscan inscriptions. In the course of the 6th cent. B.C. the influence of the Greek culture is also documented by the terracottas which decorated the Temple of Apollo, by important ceramics and architectural elements that were part of the so-called Doric Temple. During the 5th cent. B.C., after the defeat of the Etruscans by the Greeks of Cumae and the Syracusans in the battle of Cumae in 474, the entire fertile Campanian countryside was occupied by Samnite peoples from the mountain hinterlands, both as a result of military operations and through a slow gradual penetration and assimilation with the local population. This was probably when Pompeii spread out over the entire lava ridge and was surrounded by walls.

It was in the 4th cent. B.C. that Pompeii began its great urban expansion along a grid layout, and the buildings began to be constructed in limestone. A new series of conflicts broke out in that same century between the Samnites who had become city dwellers and new waves of Samnite peoples from the mountains. The intervention of Rome played a determining role and at the end of these struggles, known as Samnite wars (343-290 B.C.), Rome

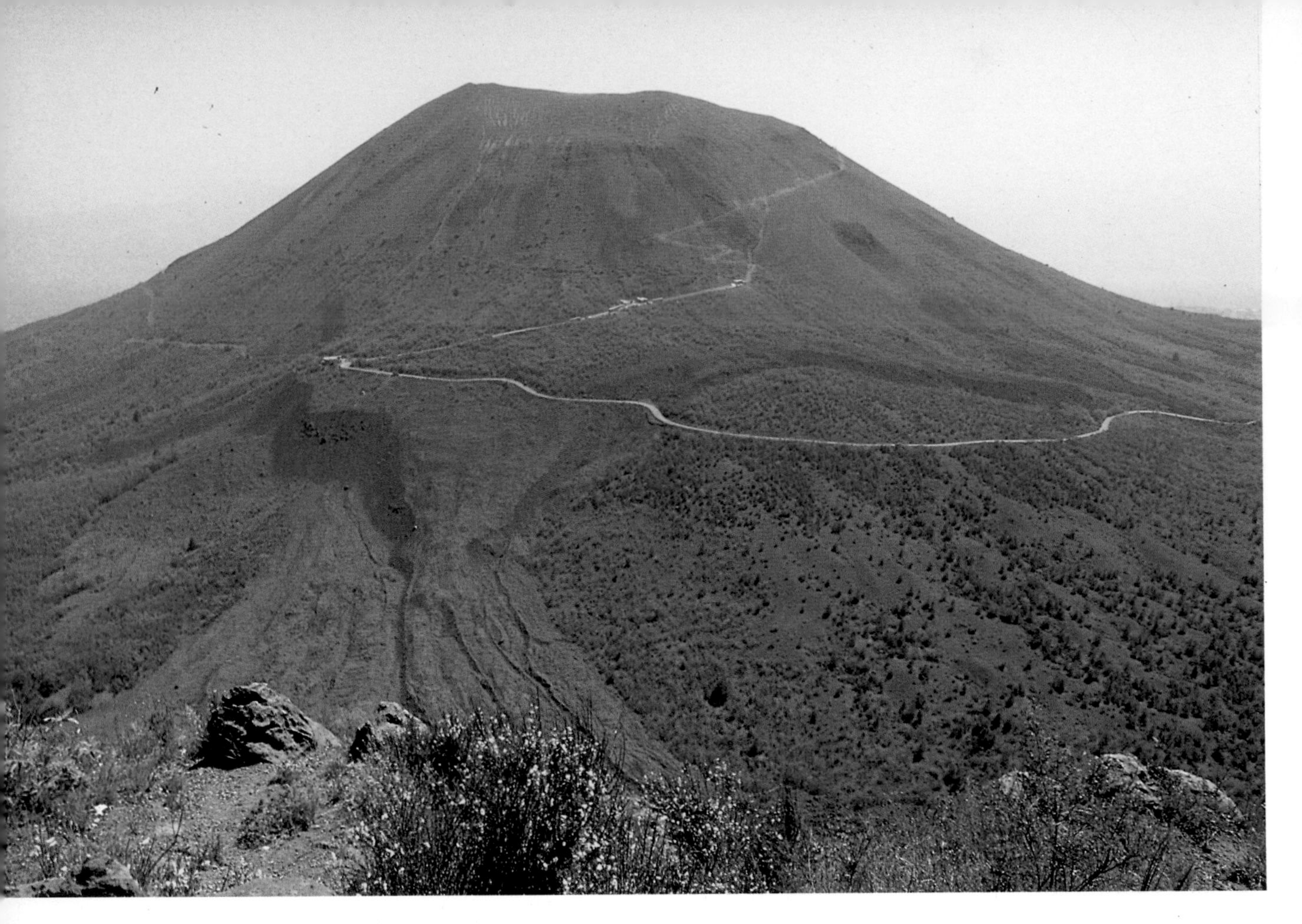

A view of Vesuvius, which erupted in A.D. 79 and buried Pompeii. Opposite: a reconstructed model of the Temple of Bacchus, situated outside the urban area of Pompeii.

dominated all of Campania. The part played by Pompeii was minor, both here and in the war with Hannibal (218-201 B.C.). In fact, while victorious Rome subjected most of the Campanian cities which had sided with Hannibal to heavy sanctions and deprived them of their liberty, the position of Pompeii was not particularly unfavorable. To the contrary, with the dominion of Rome over the Mediterranean, merchandise moved more freely and in the course of the 2nd cent. B.C. the city's economic growth accellerated, particularly with the production and exportation of wine and oil. This state of well-being was reflected in the spurt in public and private building: in this period the Temple of Jupiter and the Basilica were built in the area of the Forum, which, together with the Triangular Forum, was restructured, while in the field of private undertakings a patrician dwelling such as the House of the Faun competes both in size and magnificence with the dynastic palaces of the Hellenistic East. Pompeii sided with the Italic allies in the battle for the right to Roman citizenship which led to the Social Wars (90-89 B.C.).

In 89 B.C. the city was besieged by Sulla and conquered without particular consequences. It was transformed into a municipium *and governed by the magistrature of the* quattuorviri *between 89 and 80 B.C., when it was turned into a military colony named Cornelia Veneria Pompeianorum by Publius Cornelius Sulla, nephew of the dictator. This was when the* ordo decurionum, *or local senate was formed, through the admission of pro-Sullan elements to whom the principal magistratures were also entrusted. Economically the city continued to flourish and new important public buildings, such as the Amphitheater and the Odeion, were created.*

The Imperial period opened with the entrance into Pompeii of new families favorable to Augustus and a wholehearted adhesion to the new political ideology manifested in a propagandistic public building program, such as the Building of Eumachia and the Temple of the Fortuna Augusta. After an obscure period of political crises under Claudius, the situation was fully normalized under Nero. It was under his reign, in A.D. 59, that the bloody riots in the Amphitheater between Pompeians and Nucerians took place. In A.D. 62 a disastrous earthquake heavily damaged the buildings in the city. The following years were dedicated to the challenging job of rebuilding, which was still in progress when Pompeii was completely buried under a dense hail of volcanic cinders and ash in the fatal eruption of Vesuvius on August 24, 79 A.D. A moving eyewitness account of the tragedy has been left us in two letters sent to Tacitus by Pliny the Younger.

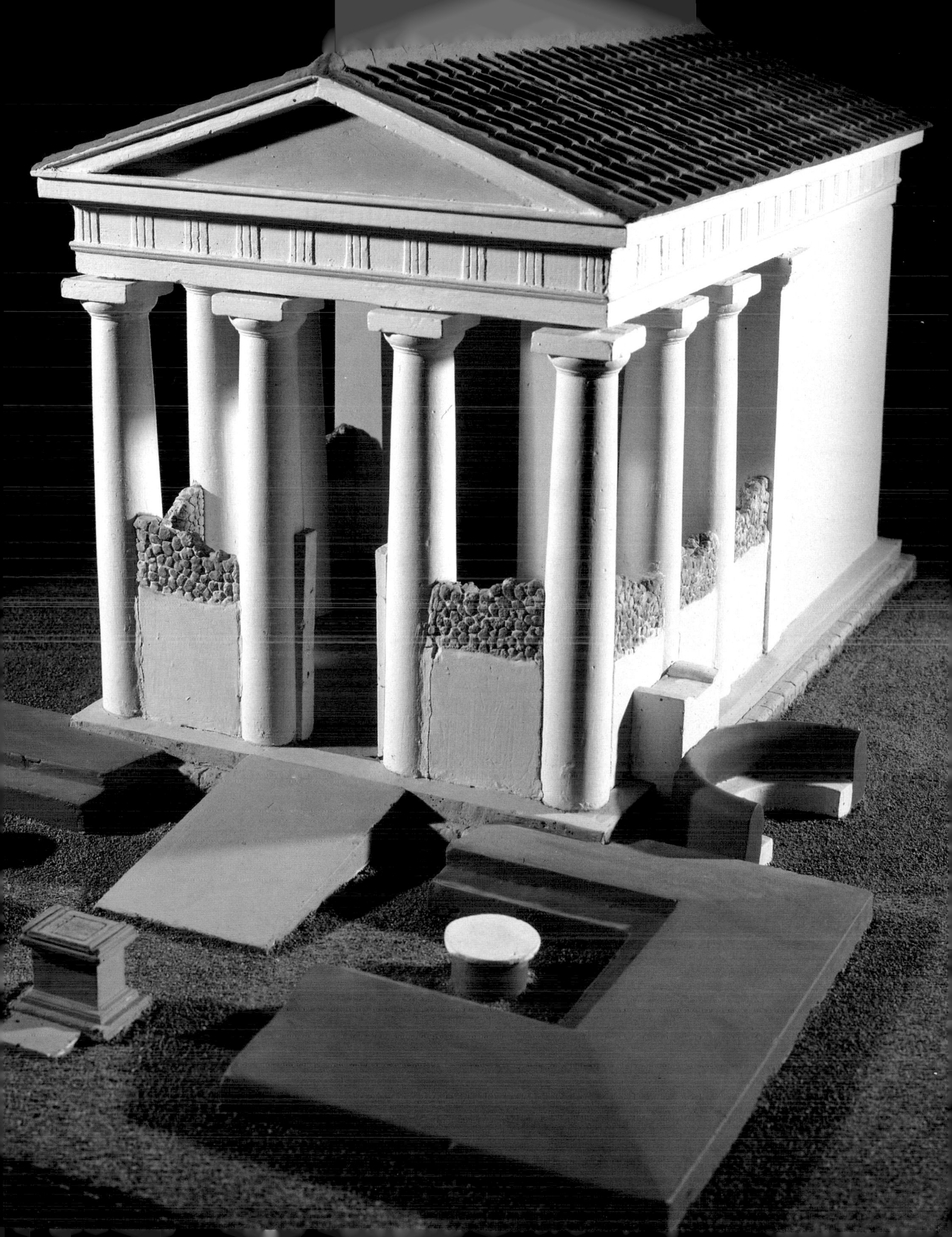

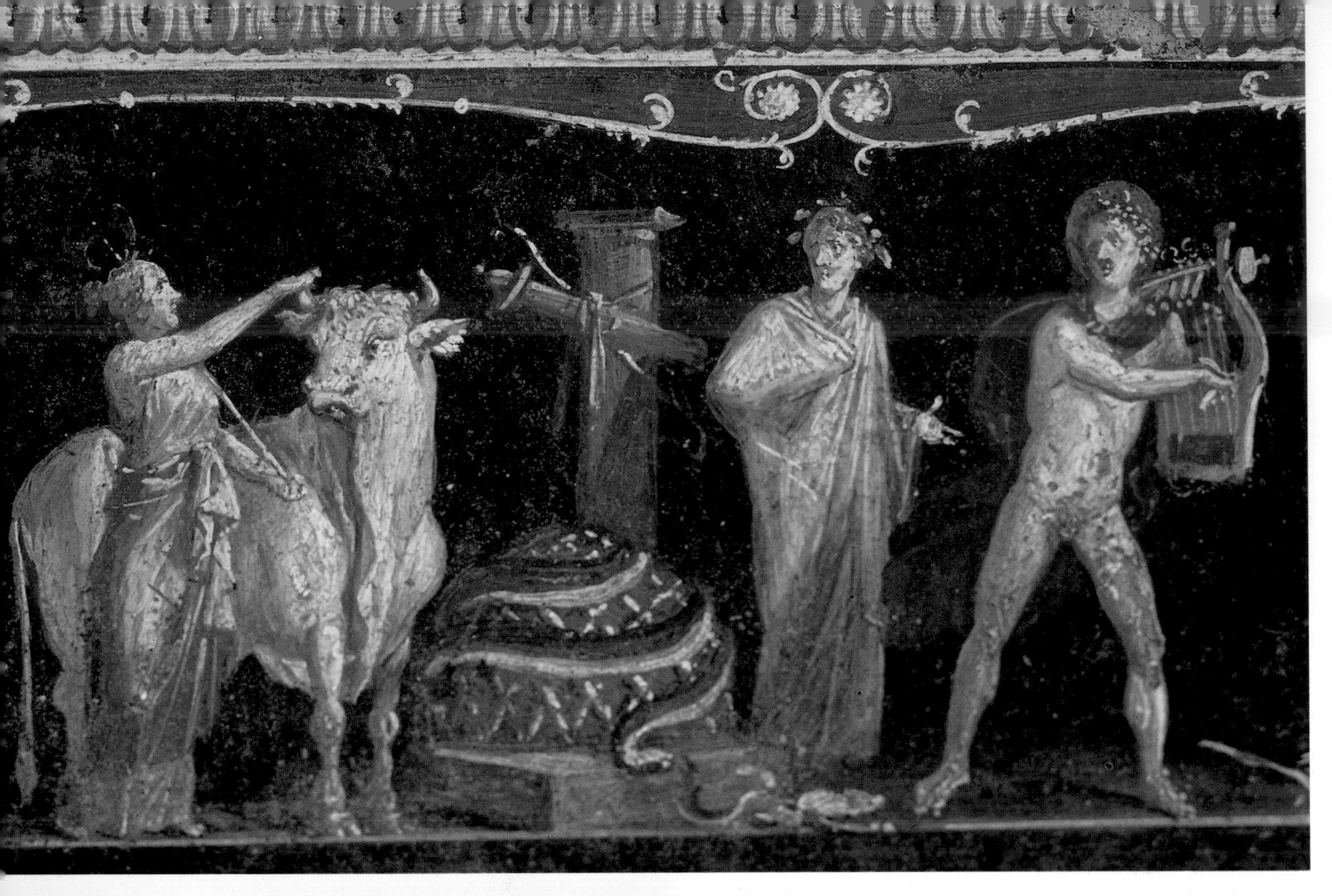

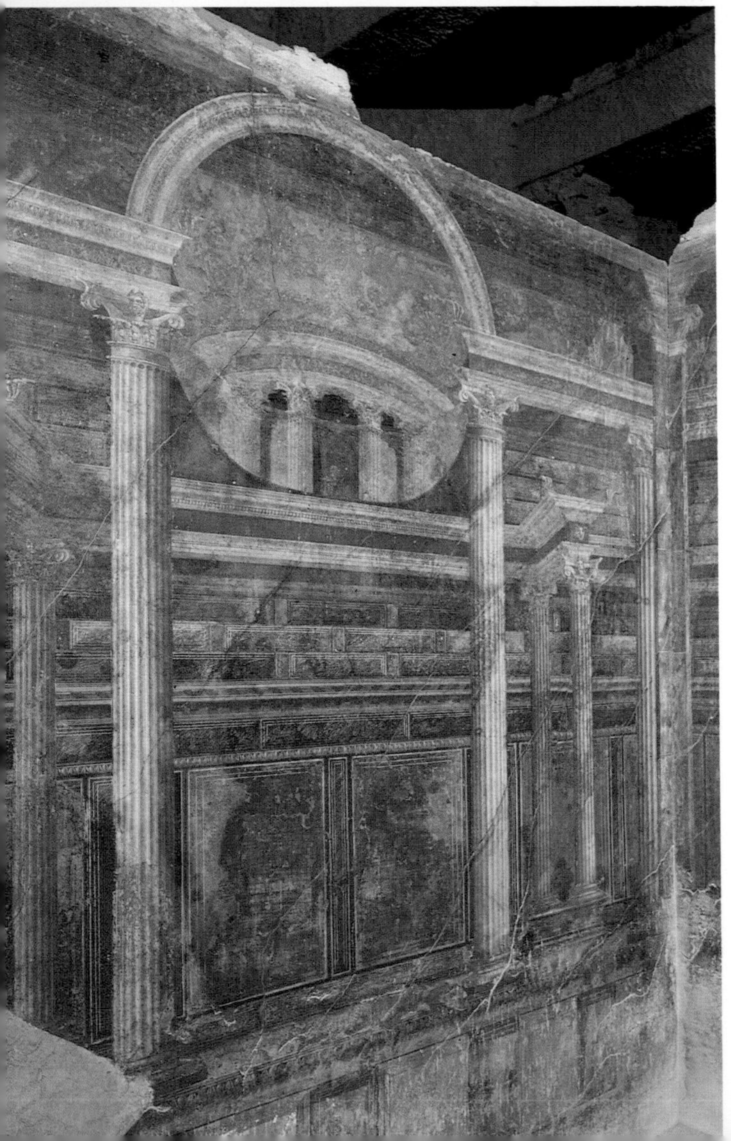

Above: the Style IV fresco inside the House of the Vettii, depicting Apollo overcoming the Python. Left: detail of a room decorated with Style II simulated architecture.

THE STYLES OF PAINTING

Style I *(or "incrustation") spread through the Roman world in the 2nd cent. B.C. when it became fashionable to paint the inner walls of private dwellings as well as of public and religious buildings. This decorative mode was of Greek derivation, directly inspired by the isodomic masonry technique of 6th and 5th cent. B.C. architecture, and used polychrome stucco to reproduce the projecting elements such as the dado, the middle zone in large panels, the upper zone in smaller panels, the cornices, and sometimes the pilasters which articulate the walls vertically. The lively color contrasts are no more than a translation into the pictorial idiom of the Hellenistic innovation of employing various types and colors of marble, in the realization of the single elements.*

Style II *(or "architectural") became popular in the years when Sulla's military colony was established (80 B.C.). The decoration on the walls proposed perspective views with architectural elements illusionistically articulated on different planes with foreshortenings and complex perspective effects which culminated in breaking through the wall towards an imaginary open space. The immediate models were the illusionistic stage sets of the Hellenistic-Roman theater and the new "baroque" fashions of 2nd-1st cent. B.C. architecture.*

Style III *(or "ornamental") was a reaction to the baroque solutions of the illusionism of Style II, together with the*

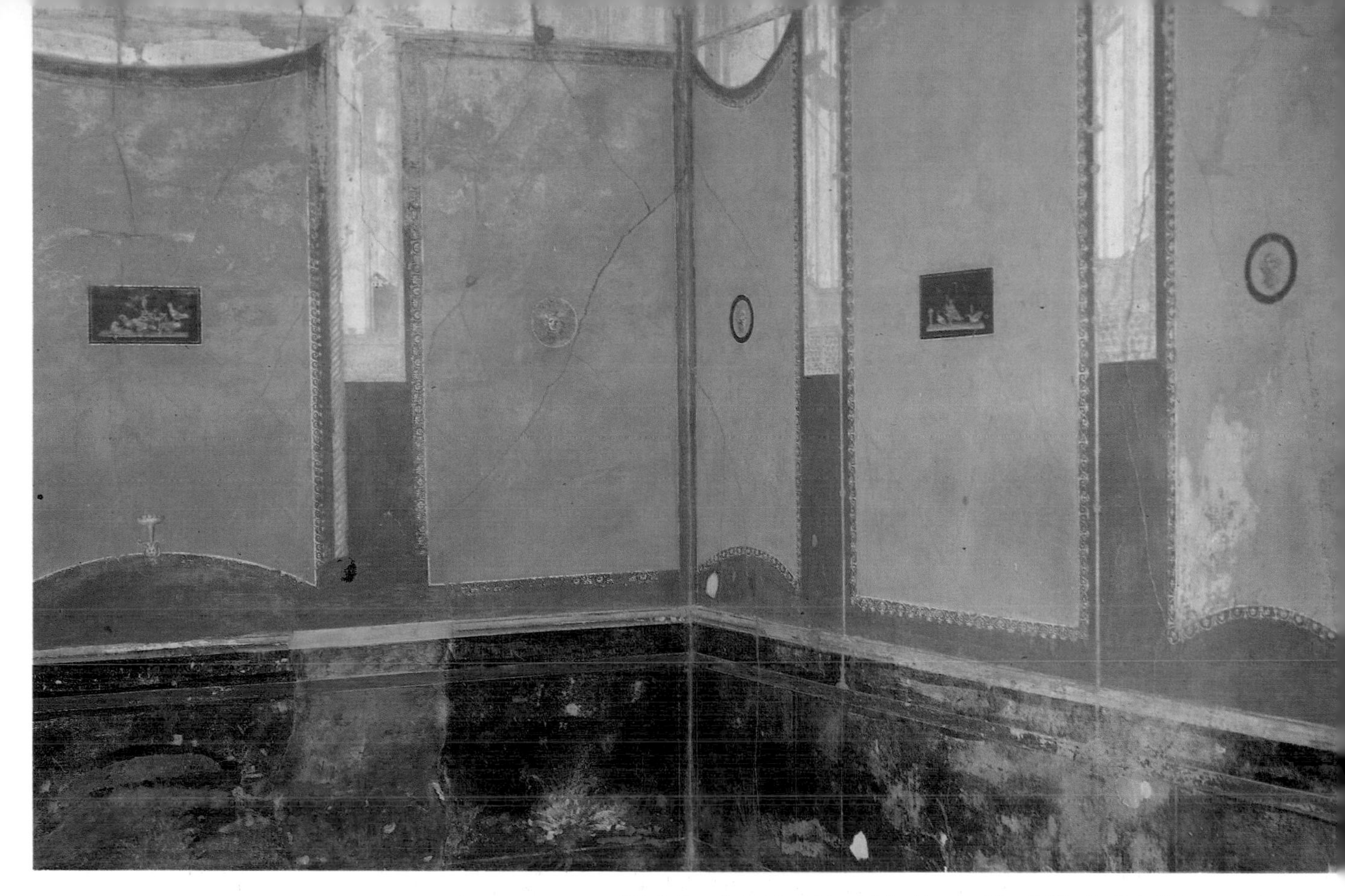

Above: the wing of the atrium of the House of the Vettii with Style III frescoes.

preference for academic classicism typical of the art of the Augustan period. The walls are once more simple flat surfaces which mark the boundaries of an enclosed space and are subdivided horizontally and vertically into monochrome areas articulated by slender architectural and decorative elements. The focal point is a painting in the center, generally of mythological, religious or idyllic subject, set inside an aedicule flanked by panels with small scenes suspended in the center which depict miniature figures and landscapes; in the upper zone slight perspective architectural elements in the manner of Style II occasionally survive. Worthy of note are the frequent use of Egyptian-style decorative elements and the appearance of an impressionistic technique typical of Alexandrine "impressionistic" painting, which in a certain sense contrasts and enlivens the sober balanced classicism of Style III.

***Style IV**, which became popular in the period of Claudius and Nero, exhibits the typical eclecticism of Roman art in its broad variety of decorative schemes inspired by both Style II and Style III. The colors are more decided and tend to contrasting lively color effects, the decorative elements multiply and crowd together, alternating with illusionistic architectural views and pictures of mythological subjects often painted in the impressionistic technique. A particular type is that of suspended carpets with small pictures and figures in the center, inspired by the Hellenistic fashion of hanging decorative tapestries on the walls.*

DOMESTIC ARCHITECTURE

Pompeii, thanks to the exceptional completeness of archaeological documentation, provides a fairly exhaustive picture of the evolution of domestic architecture of the "Italic" type, both as regards upper class houses as well as the more modest dwellings. The basic nucleus for all further development was the atrium house, of which one of the oldest and most important examples in Pompeii is the House of the Surgeon dating to the 4th cent. B.C. Domestic life revolved around the atrium which had two basic functions: it provided light for the house, which was conceived of as a closed organism with high enclosing walls, through an opening in the roof, and it collected rain water in an impluvial basin at the center of the floor under this opening, from whence the water was carried off into a cistern. The lararium *for the tutelary gods of the household was in the atrium and in the earlier examples the kitchen with the hearth, around which the family consumed its meals, was also there. A short corridor (*fauces*) led to the atrium around which there was a series of small rooms which served as bedrooms (*cubicula*), as well as two open areas at the ends of the side walls, used for the ancestor cult (*alae*). The back wall was occupied by the* tablinum, *a room originally used as bedroom for the husband and wife and later transformed into a dining room or reception hall. Next to it was a corridor which led to the* hortus, *a small garden enclosed by a high wall.*

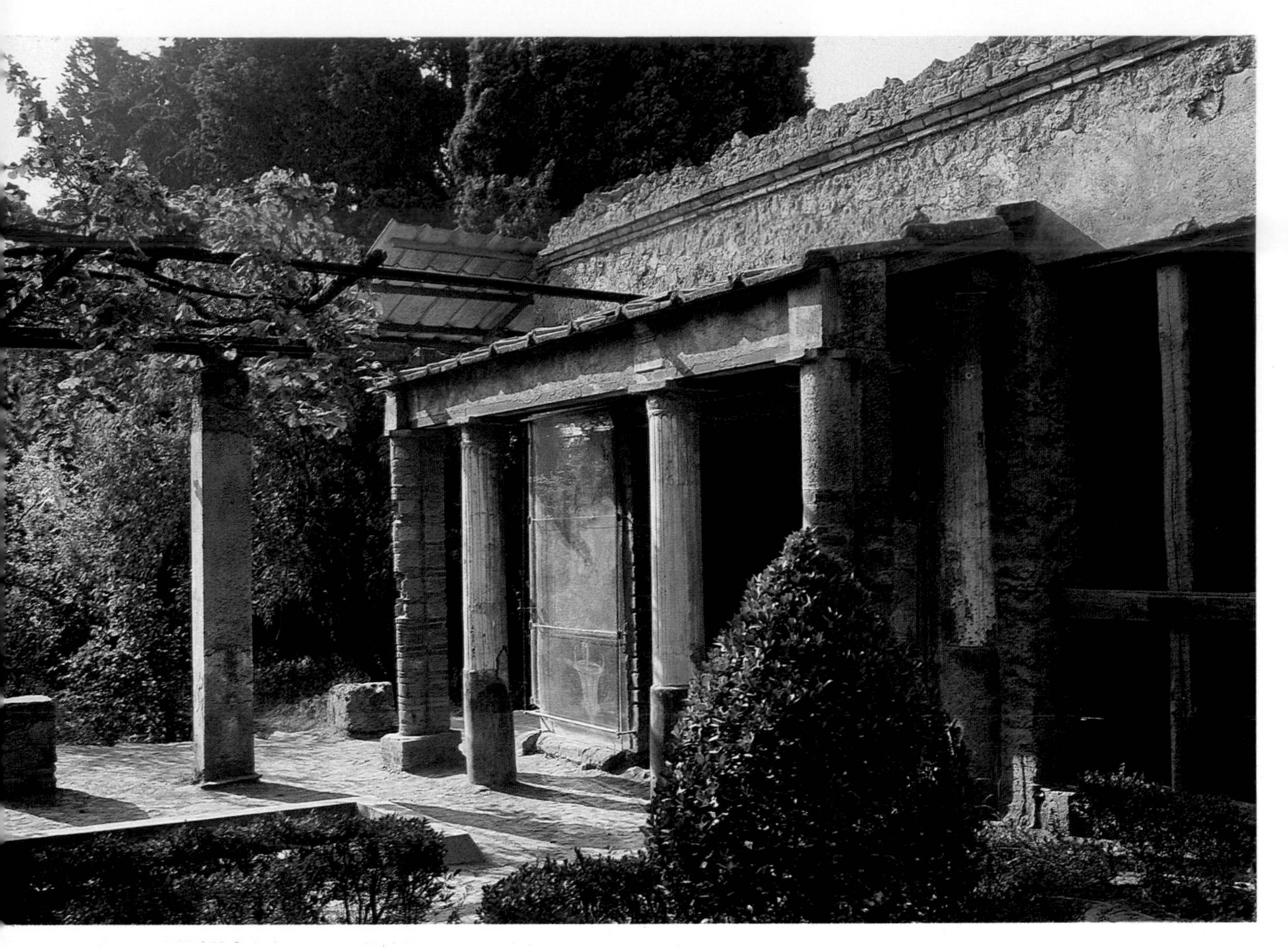

Above: the small entrance portico to the presumed shrine of Isis inside the House of Octavius Quartio.

In the 2nd cent. B.C., after Rome's conquests in the East, the influence of Hellenistic architecture led to the fusion, in the ambience of the patrician dwelling, of the atrium house with the Greek type centered around the peristyle, a courtyard garden, often with basins, surrounded by a columned portico off which the various rooms opened. Another element adopted at this time by the Italic house was the triclinium, *a dining room generally situated next to the* tablinum *and with three convivial couches from which meals were taken in a reclining position in Greek style. The introduction of the peristyle in place of the original* hortus *led to the development of other rooms for daily use (*diaetae*) and reception (*oeci*) next to it, as well as occasionally the creation of baths. As time passed the layout of the various elements became more complex. A particularly significant example is the imposing House of the Faun.*
The houses of the lower classes of small shopkeepers, artisans, freedmen, were much smaller and simpler in plan. Often they were lined up in a single large building with the various entrances on the facade. Inside, the various rooms were articulated around a covered atrium without an impluvium *(*atrium testudinatum*), with a first floor facing onto it, used for the bedrooms. The increase in population in Pompeii in Imperial times meant that housing was in great demand and as a result apartment houses of as many as three floors were built.*
The shops, workshops, laboratories, of which Pompeii furnishes us with an exceedingly vivid and significant picture, were often part and parcel of the owner's living quarters, which were behind the shop or on the floors above.
It was also fairly frequent to find shops set up in rooms that opened off on either side of the entrance to an upper class dwelling and which were rented out by the owners of the house.

MOSAICS

The oldest type of decorated pavement is the opus signinum, *well represented in pre-Sullan Pompeii. This type of pavement consists of fragments of bricks and potsherds set into a layer of lime, in which white tesserae of "palombino" were sometimes inserted to create a regular dot effect or a carpet of geometric pattern. At the same time the* emblemata *made their appearance - small pictures set at the center of the pavement and depicting scenes that were inspired by the models of great Greek painting. In Sulla's time the mosaics reflected the taste for the schemes of Style II wall painting, with illusionistic perspectives in boxes made of tesserae that became gradually lighter in color and with patterns of rhombs with borders of cubes and perspective meanders. Toward the end of the republican period simpler black and white mosaics became popular. They had geometric decorations and figures, surrounded by borders of wave meanders, dentate bands, checkerwork. Sober geometric mosaics also characterize the period of the early empire; with the Claudio-Neronian period there is an increase in traditional ornamental elements which crowd the composition, while the figured mosaics reflect the luminarist acquisitions that had been experimented in contemporary Style IV painting.*

SCULPTURE

The sculpture found in Pompeii generally falls into a category of artisan production that satisfied requests of a decorative, celebrative-political, religious, and sepulchral nature.

Pompeii was after all a provincial city, where the clients were prevalently middle class and there was no particular demand for real works of art.

This explains the essentially "practical" nature of Pompeian sculpture which consisted primarily of small-size statues although there were also figures that were larger than life such as some of the examples from the Temple of Jupiter. Copies of famous works, such as that of the Doryphorous, are extremely rare. A variety of materials was used for the sculpture: marble, tufa, limestone, terra cotta, bronze.

The discovery of fragments from various statues as well as famous pieces such as Apollo playing the lyre, the so-called Caligula on horseback, Apollo and Artemis archers, show that bronze was more common than previously thought.

Portraiture appeared after the establishment of Sulla's colony, initially in the field of funerary and honorary sculpture, and then, after the empire, with the representations of the various members of the imperial family.

Below: the elegant mosaic in chiaroscuro, depicting two tragic masks and garlands, found in the House of the Faun and now in the Museo Nazionale in Naples.

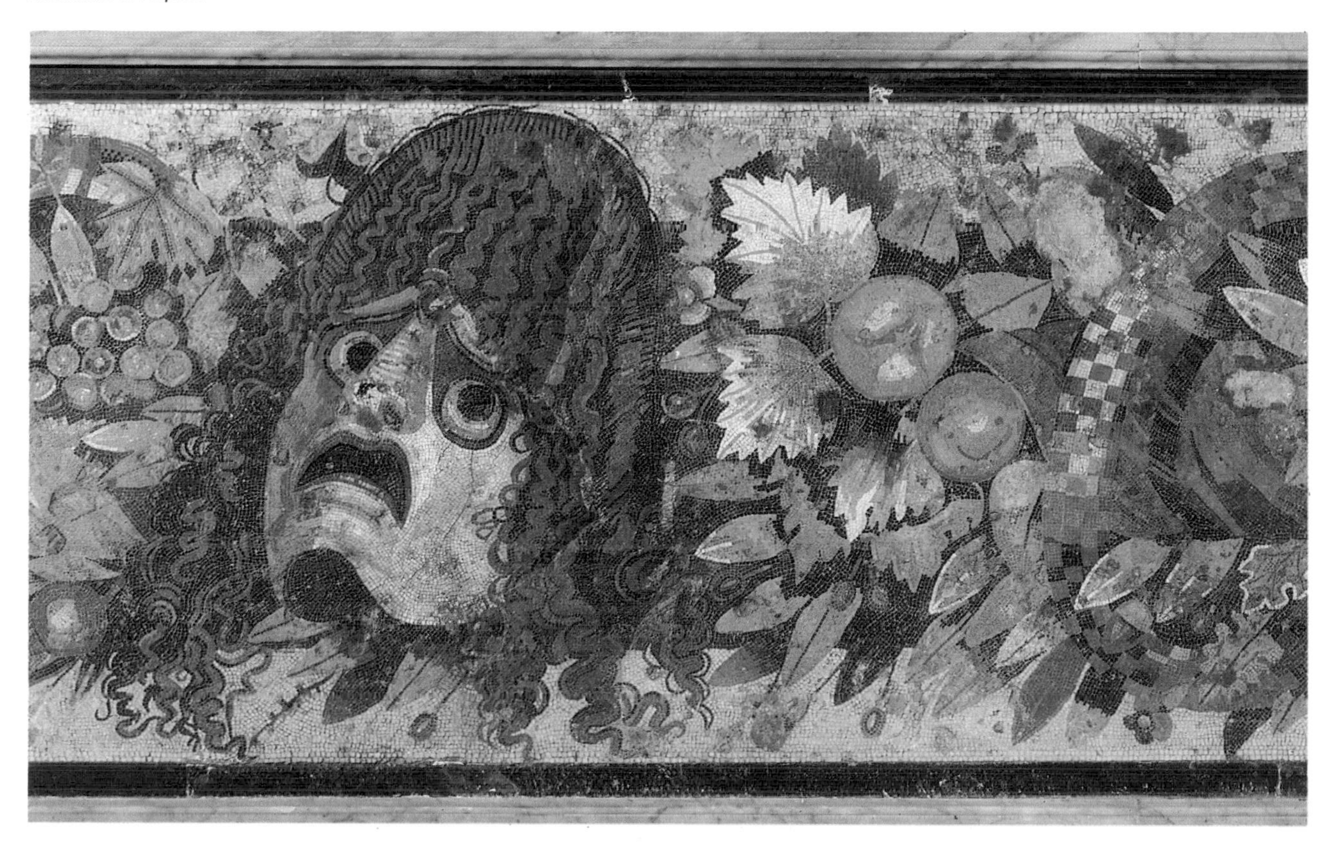

I PART

Porta Marina - Suburban Villa - Antiquarium - Temple of Apollo - Basilica - Forum - Public Buildings on the South Side of the Forum - Building of Eumachia - Temple of Vespasian - Sanctuary of the Lares Publici - Macellum - Temple of Jupiter - Arches on the North Side of the Forum - Horrea or Forum Olitorium

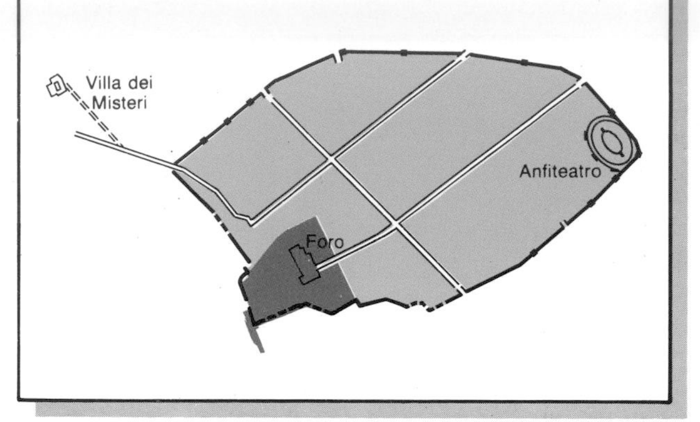

1 - PORTA MARINA

As the name indicates, this was the gate facing the sea, set in the western side of the hill on which the town rose. It is the most recent of Pompeii's city gates, built in *opus incertum* in lava stone. It consists of two passageways with barrel vaults, one meant for pedestrians and one for vehicles and animals.
Later these two passageways were joined at the back in a single vaulted gallery, which is what we see today.
In the 1st cent. B.C. various villas were built near the city walls on this side with its magnificent panorama of the coast.

2 - SUBURBAN VILLA

This villa near the Porta Marina was discovered after the bombardment of 1943. It dates to the Imperial period and is set against the outer side of the city walls, whose function had changed with the *pax augustea* and from here it enjoyed a marvelous view of the sea. The building

The two vaulted passageways of the Porta Marina, for pedestrians and for vehicles.

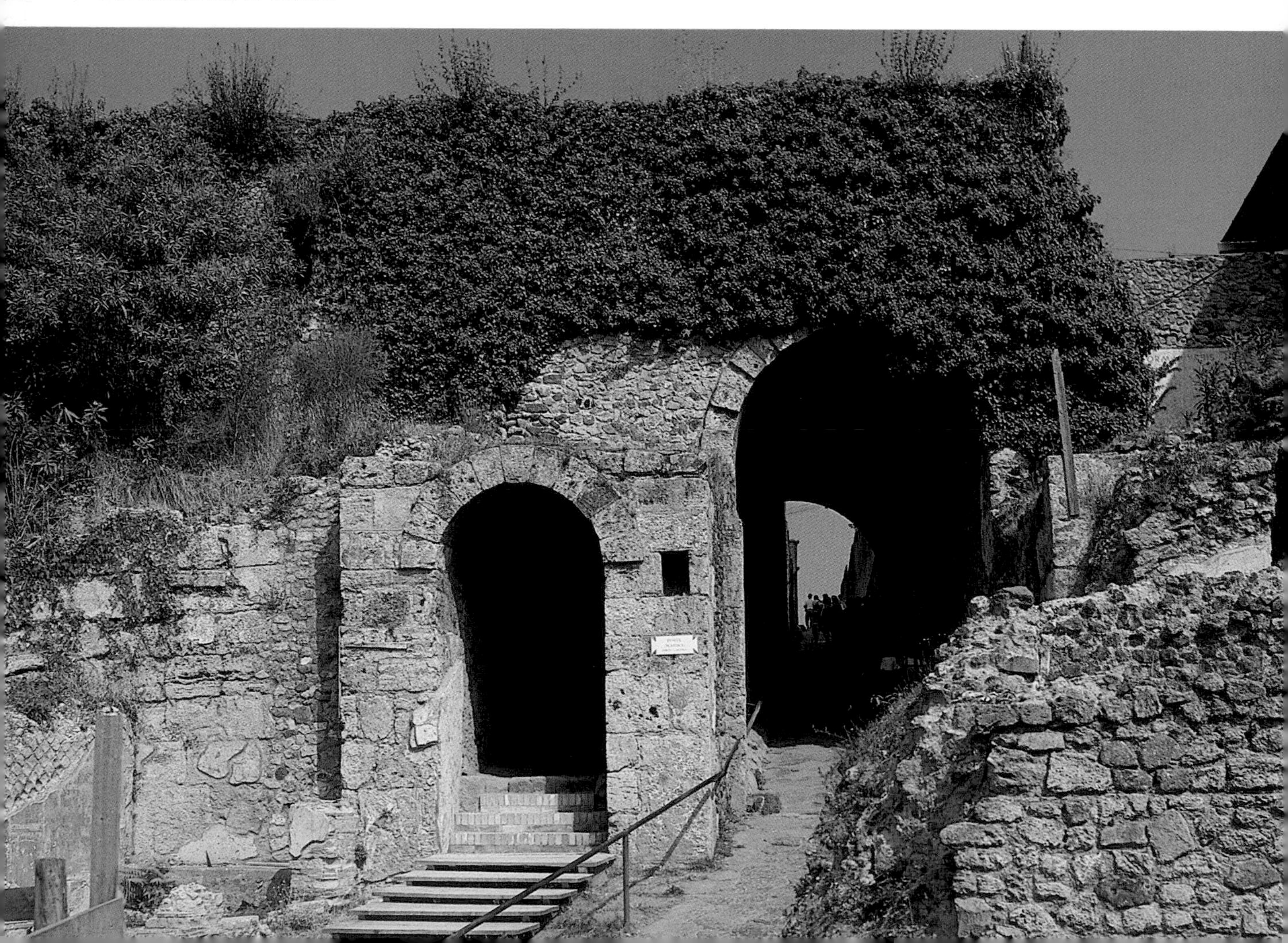

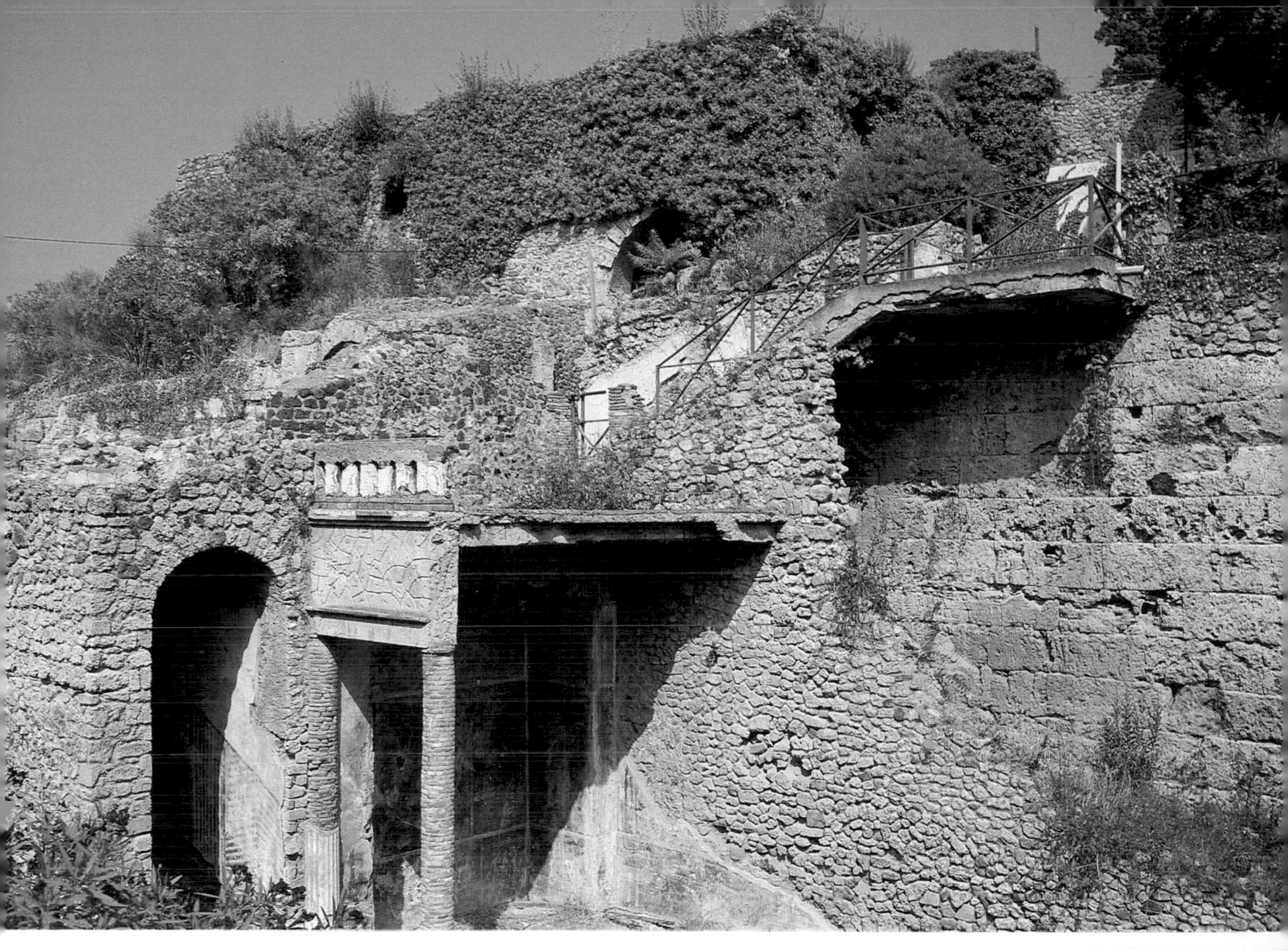

On this page: two views of the suburban villa next to the Porta Marina: the remains of the portico and the city walls can be identified at the top.

seems to have been abandoned after the earthquake of A.D. 62.
Stretches of walls can still be seen behind a long colonnaded portico, in front of which is a garden that covers an older road that led to the Porta Marina. A series of rooms opens off the portico: the main room is a large triclinium with an antechamber, originally paved with hexagonal tiles and a complex painted decoration which represented one of the first examples of Style II (late 1st cent. B.C.), restored in Style IV in the middle of the 1st cent. A.D. The main band on the walls, surrounded by elegant accessory decoration, is occupied by three large pictures of Cretan subjects: Theseus killing the Minotaur with Athens in the background; Theseus abandoning Ariadne on the island of Naxos; and Icarus and Daedalus. The upper band contains cupboard doors with portraits of poets.
Next to the triclinium is a cubicle with an alcove with white-ground walls and another alcove with two small pictures of mythological subject. Behind the cubicle a second triclinium looks out through a three-light opening onto another garden. The fresco on the walls depicts a satyr and a maenad.

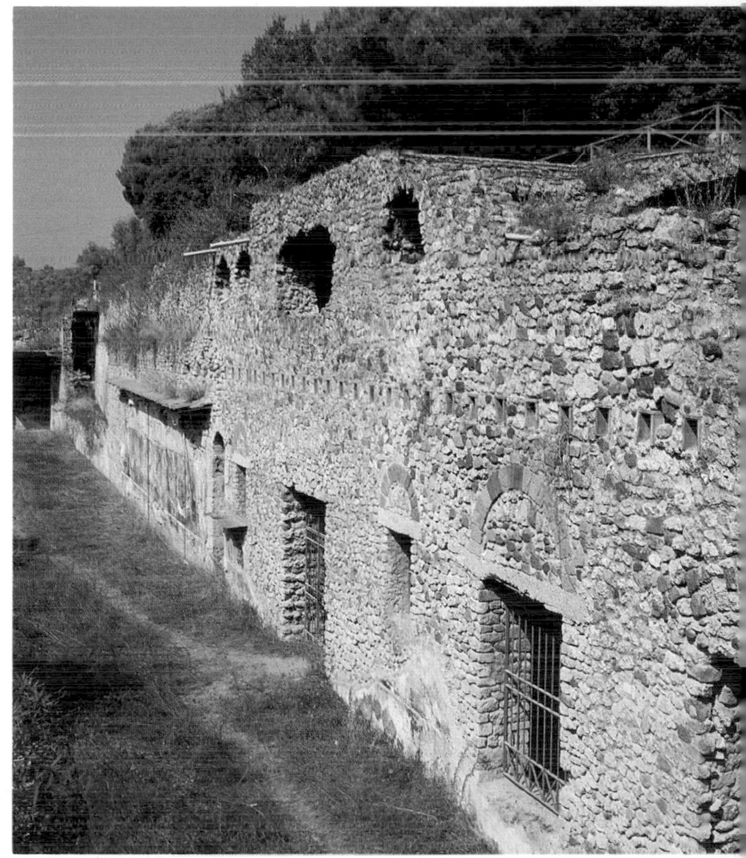

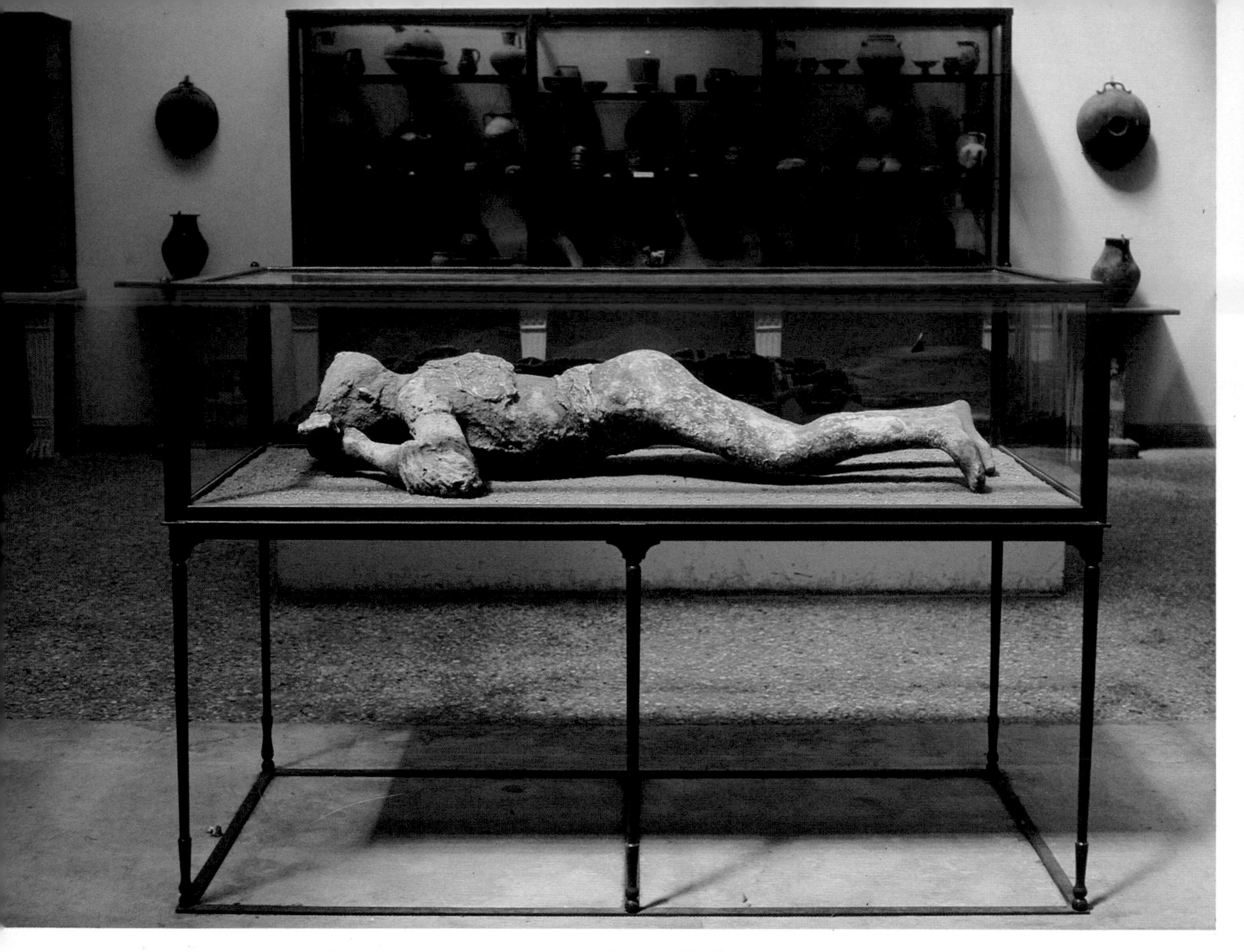

Above: a room in the Antiquarium. Right, above: the portico of the Temple of Apollo with the statue of the God and, below, the remains of the sanctuary and the altar.

3 - ANTIQUARIUM

The Antiquarium in Pompeii, at present being reorganized, was founded in 1861 and rebuilt with new museum installations after being destroyed by bombs in World War II. The Antiquarium contains material from the different phases of life in the city and the surroundings, thus supplying an explanatory chronological survey of the cultural vicissitudes of this exceptionally well-documented archaeological site.
The protohistoric phase is represented by tomb furnishings from the inhumation cemetery in the Valle del Sarno, dating to the Iron Age between the 9th and the 8th cent. B.C. The archaic period is represented by terracottas from the Doric Temple and the Temple of Apollo, as well as Corinthian pottery, Attic black-figure and red-figure pottery, and Etruscan bucchero, dating to between the 6th and 5th cent. B.C. From the Samnite period there are the tufa pediment and the altar from the Temple of S. Abbondio dedicated to Dionysius (3rd-2nd cent. B.C.) and figured capitals with Dionysiac subjects dating to the same period and from the entrances of some of the houses on the Via Nolana.
From the Roman period are a cloaked statue of Livia, Augustus' wife (from the Villa of the Mysteries), and the portraits of Marcellus, Augustus' nephew, of C. Cornelius Rufus (from the house of the same same), of Vesonius Primus (from the House of Orpheus). Domestic ware, tools and instruments for work, the remains of food such as carbonized loaves of bread, eggs and other things also date to Roman times. Casts of some of the bodies of the victims of the eruption are also to be found here.

4 - TEMPLE OF APOLLO

This imposing religious complex stands along the western side of the forum but does not communicate with it. The fact that Corinthian, Attic black-figure and red-figure pottery and Etruscan bucchero with dedicatory inscriptions have come to light in the area of the temple testifies to the existence of a cult of Apollo in Pompeii, undoubtedly imported from Greece via the Greek colonies in Campania as early as the first half of the 5th cent. B.C. The ground plan as we know it dates back to no earlier than the Samnite period (2nd cent. B.C.) and was inspired by Hellenistic models. It was frequently modified until the restoration after the earthquake of A.D. 62, and this had not yet been terminated when the eruption of A.D. 79 took place.
The actual temple stands at the center of a peristyle of 48 columns with the entrance on the south side, from the Via Marina. Originally the colonnade of the portico was

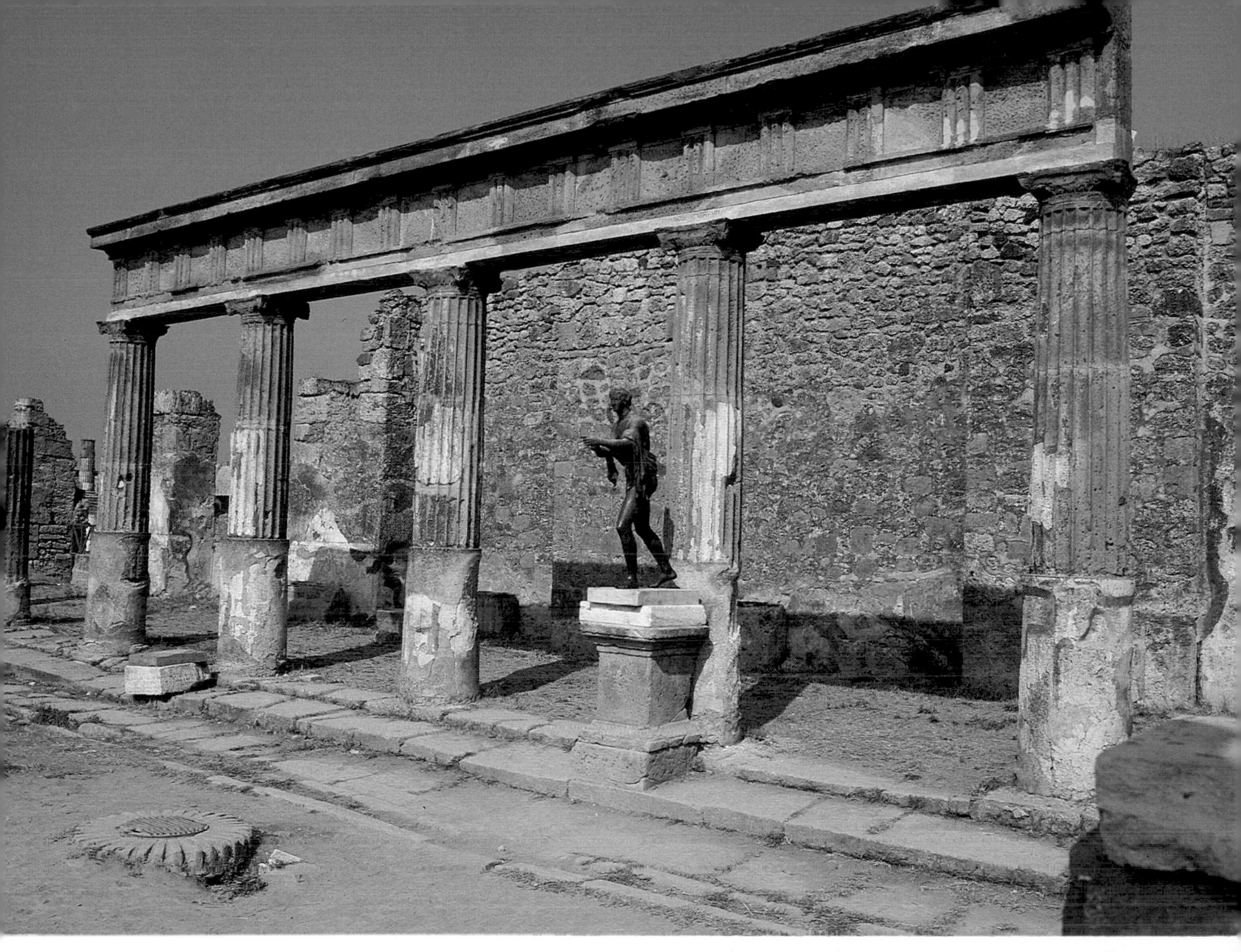

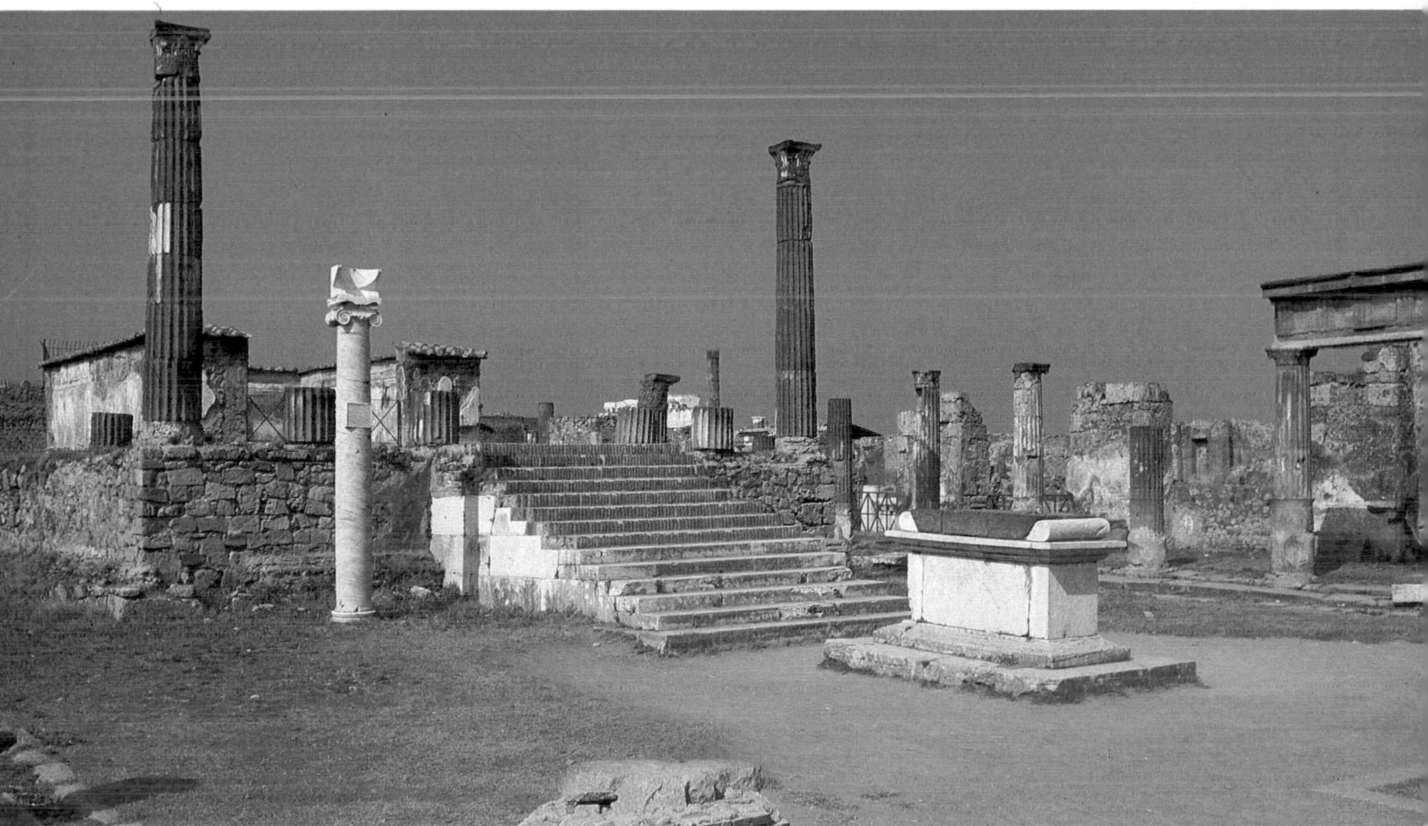

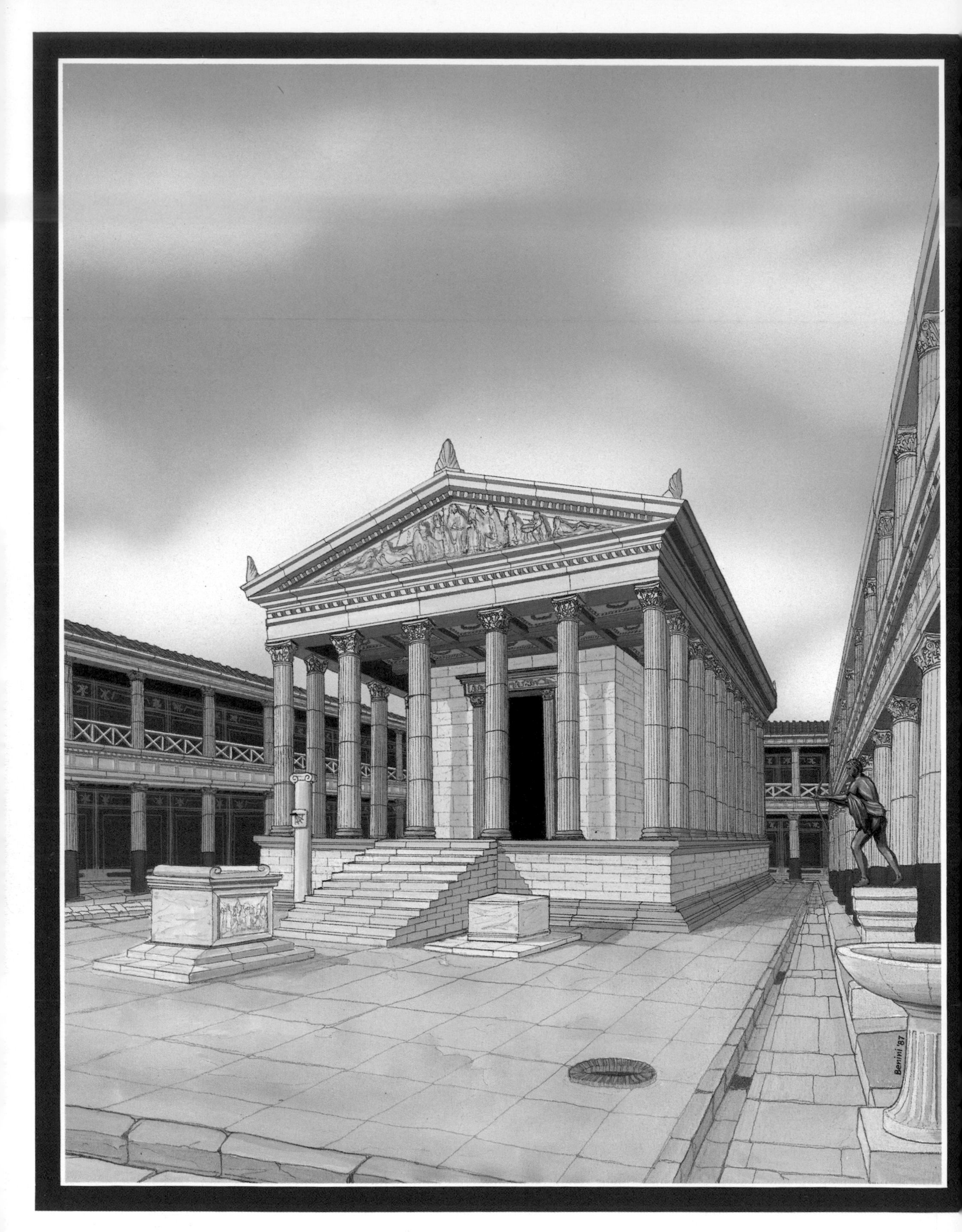

Above: the reconstruction of the Temple of Apollo, to be compared with the extant remains shown on the facing page, above.
Below: the bronze statues of Apollo (left) and Diana (right).

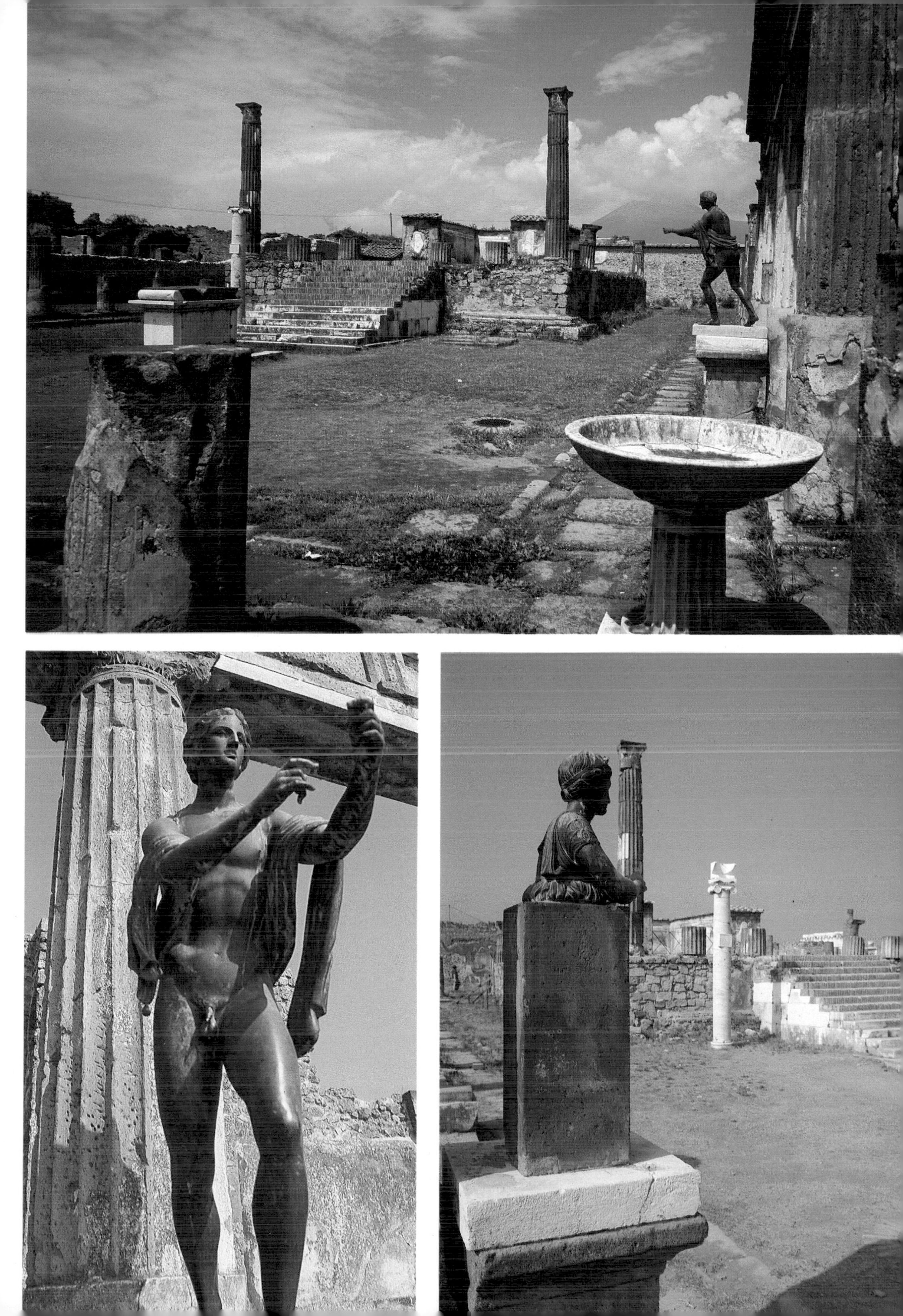

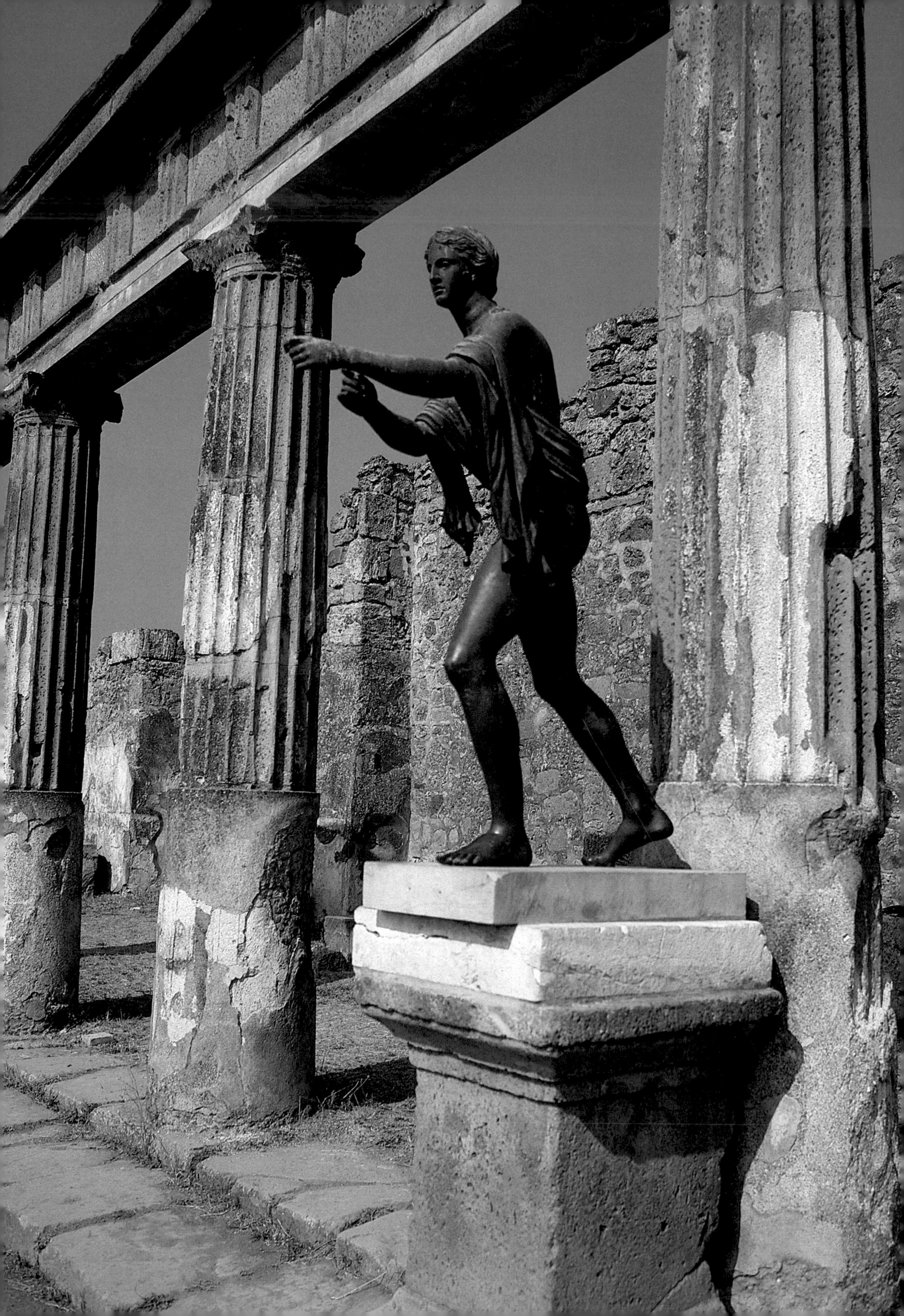

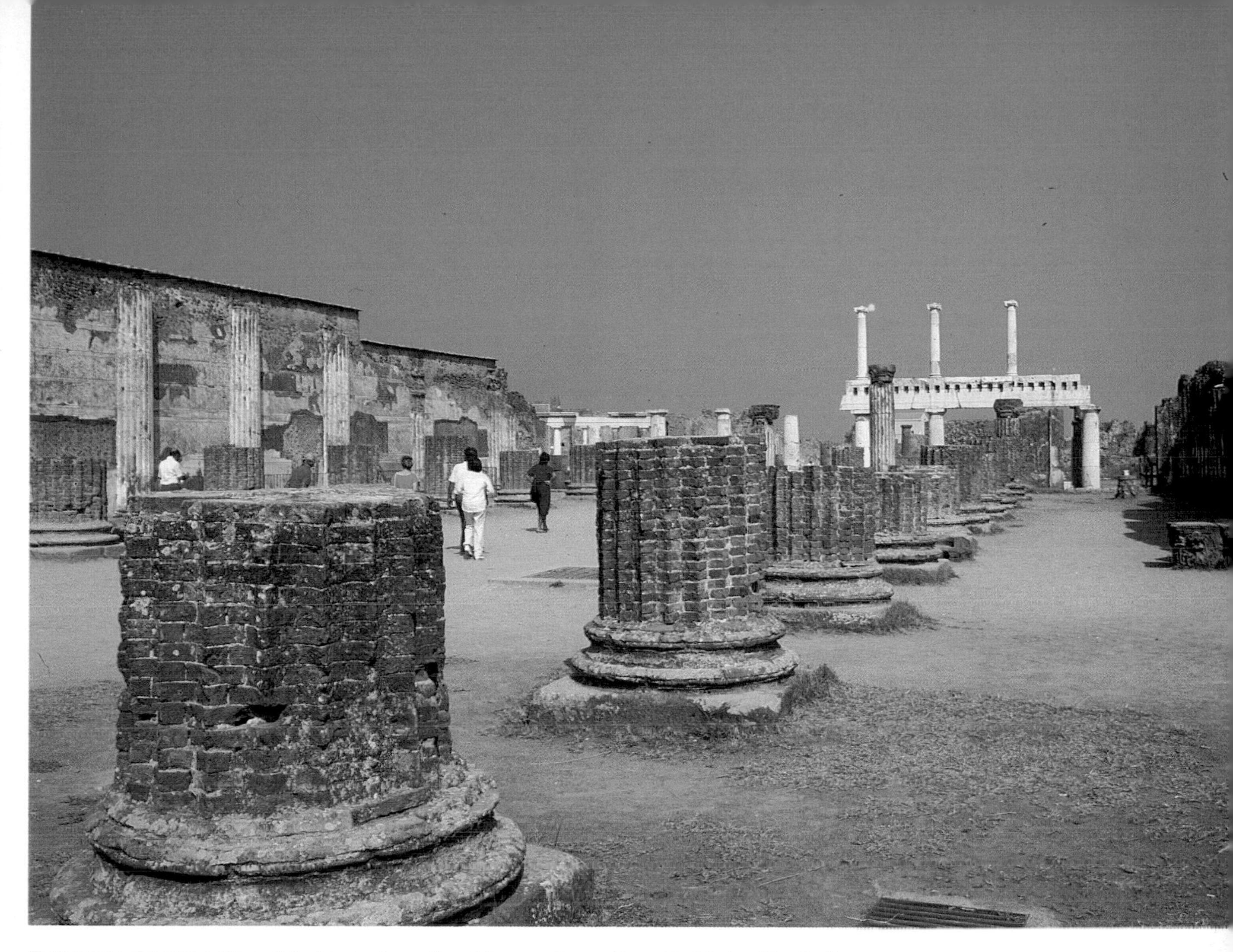

Facing page: the bronze statue of Apollo near the portico of the sacred area. Above: the interior of the Basilica.

Doric with a Doric entablature with metopes and triglyphs, on top of which stood another tier of smaller columns. After the earthquake, a heavy layer of stucco transformed the columns into the Corinthian style, the entablature was redecorated with a frieze of griffins supporting garlands and the upper tier of columns was not replaced.
The original aspect of the complex was considerably modified when openings the sanctuary had on the east side, overlooking the forum, were walled up and transformed into niches decorated in Style IV painting with subjects from the Iliad. Around 2 B.C. the *duoviri* M. Holconius Rufus and C. Egnatius Postumus had a high wall raised on the west side. As explained in an inscription, it was built so that the sanctuary could not be seen from the windows of the houses that faced in this direction. The temple was thus isolated at the center of an enclosing wall, completely altering the idea behind the original Greek architectural model upon which it was based. Various statues were found in front of the columns of the portico: the bronze statue of Apollo with a bow was near the east side, while on the west the statue of his divine sister Diana was situated, with an adjacent cult altar. Both statues have now been replaced by copies. The marble statues of Venus and Hermaphrodyte may have been set along the south side temporarily while the nearby Temple of Venus to which they probably belonged was being remodelled. Lastly, on the east side there was also a herm with a youthful version of Hermes, of the type associated with the god as protector of the palaestra.
The Temple of Apollo is a peripteral structure with six Corinthian columns on the front and nine on the sides, set on a podium with an entrance staircase on the front. The cella is paved with a central carpet of rhombs in polychrome stone mosaic bordered by three bands. The outer one was decorated with a meander design in perspective. Near the entrance, in the pavement, a dedicatory inscription in Oscan referring to the *quaestor* Oppius Campanus was found. The oval tufa *omphalos* inside the cella is the symbol of the Delphic Apollo. The cult statue has not been found and all that remains is the base at the back wall. The temple is architecturally heterogeneous, for it includes elements appertaining to the Etruscan-Italic tradition such as the podium and the flight of stairs on the front, and Greek, such as the peripteral module and the Corinthian order.
In front of the building is the marble cult altar with the dedicatory inscription of the *quattuorviri* M. Porcius, L. Sextilius, Cn. Cornelius, and A. Cornelius, figures who belonged to the early phases of Pompeii's political history when it was a Sullan colony (80 B.C.). The sundial, dedicated by the Augustan *duoviri* L. Sepunius Sandilianus and M. Herennius Epidianus was set on an Ionic column near the temple stairs.

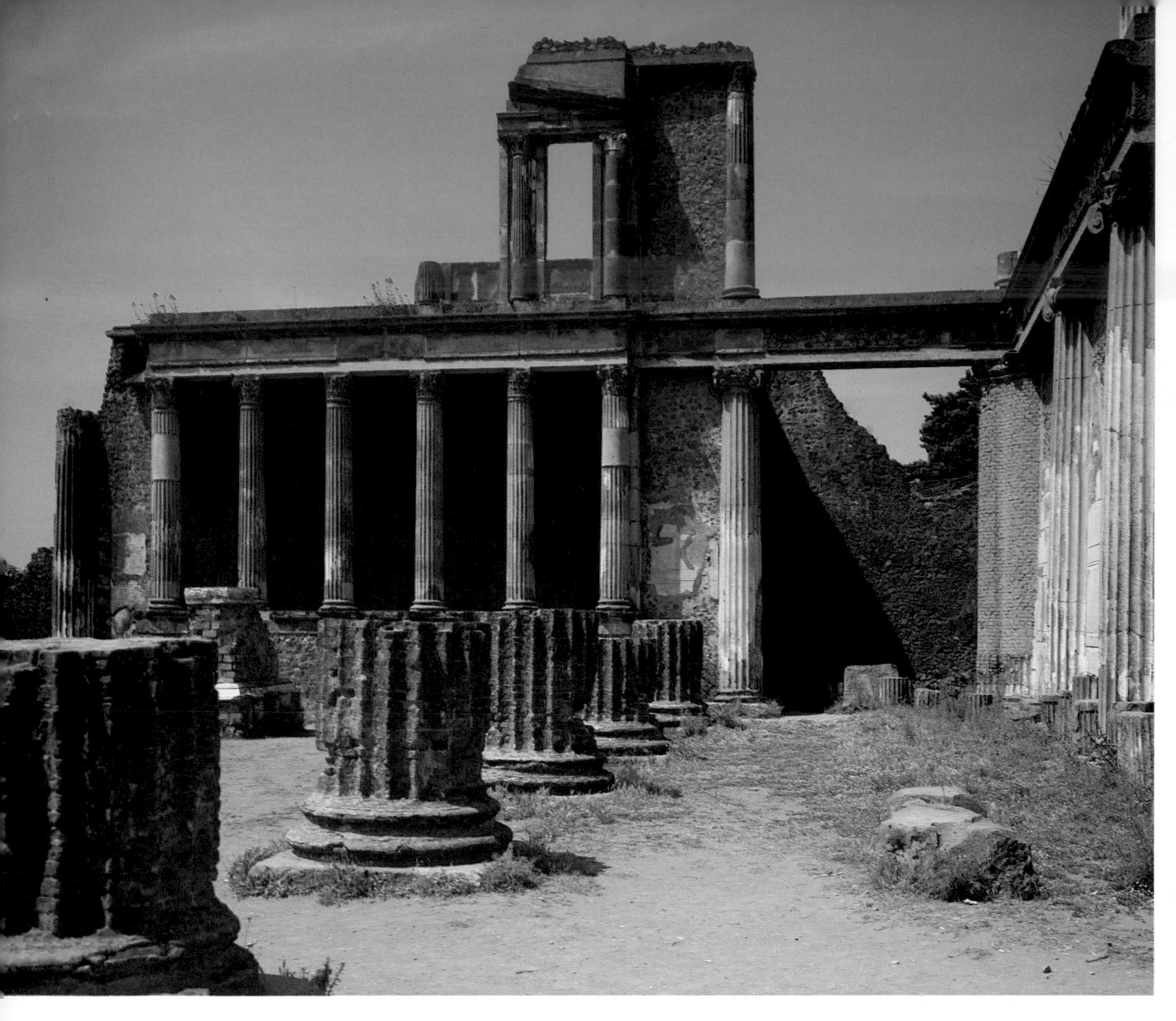

Above: the interior of the Basilica with the Tribune at the back and, opposite, the reconstruction of the same side of the building.

5 - BASILICA

The Basilica, identifed as such by graffiti on the intonaco of the walls (*bassilica*), stands near the west corner of the Civil Forum. It is one of the oldest known examples of this type of building, the beginning of a long tradition which would evolve in its final form into the model for the Christian basilicas.
In Pompeii the Basilica can be dated to the last quarter of the 2nd cent. B.C. on the basis of roofing tiles with the factory mark in Oscan *Ni-Pupie*, the name of a magistrate in the Samnite period, and of inscriptions scratched into the oldest intonaco of the walls, also written in Oscan. The building already reflects some of the structural conventions later codified by Vitruvius in his *De Architectura* for the basilicas, but differs in the proportions of the volumes and because the entrance is on the short side, overlooking the Forum, instead of on the long side; as a result the tribunal is also on the short back wall, on an axis with the entrance.
The main entrance consists of five openings scanned by piers, which lead to an uncovered vestibule, to the south of which is a room with a deep well for water inside. The vestibule leads to the real entrance to the Basilica which has a facade raised up on four steps, with four Ionic columns flanked by two side doors. The interior has a nave and two aisles: the nave is bordered on its four sides

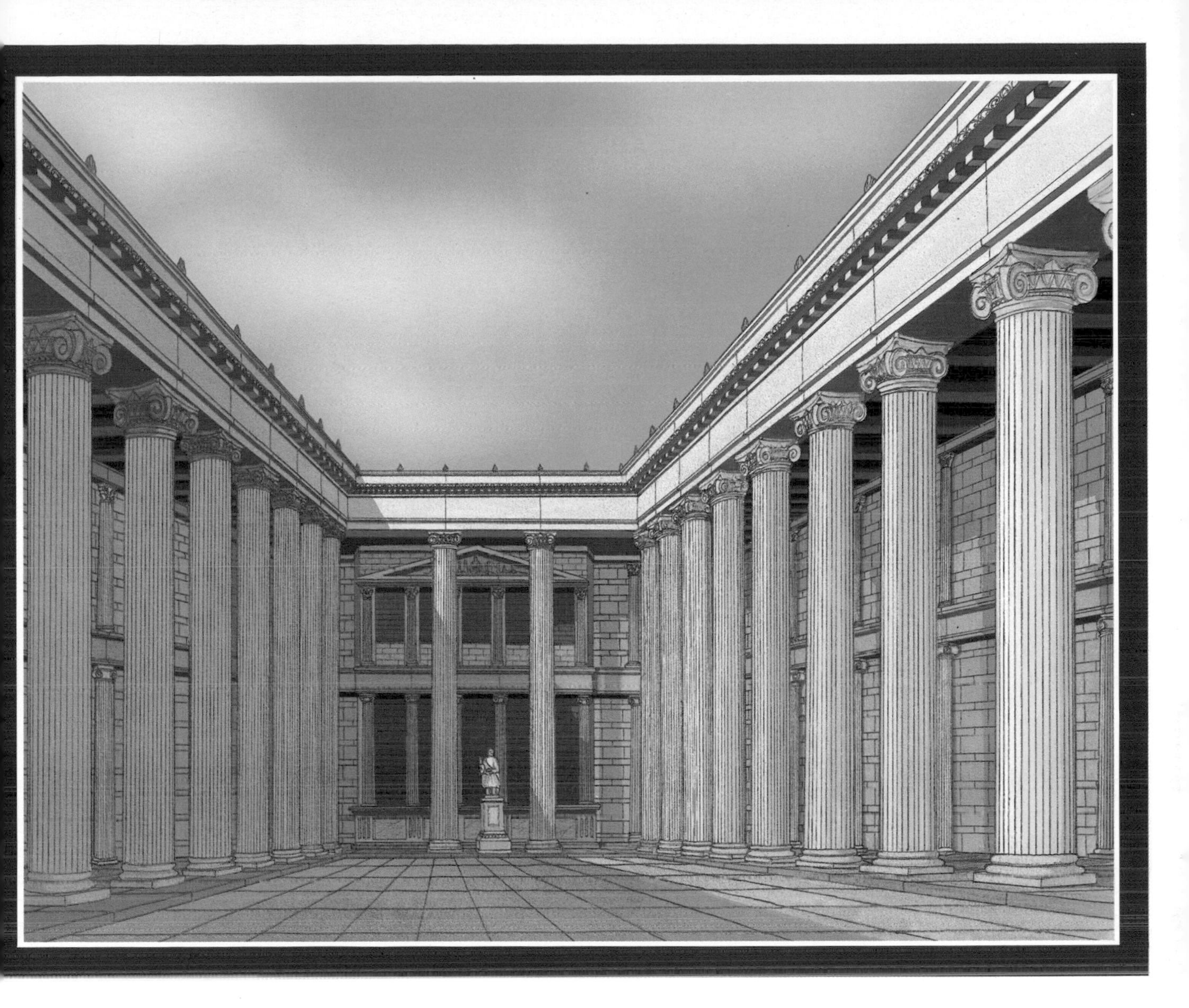

by twenty-eight large columns, each built of tiles which were cut along the flutes and then covered with stucco. A row of Doric half columns is set along the aisles. Originally they were topped by a second tier of Corinthian half columns. The roof must have been with a single truss and the intercolumniations between the half columns of the upper tier must have been left open to allow light to enter the Basilica.

There were two secondary entrances at the center of the long sides. The back wall was occupied by a tribunal, a podium with an elevation of two superposed tiers of six Corinthian columns; two rooms at the sides have entrances framed by an Ionic column and two Doric half columns in the corners. In the space between these two rooms and the tribunal, two flights of stairs lead to an underground vaulted room. The tribunal, access to which was via two wooden staircases, was reserved for the judges who directed the trials from here and pronounced their verdicts. The Basilica played a leading role in the civil and commercial life of the city. Justice was administered here, but important business meetings were also held, the most pertinent economic and legal affairs were handled and authoritative scholars have found a comparison to modern Wall Street quite apt. The numerous graffiti found on the walls inside, which were originally decorated in Style I, are now in the Museo Nazionale in Naples. The subjects were varied ranging from witty to erotic to political.

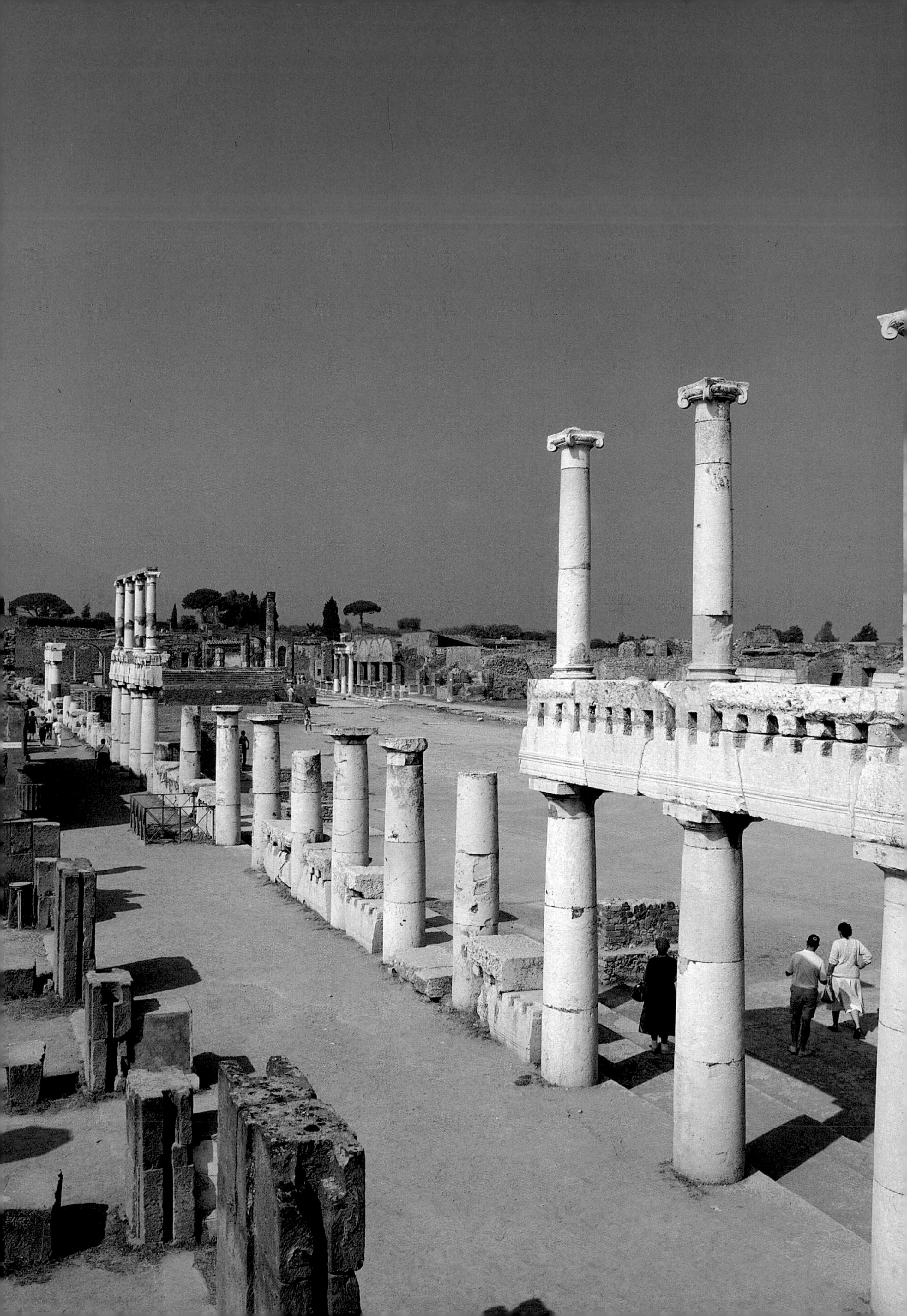

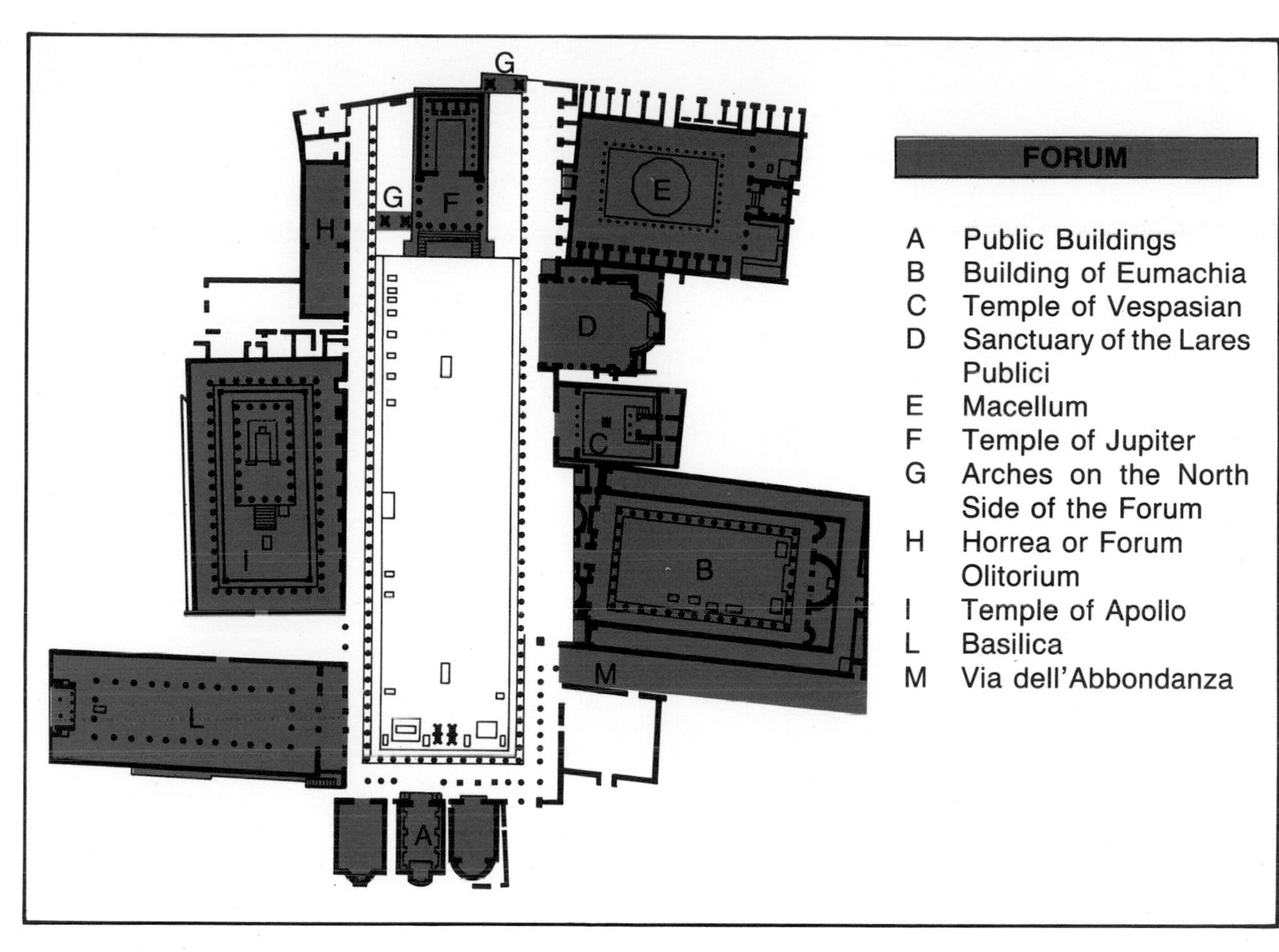

Opposite: a stretch of the portico in the forum with the Temple of Jupiter in the background.

THE FORUM

GENERAL BACKGROUND

The Forum of Pompeii occupies an area which lies at the confluence of important old communication routes between that city and Naples, Nola and Stabia. It was the center of the city when it was first founded, and even after the great expansion of Pompeii it continued to play a fundamental role in the politcal, religious, and economic life of the city even though it now lay on the outskirts. Unfortunately most of what we know is limited to the more recent phases of the layout of the Roman Forum, both as far as the shape and size of the piazza are concerned as well as for the types of buildings which surrounded it. Up until the 2nd cent. B.C., a relatively late period, the area of the Forum, which was certainly smaller than it is now, was used only for markets. It was not enclosed by porticoes and seems to have been surrounded by a series of shops and modest buildings, the foundations of which indicate that the square was irregular in shape. But the religious complex of the Temple of Apollo already existed in the 6th cent. B.C. It was originally in communication with the piazza and still constitutes part of the western side, although the orientation diverges slightly.

The great transformation of this market place into a monumental area to be used as the site for public buildings and official religious structures took place in the 2nd cent. B.C. The piazza was enclosed on three sides by two tiers of porticoes in tufa, Doric below and Ionic above, separated by an entablature of metopes and triglyphs. A Latin inscription found in front of the Basilica informs us that this portico was built by the quaestor *Vibius Popidius. Now the office of* quaestor *is not among those documented in Roman Pompeii, but since the inscription is in Latin and not in the Oscan tongue, the portico was probably built some time around the conquest by Sulla, and certainly before its institution as the colony of Cornelia Veneria Pompeianorum in 80 B.C. The paving of the piazza in slabs of tufa, about 40 cm. lower than the present level, also belongs to this phase. The base of the portico is raised above the level of the piazza by three steps, thus closing the area of the forum to wheeled traffic.*

It was also in the course of the 2nd cent. B.C. that the Fo-

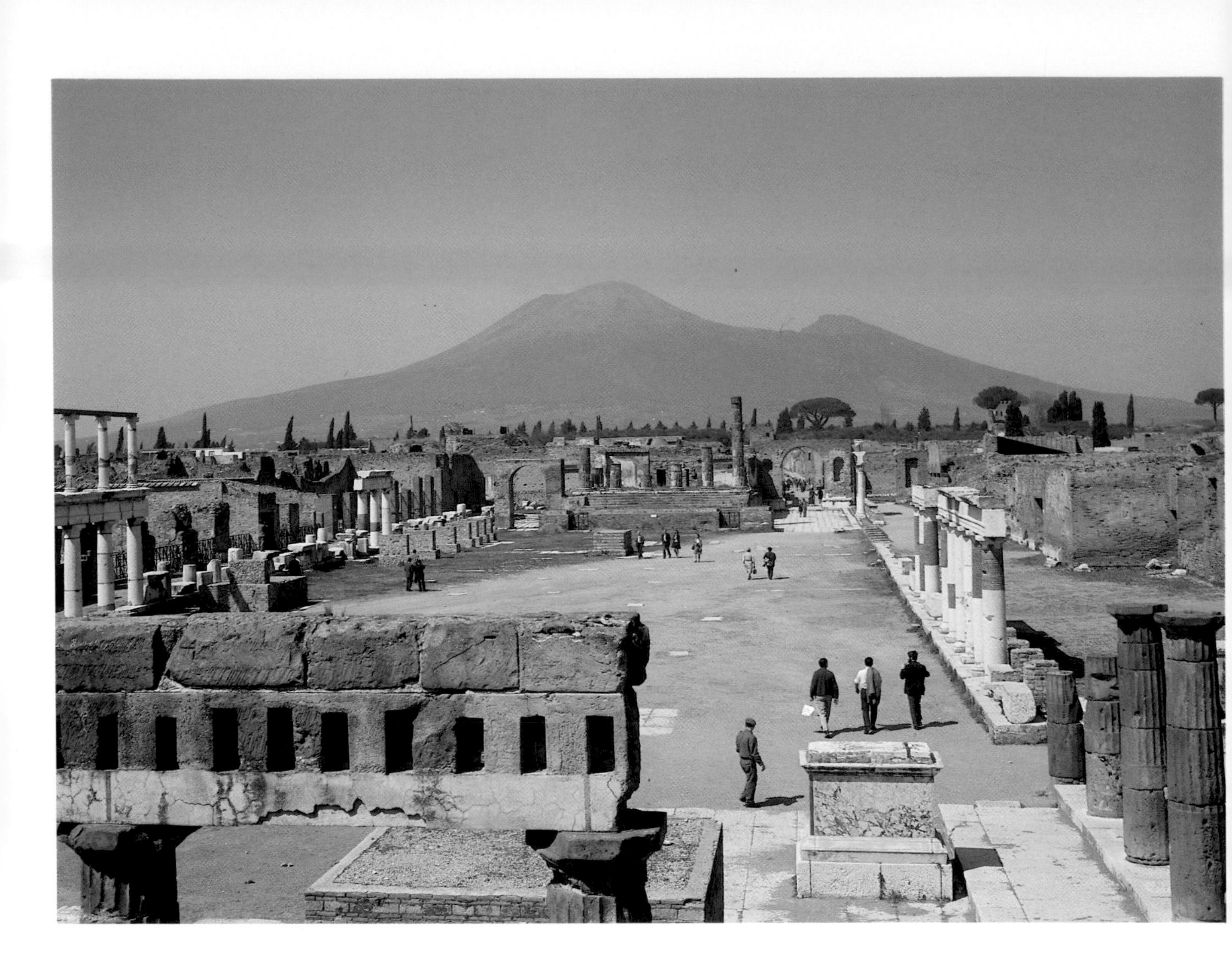

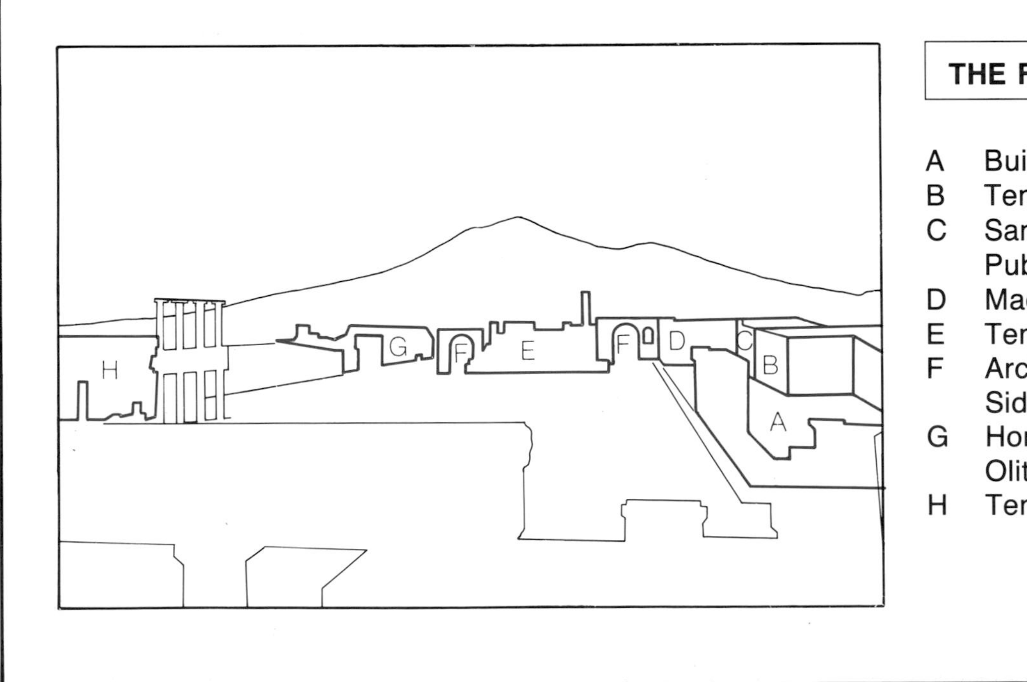

THE FORUM AS IT IS

A Building of Eumachia
B Temple of Vespasian
C Sanctuary of the Lares Publici
D Macellum
E Temple of Jupiter
F Arches on the North Side of the Forum
G Horrea or Foro Olitorium
H Temple of Apollo

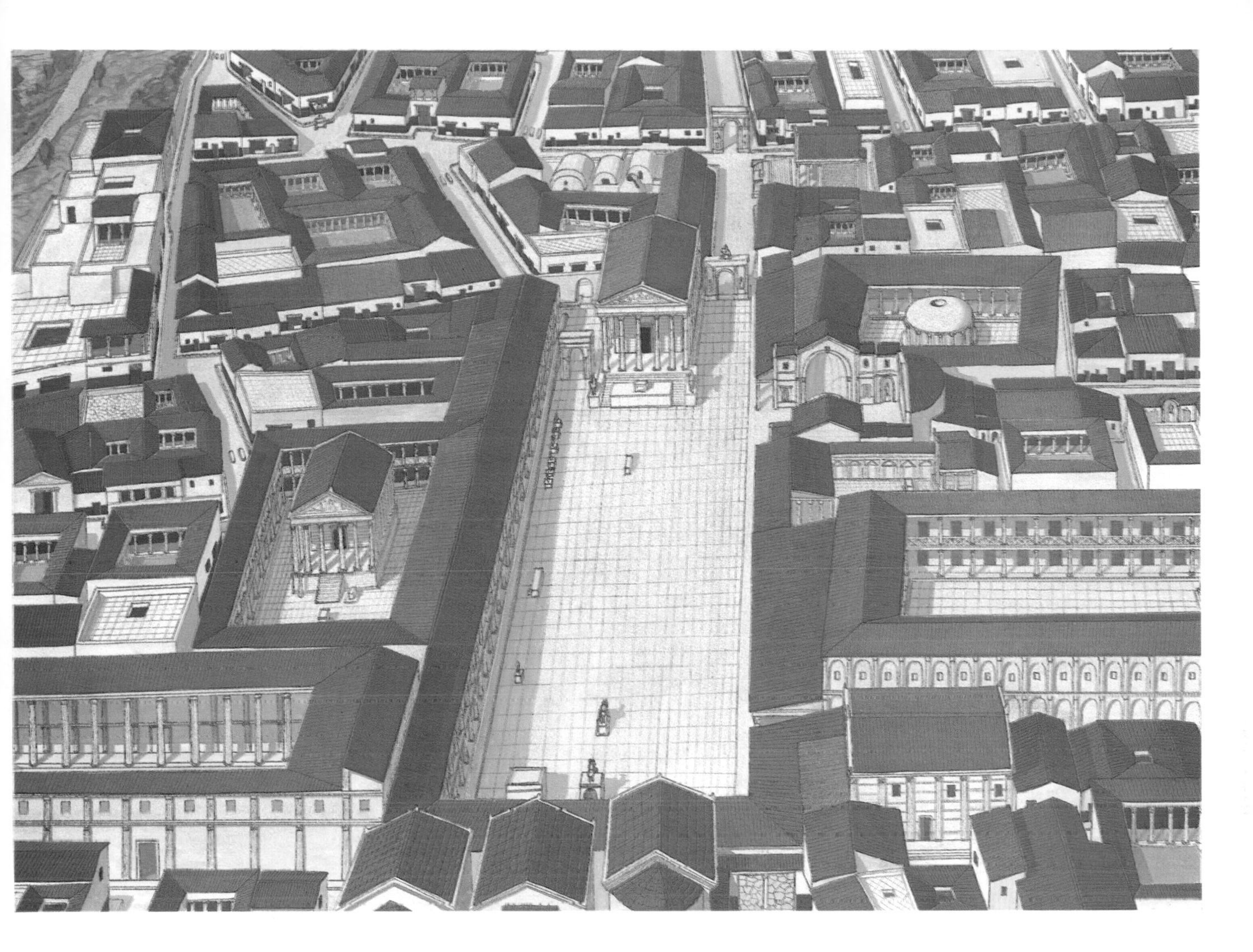

THE FORUM AS IT WAS

- A Building of Eumachia
- B Temple of Vespasian
- C Sanctuary of the Lares Publici
- D Macellum
- E Temple of Jupiter
- F Arches on the North Side of the Forum
- G Horrea or Forum Olitorium
- H Temple of Apollo
- I Basilica
- L Public Buildings

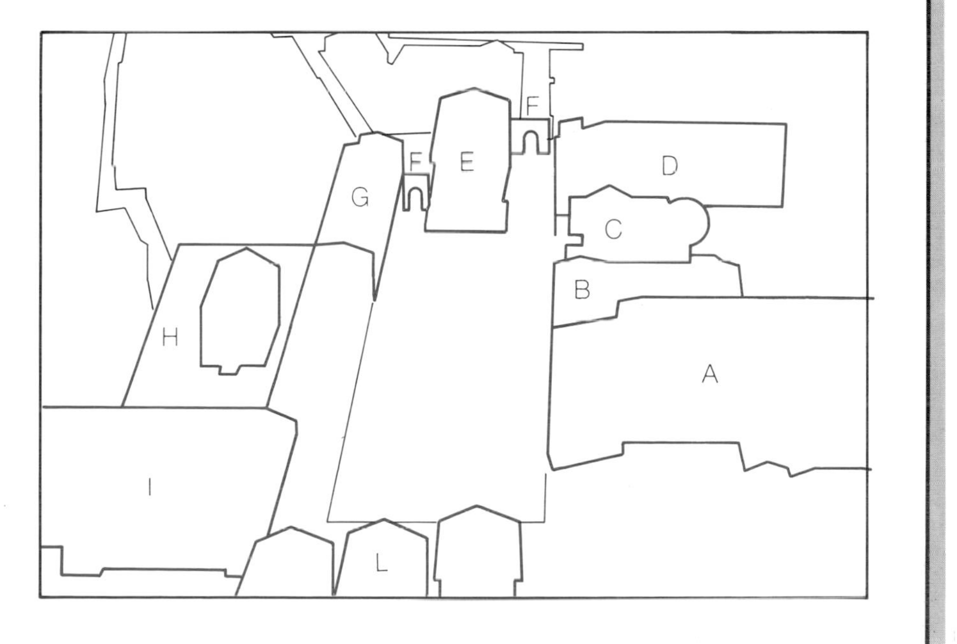

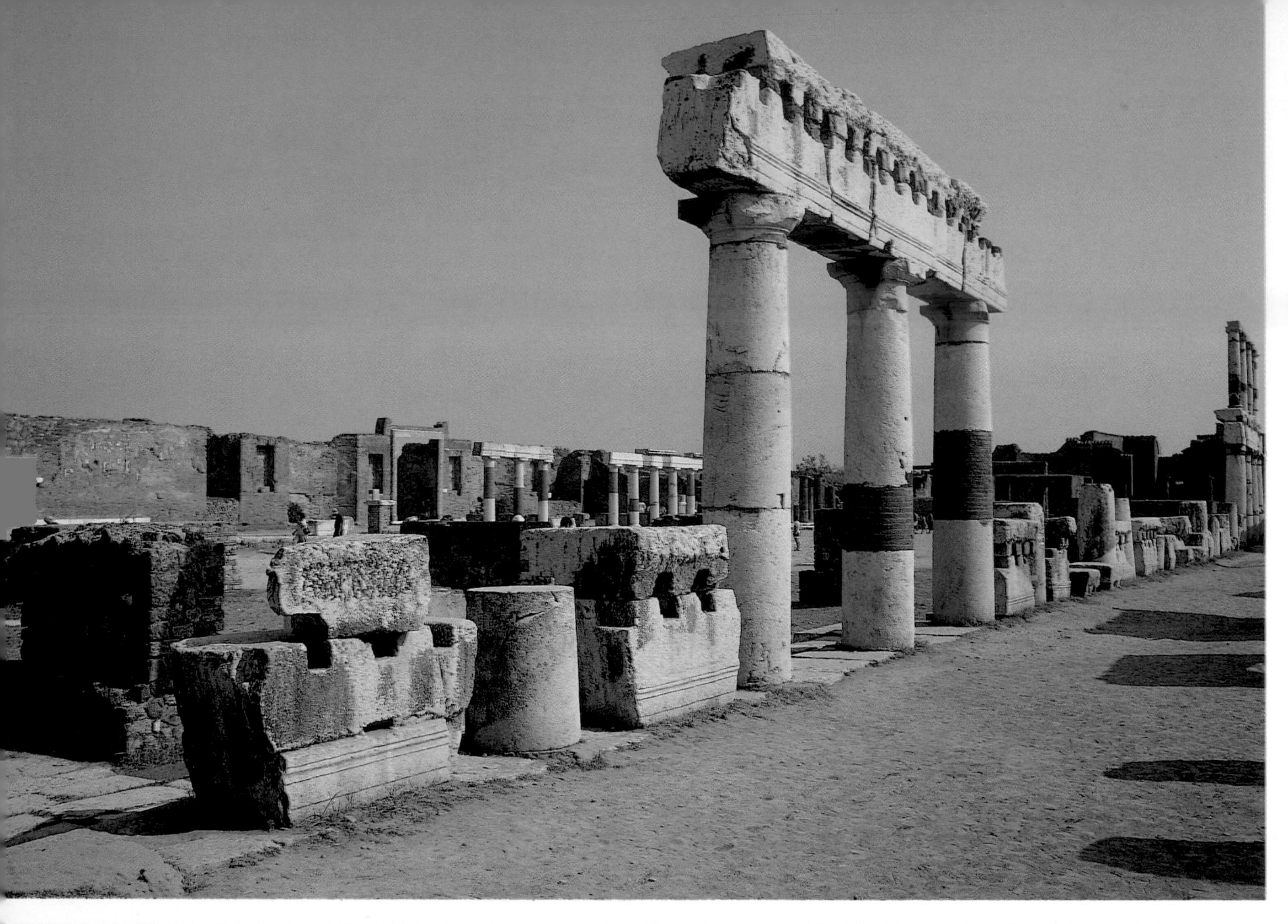

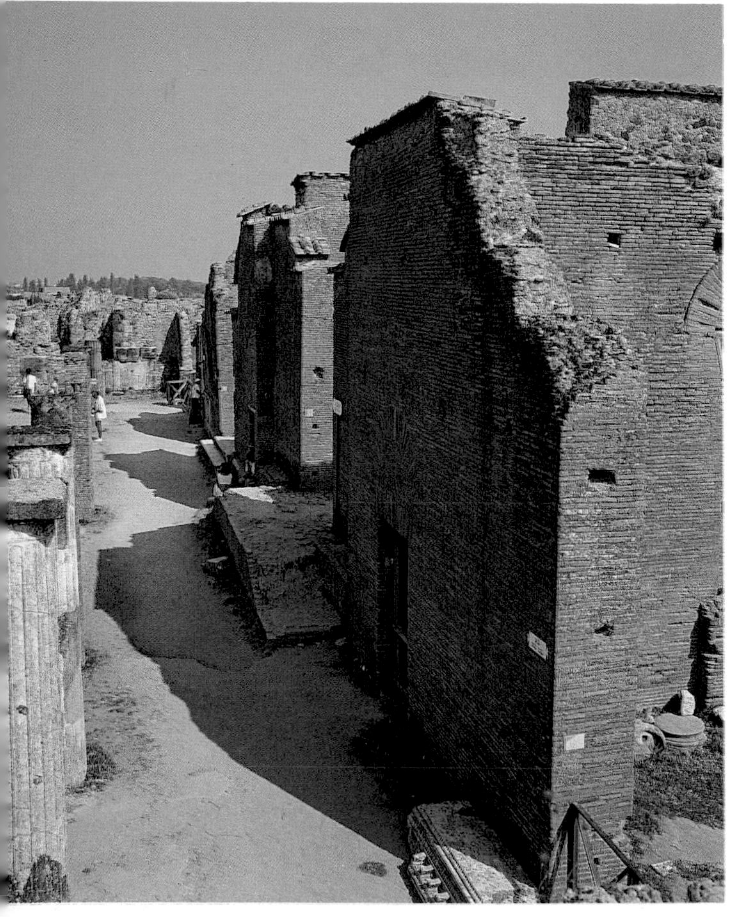

Above: a stretch of the Forum and, on the left, the south side with the public buildings.

rum acquired its definitive size: the north side was shut off by the creation of the large Temple of Jupiter (later transformed into Capitolium), while the south side was enlarged by building the Basilica, seat of the administration of justice and commerce, the Comitium for the elections and the three municipal buildings. A mensa ponderaria *(weights and measures standard) already existed in the Samnite period, set in a niche in the external wall of the enclosure of the Temple of Apollo. The Samnite weights and measures were then modified according to those of the Augustan period.*
*In the years after the establishment of Sulla's colony, building activity was concerned primarily with the theaters and the realization of the Amphitheater. In the early Imperial period new buildings also appeared in the Forum. The east side of the square was occupied by the Building of Eumachia, the wool market, probably meant for more important commercial transactions, by the Temple of Venus and the Sanctuary of the Lares Publici (protecting divinities of the city). In the Augustan period the repaving of the piazza in travertine was begun as well as the replacement of the tufa portico with one in travertine, never completed because of the earthquake of A.D. 62 and the eruption of A.D. 79. The orators' tribune (*suggestum*), situated on the west side of the piazza, is also incomplete. None of the many statues whose bases are still visible in the area of the Forum was ever found. They may have been damaged and were never set up again after A.D. 62. Gladiatorial games were also held in the Forum until the Amphitheater was built.*

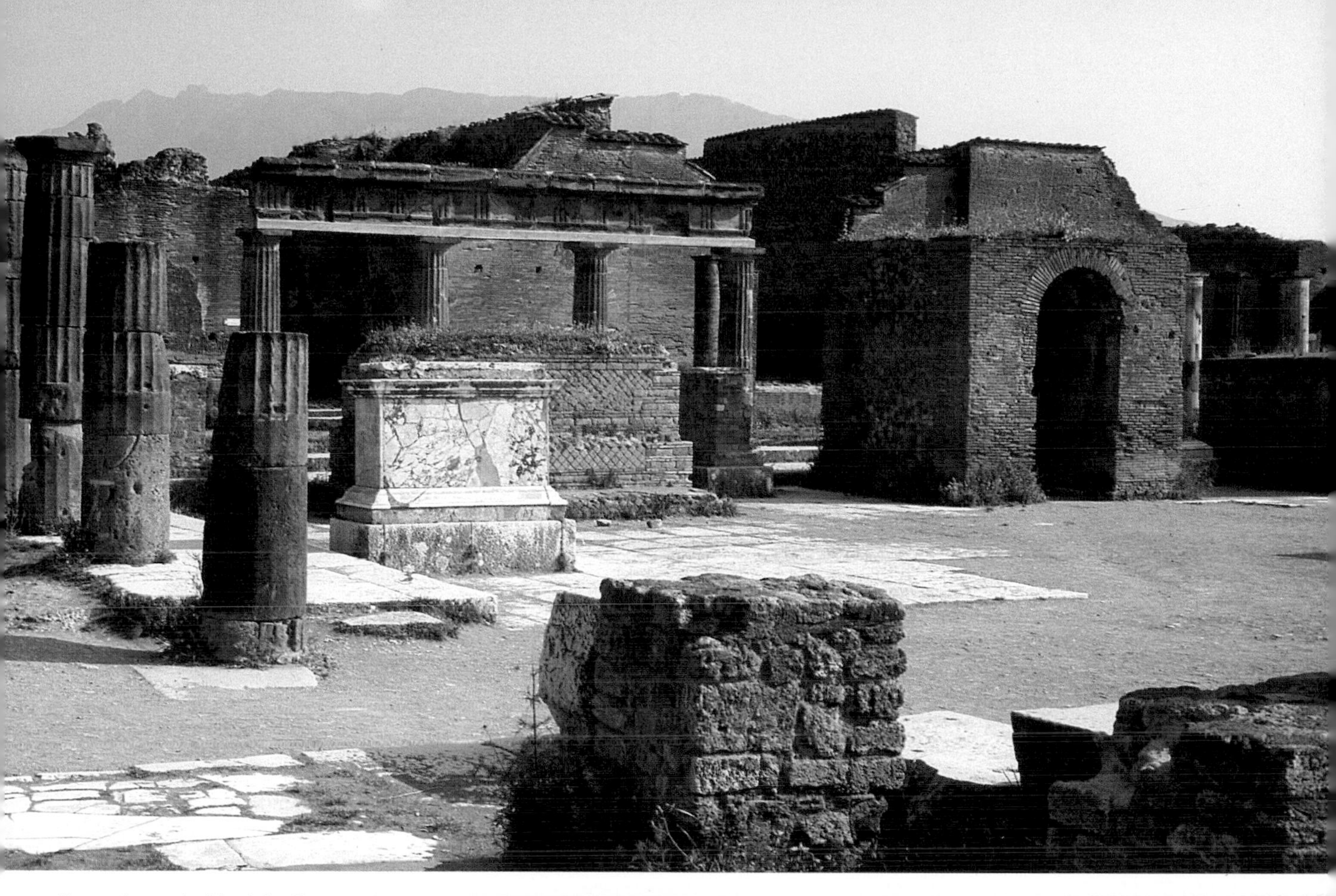

Above: the south side of the Forum and, on the right, the model of the area.

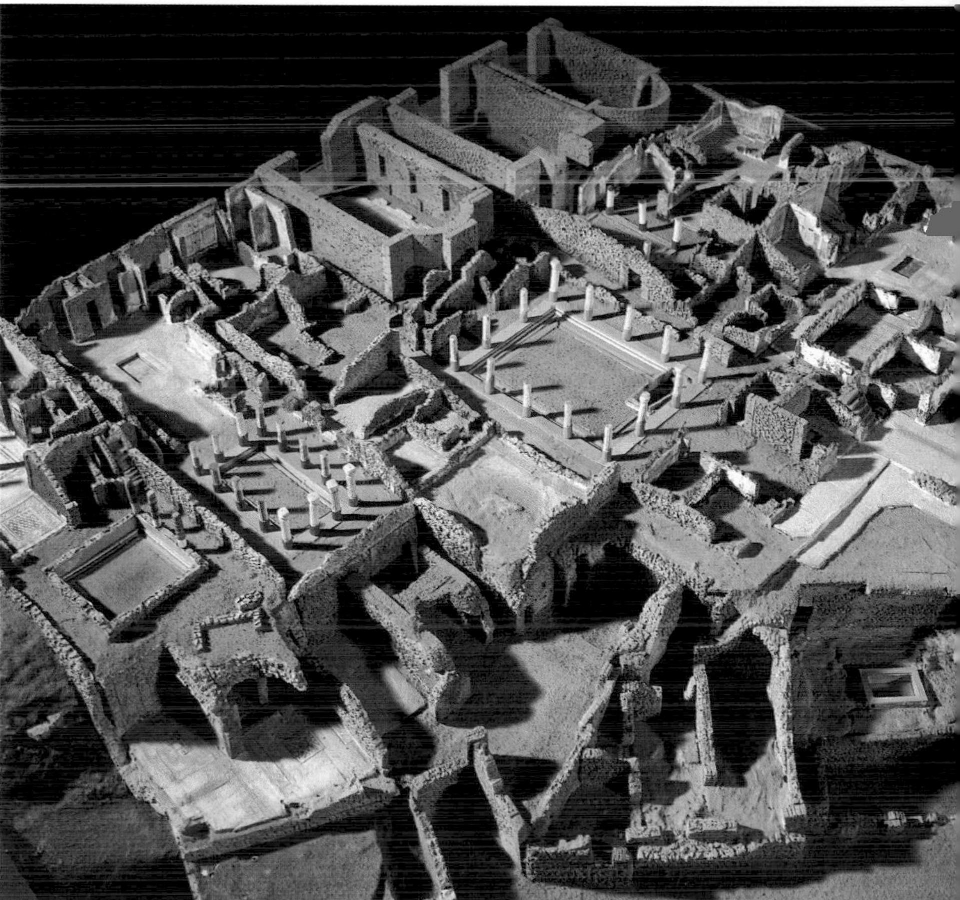

6 - PUBLIC BUILDINGS

Three buildings of almost identical size, meant to house the principal magistratures of the city, are lined up along the south side of the Forum. All three reveal remodelling in brick that dates to after the earthquake of A.D. 62. The eastern building, towards the Via dell'Abbondanza, is the one that suffered least damage. It is a rectangular building with an apse at the back. It was here that the *duoviri*, the principal magistrates of the city, exercised their functions. The building in the center has a podium and a series of piers along the interior side walls. The supposition is that the civic administrative documents were kept in wooden cupboards which would have been set into the niches that were thus formed. The western building was the headquarters of the *decurioni* who comprised the *Curia*, the city's senate. There are niches for statues in the side walls and in the apse at the back.

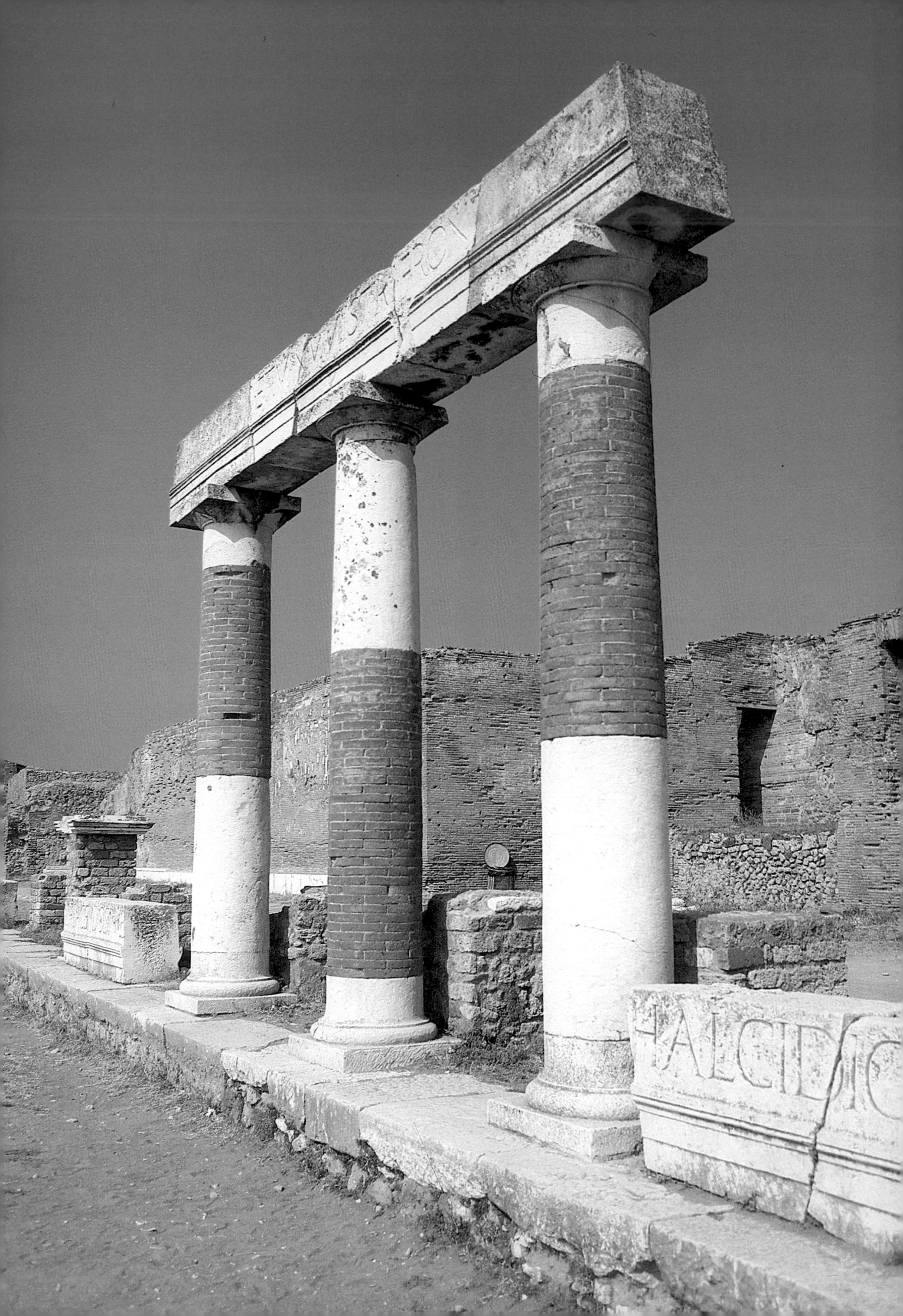
ALCID

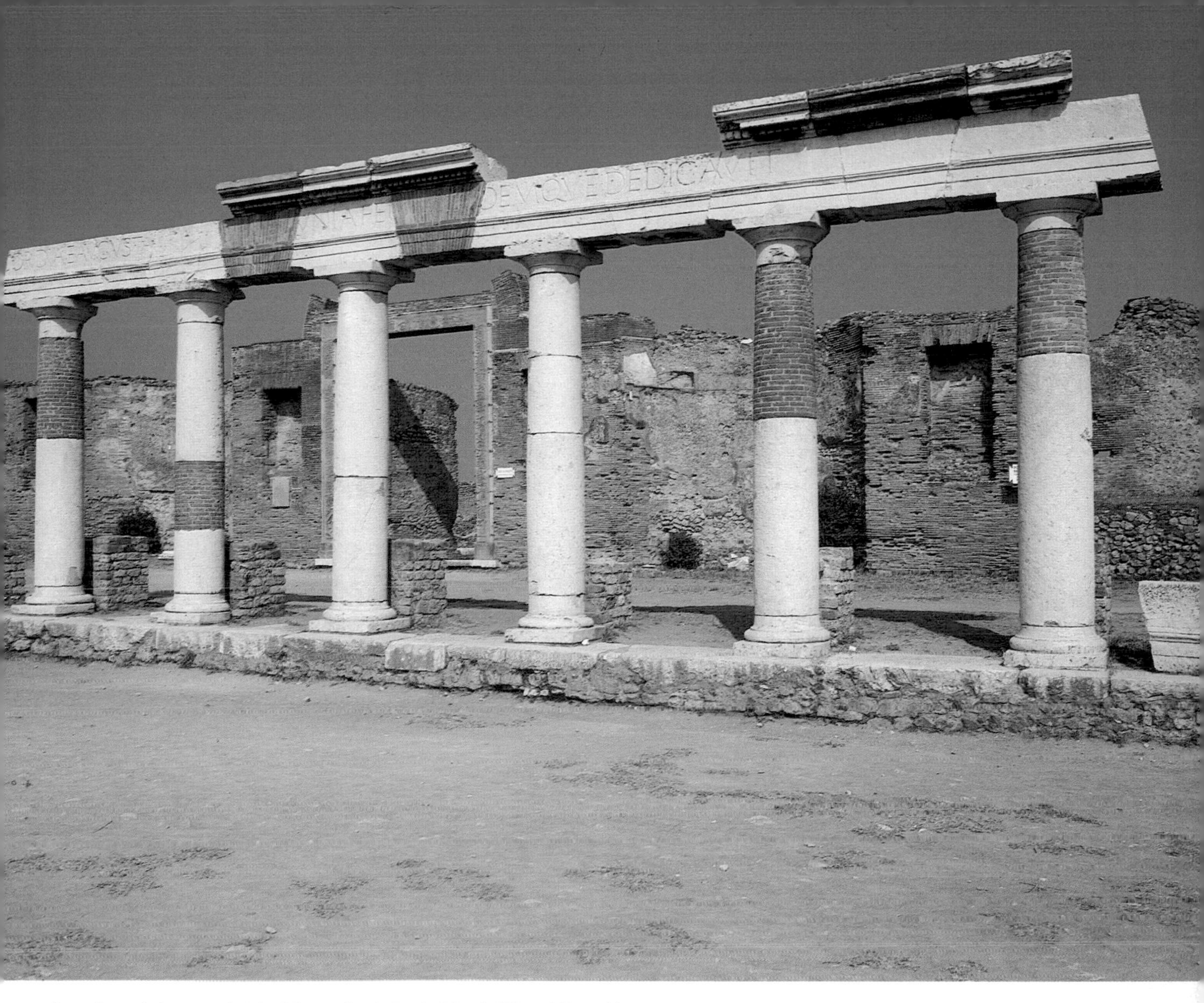

Opposite and above: a stretch of the portico in front of the building of Eumachia.

7 - BUILDING OF EUMACHIA

The large building situated on the eastern side of the Forum, between the Temple of Vespasian and the Comitium, was built, according to the two inscriptions on the architrave of the portico in front of it and near the entrance on Via dell'Abbondanza, by the priestess of Venus Eumachia, patron of the *fullones*, who dedicated it to the *Concordia Augusta* and the *Pietas*. These were programmatic concepts bound to Tiberius and his mother Livia and the building must be dated to this period.

The facade, rebuilt in brick after the earthquake of A.D. 62, is preceded by a portico with two tiers of columns and has two large raised niches at the sides which were meant for the auctioneer at public auctions. Another two semicircular niches are framed by a pair of smaller niches which contained the statues of Aeneas, Romulus and, probably, of Caesar and Augustus. Extant inscriptions on the bases of the first two list the deeds of the personages represented (*elogia*) and thus clearly indicate that it was modelled on the Forum of Augustus in Rome. The entrance is framed by a particularly fine marble cornice, decorated with scrolls and birds, which must have belonged to the first phase of the building for it is too short. A corridor flanked by two rooms, in one of which is to be found the large container for urine which the *fullones* used to cleanse the cloth, leads to a large interior courtyard with a two-tiered colonnaded portico on four sides. On the back part a porch-like structure marks the presence of the large apse behind, preceded by two columns topped by a pediment, containing the cult statue of the Concordia Augusta. A cryptoporticus lit by large windows runs along three sides behind the walls of the porch. In the back wing, behind the apse, is a niche with a statue of Eumachia dedicated by the *fullones*.

Just what the building was used for is problematical. Its obvious propagandistic intent in favor of the imperial family leads one to believe that it must have been something more important on an economic and commercial level than a simple wool market, a hypothesis some of the evidence has engendered.

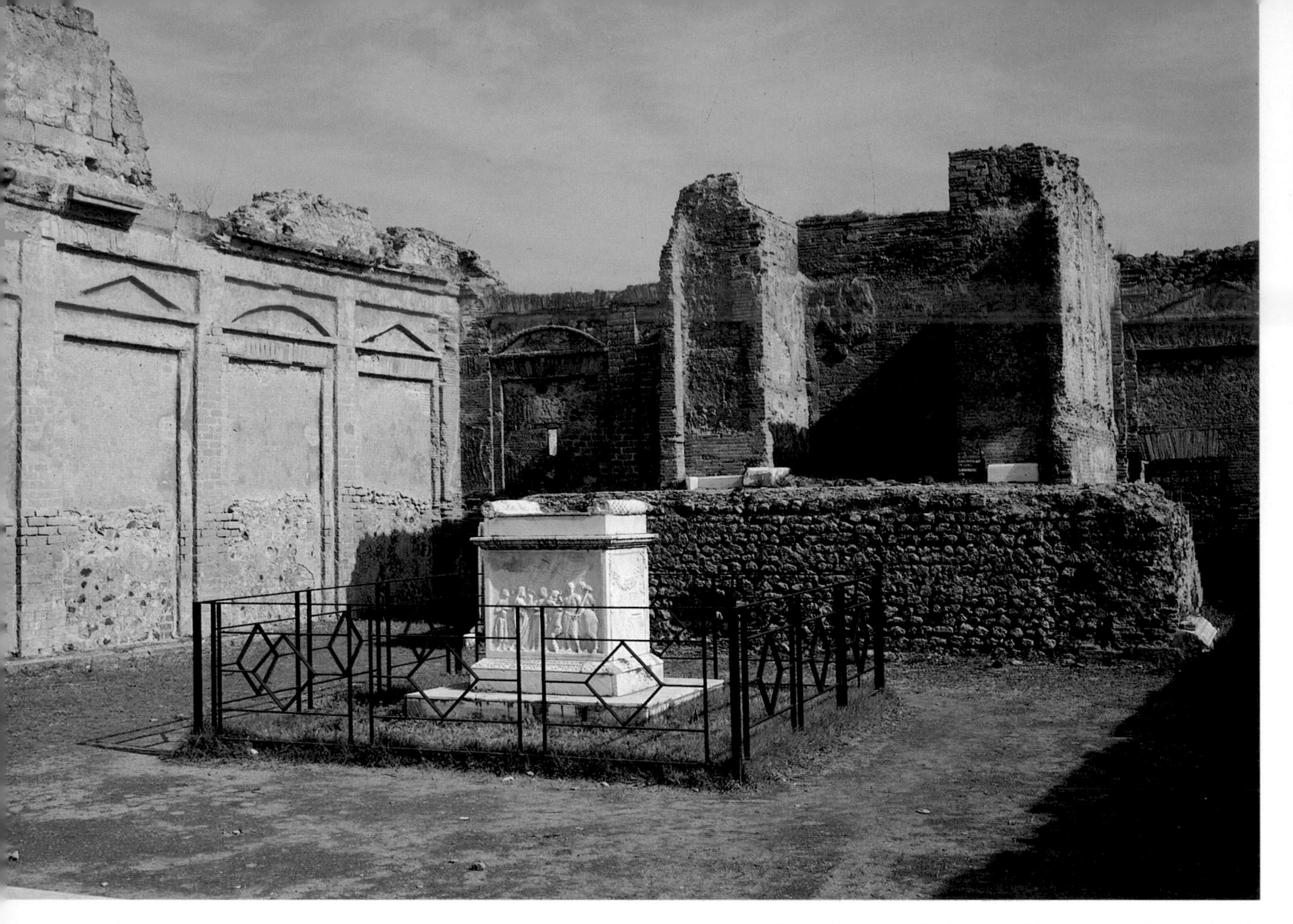

Above: the area of the Temple of Vespasian and, opposite, the reconstruction of the sacred area as it originally was.

8 - TEMPLE OF VESPASIAN

It is situated on the eastern side of the civil Forum between the Sanctuary of the Lares Publici and the Building of Eumachia. The limited space available determined the irregularity of the plan, set at an angle with respect to the axis of the square of the Forum.
The facade is in brick, parallel to the axis of the portico, projecting forwards more than the adjacent Building of Eumachia. An entrance door here leads into a vestibule and then to the court preceded by four columns, with perimetral walls in blocks of tufa reinforced at the corners and with piers in brick. The walls were simply intonacoed and decorated with a pattern of large blind windows framed by pilaster strips and with triangular and curved pediments set over them. A provvisory system for channeling rain water had been installed in the courtyard in preparation for the paving that was to come.
The temple stands at the center of the back wall of the courtyard, with a cella in brick with two antae, set on a tall podium and accessible from the back via two side-stairs. The cella, which still has the base on which the cult statue was set inside, was originally preceded by a tetrastyle porch.
A marble altar, its four sides decorated with reliefs, stands at the center of the courtyard in front of the aedicule. The principal side depicts a scene of sacrifice of a bull: a priest, *capite velato* (with his head covered), performs libations on a tripod, assisted by *camilli* with objects for the rite; behind him are two lictors and a flute player. In front of the priest is the *victimarius* with a two-edged axe and an assistant leading the bull to sacrifice. In the background of the scene is depicted a tetrastyle temple to be identified with the aedicule of the back side. The reliefs on the north and south sides show the objects used in cult ceremonies: the augur's curved staff, the box which contains the incense, the small tablecloth, the patera for the libations, the pitcher, the ladle. Lastly, on the relief facing the temple aedicule there are two laurel trees, attribution of the emperor Vespasian (formerly of Augustus), between which is hung a garland of oak leaves, the civic garland which since Augustus has been the symbol of imperial authority. The temple then was dedicated to the Genius of Vespasian and had not yet been finished when the eruption of A.D. 79 took place. A door in the back wall of the courtyard leads to three rooms used by the personnel in charge of the temple and as storerooms.

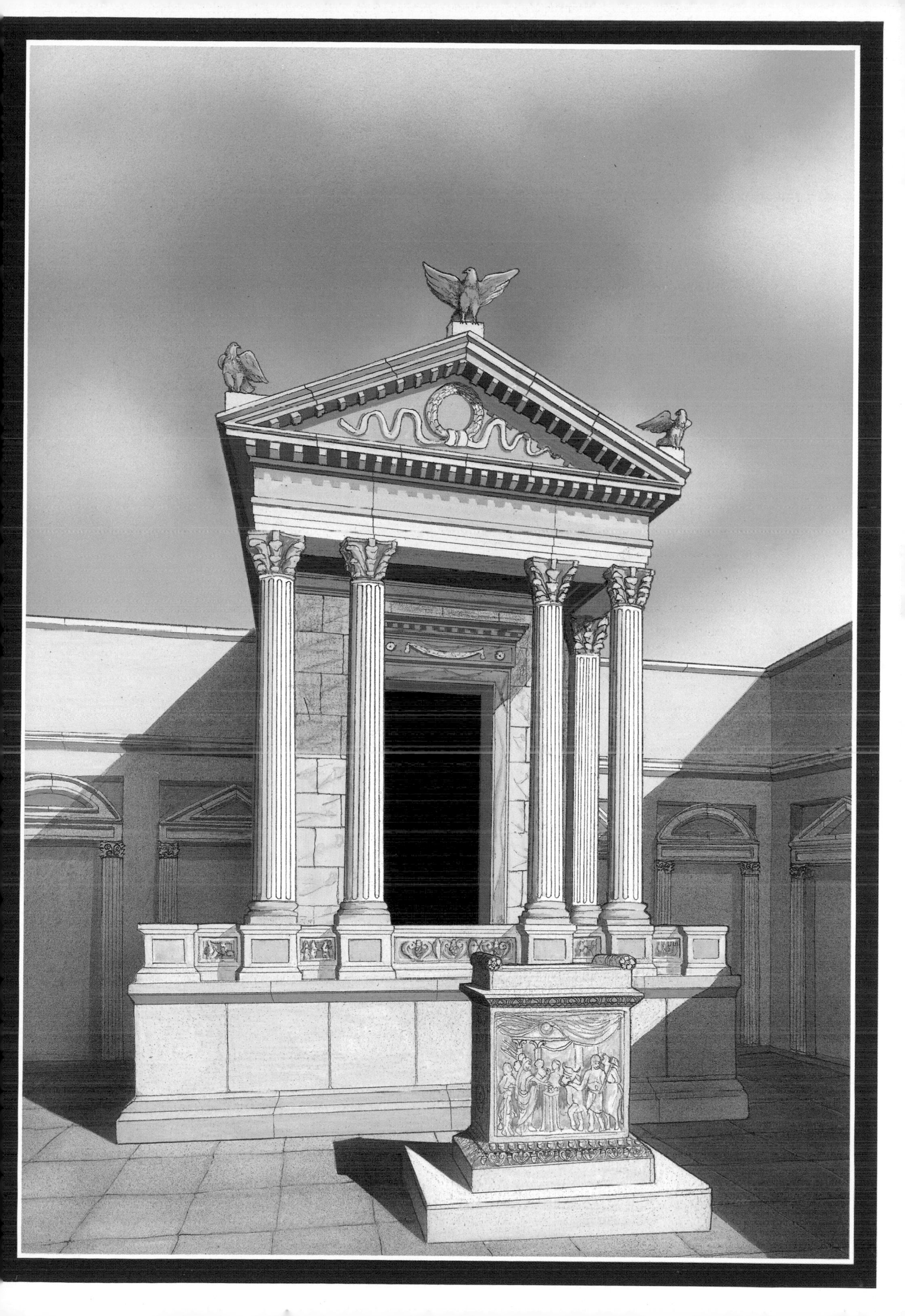

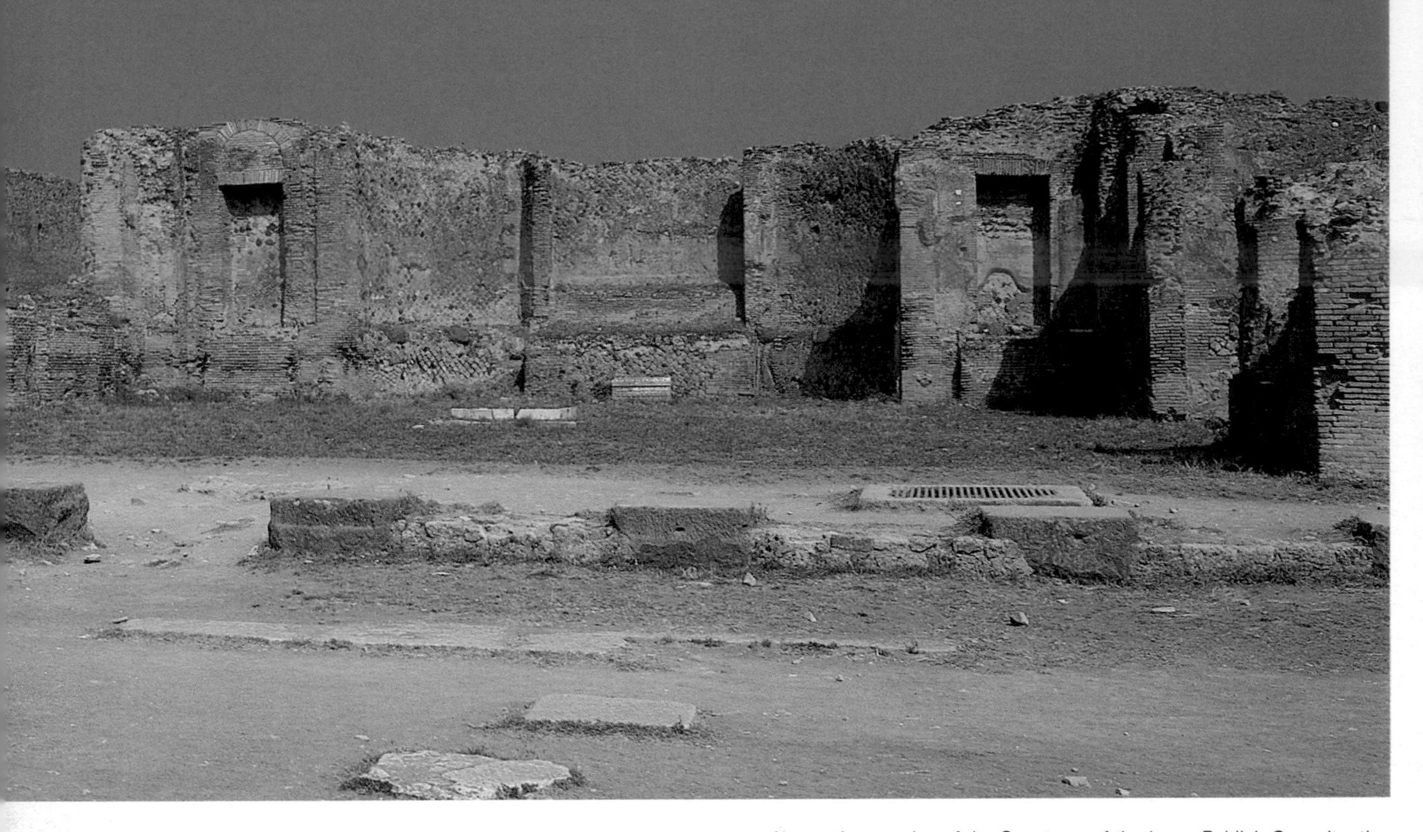

Above: the remains of the Sanctuary of the Lares Publici. Opposite, the portico in front of the shops of the Macellum.

9 - SANCTUARY OF THE LARES PUBLICI

The sanctuary consists of a large unroofed atrium and a vast apse which occupies the back wall. The few remains of an *opus sectile* pavement and a central altar are preserved in the atrium. The two side walls seem to be articulated by six symmetrically facing niches, crowned by triangular pediments, and by two large rooms, also symmetrical, preceded by two columns. Statues were originally set in the niches and in the two rooms. As mentioned, the back wall of the building consists mostly of a large apse with a triangular pediment. A row of purely ornamental columns is set on the socle which runs along the wall of the apse. At the center of the wall is an aedicule with two columns which support an entablature and a pediment, and which contains the cult statues. The sanctuary, in brickwork, *reticulatum* and *incertum*, was not completely finished at the moment of the eruption in A.D. 79. The architectural inspiration, based on luministic contrasts created by the niches and the columns which animate the internal walls, could go back to the period of Nero. It has been proposed to identify the altar of this sanctuary with the one depicted in the lararium of the House of L. Caecilius Iucundus, in the scene of sacrifice made by the citizens to invoke divine protection after the earthquake of A.D. 62.

10 - MACELLUM

The Macellum, or the food market of Pompeii, stands in the northeast corner of the Forum. It was set here for two reasons - firstly because a supply center was needed in a central zone of the city, and secondly because its position at the edge of the Forum square would not obstacle its functions.
Its orientation does not lie on an axis with that of the Forum and in an attempt to compensate for this the shops decrease in depth from north to south. The building has three entrances, the main one on the west side divided into two passageways by an aedicule set in the center. From here there is access to the rectangular courtyard which originally had colonnaded porticoes on four sides, as indicated by the remains of travertine steps which must have served as stylobate for the columns, of which however no traces have been found since the building was being reconstructed after the damages suffered in the earthquake of A.D. 62.
At the center of the courtyard twelve bases housed the supporting posts of the conical roof of a twelve-sided building used as a fish market, which was cleaned by the flow of a fountain as shown by the great quantity of fishbones and scales found in a drainage channel which began at the center of this area.

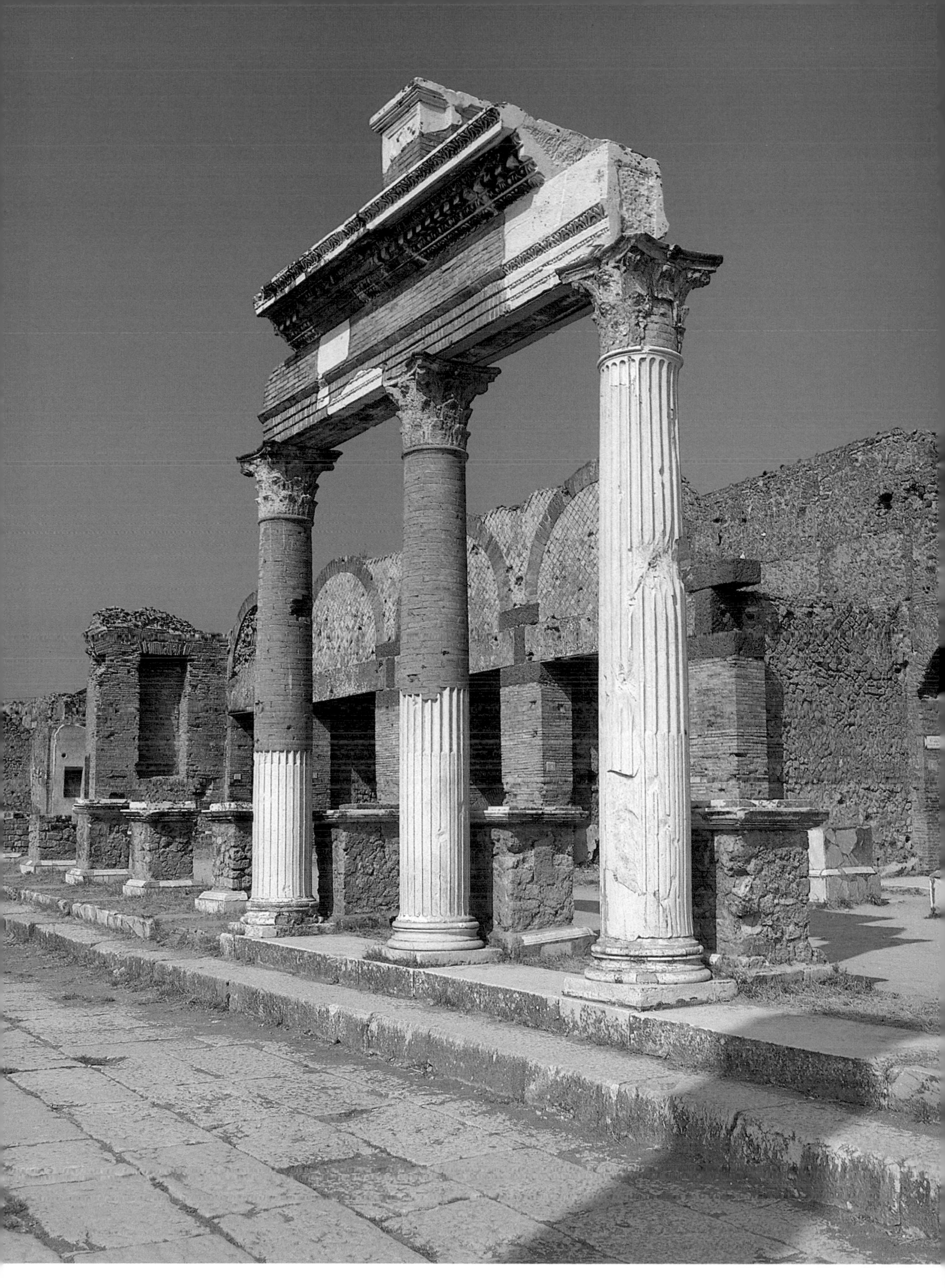

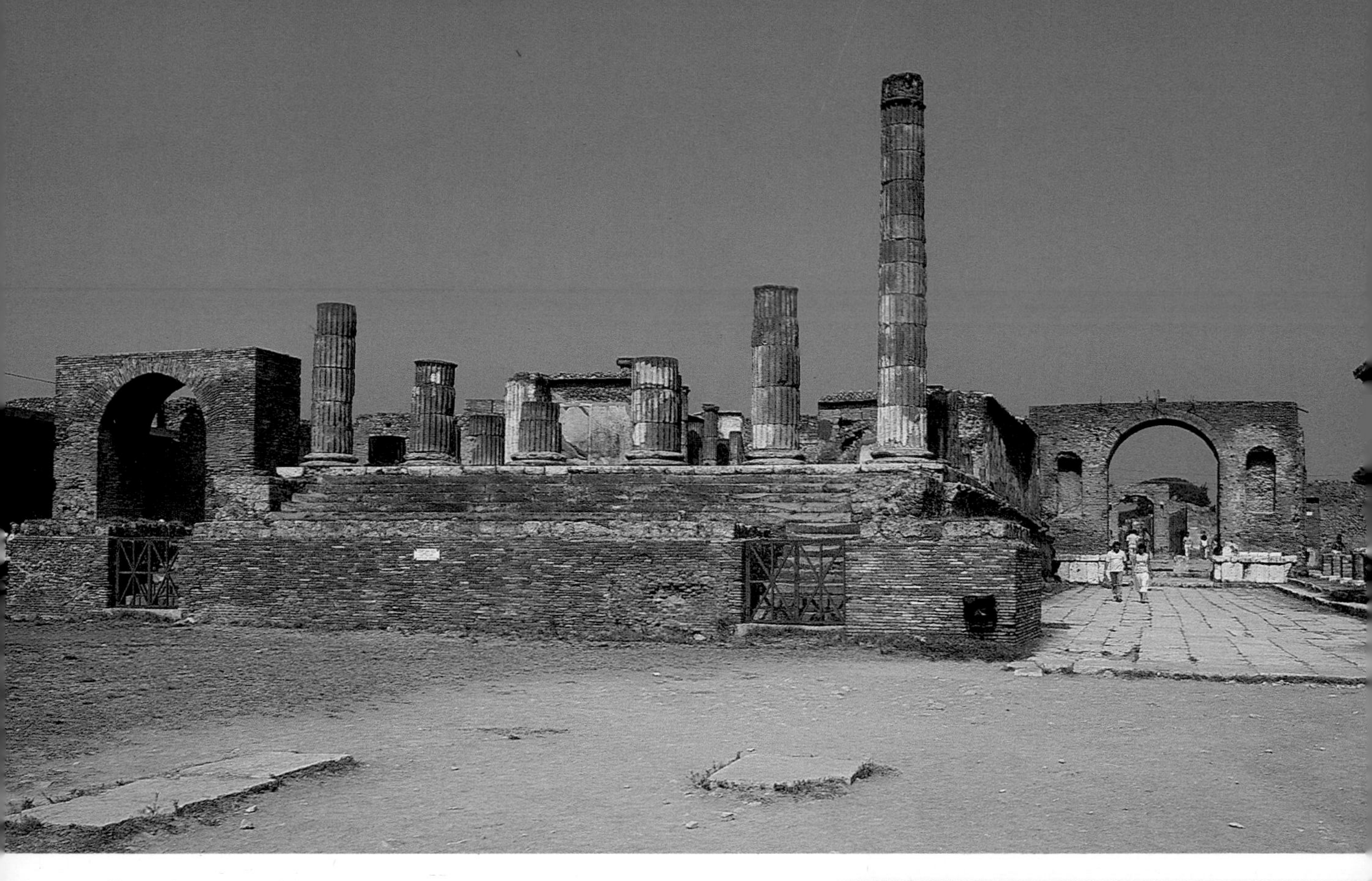

Above: the remains of the temple of Jupiter and, alongside, the reconstruction of the temple and the contiguous arches.

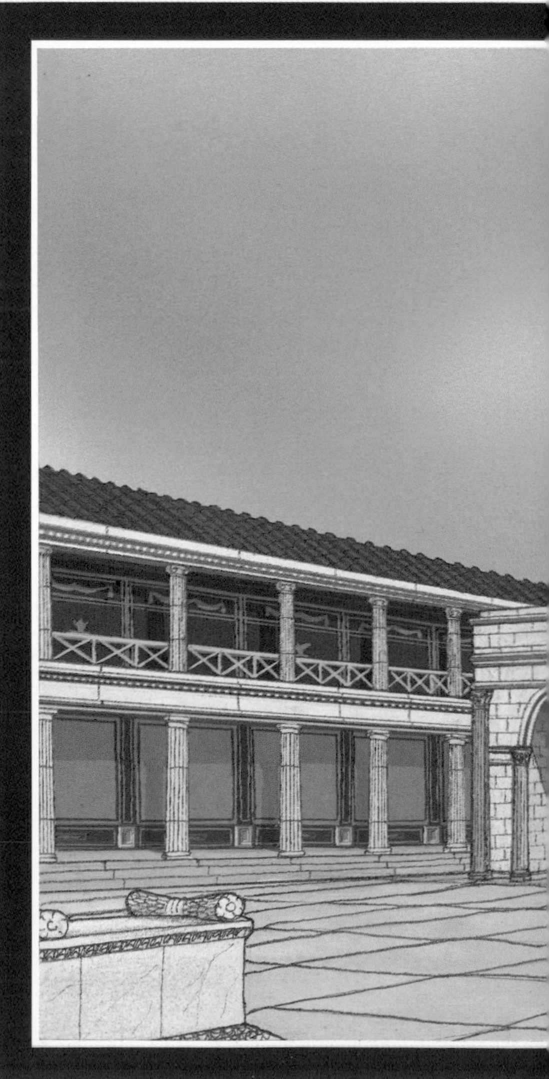

11 - TEMPLE OF JUPITER

On the short south side of the Forum square, the temple is dedicated to the Capitoline triad of Jupiter, Juno and Minerva. It was first built around the middle of the 2nd cent. B.C. as part of the enlargement and new orientation of the forum.
The podium, built in *opus incertum*, dates to the founding of the temple and inside houses rooms (*favissae*) comprised of three aisles and covered with vaulting which were to be used as storage chambers for the ex-votos and as storerooms. The temple was prostyle with six Corinthian columns on the front and three on the sides, and with piers at the outer corners of the cella, with composite capitals. In its earlier 2nd-cent. B.C. version the pronaos and the cella were shorter than what we see now and the entrance staircase on the front reached up to what is now the second intercolumniation. The cella had no aisles and was without an internal colonnade.
With the second phase, dated to the 2nd cent. B.C., the temple assumed its present size, with a very deep pronaos and the staircase which is divided into two flights below so as to include at the center a platform on which the altar was set. There must have been equestrian statues on either side of the staircase, for which only the bases remain. The cella was divided into three aisles by two rows of columns set in two tiers, Ionic below and Corinthian above, set along the side walls. The side aisles were thus extremely narrow.
The first wall decoration was painted in Style I in faux marble incrustation, probably replaced in the Sullan period by paintings in Style II. At the back of the cella a tripartite podium, with an elevation of half columns and three-quarter columns at the corners, held the statues of the Capitoline triad, of which a large head of Jupiter still remains.
A third phase in the restoration of the temple took place in the time of Tiberius. The tripartite podium of the cella was enlarged and faced in marble, the pronaos was repaved in travertine, the external walls and the podium were freshly stuccoed and the interior walls of the cella were redecorated with Style III painting.
An idea of what the Temple of Jupiter looked like can be had from a representation in the household shrine of the House of Caecilius Iucundus, in which the equestrian statues on either side the staircase are also visible.

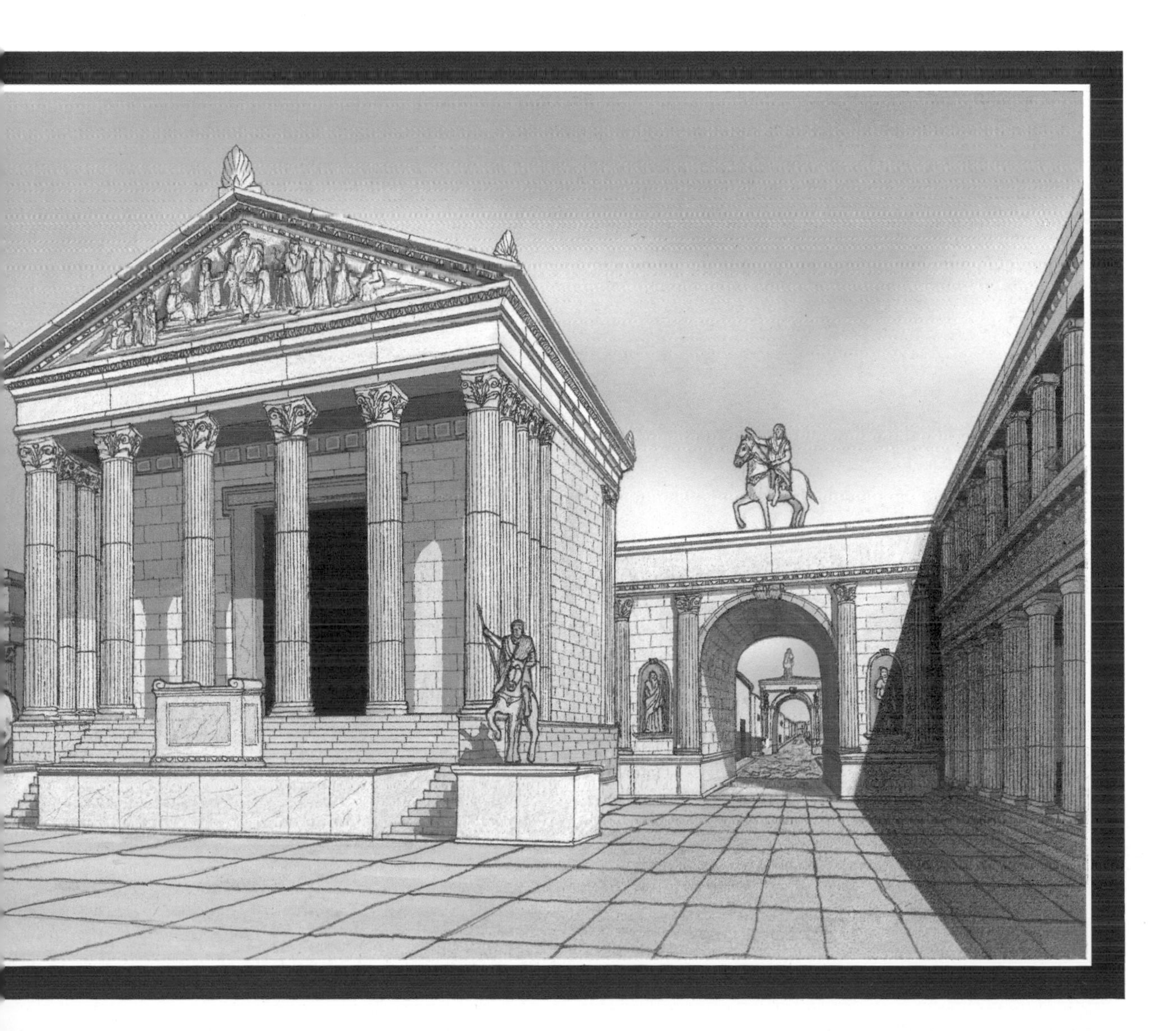

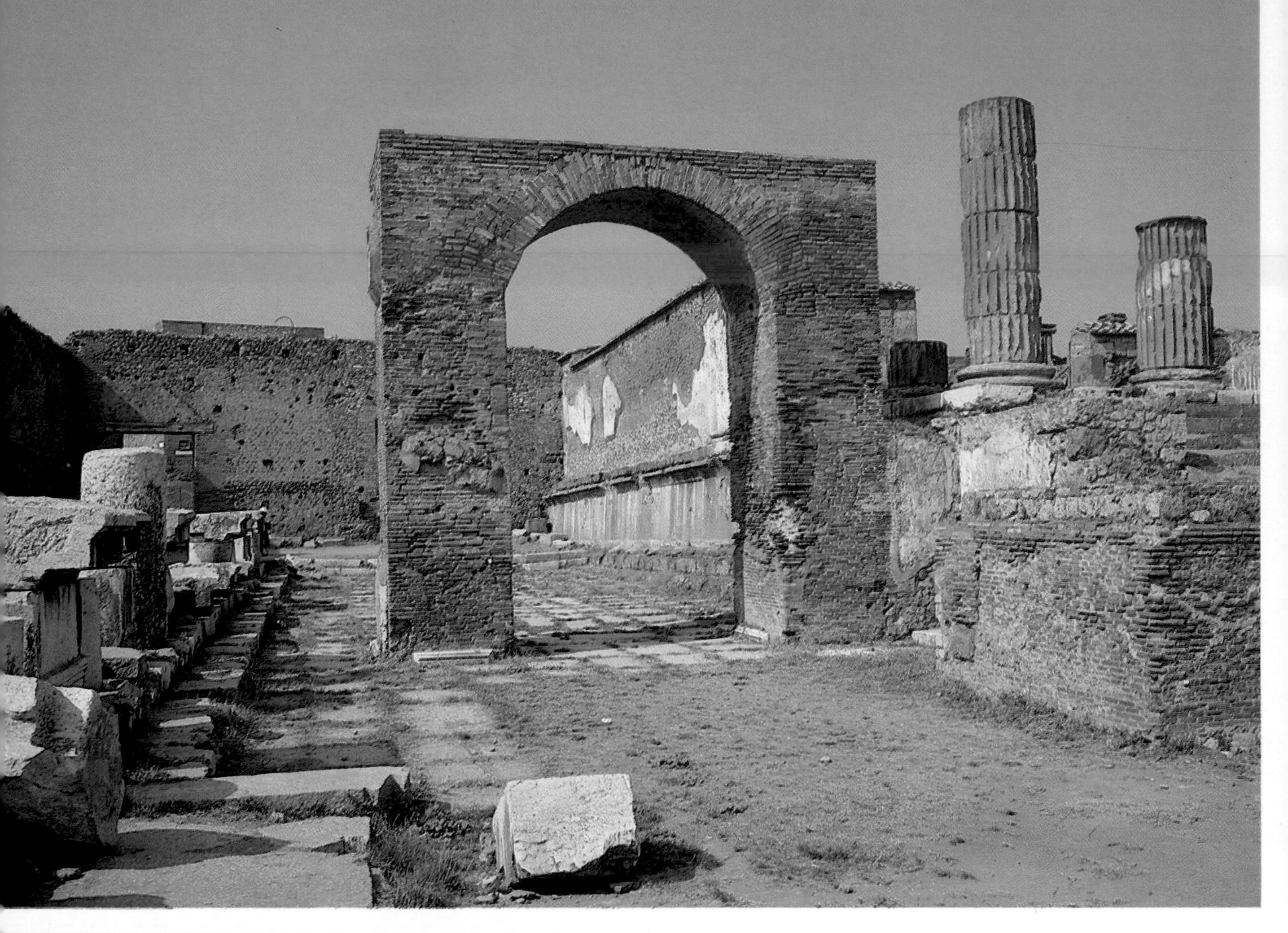

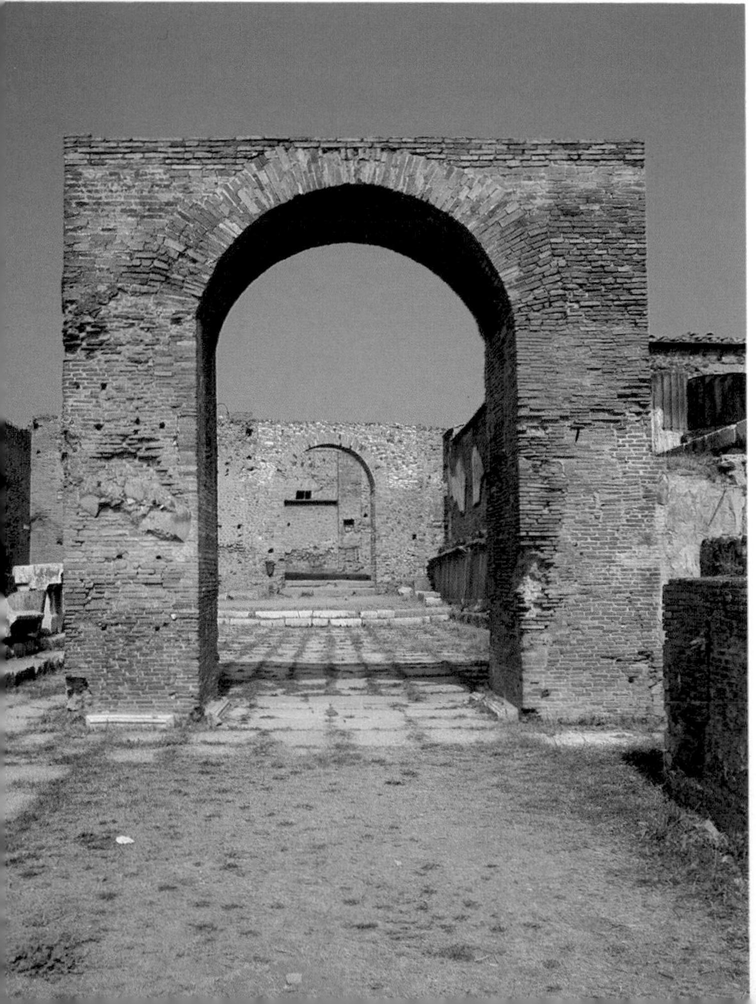

This Page: the honorary Arch to Drusus. Opposite: the two sides of the honorary Arch of Tiberius or Germanicus.

12 - ARCHES ON THE NORTH SIDE OF THE FORUM

The northern side of the Civil Forum is shut off by the mass of the Temple of Jupiter, flanked by two honorary arches in brick. Nothing is left of their original marble revetment. The western arch, situated at the height of the temple colonnade, was dedicated to Drusus; it originally had a pendant arch on the other side of the temple, which was torn down so as to leave open the view of the arch behind attributed to Tiberius or to Germanicus.

It was built further back from the temple and constitued a monumental entrance to the Forum. The uncertainty of the attribution is due to an inscription by Germanicus in which his son Nero is named, that was found nearby and which probsbly belonged to the arch. On either side of the passageway, facing the Forum, are two niches in which the statues of Nero and Drusus werw set. They were Germanicus' sons but also heirs to the throne after the death of the son of Tiberius. The bases of the marble columns which decorated the front and back of the arch are still extant. The attic must have been crowned by an equestrian statue of Tiberius or Germanicus.

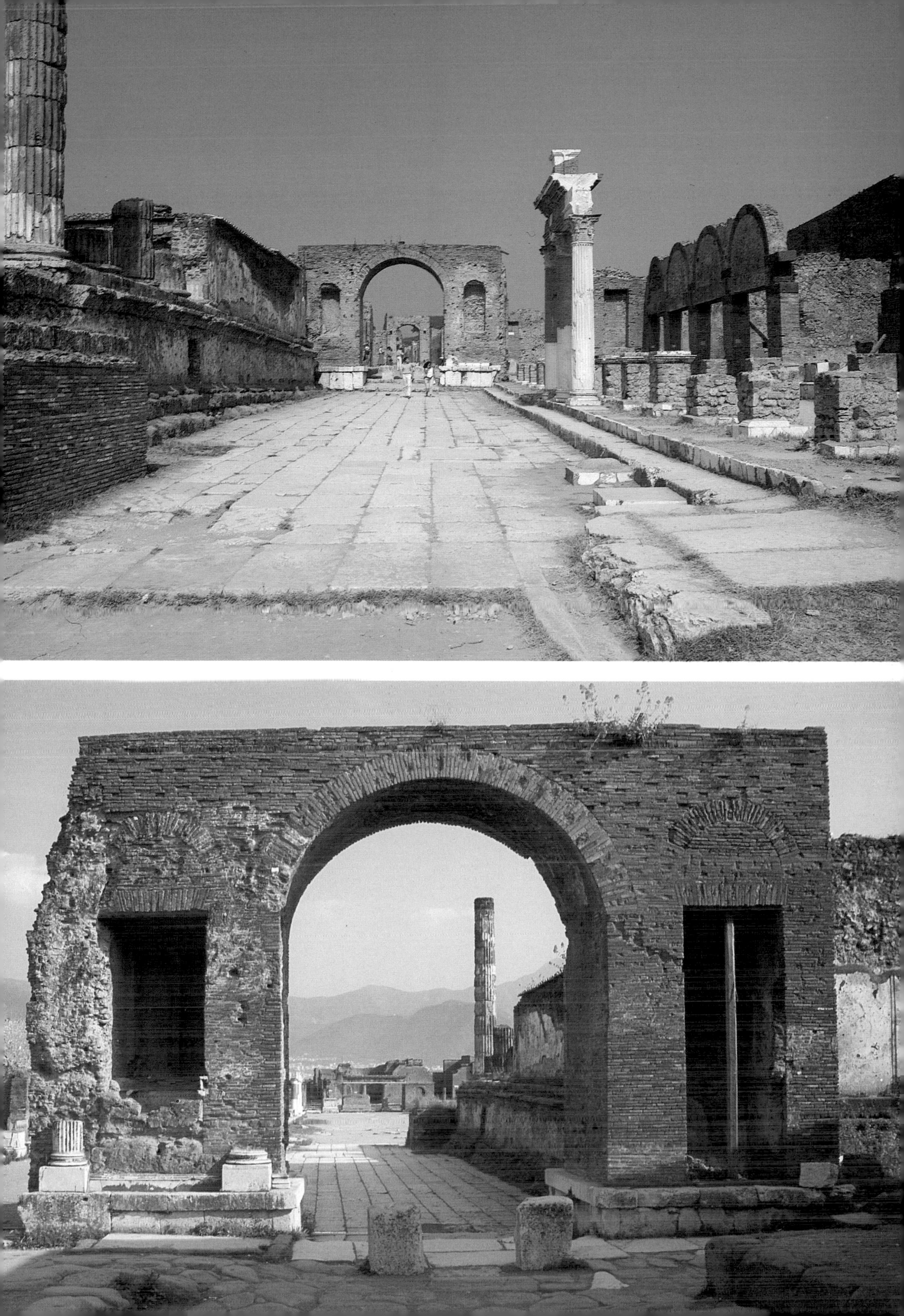

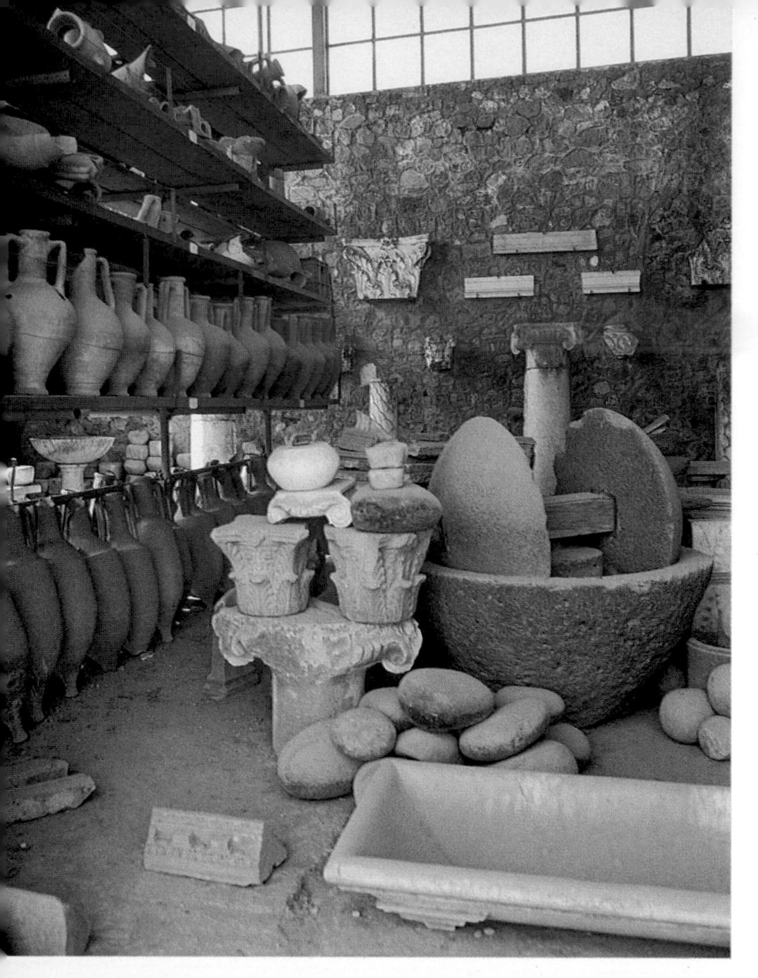

13 - HORREA OR FORUM OLITORIUM

This building is situated along the west side of the Civic Forum to the north of the Temple of Apollo. An open portico, it faces on the Forum square and on the facade has eight large piers in brick which frame eight entrances. It was to house the warehouses and the grain market, but it had not yet been finished when the eruption of A.D. 79 struck. The internal walls are of rough masonry with no trace of intonaco and the roof had not yet been built.

Left: a millstone, architectural fragments, stone weights and amphorae inside the Forum Olitorium. Below: the piers on the facade of the Horrea.

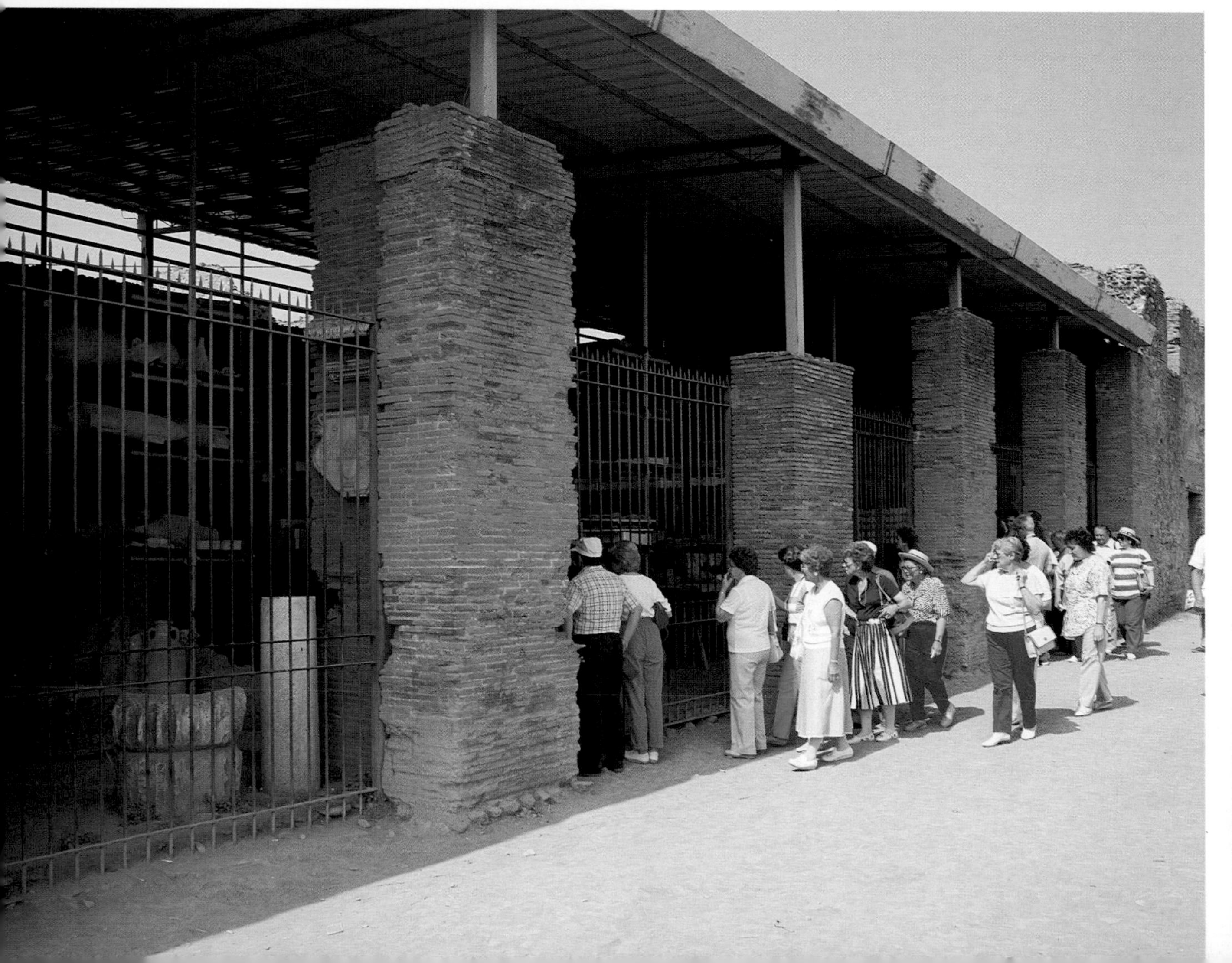

At present, covered by a modern shed roof and closed by a gate, the portico is used as the storeroom for the archaeological finds. It contains a large quantity of amphoras and pottery of daily use, oil presses, capitals and architectural elements as well as casts of the victims of the eruption from the Antiquarium. Of particular interest is the 'muleteer' who, crouched up, tries to protect his face with his hands from the terrible exhalations. He was found next to the skeleton of his mule, under the portico of the Large Palaestra. Inside a case is the cast of a dog who was chained near the entrance of the House of Vesonius Primus, struck as he tried in vain to free himself.

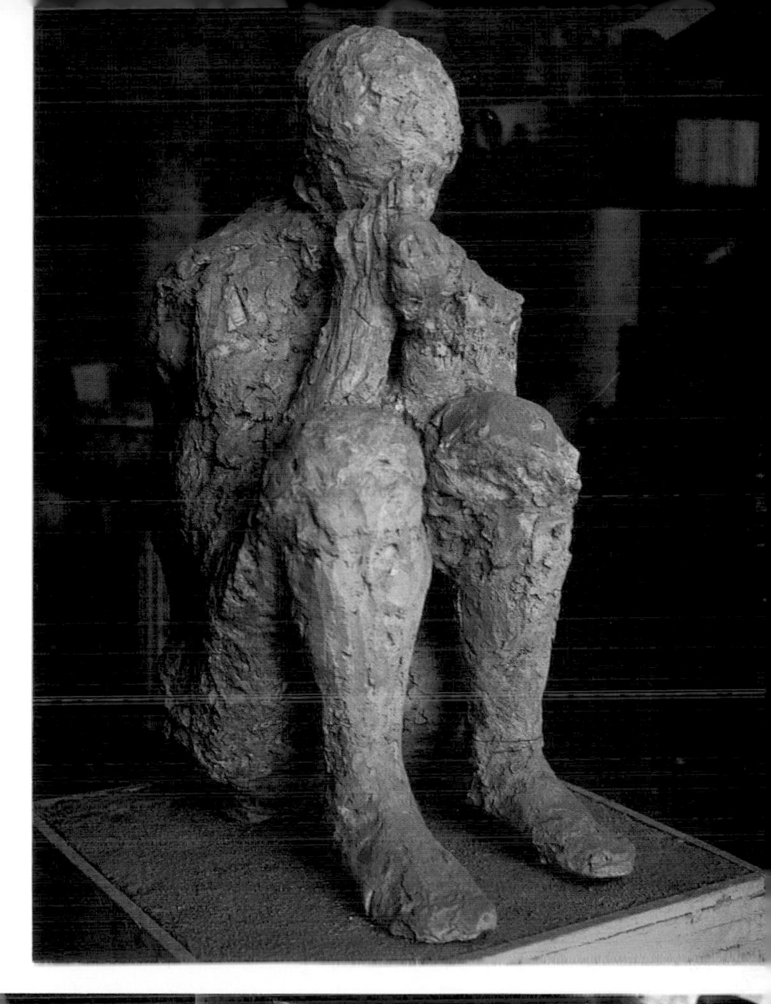

Right: the famous cast of the « muleteer », victim of the exhlations of the eruption, found in the Large Palaestra. Below: a series of amphorae from the houses of Pompeii.

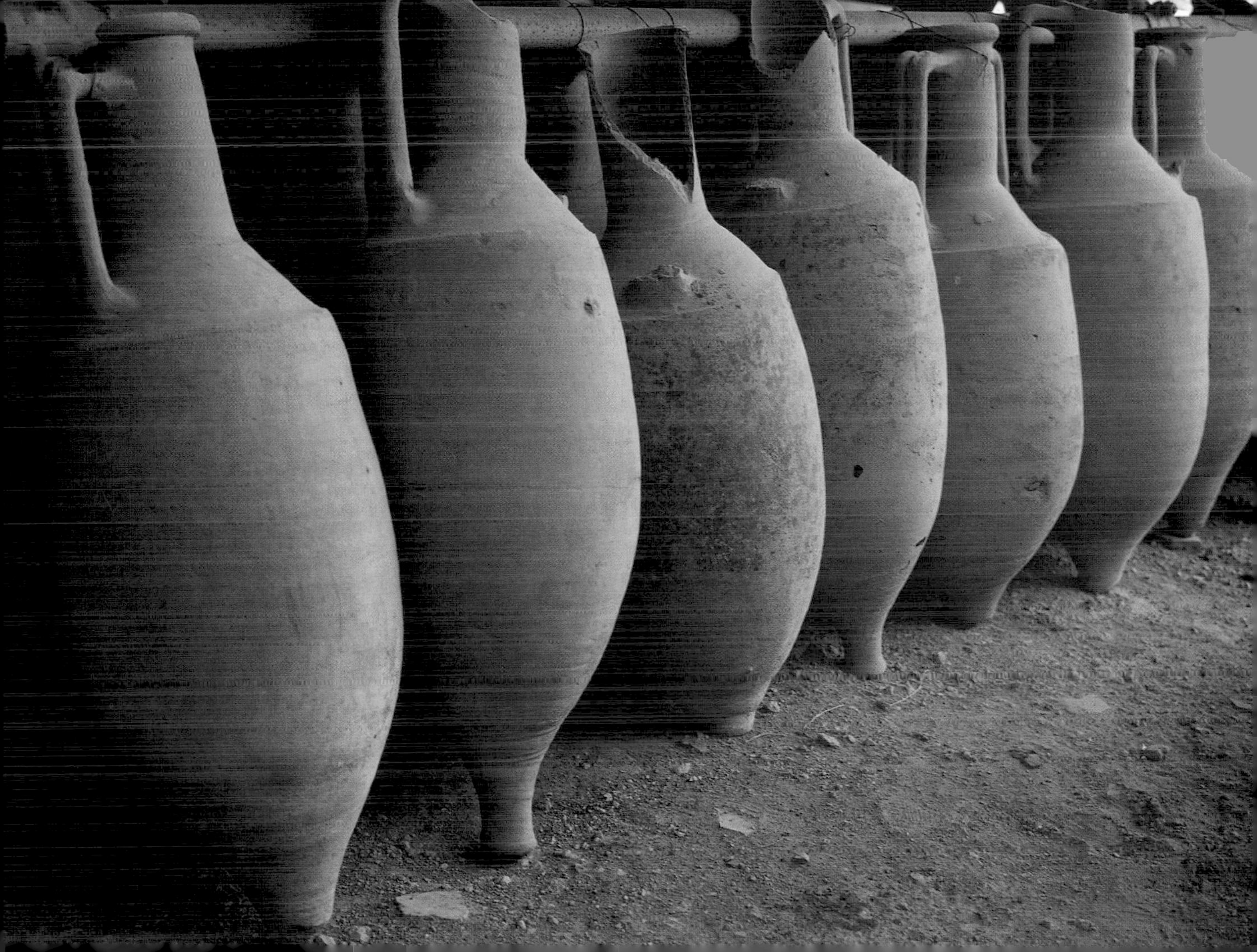

II PART

Via dell'Abbondanza - Triangular Forum - Doric Temple - Large Theater - Odeion - Gladiators Barracks - Temple of Isis - House of Menander - House of the Ceii - House of the Diadoumeni - Fullonica Stephani - Thermopolium with Lararium - Thermopolium of Asellina - House of Trebius Valens - House of Paquius Proculus - House of Octavius Quartio - House of Venus in the Shell - House of Iulia Felix - Amphitheater - Large Palaestra - Necropolis of Porta Nocera

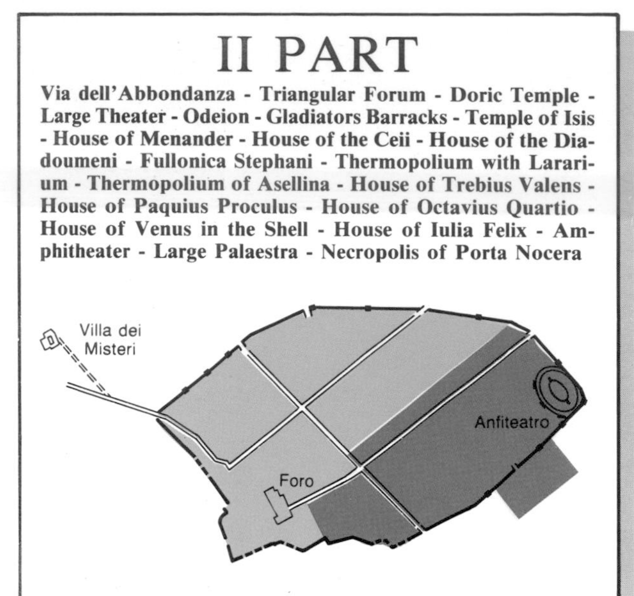

14 - VIA DELL'ABBONDANZA AND INTERSECTION OF HOLCONIUS

The Via dell'Abbondanza was one of the two principal *decumani* of the city (the other consisted of Via di Nola and its extensions into Via della Fortuna and Via delle Terme), in other words the east-west street axis which traversed the entire urban area, even if in Pompeii the orientation is more southwest-northeast. The western stretch of Via dell'Abbondanza connects Via Stabiana, that is the *cardo maximus*, with the Forum square, after which the street continues as Via Marina, leading out of the Porta Marina. This first stretch of Via dell'Abbondanza, which belongs to the earliest phases of Pompeii's city plan as it grew up around the area of the Forum, later, when the city's town plan was considerably enlarged, was continued beyond the Via Stabiana, following a course that was exactly parallel to the *decumanus* of Via di Nola, until it reached the Porta di Sarno. This large thoroughfare connected the most important centers of city life with each other, from the Forum, to the Stabian Baths, up to the zone of the Amphitheater and the Large Palaestra. The maximum width was about 8.50 m. and it seems that in the stretch towards the Forum it had been newly paved by the *aedili*. The intersection formed by the crossing between Via dell'Abbondanza and Via Stabiana, that is between the *cardo maximus* and the

This and opposite page: Via dell'Abbondanza and the fountain from which it takes its name.

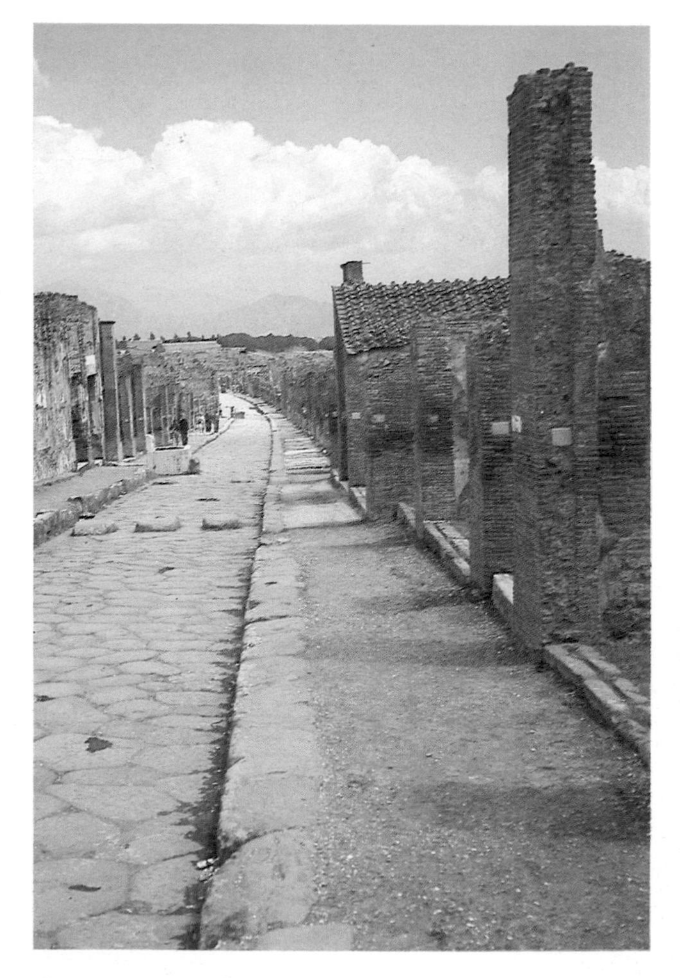

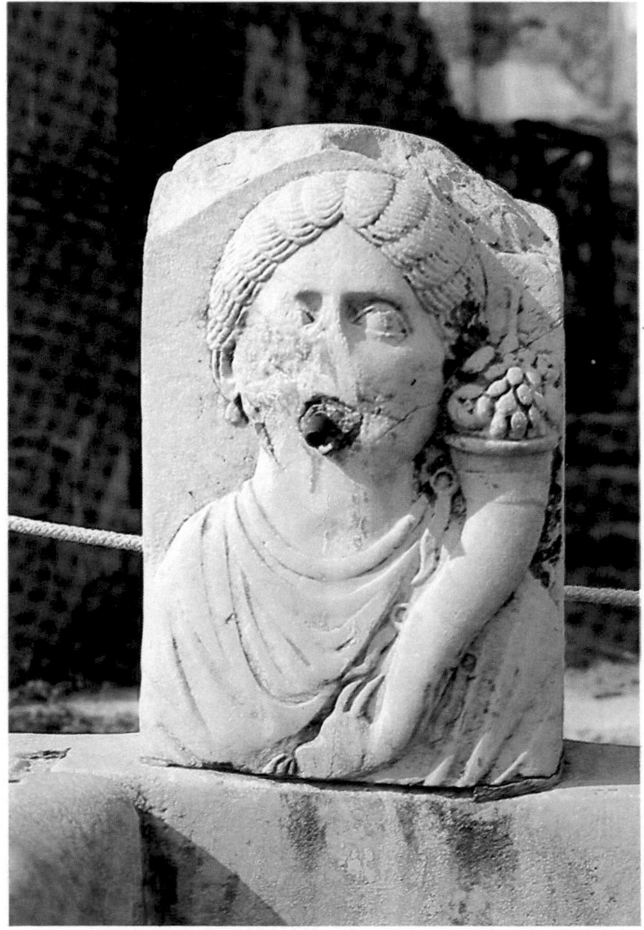

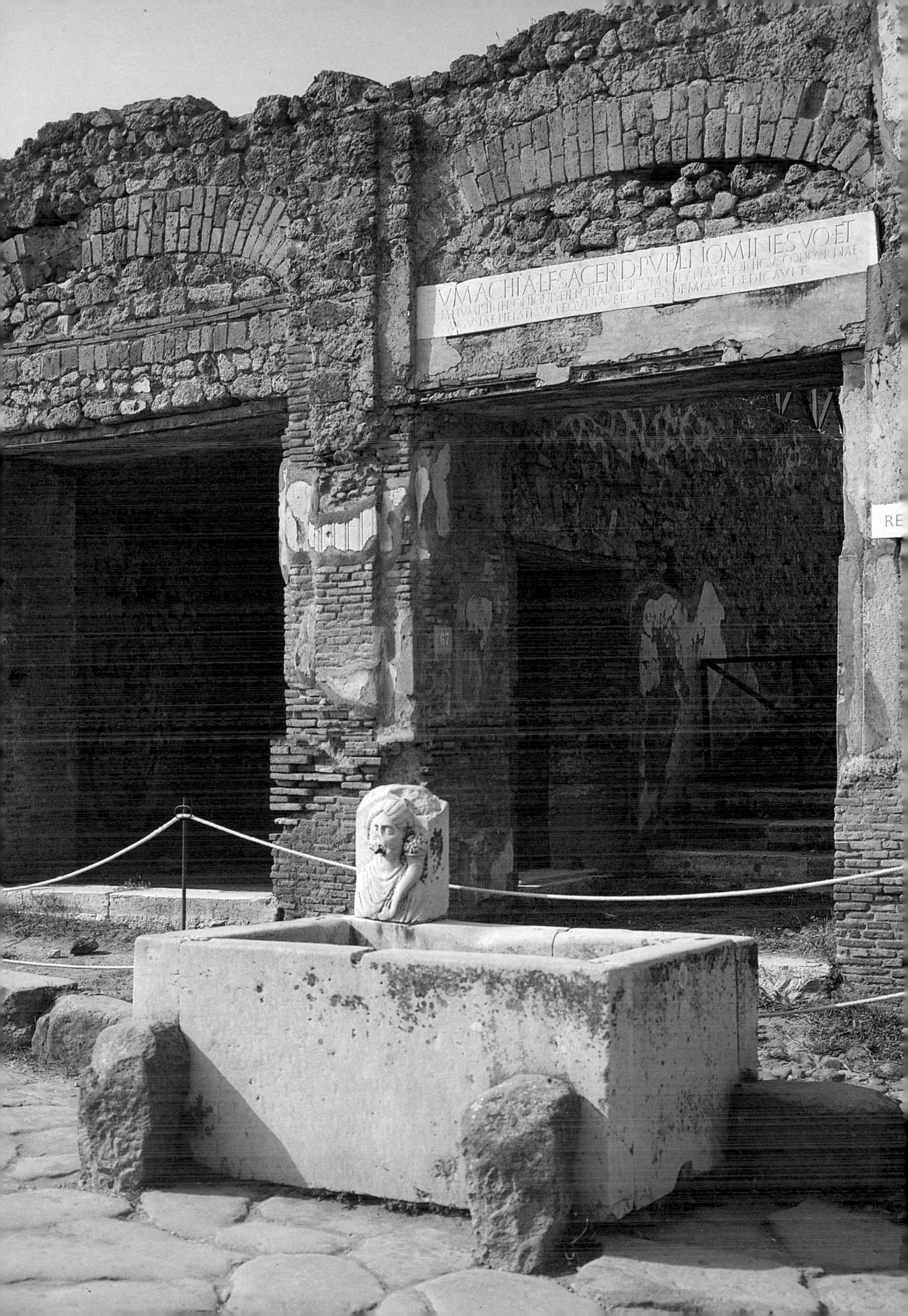
V·MACHIA·L·F·SACERD·PVBL·NOMINE·SVO·ET

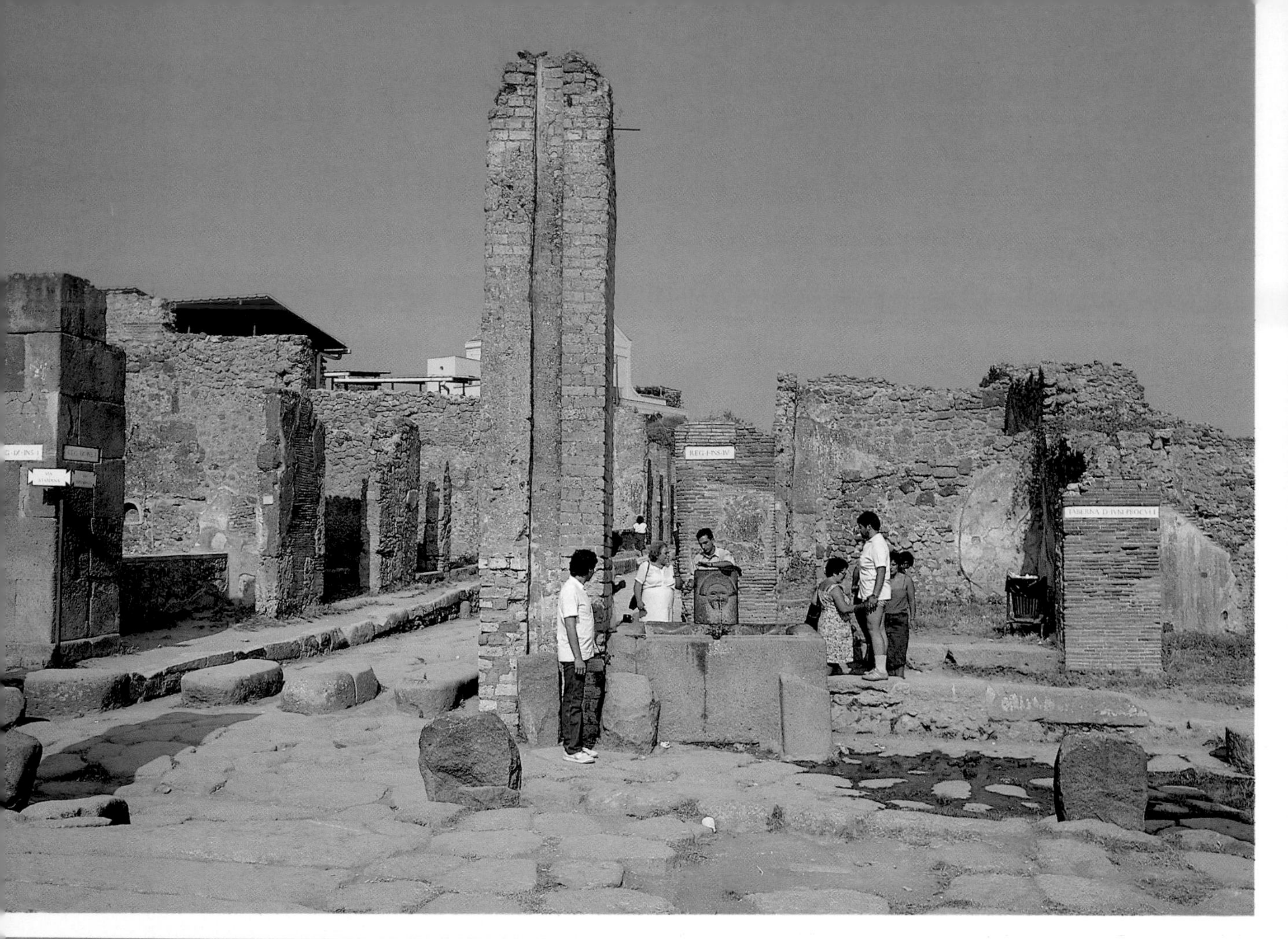

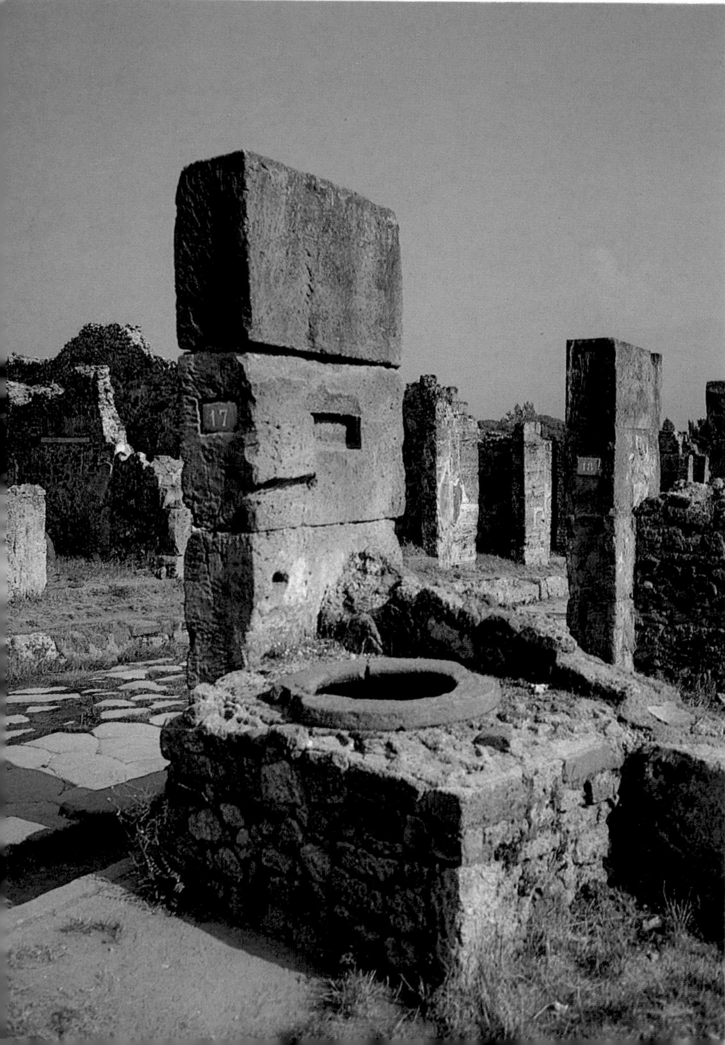

Above: the Intersection of Holconius as it is now and, on the left, a shop nearby. Opposite: a reconstruction of the intersection.

decumanus maximus is known by the name of Holconius for on a base near one of the four piers which supported a four-sided arch there was originally the wreathed statue of M. Holconius Rufus, one of the outstanding political figures in Pompeii of the Augustan period. The house attributed to him stands nearby. On one side of the intersection is the fountain with a basin in which is represented the *Concordia Augusta* with a cornucopia, erroneously identified with the personification of Abundance, from which the street takes its conventional name.

15 - TRIANGULAR FORUM AND DORIC TEMPLE

The so-called Triangular Forum is situated on the far end of a lava outcrop to the southwest of the Large Theater and the Quadriporticus of the Gladiators, in a striking position overlooking the plain below. This area came to look as it does now in the Samnite period, in the 2nd cent. B.C., as part of the town-planning project for the restructuration of the theater area.
The complex can be reached through a propylaeum with six Ionic columns and a fountain in front, which opens in the northern tip of the triangular piazza. It has a portico with ninety-five Doric columns on three sides, while the southwest side has been left open with its fine panorama towards the sea. Right inside the entrance, near the north portico, were a fountain and the base of a statue

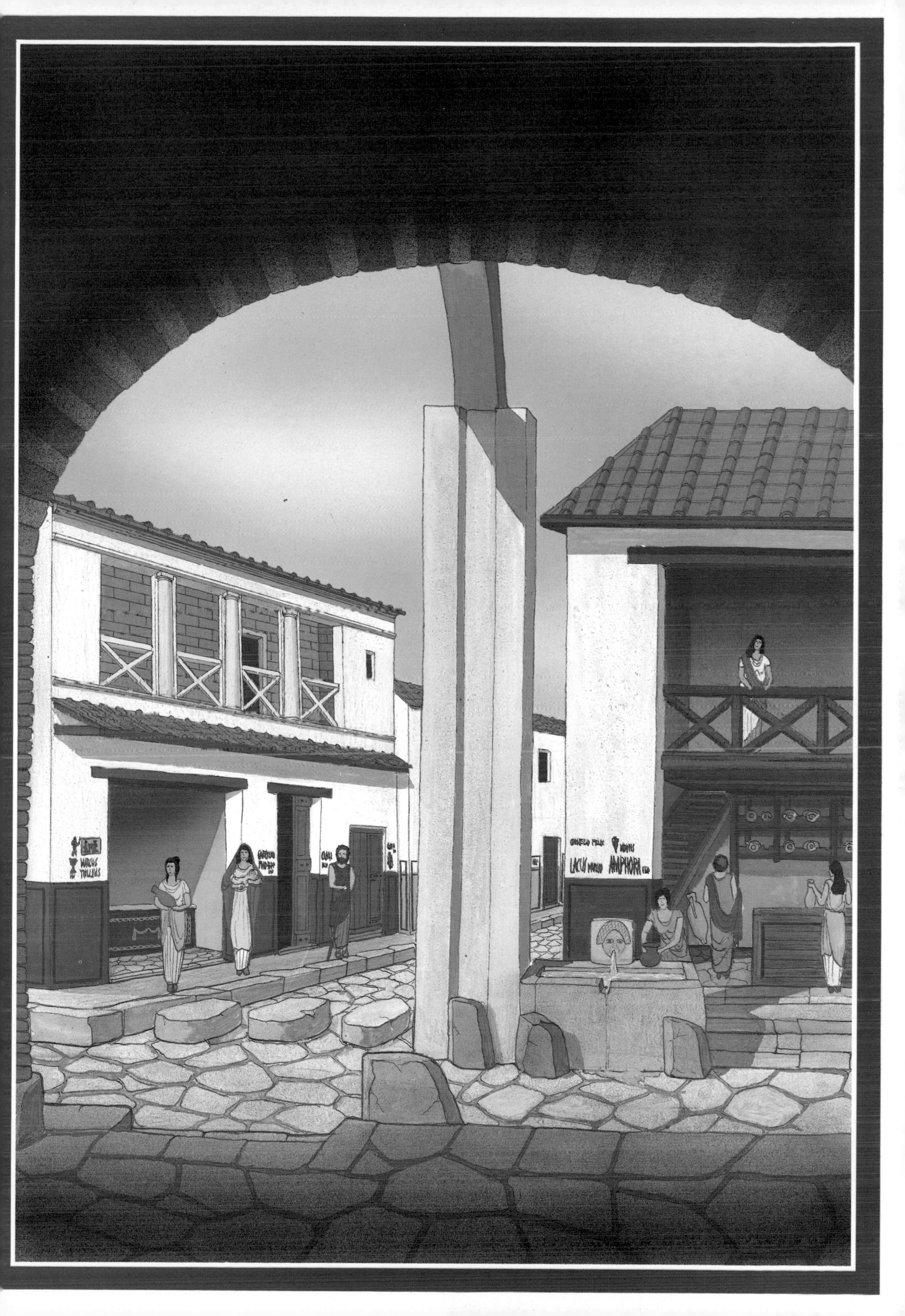
MARCUS
AMPHORA

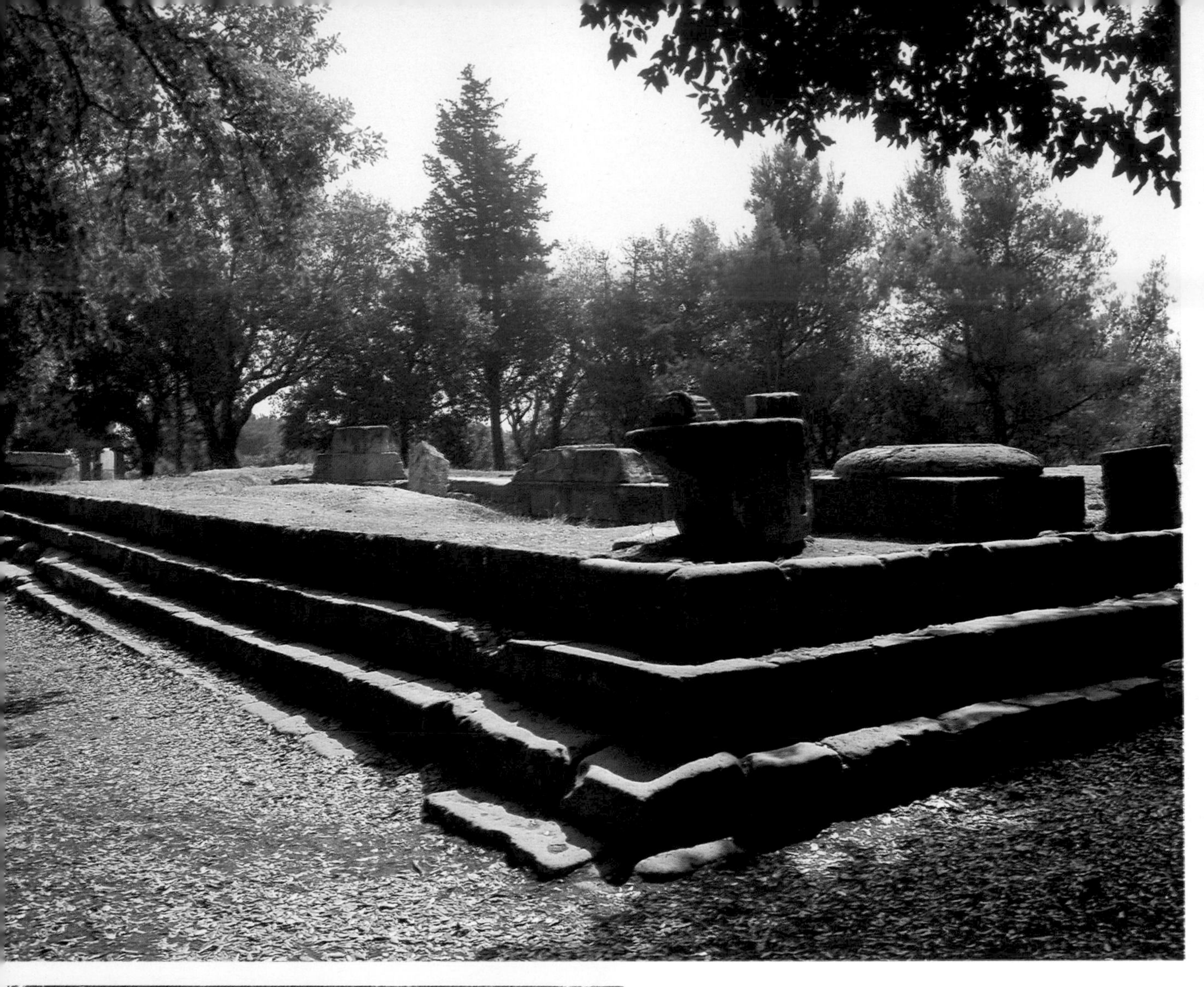

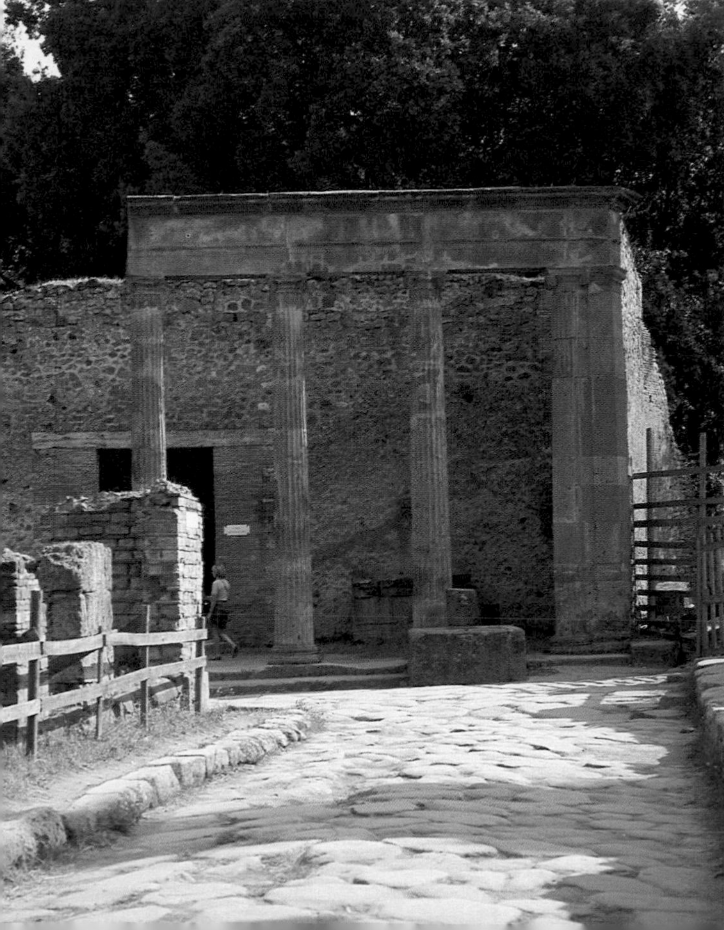

dedicated to Marcellus, Augustus' grandson. The archaic Doric Temple stands in the center of the piazza, with nothing left now but the foundations. To judge from the few surviving architectural elements, it was founded in the second half of the 6th cent. B.C. It is difficult to establish what the original plan was, for it is poorly preserved and was frequently remodelled in the course of the centuries. Renovation dating to four different phases has been identified, to between the end of the 6th and the 2nd cent. B.C. Two divinities, Hercules and Minerva, represented in some of the antefixes, were probably worshipped here.
The double rectangular enclosure in front of the facade of the temple probably represents the *heroon* for the cult of the mythical founder of the city. Three tufa altars are found next to it. Not far from the *heroon*, a *tholos* with seven Doric columns encloses a well cut into the lava rock. As shown by an inscription in Oscan, this building was built by the *meddix* (an important public office in the Samnite period) Numerius Trebius. Near the northwest corner of the temple a semicircular bench with lion feet (*schola*) and a sundial behind it were set up in the Augustan period by the *duoviri* L. Sepunius Sandilianus and M. Herennius Epidianus, both of whom also dedicated the sundial in front of the Temple of Apollo.

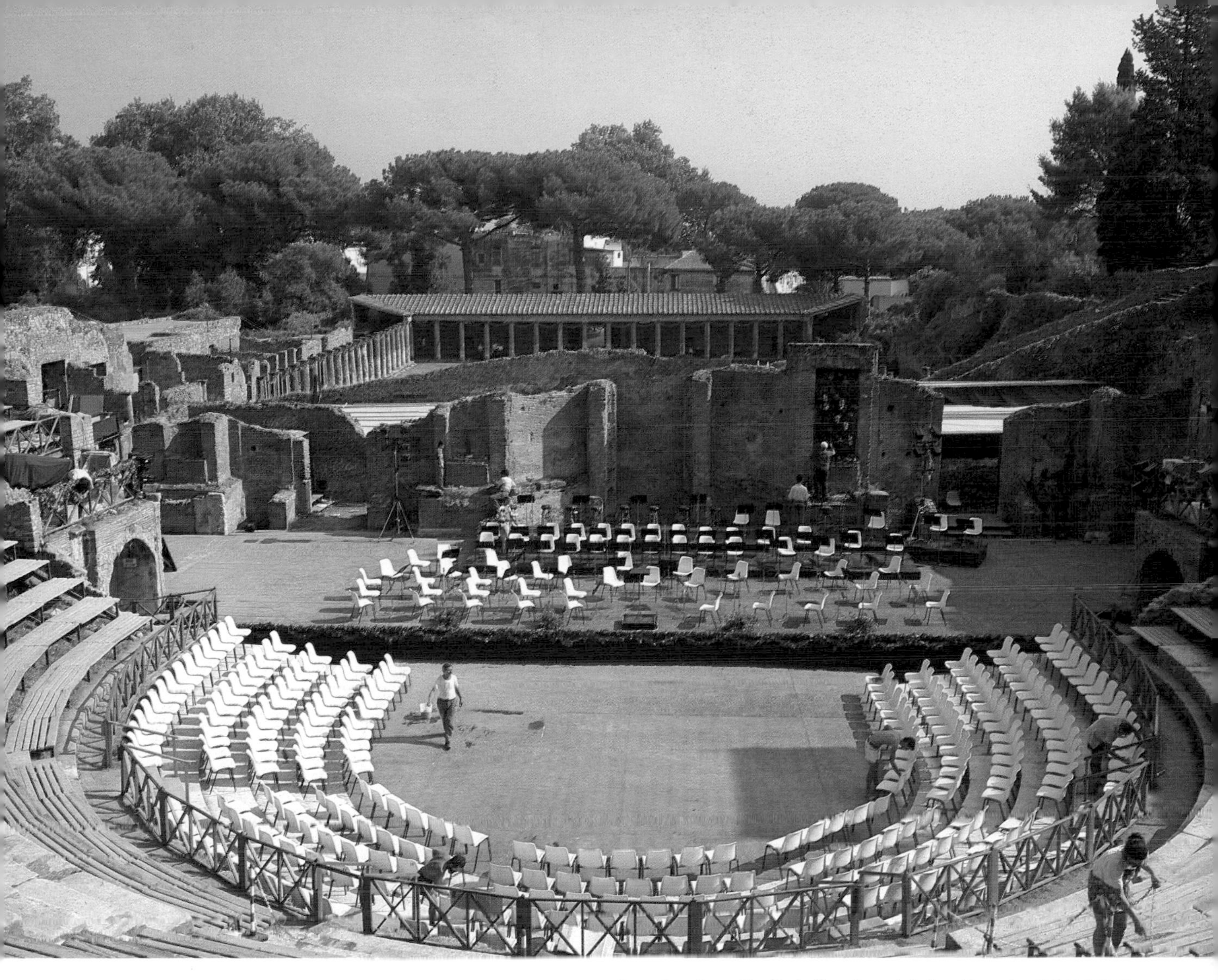

Opposite, above: the Doric Temple and, below, the columned entrance of the Triangular Forum. On this page, above, the interior of the cavea of the Large Theater.

16 - LARGE THEATER

Built in the Hellenistic period, between the 3rd and the 2nd cent. B.C., the theater of Pompeii obviously assimilated all the architectural canons of the Greek theater, which remained basically the same despite the various modifications the building was subject to. The *cavea* was in fact set into the natural slopes of the lava ridge and not raised on masonry substructures; the orchestra is in horseshoe shape and not semi-circular, a mode which was also of Greek origin and which was to encounter greater favor in the Roman-Italic ambience. Moreover the specific position of the building can be traced back to the sacral character of the theater performances which was strongly felt in the Greek world, and which is here manifested in the fact that it communicates directly with the so-called Doric Temple and the ancient sacred area of the Triangular Forum which it included.
The theater as we see it now has many elements due to restoration carried out in the Augustan period, as stated in various inscriptions, under the patronage of Marcus Holconius Rufus and his brother Marcus Holconius Celer, members of a wealthy family who held the most important civic offices in the city. The architect responsible

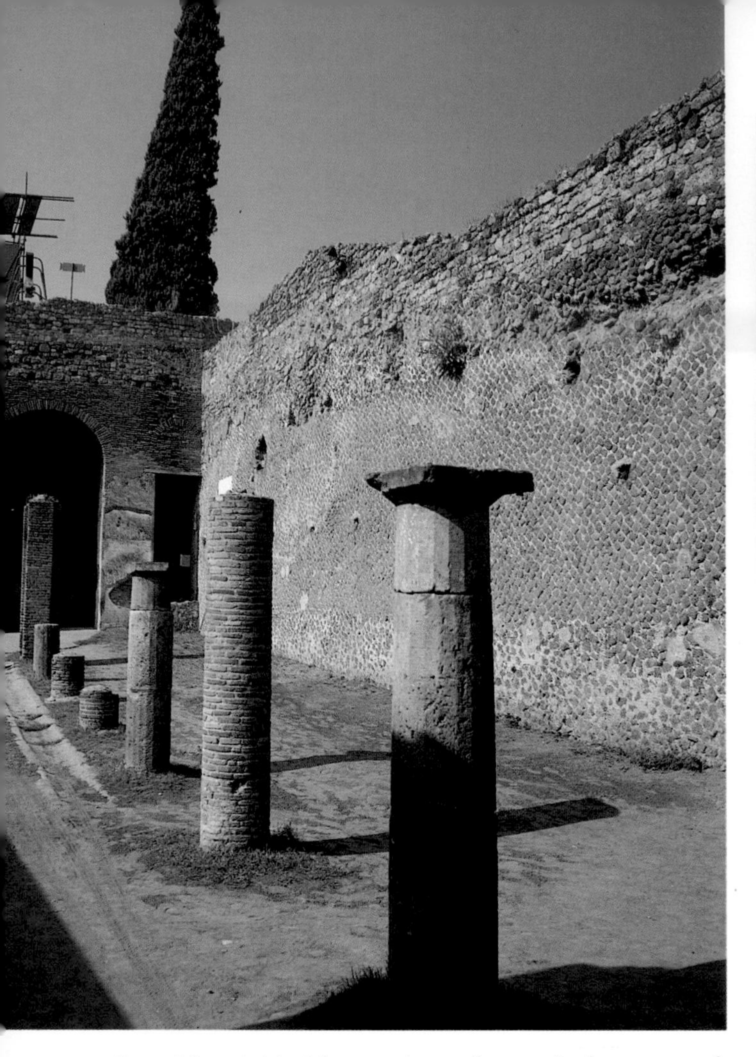

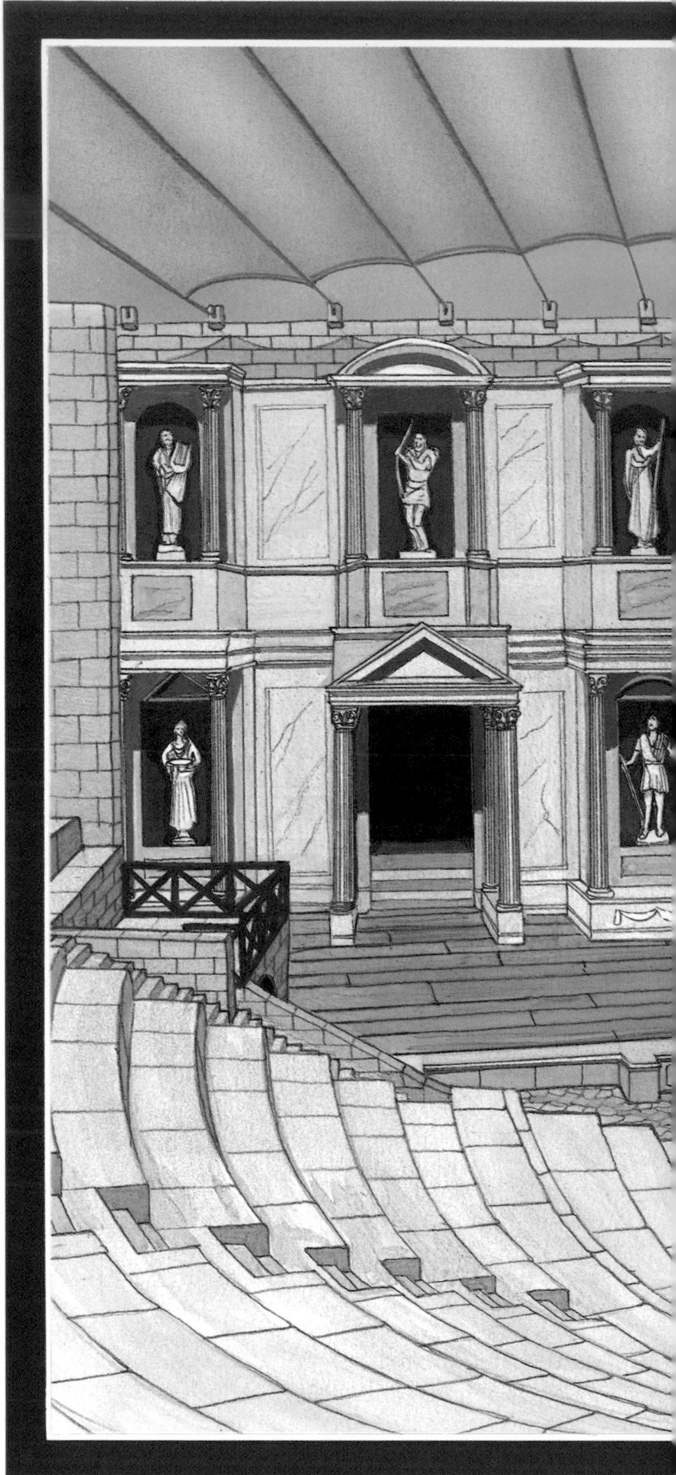

Above, left: a stretch of the secondary portico near the frons scenae of the Large Theater and, on the right, the reconstruction of the interior of the Theater.

for the renovations and the innovations was the freedman Marcus Artorius Primus: he built the annular gallery (*crypta*) on which the *summa cavea* rests, and installed the *tribunalia*, or boxes of honor above the vaults of the covered *paradoi*. The *paradoi*, or two corridors which led to the orchestra seats at the end of the *cavea*, were originally uncovered according to the Greek model and were vaulted over around 80 B.C., shortly after the installation of Sulla's colony, perhaps under the influence of the Odeion nearby which had just been built. The head of a satyr set into the keystone of the arch of the western *parados* seems to date from this period.
The *cavea* is subdivided by corridors into *ima*, *media* and *summa*, which are in turn divided vertically into five sectors (*cunei*) and could accommodate as many as 5000 spectators. In its four rows of broad low tiers the *ima cavea* housed the seats of the decurions (*bisellia*). At the center of the lowest of the twenty rows of tiers in the *media cavea*, with the best possible view, was the place reserved for Marcus Holconius Rufus, as an inscription in bronze letters tells us. The wooden poles which supported the *velarium* were set into the outer wall of the *summa cavea* and this canopy may have been tied to the shed which covered the *frons scenae* by a system of cords. Basins for waterworks were installed in the orchestra, since it was no longer used by the chorus for dances or scenic movements. The walls of the *paradoi* acted as a connection between the *cavea* and the podium of the stage (*proskenion*) which touch on them and form a continuous straight front. Access is via the three small staircases. The housing for the poles of the curtain, which was

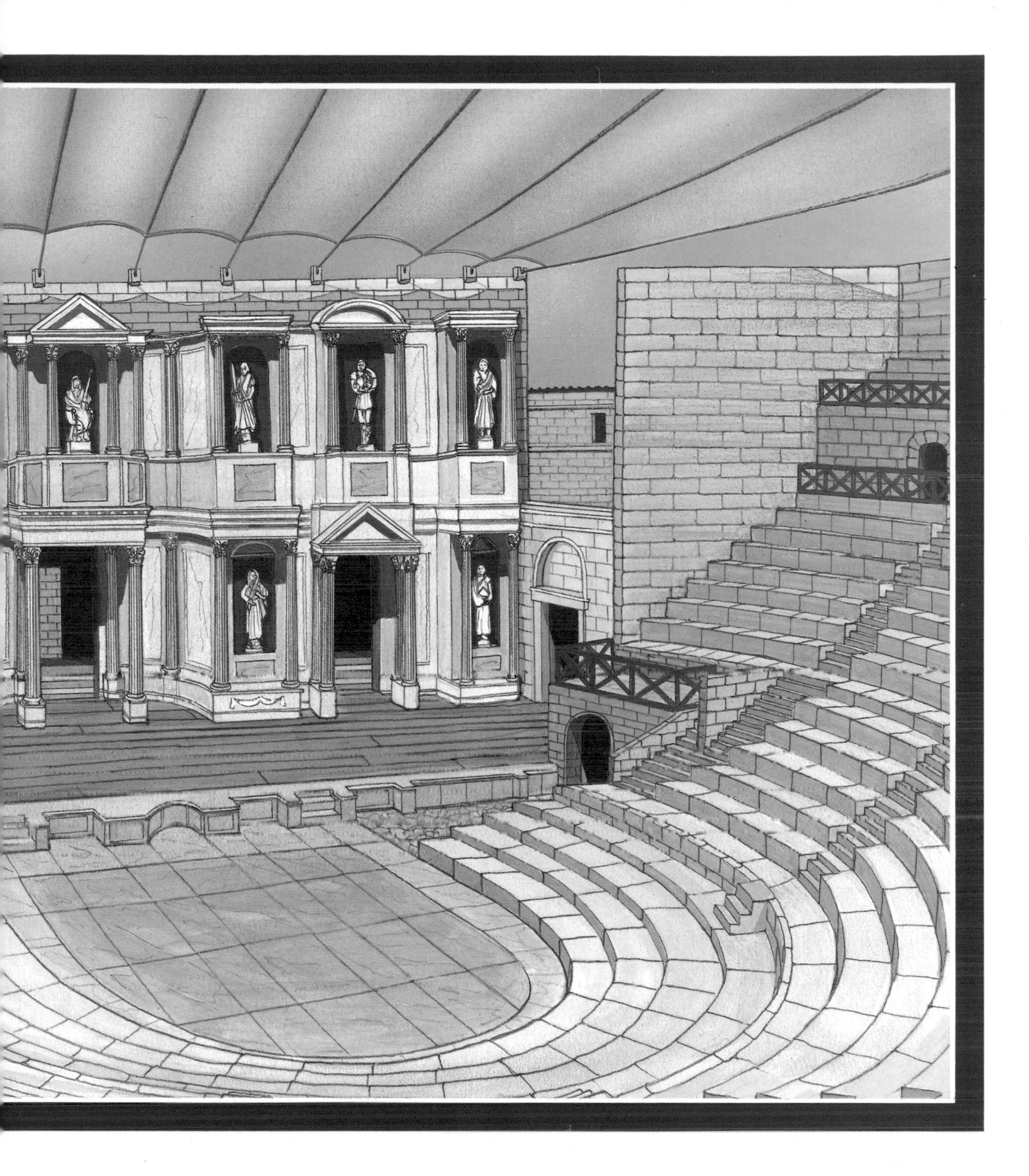

raised from below instead of being dropped down from above, can still be seen. The *frons scenae* behind dates to after the earthquake of A.D. 62 and originally consisted of two stories, enlivened by a large apse in the center and two square niches at the sides, in imitation of the facade of a palace. A series of lesser niches framed by columns enriched the elevation. They contained various statues, including one of Marcus Holconius Rufus, set here on the occasion of his fourth *duovirato* in 3-2 B.C., and that of his brother Marcus Holconius Celer. Three doors in the *frons scenae* lead to a spacious rectangular room behind, which must have served as dressing room for the actors. In its first version the *proskenion* was not raised and the *frons scenae* was straight with two avant corps (*parascenii*) at the sides, the latter an element of Italic origin, set at an angle. Nothing remains of the *cavea* except the four platforms of the *ima cavea*, a few tiers of the *media* and the bare traces of the *summa*.
Recently work has been effectuated in the theater so that it can once more be used as such.

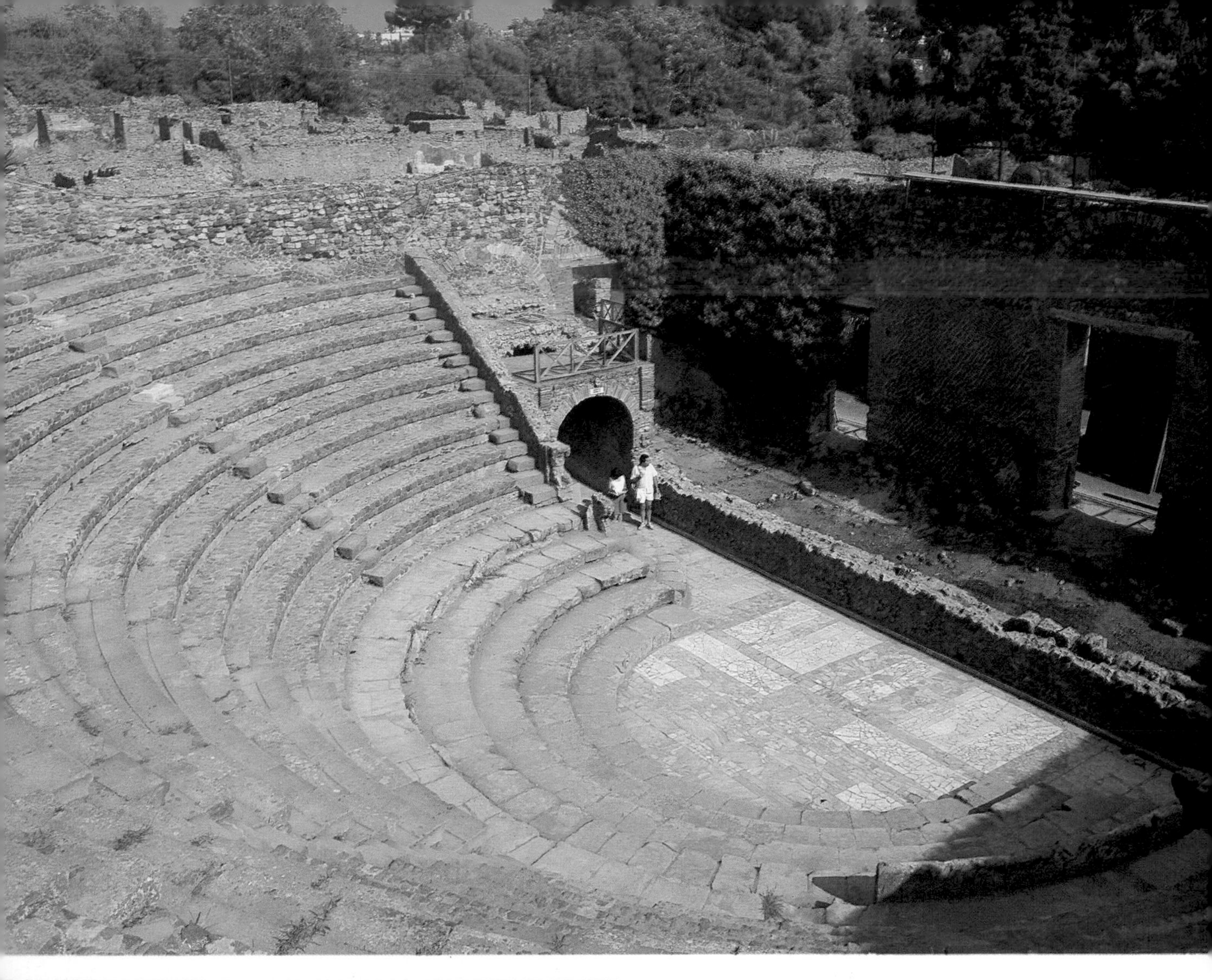

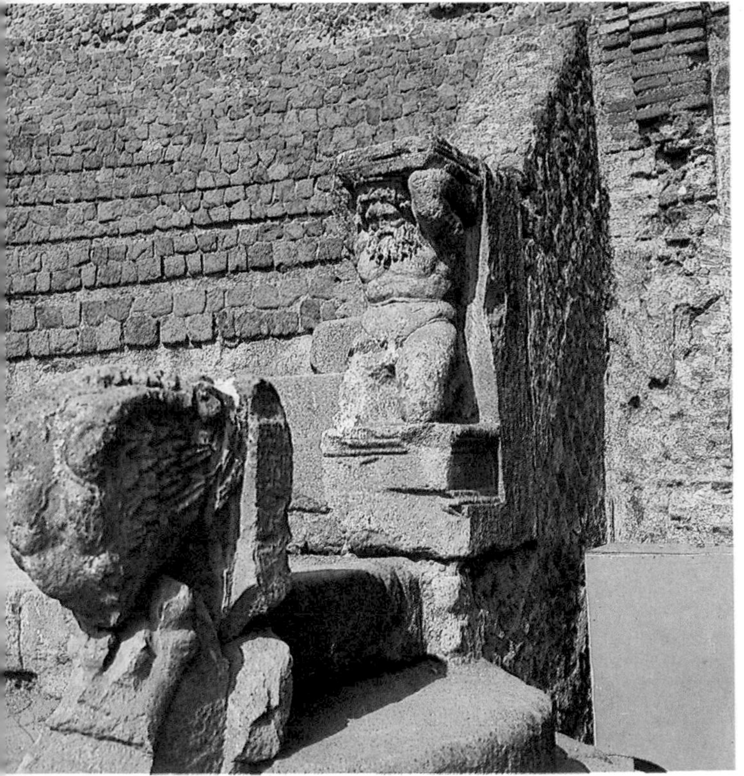

Above: the interior of the Odeion and, on the left, one of the kneeling atlantes figures decorating the head of the cavea.

17 - ODEION OR SMALL THEATER

Situated near the Large Theater, the construction of the *odeion* had evidently already been foreseen in the town plan of the entire area in the Samnite period, even though it was not to be built until Pompeii was transformed into a colony by Sulla (80 B.C.).
Two inscriptions inform us that the two Sullan *duoviri* Q. Valquo and M. Porcius were responsible for having the structure built. It consists of a theater *cavea* inserted into a square perimetral wall on which the roof rested. The Odeion was in fact meant for a more intimate type of spectacle, such as musical auditions, poetry recitals, mime. The seating capacity is about 1500.
Architecturally there are evident affinities with the neighboring Large Theater, except that here the orchestra is semicircular. The *paradoi* (entrances) are vaulted and support the *tribunalia*, reserved for particularly important spectators. The first four tiers of the *cavea* were for the seats of the city's decurions, the *scena*, as well as the *frons scenae*, are straight. The latter has five doorways which lead to a room behind that served as a dressing room. The orchestra was paved in marble in the Augustan period. The lower part of the end walls of the *cav-*

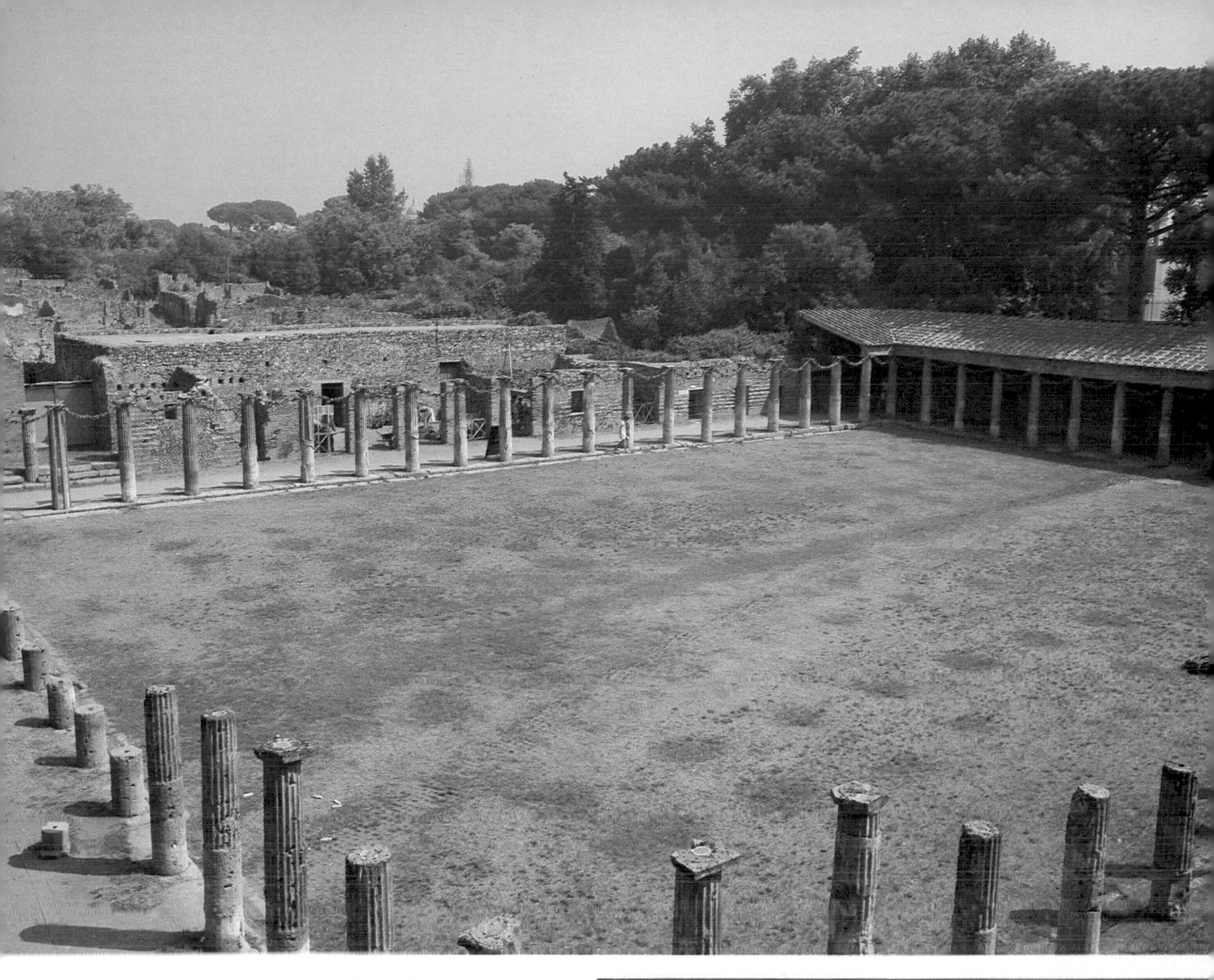

Above: the large quadriporticus of the Gladiators Barracks. Right: the helmet of a gladiator found here (Museo Nazionale, Naples).

ea are decorated with kneeling atlantes figures in tufa. The architectural model for the Odeion is to be found in the *bouleuteria* (seats of the city councils) of the Hellenistic period such as the one in Miletus, datable to around 170 B.C.

18 - GLADIATORS BARRACKS

A large quadriporticus stands behind the stage of the Large Theater and is connected to it, in line with the Vitruvian canon which, according to the Greek model, provided for a porticoed area in which the spectators could walk and converse during the intervals between spectacles. This example in Pompeii is one of the oldest known in Italy for this type of building and it dates to the early 1st cent. B.C. The quadriporticus, composed of 74 Doric columns, can be reached from an entrance with three Ionic columns set near the north corner. After the earthquake of A.D. 62 the complex lost its original function and was turned into barracks for gladiators. The monumental entrance was walled up and a guard post was set near an entrance doorway. In this phase a series of rooms on two floors was realized. The northeast side houses the sector for the mess with a spacious exedra

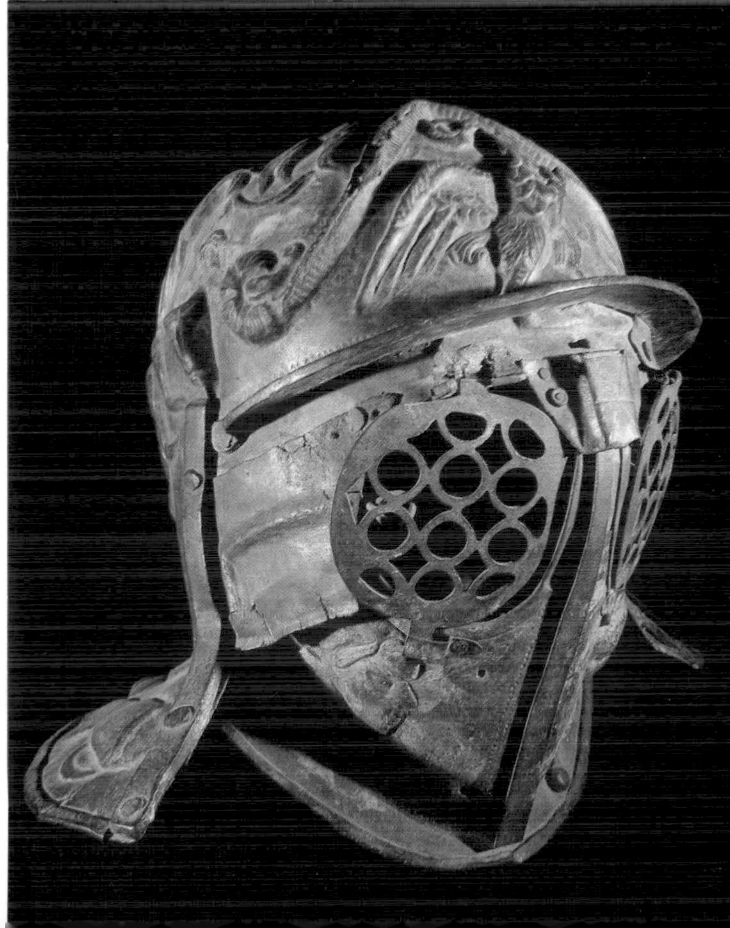

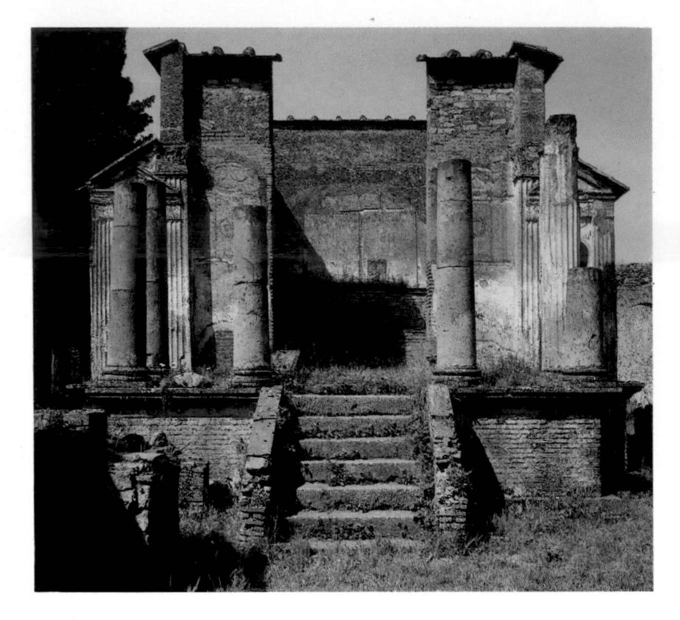

Above and alongside: the Temple of Isis as it is and the reconstruction.

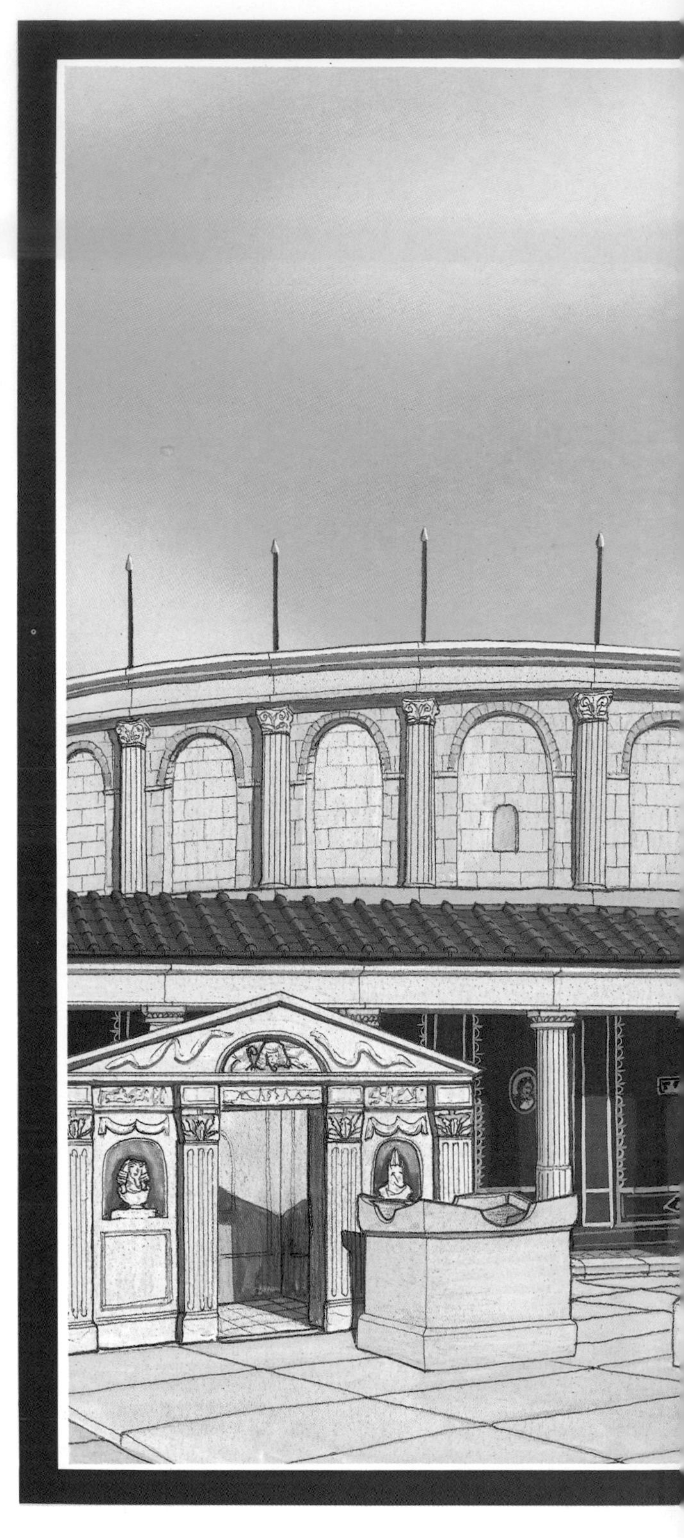

preceded by four piers which comprised the dining room, and a large kitchen with annexed storerooms. The apartment of the *lanista* or instructor was on the top floor while the gladiators were lodged in the cells arranged along the sides of the quadriportico. In some of them helmets and richly decorated parade armor was found, as well as eighteen cadavers and the skeleton of an infant in a basket.
An exedra at the center of the southwest side has frescoes in Style IV depicting Mars and Venus and trophies of gladiators' arms. A room in the southwest side served as a prison as shown by the iron shackles fastened to a beam, although the four bodies found here were not chained. A monumental staircase on the northwest side led to the Triangular Forum. The skeletons of a stableboy and mule were found in a stable nearby.

19 - TEMPLE OF ISIS

It is situated to the north of the Large Theater, between the Samnite Palaestra and the Temple of Jupiter Meilichio. As we are told in an inscription on the architrave, this religious complex was restored after the earthquake of A.D. 62 by a private individual, the wealthy freedman Numerius Popidius Ampliatus in the name of his son Numerius Popidius Celsinus. The temple was first built around the end of the 2nd cent. B.C. The sacred area is bounded by a high wall with a colonnaded quadriporticus inside, at the center of which the temple stands. The ground plan is unique - the cella, which is wider than it is deep, is set on a tall podium and is preceded by a pronaos with four columns on the front and two on the sides. The main entrance consists of a flight of stairs on the front of the building, while a subsidiary staircase is on the south side. Two niches with triangular pediments, on either side of the cella outside the columns of the pronaos, housed the statues of Harpocrates and Anubis, divinities connected with the cult of Isis. On the exterior wall of the back of the temple there is a third niche for the simulacrum of Dionysius between two ears in stucco, symbols of the god's benevolence in giving petitions a hearing.
A podium whose hollow interior was meant for the cult

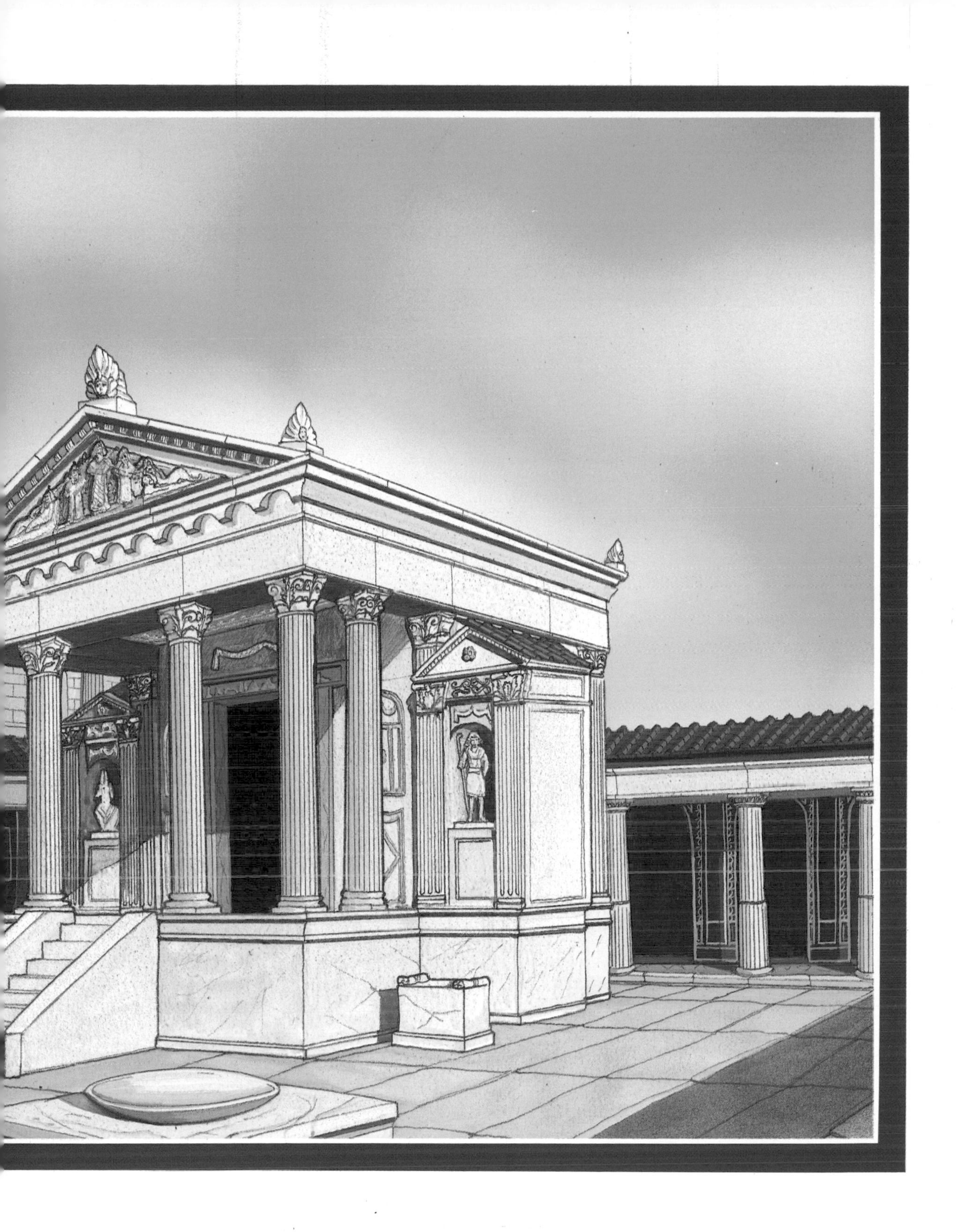

statues is in the cella. When excavations were in course, a large marble hand, two human skulls, and other ritual objects were found here. The decoration on the outside of the temple consisted of white stucco panels and a polychrome frieze of volutes. The walls of the portico were painted with a pattern of red panels, at the center of which were priests of Isis, framed by architectural elements and small landscape scenes. A statue of Venus and the bronze herm of C. Norbanus Sorex, an actor, were found in the south corner, while a statuette of Isis dedicated by the freedman L. Caecilius Phoebus was found near the west corner. The entrance to the courtyard, flanked by two piers with engaged half-columns, is at the center of the east side.

A shrine with a fresco, now transferred, depicting a priest before Harpokrates, is in the wall across the way.

A square unroofed building in the southeast corner of the courtyard is the so-called *Purgatorium*, in which purifica-

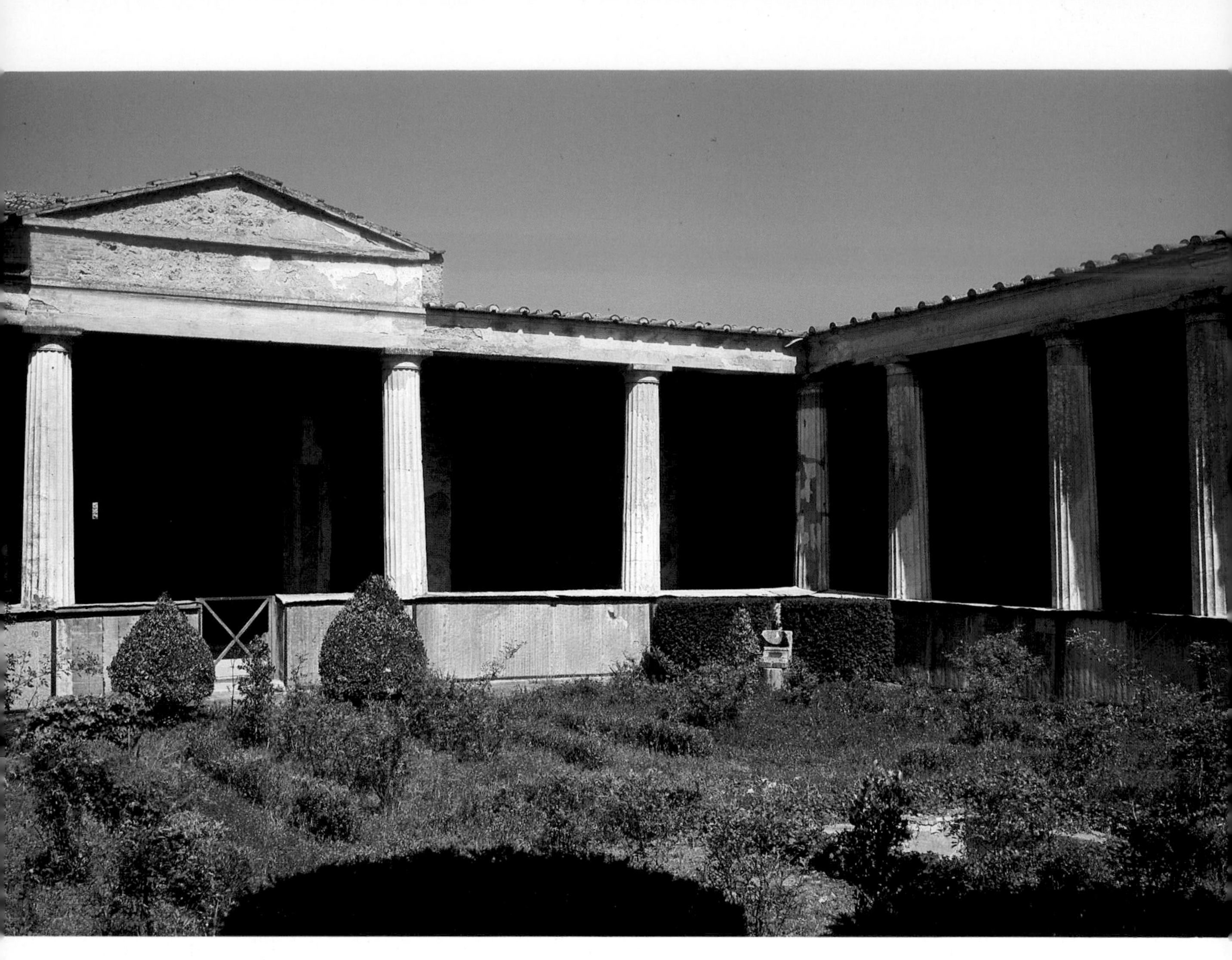

Above: the large peristyle around the garden of the House of Menander.

tion rites were held. A staircase leads to a vaulted subterranean chamber, which contains a basin for lustral water. The facade has a broken triangular pediment and a frieze with two processions of priests converging towards the center. Mars with Venus and Perseus with Andromeda are shown on the side walls.
The most important of the various altars set up in the courtyard and between the columns of the portico is the one between the *Purgatorium* and the temple. The remains of the sacrifices were collected in a well that was fenced off in the northeast corner of the courtyard.
A series of living quarters for the priests opens off the south wall of the portico, whiile the west wing is almost completely occupied by the elevation of the *Ecclesiasterion* with five arched entrances. This large hall was where those initiated in the cult of Isis met. When it was discovered, the names of Numerius Popidius Celsinus, his father, and his mother Corelia Celsus, could be read on the pavement. The walls are frescoed with five panels of sacred subjects in Egyptian style and representations of Io in Egypt and Io in Argos. The remains of an acrolythic statue were found in front of this room. Two other rooms which communicated with the *Ecclesiasterion* were clearly used for cult purposes.

20 - HOUSE OF MENANDER

As indicated by a bronze seal found in the servants' quarters, this imposing mansion belonged to Quintus Poppaeus, a member of the important *gens* of the Poppaei related to Nero's second wife, Poppaea. The first version of the house, limited to the rooms articulated around the atrium, dates to the middle of the 3rd cent. B.C. It was renovated a century later, but the ground plan and the decoration as we know it date to the early Augustan period when a revolutionary enlargement of the dwelling was terminated with the addition of the peristyle, the baths and the servant's quarters. At the time of the eruption the decoration and some of the structures were being restored.
Benches for the *clientes* were built along the facade. The entrance is framed by two Corinthian piers. The vestibule leads to the large Tuscan atrium, with a marble basin for rain water (*impluvium*) in the center and the walls frescoed in Style IV with medallions containing the head of Zeus-Ammon and tragic masks. Set into the west corner is a lararium in the form of a small temple with a double pediment. The three rooms on the west side were a

storeroom and two cubicles. A kiln for the restorations in progress had been temporarily installed in the spacious room on the east side. The adjacent *ala* has three pictures of stories from the Iliad: Cassandra pursued by Ulysses clings to the simulacrum of Athena, with her father Priam looking on, while Menelaos drags away Helen by her hair; Cassandra opposes the entrance of the wooden horse into Troy; Laocoön and his sons are strangled by the serpents. The back wall is taken up by the tablinum, flanked by two corridors that lead to the peristyle; one of these, walled up and transformed into a closet, contained a set of locally made dishes.
The large garden is enclosed by a peristyle with decorated plutei set between the columns. The room that faces out near the northwest corner has an elegant wall decoration on a green ground in early Style IV with complex stylized motifs, with vine scrolls and cupids and medallions with portraits; a frieze with figures is a playful version of the wedding of Pirithous and Hippodameia, with the drunken Centaurs carrying off the Lapith women; on the pavement is a Nilotic mosaic with villas and pygmies on boats. The west side of the peristyle consists of the baths which are articulated around a columned atrium with traces of a frieze with caricatures of gods and mythological figures. After the dressing room with its mosaic pavement comes the *calidarium* with wall paintings in Style IV. The pavement mosaic depicts a marine setting with an ithyphallic negro swimming and another hunting a monster, while near the entrance there is the figure of a servant carrying two containers, with his phallus protruding from his loincloth. On the western side of the atrium is a terrace with a large exedra to take the sun. Subterranean chambers lie beneath the baths and here a treasure of 118 pieces of silverware weighing twenty-four kilograms was found in a chest, while a casket contained gold jewelry and 1432 sesterces. Next to these cellars is a garden with an annexed kitchen and latrine.
The south arm of the peristyle has a series of rectangular and semicircular exedras and a cubicle. The first exedra from the right, decorated in Style IV, contains a lararium and it was possible to make casts of the impressions left by the wood and wax statuettes of the Lares. In the third exedra is the famous painting with the playwright Menander, which gave the house its name, while tragic and satiric masks are on the other walls. An *oecus* with yellow walls painted in Style IV with Dionysiac motifs and pictures opens on the east side. The adjacent triclinium is the largest found in Pompeii and above on one wall has a large window with a pediment. A corridor right next to it leads to an isolated cubicle.
The servants' quarters are reached via a ramp near the eastern corner of the peristyle. Here are to be found a sta-

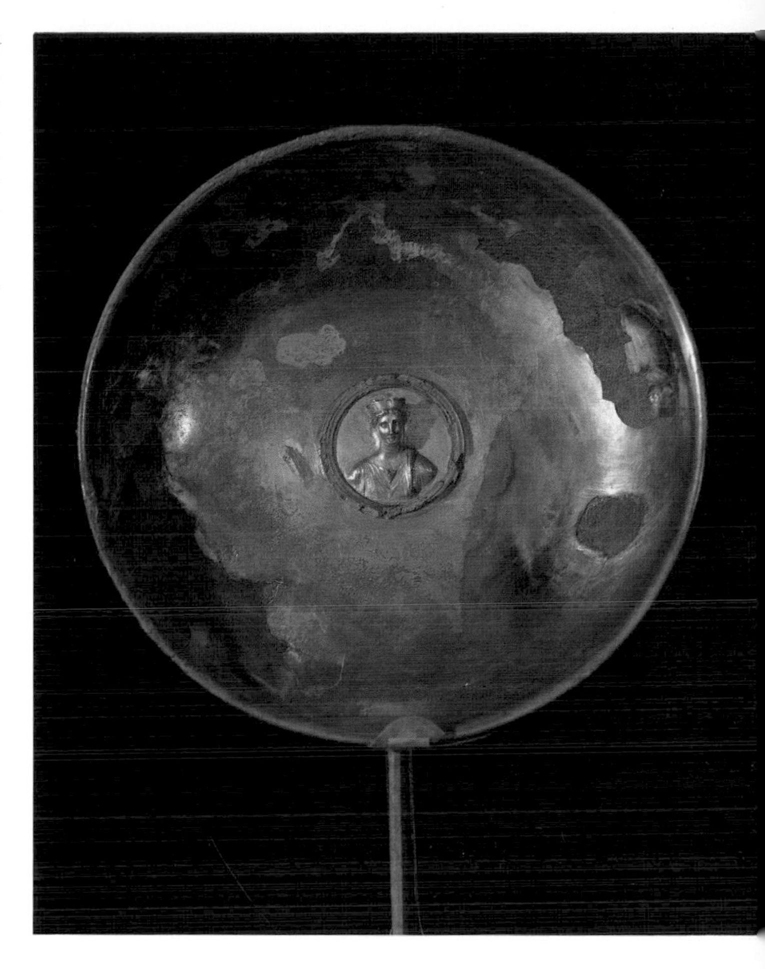

Above: silver cup with golden medallion from the House of Menander. Below: the model in the Museo della Civiltà Romana (Rome) with the reconstruction of the cross section of the House of Menander.

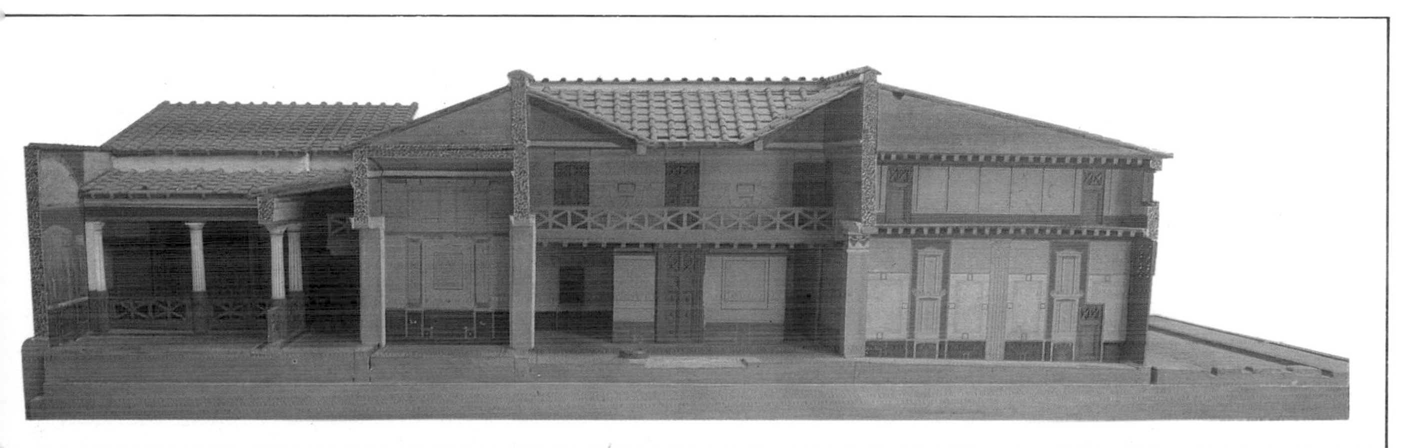

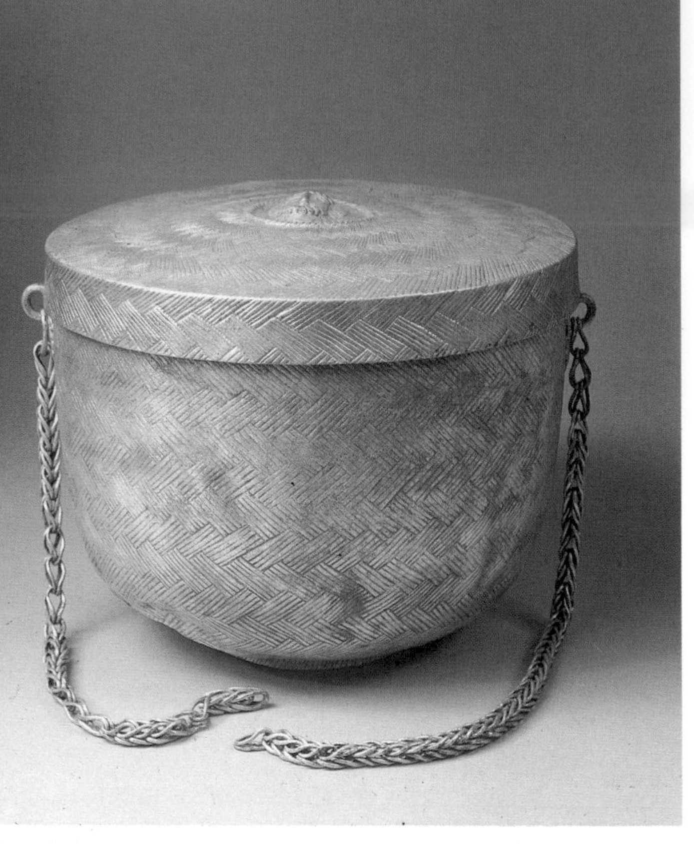

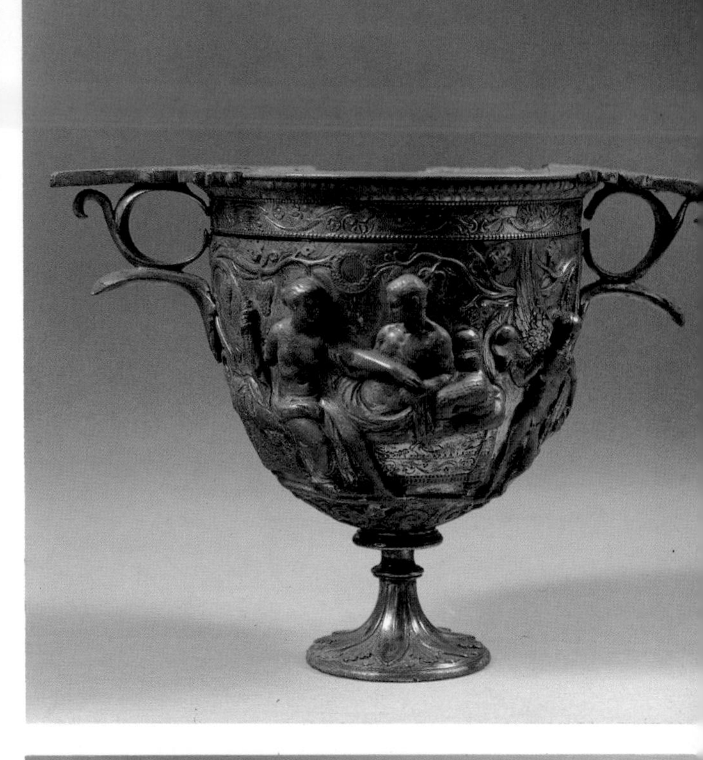

This page: various objects in silver from the House of Menander now in the Museo Nazionale in Naples: above, left, a casket and, on the right, a chalice; below, a pail.

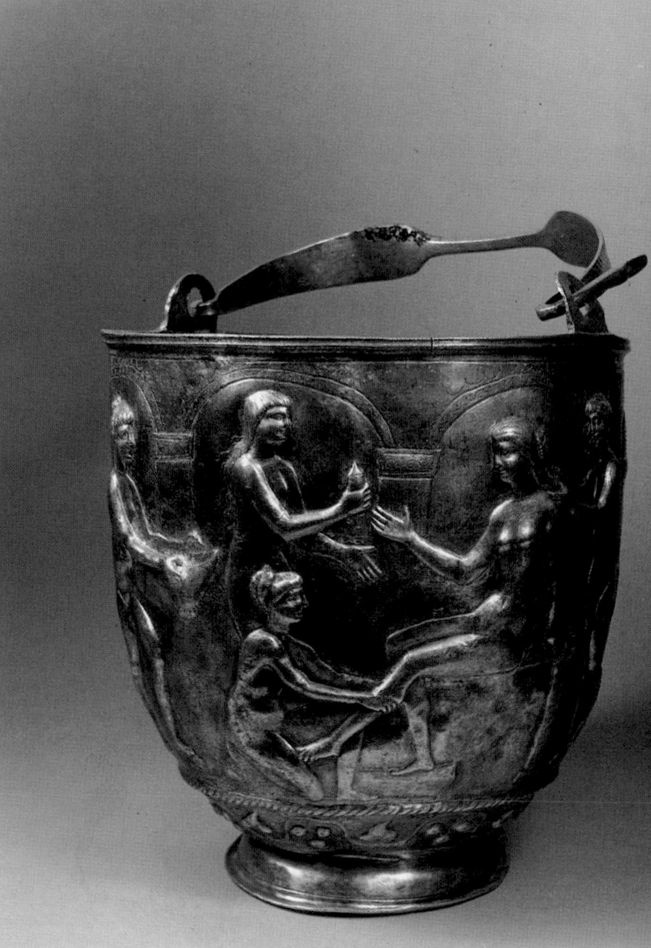

ble, store-rooms, a latrine and, on the upper floor, the lodgings for the servants. This sector had an independent entrance through the living quarters of the *procurator*, a man by the name of Eros as his seal tells us. His cadaver was found in a cubicle lying on the bed, next to the body of a little girl and his life savings. Various farm tools in iron were hung on the walls.

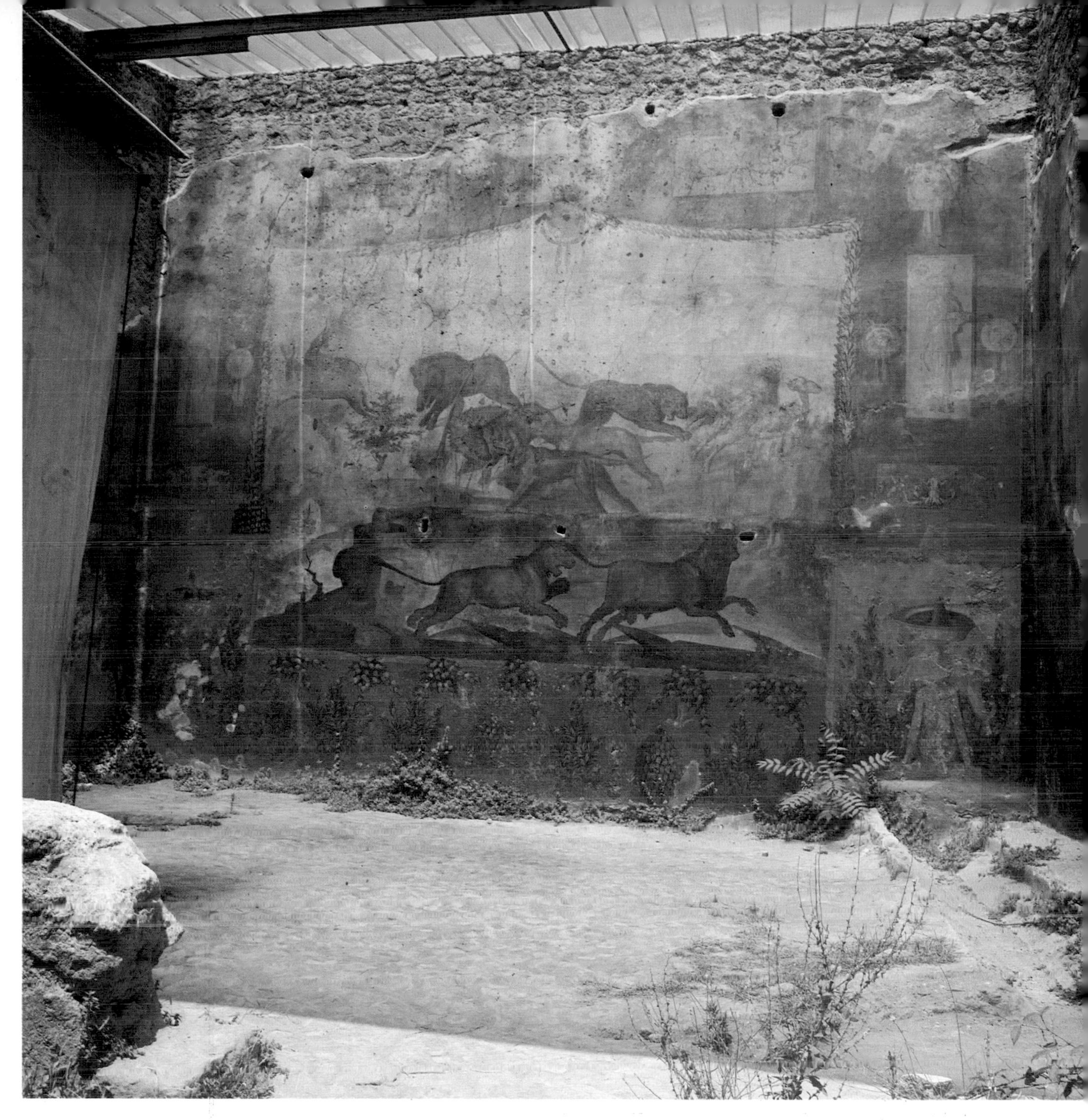

Above: the frescoes with scenes of the hunt in the House of the Ceii.

21 - HOUSE OF THE CEII

The house has been attributed to a certain Ceius on account of the election slogans painted on the facade. Outside, the front of the house is faced with stucco in imitation of *opus quadratum*, and has a projecting shed roof. The cast of the double-leafed entrance door still exists. The vestibule leads to the tetrastyle atrium onto which four rooms open: on the south, to the right of the vestibule, there is a cubicle (bedroom) with Style III wall paintings which show a poetess and a lyre player, while on the left a kitchen has a flight of stairs that lead to an upper floor meant for the servants. On the north side of the atrium there are a tablinum and a triclinium with Style III paintings showing Dionysius pouring wine for a tiger and a maenad.

The cast of a closet is in the atrium. Along the west wall are the remains of a staircase for a first floor that was being built over the tablinum. The garden has a canal that was fed by a fountain-nymph opposite a sphinx on the other side, with a basin to receive the water. The wall paintings depict hunting scenes with animals and Nilotic landscapes with pygmies, hippopotami, crocodiles and Egyptian style buildings.

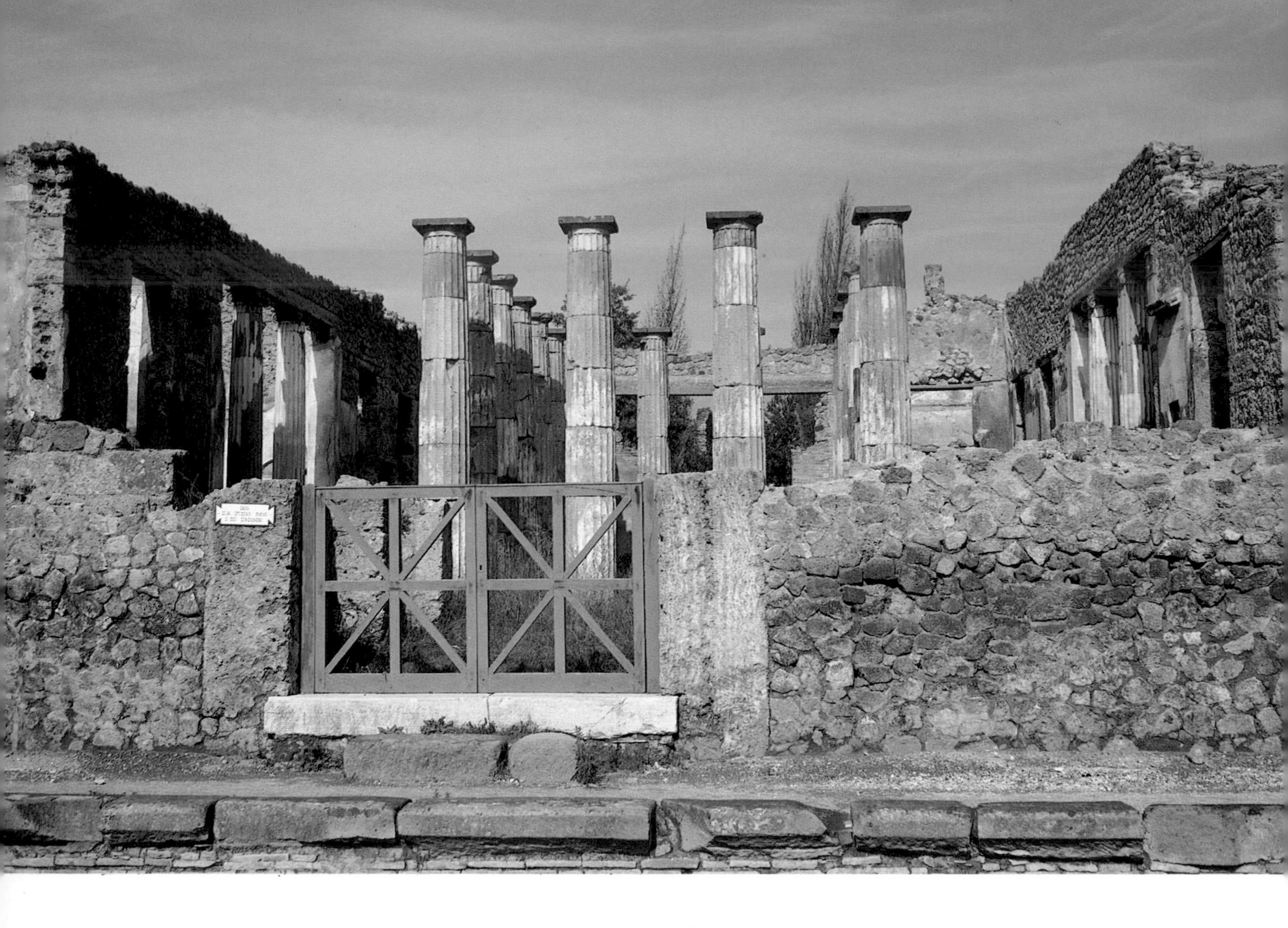

22 - HOUSE OF THE DIADOUMENI

This large house, built in the Samnite period in the second half of the 2nd cent. B.C., must have belonged to Marcus Epidius Rufus or Marcus Epidius Sabinus, to judge from the number of times these two names appear in the election propaganda on the facade and on the walls of the neighboring buildings.
Outside, a two-step podium runs along the facade, an unusual architectural feature. Beyond the entrance vestibule is an atrium of Corinthian type of an imposing size, with sixteen columns with Doric capitals set around the impluvium basin in the center. This is the most striking of the rare Corinthian atriums in Pompeii (in other words with a row of columns set along the sides of the impluvium). All around were various rooms, but unlike the canonic scheme, here the *alae* were at the center of the side walls instead of at the back. They were preceded by a pair of Ionic columns and the corner piers had capitals with the heads of maenads or divinities.
In the *ala* of the northwest side there is a shrine which the dedicatory inscription on the podium tells us was erected by two freedmen named Diadumeni (hence the name of the house) in honor of the Lares and the Genius of their master Marcus, certainly one of the two public personages cited above.

23 - FULLONICA STEPHANI

This is the only one of the laundries in Pompeii that had not simply been adapted from a building that was already there, but was an actual restructuring of a patrician house, rationally conceived to best fulfill this new function. It was excavated in 1911 and was found in good shape so that the specific uses of the various rooms could be identified.
Both the final phase in the preparation of fabrics, the end process for removing the last traces of dirt, as well as the public service of washing and pressing garments, took place in the *fullonicae*. The name of the probable owner of this laundry, a man named Stephanus, has been deduced from the programs of election propaganda that are painted near the entrance, which also inform us that women as well as men worked in the *fullonica*.
The entrance door was normally closed from the outside by a latchbolt. During the excavation a skeleton was found inside, with a considerable sum of money nearby (1089.5 sesterces), which may have been the laundry's last intake, unless it was the patrimony of a simple fugitive who had sought refuge here. The entrance is very wide facilitating the movement of the clients. The remains of a press (*torcular* or *pressarium*) for "ironing" clothes was found in the first room. From here to the atrium

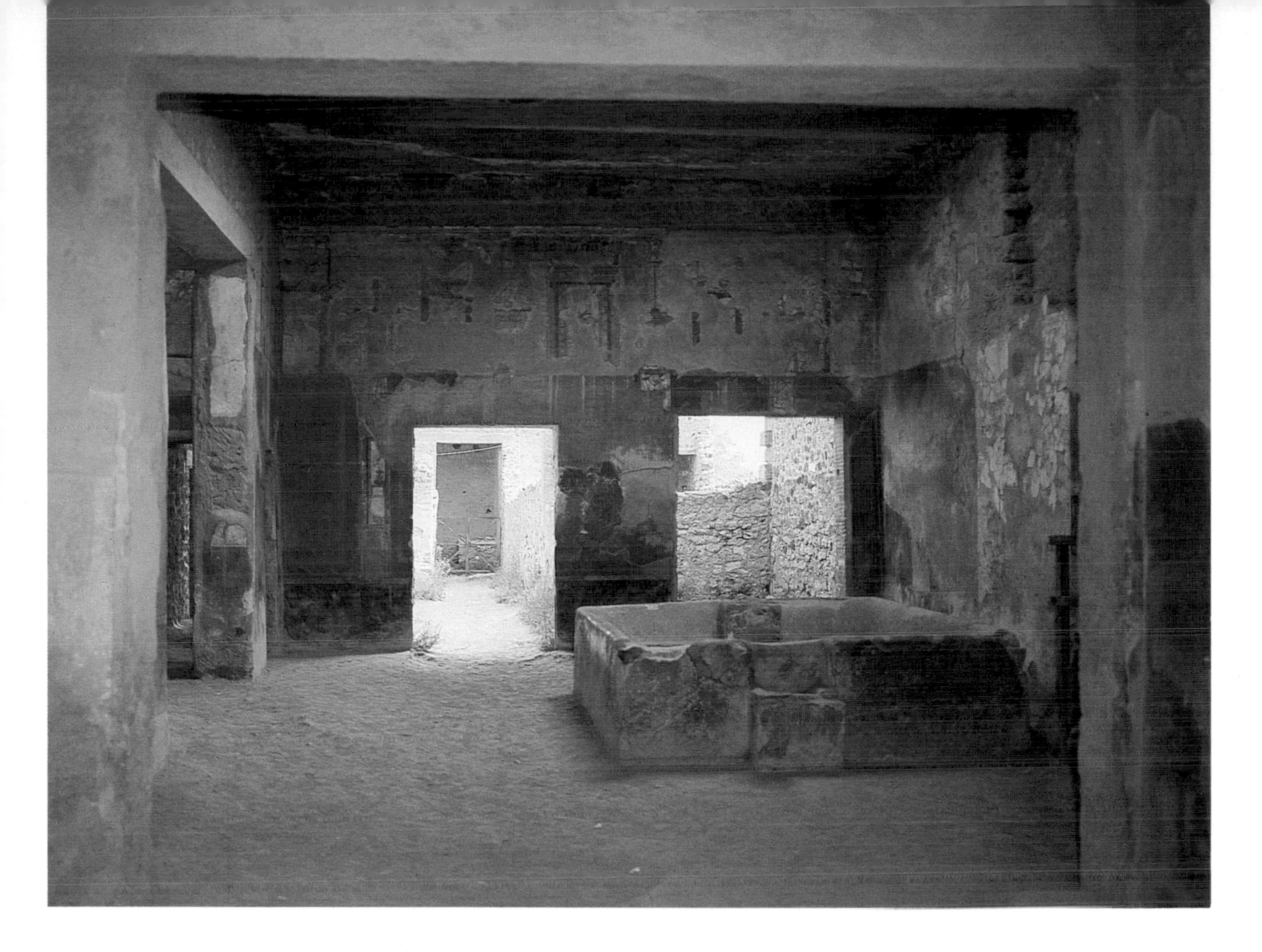

Opposite, above: the remains of the facade of the House of the Diadoumeni with the columns of the Corinthian atrium. This page: the atrium of the Fullonica Stephani with the tub for washing the cloth.

where the impluvium basin at the center has been transformed into a tub for washing, with the addition of a parapet. The roof of the atrium does not slope down but is flat with a skylight in place of the *compluvium* (the only known example in Pompeii) to provide a surface where the cloths could be spread out to dry in the sun.
Beyond the small garden with the peristyle are the other installations: three tubs for washing, intercommunicating but without a drainage system, and five oval basins for trampling (*lacunae fullonicae* or *saltus fullonici*) where the workers washed the fabric by trampling on it after having soaked it in a mixture of water and degreasing alkaline substances such as soda and human or animal urine. Containers for the urine used in washing were found near these basins. It is a curious fact that while after Vespasian the urine was available from the public latrines which he had created involving the payment of a tax, before that the *fullones* invited their clients or simple passersby to urinate in amphoras from which the neck had been removed and which were set in the lanes and near the entrances of the *fullonicae*.
The next step in the procedure was to soften the fabrics which had been hardened by the urine by treating them with a special type of clay (*cretae fullonicae*) and then to the scutching and a thorough rinsing that would eliminate the substances used in the previous steps. These procedures were then followed by carding to raise the nap, clipping, brushing and finally pressing. This *fullonica* also had service rooms for the personnel such as a latrine and a kitchen.

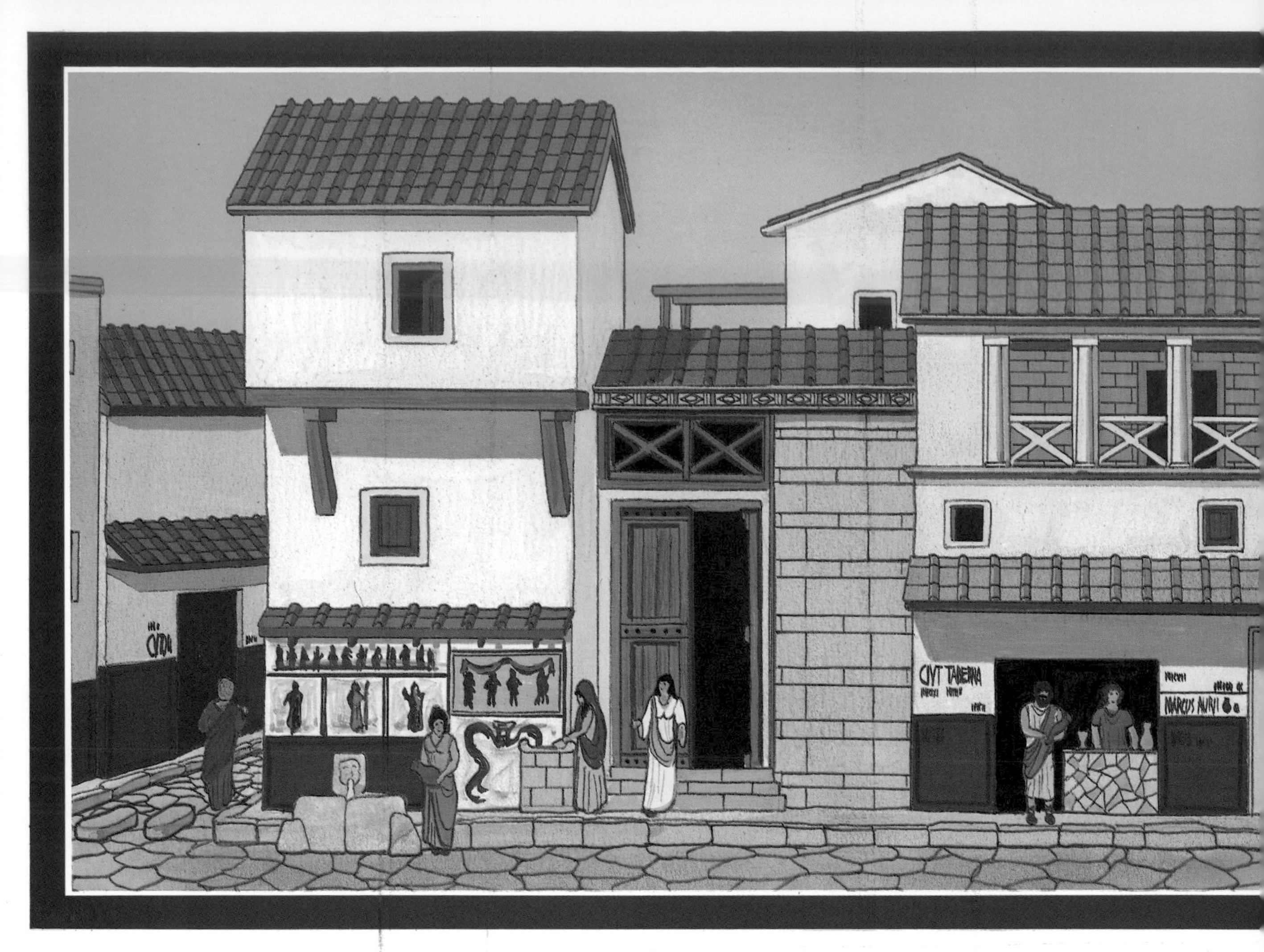

Above on both pages, a reconstruction of Via dell'Abbondanza and its shops. Opposite: a stretch of the same street as it looks now.

24 - SHOPS OF VIA DELL'ABBONDANZA

In 1911-1912 excavation campaigns were begun in Pompeii aimed at uncovering a long stretch of Via dell'Abbondanza and the buildings which lined it, in the direction of the Porta di Sarno. The excavation and careful restoration have provided us with a vivid image of what daily life was like in one of the main thoroughfares in the city, with its shops and their signs to attract clients, its two-story buildings with balconies overlooking the street, the election and propagandistic inscriptions on the walls, the graffiti left by passersby.
In the years after the earthquake of A.D. 62 the Via dell'Abbondanza was apparently becoming the real heart of commercial activity in Pompeii, especially in the area around the intersection with the Via Stabiana. Shops above all were being rebuilt or newly constructed, while the actual dwelling houses had not yet been restored when the eruption took place in A.D. 79. This, for example, was the case with the bakery of Sotericus, the only one facing onto this street, realized after A.D. 62 by adapting two ruined houses. Next to it is the *caupona* (tavern) which also belonged to Sotericus, with a sign that was originally painted with the personification of Roma-Virtus wearing a helmet and where the obscene graffiti left by the clients refer to the amatory services provided by the waitresses and the hostess. In addition to various taverns, a wide variety of shops lined the Via dell'Abbondanza: laundries, dyers, workshops where felt was made, smithies - in one, which belonged to a man named Verus, was found a *groma*, an instrument used by surveyors in measuring lots of land. In the stretch of street near the Porta di Sarno, already in the suburbs, the shops become less frequent and the houses, like the one of Octavius Quartio and Iulia Felix, resemble suburban villas in their size and layout more than city dwellings.

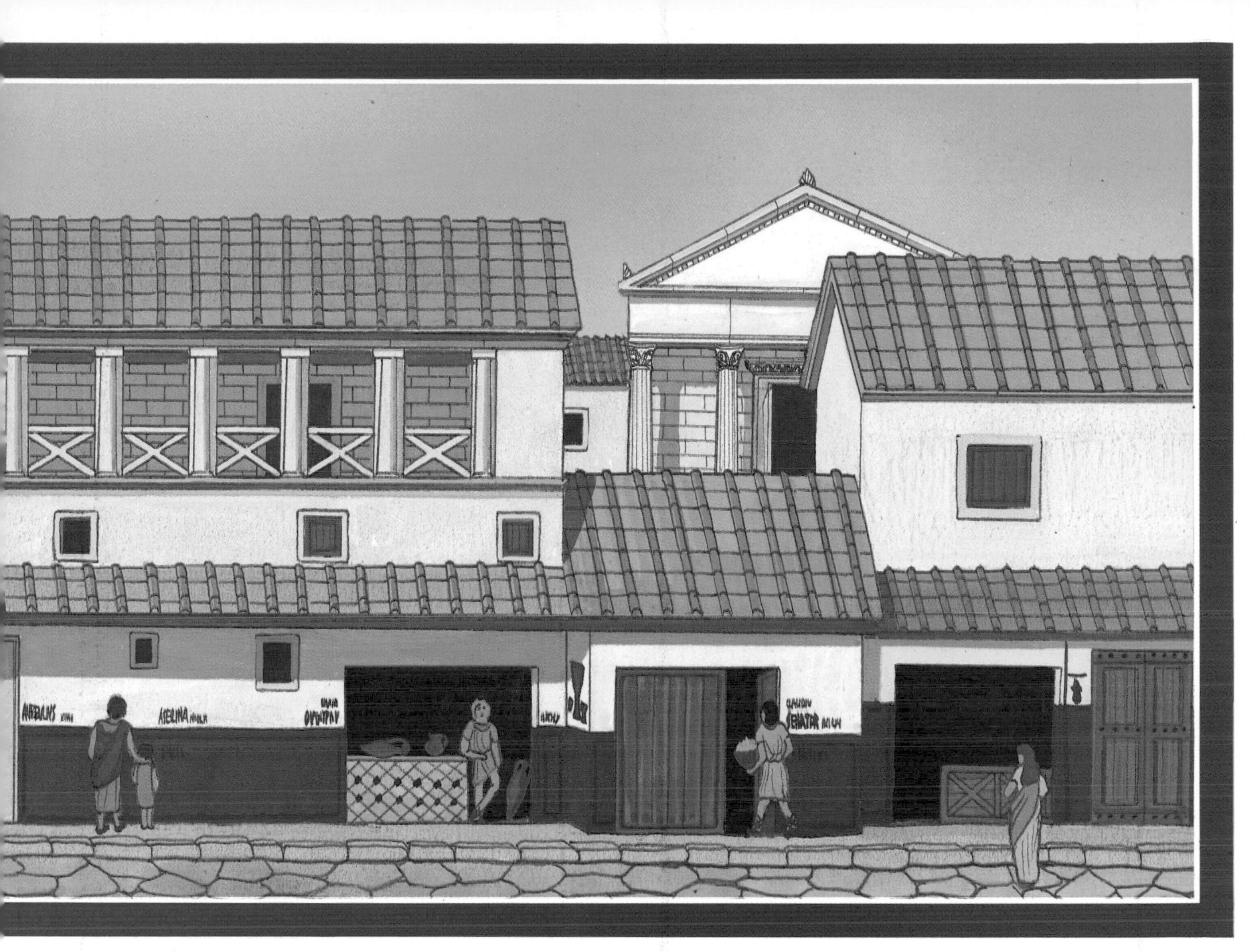
ASELINA
SENATOR

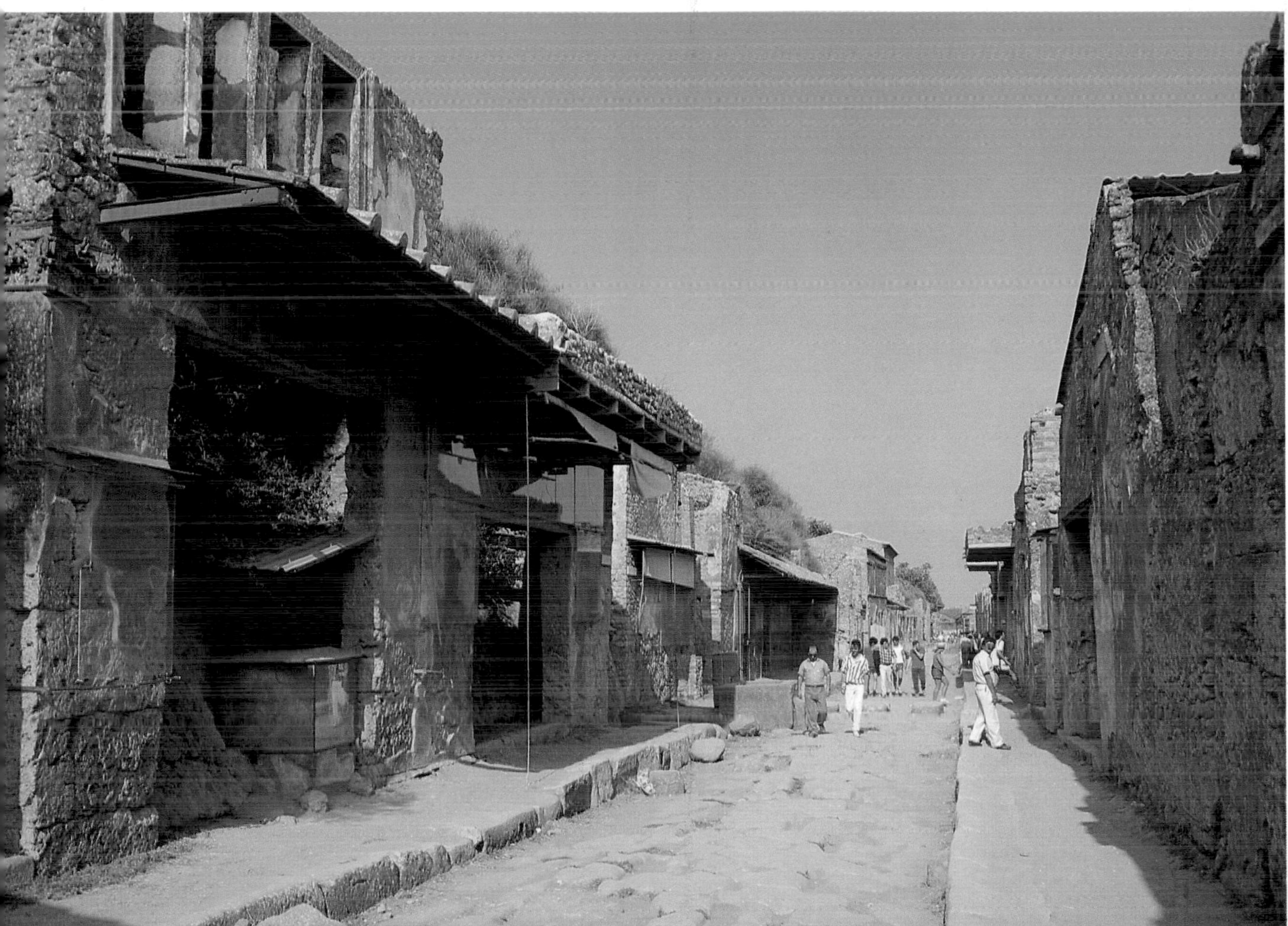

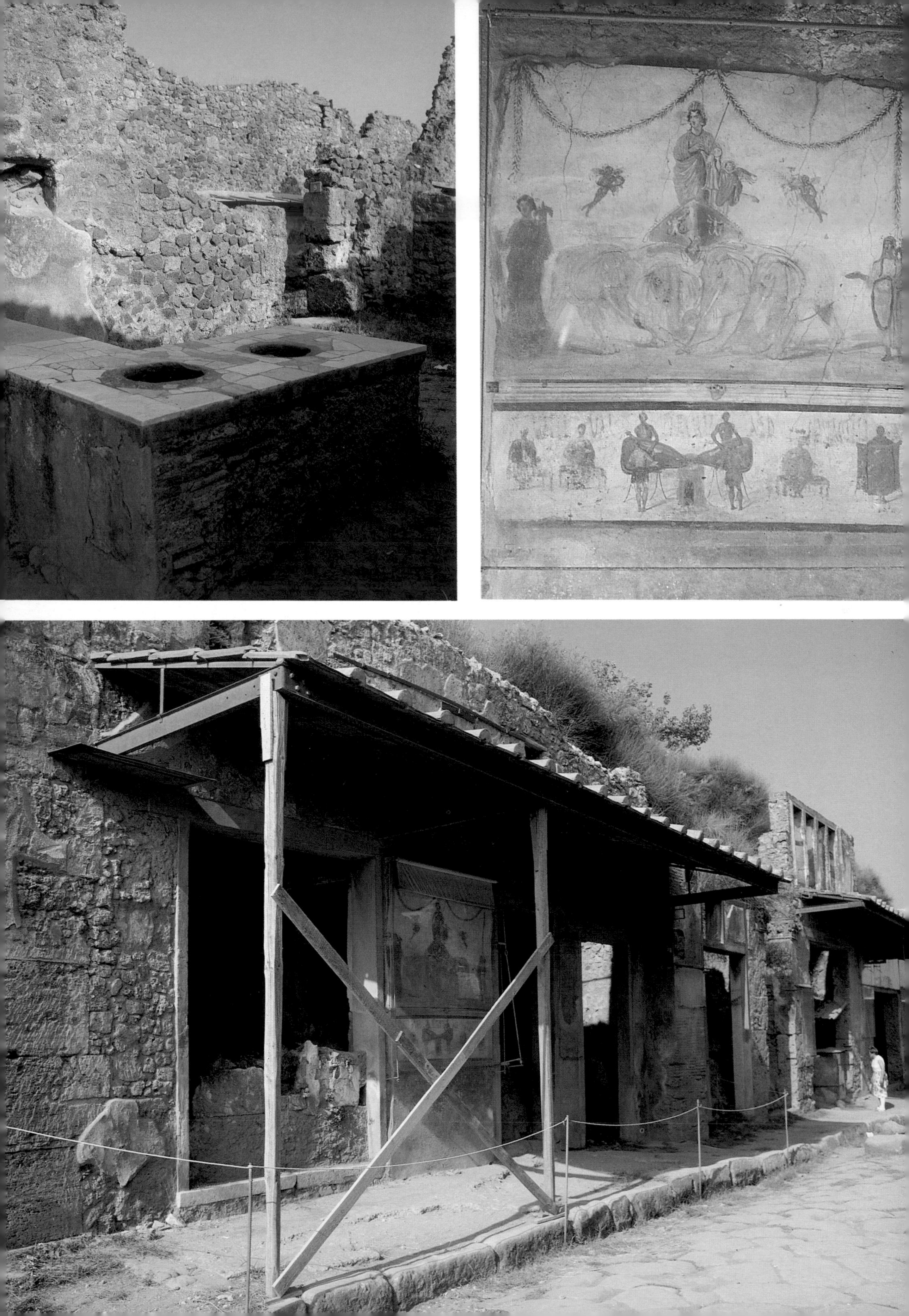

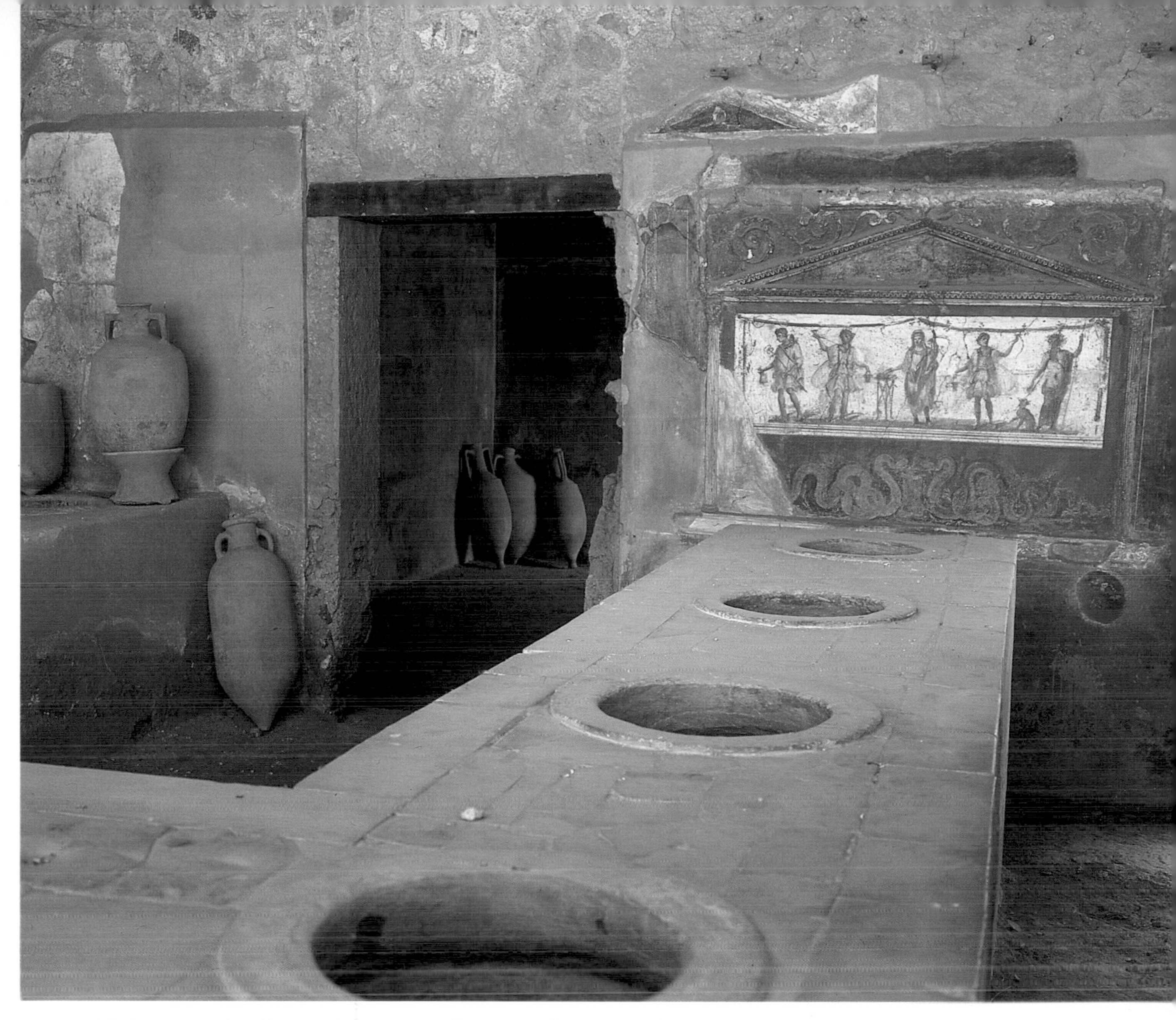

Opposite, left: the counter of the Thermopolium next to the House of the Sacerdos Amandus and, on the right and below, the fresco on the facade of the workshop of Verecundus, with Venus on elephants (above) and felters (below). This page: the interior of the Thermopolium with the Lararium.

25 - THERMOPOLIUM WITH LARARIUM

This thermopolium is situated in Via dell'Abbondanza and has the usual L-shaped counter, with the long side facing the entrance and the other side at right angles towards the interior, with built-in holes for the containers for drinks and hot food served there. A similar simple counter runs along one of the side walls.
When it was excavated, the last day's earnings, 683 sesterces in small coins, were found in one of the jars in the counter. A lararium with a temple-like facade in stucco, with small Corinthian columns and a triangular pediment, is on the back wall. Inside is a white-ground band in which the Genius of the owner of the shop, flanked by the Lara, is depicted offering libations in favor of the gods. Below are painted two serpents moving towards an altar, a subject commonly found in domestic shrines, symbol of fertility and procreative power.
A door near the lararium leads to a back room which communicates with the atrium of the house of the owner of the thermopolium, the entrance to which is in a secondary side street off Via dell'Abbondanza. A cubicle is decorated with pictures of birds on white walls, while the tablinum has as yet no painting. A triclinium with fine late Style III wall painting opens onto a small garden. The dado is painted with plant motifs while, above, a shrine is flanked by architectural views, panels with a picture in the center, candelabra. A painting depicting the Rape of Europa, who is shown on the back of a bull, is still intact at the center of one wall. The small garden, in which numerous amphoras were found, also houses a summer triclinium.

26 - THERMOPOLIUM OF ASELLINA

This can be described as the equivalent of a modern bar with an annexed inn. An L-shaped counter has four large containers for the drinks and food to be served, with at one end a fireplace over which is the neck of a vase to let the smoke escape.
Various containers and pots were also found. Some of them are now displayed on the counter and include animal-shaped vessels for serving wine, amphoras for wine, a bronze cauldron. The room was lit by a bronze lantern hung on the ceiling. It was biphallic with a pygmy and bells to keep away the evil spirits.
Still visible at the back is the base of a wooden staircase which led to the rooms of the inn on the floor above. On the outside of the building were listed the name of the owner Asellina and the "exotic" names of the girls, apparently foreigners, (Smyrina, Aegle, Maria) who worked as waitresses in the tavern and in the rooms upstairs as prostitutes.

Left: one of the election inscriptions in Pompeii. On both pages: some of the election inscriptions and notices for sales in Pompeii.

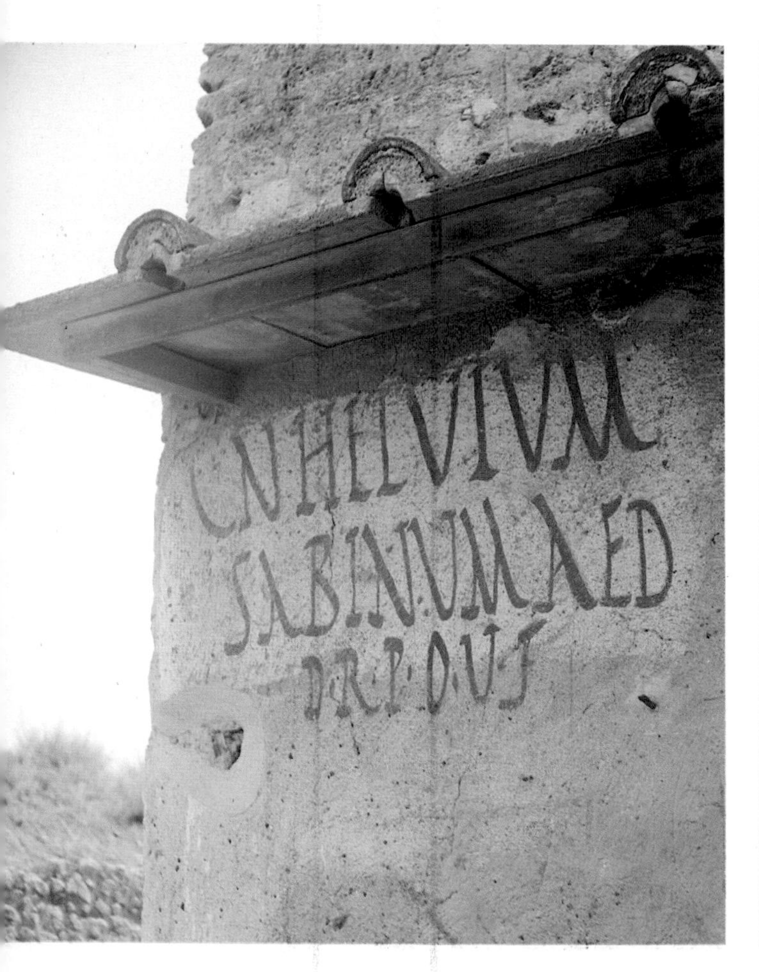

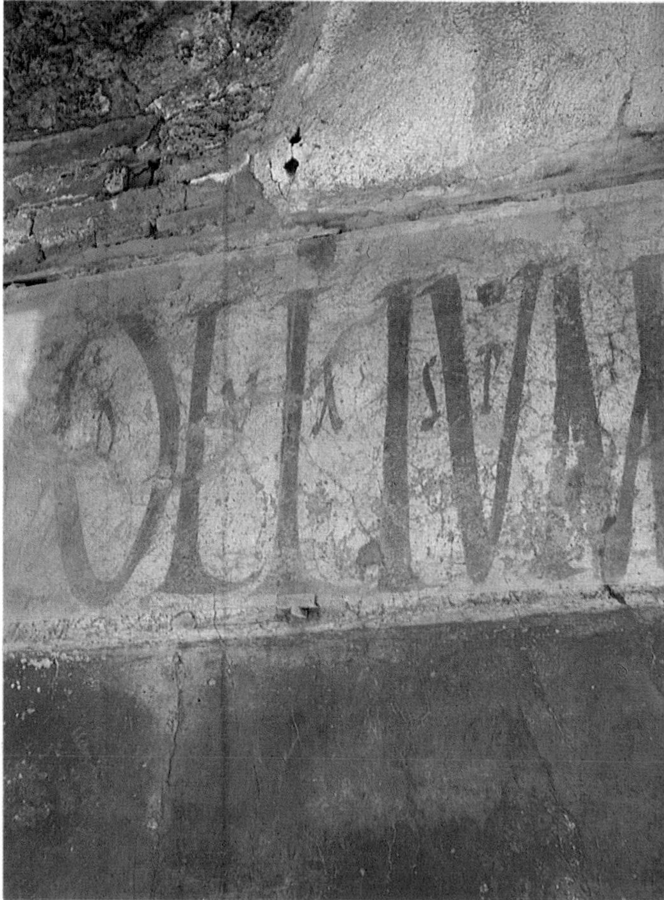

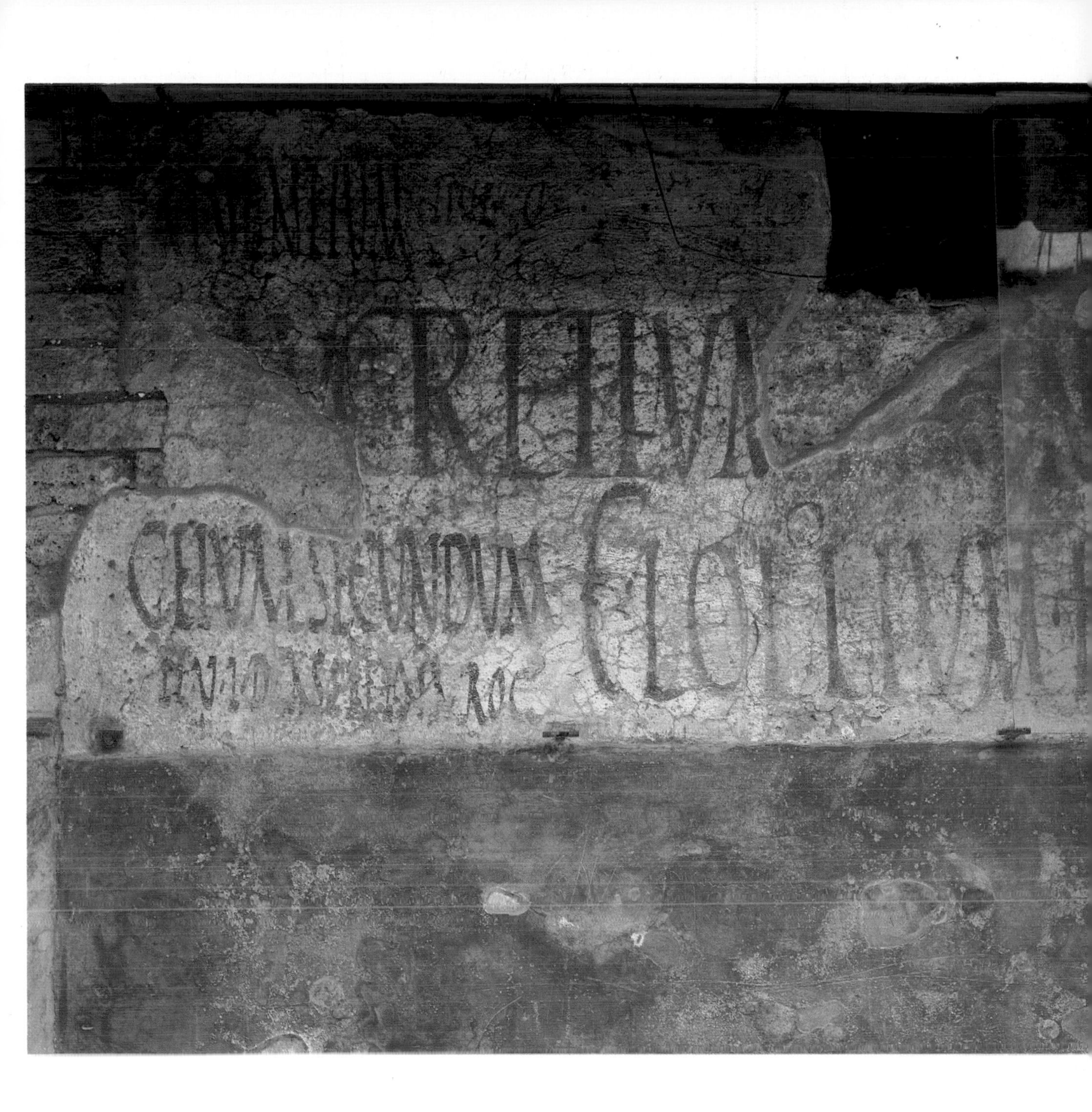

27 - ELECTION SLOGANS

On the walls of its buildings Pompeii preserves invaluable evidence of its daily life in inscriptions of various types. Of particular interest are the election programs which were painted in large red and black letters directly on the outer walls of the houses, shops and public buildings by specialized sign writers known as *scriptores*. They worked at night helped by a *lanternarius* who provided light. These inscriptions were made to the order of trade corporations, districts, or private citizens. They were part of the propaganda campaigns for candidates to municipal offices which were annually renewed in March.
The electoral message was generally very simple and direct, requesting that a certain candidate be voted for a certain office, often accompanied by praises of his honesty or virtue or promises of good government. Despite the fact that women did not have the right to vote, some of them, generally the owners of taverns or shops, such as for instance Asellina and her girls, appeared as advocates of a specific candidate.

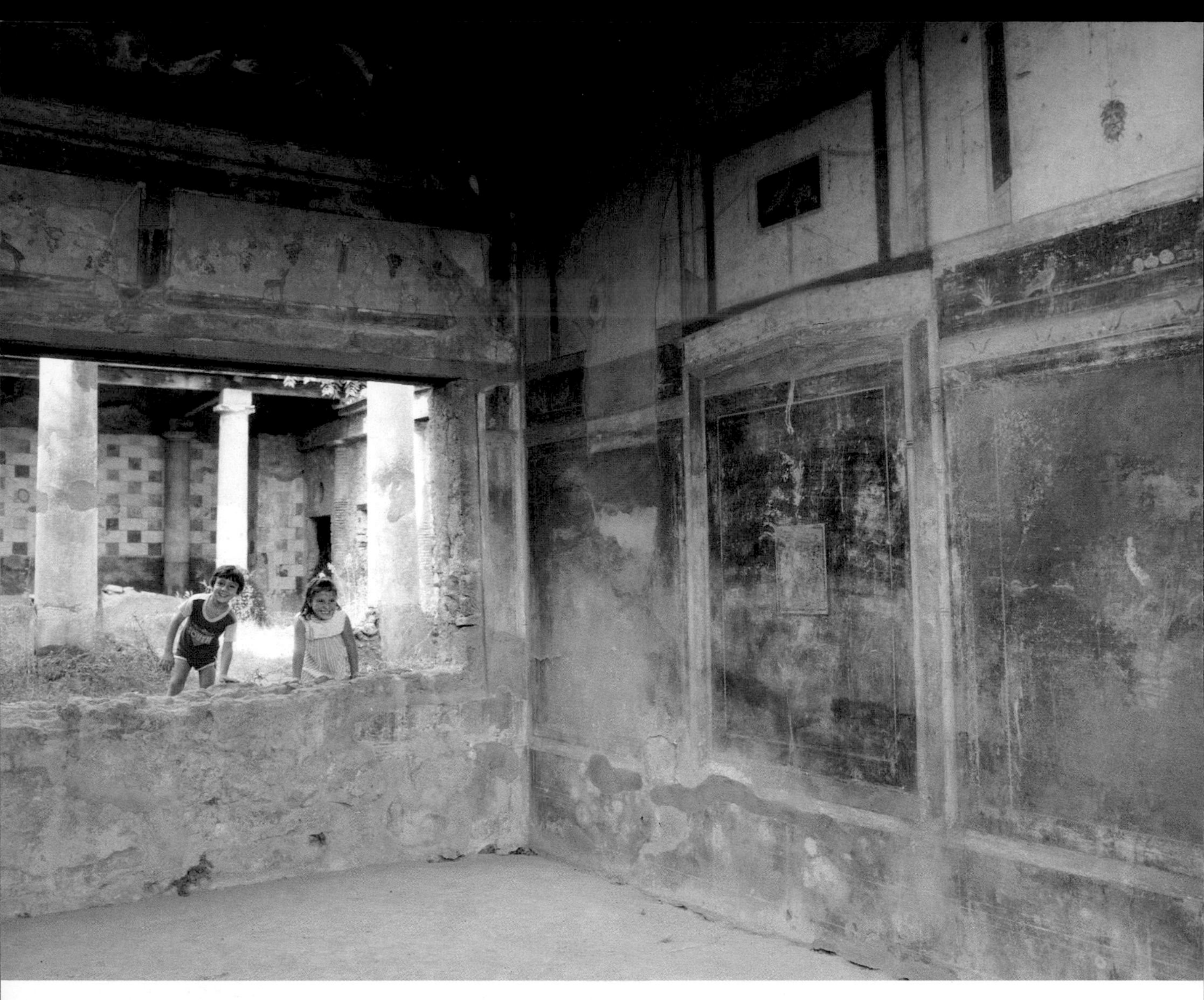

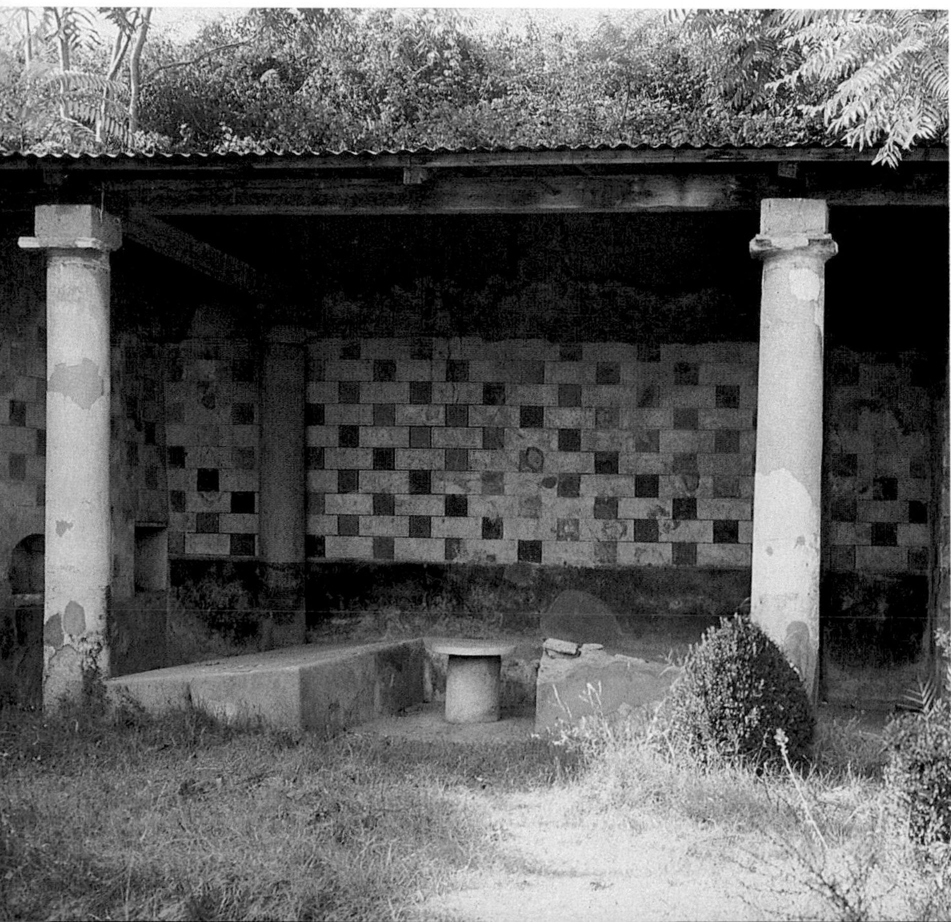

28 - HOUSE OF TREBIUS VALENS

A multitude of inscriptions covered the facade of this house, but they were unfortunately lost in the bombardment of 1943.
In the front, the house is laid out around an atrium with a basin in the center, surrounded by the various rooms. The first cubicle on the left in decorated with full Style II paintings with the name of the owner of the house, Valens, scratched into one of the walls. In another cubicle, on the right, the discovery of a casket with precious objects and ointment jars would seem to indicate that it was the mistress's bedroom. On this side there is also a rectangular hall with birds and other animals painted on the black-ground walls. As usual, the back wall of the atrium has the tablinum at the center with a

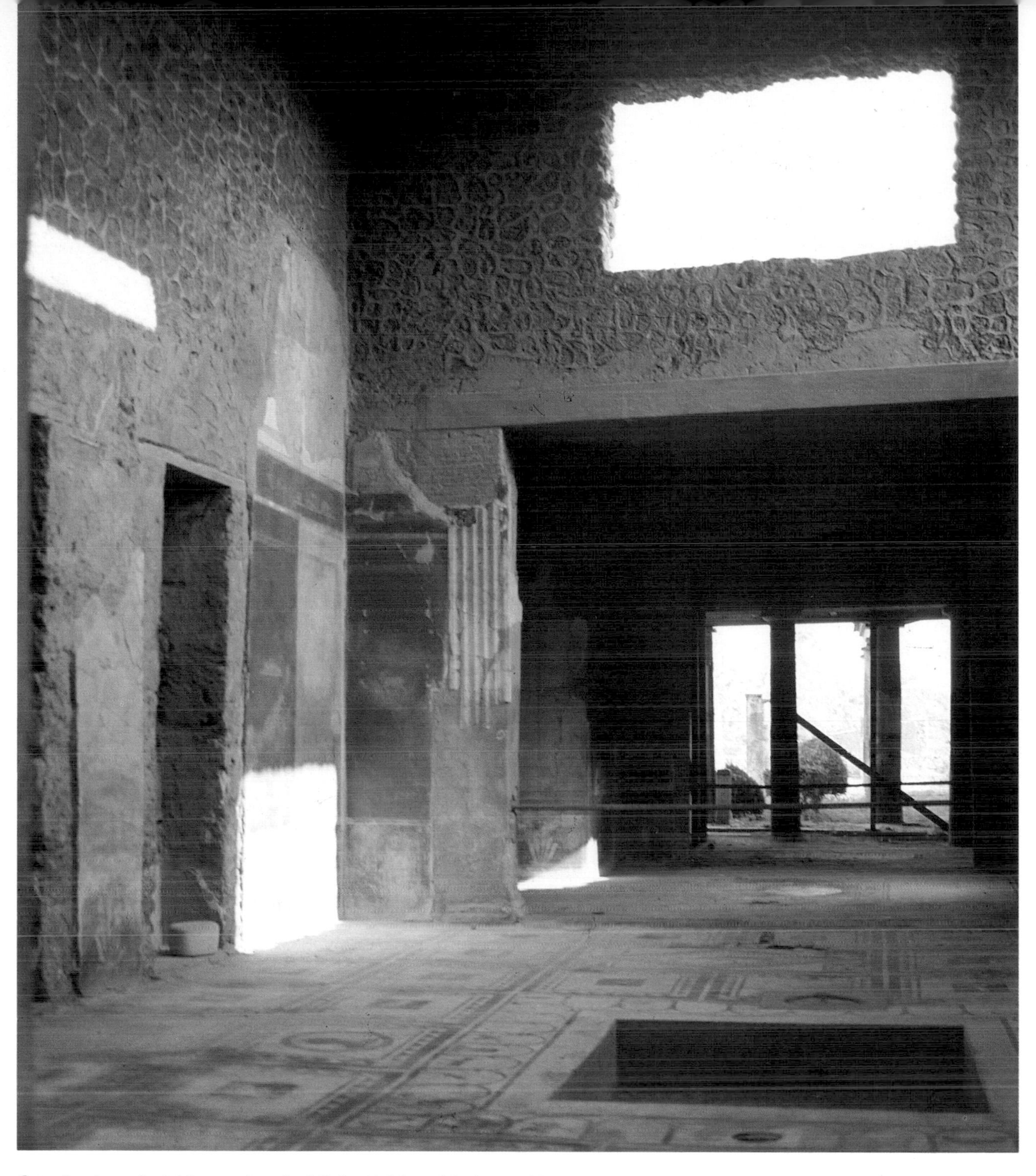

*Opposite, above: the tablinum and, on the left, the triclinium of the house of Trebius Valens.
This page: the atrium of the House of Paquius Proculus.*

large window opening onto the peristyle which can be reached through the adjacent corridor. There were waterworks in the peristyle and at the back of the garden, under a bower, there was a triclinium. In the southeast corner is a bath which consists of two small rooms, the first used as a *tepidarium* and the second, with an apse, as a *calidarium*. The walls of the peristyle are decorated with checkerwork painting and a graffito of the first line of Vergil's *Aeneid* is found here.

29 - HOUSE OF PAQUIUS PROCULUS OR CUSPIUS PANSA

The house may have belonged to one or the other of these two patrician personages whose names appear more than once in the election slogans painted on the facade. The house is Samnite in type and the tall entrance portal leads

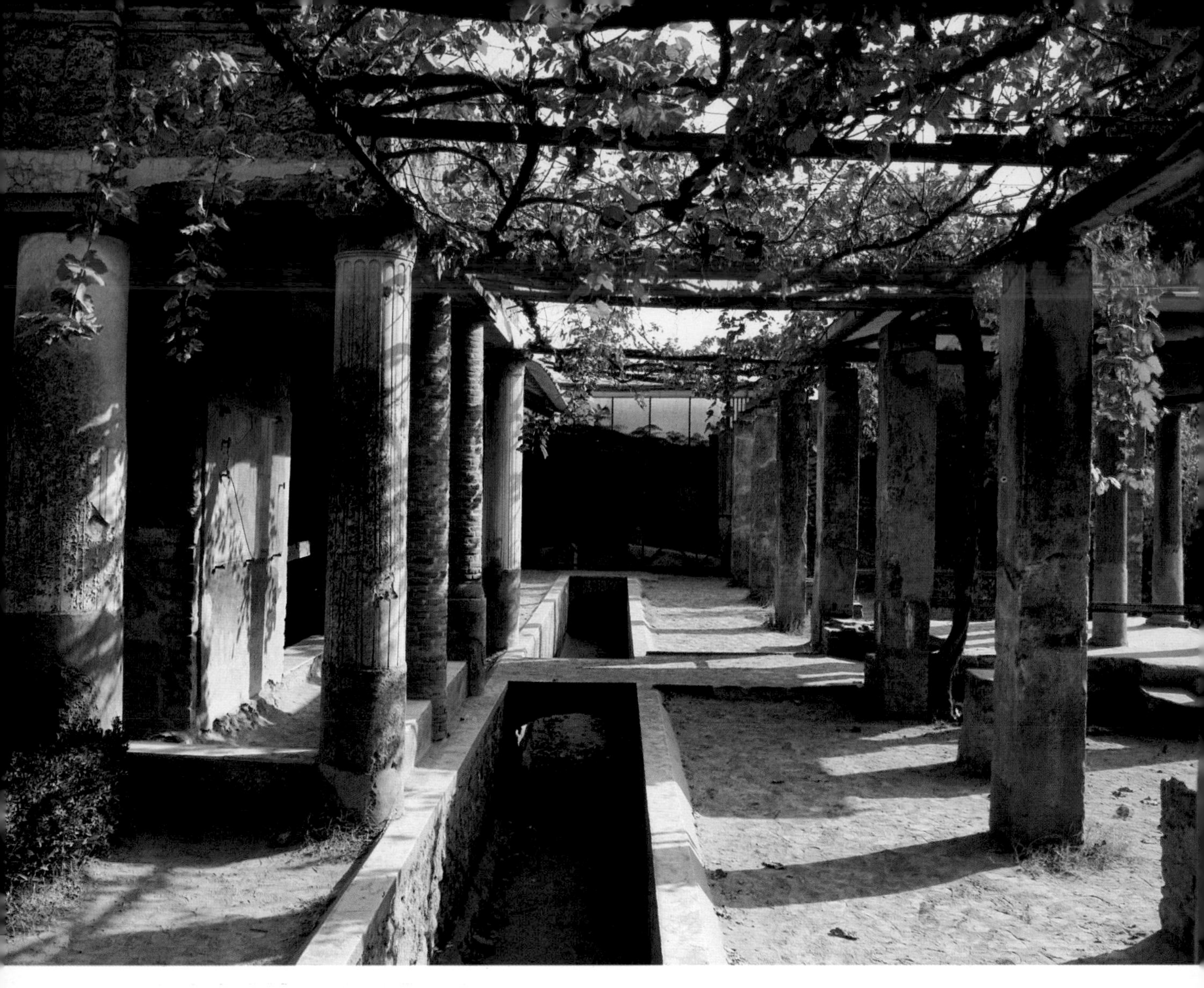

Above: the colonnade and the pergola with the biclinium on the east side in the House of Octavius Quartio.

to a vestibule with a mosaic pavement in which the portal itself and a chained dog are depicted.
Next comes the atrium decorated with mosaic panels with figures of animals. This had already been damaged in the earthquake of A.D. 62, as had the Style IV wall paintings, of which only two still lifes survive. At the center of the pavement an alabaster tondo is surrounded by a double guilloche motif, palmettes and animals in panels. After this comes a series of rooms opening onto the peristyle; in one of these the remains of the bodies of seven children who had sought shelter when the volcano erupted were found. The room in the northeast corner is the triclinium and it contains an *emblema* with a comic scene in Nilotic surroundings with pygmies fishing. One of them is falling from the boat while crocodiles and a hippopotamus with gaping jaws wait for him in the water. At the center, the peristyle has what remains of the summer triclinium which stood under a pergola with four columns near a basin. Below are subterranean chambers used as storerooms. A room at the back of the peristyle contained the humorous mosaic with an ass collapsing under the weight of a silenus.

30 - HOUSE OF OCTAVIUS QUARTIO OR OF LOREIUS TIBURTINUS

This large patrician mansion takes its name from a fictive Loreius Tiburtinus, the result of the fusion of the names of two people which appeared in the election slogans on the facade. It actually belonged to Octavius Quartio whose bronze seal was found in a cubicle where a kiln had been temporarily set up for the redecoration of the walls which was being carried out at the time of the eruption of A.D. 79. The dwelling consisted of two nuclei: the first dating to the Samnite period was traditionally centered around the atrium, the second was inspired by the more varied and animated architectural idiom of the 1st cent. A.D.
The entrance, near which are seats for the *clientes*, is flanked by two *cauponae* (taverns) which communicated with the inside of the house. The impression of the tall door reinforced with bronze bosses still exists. The vestibule leads to the Tuscan atrium with a central impluvium,

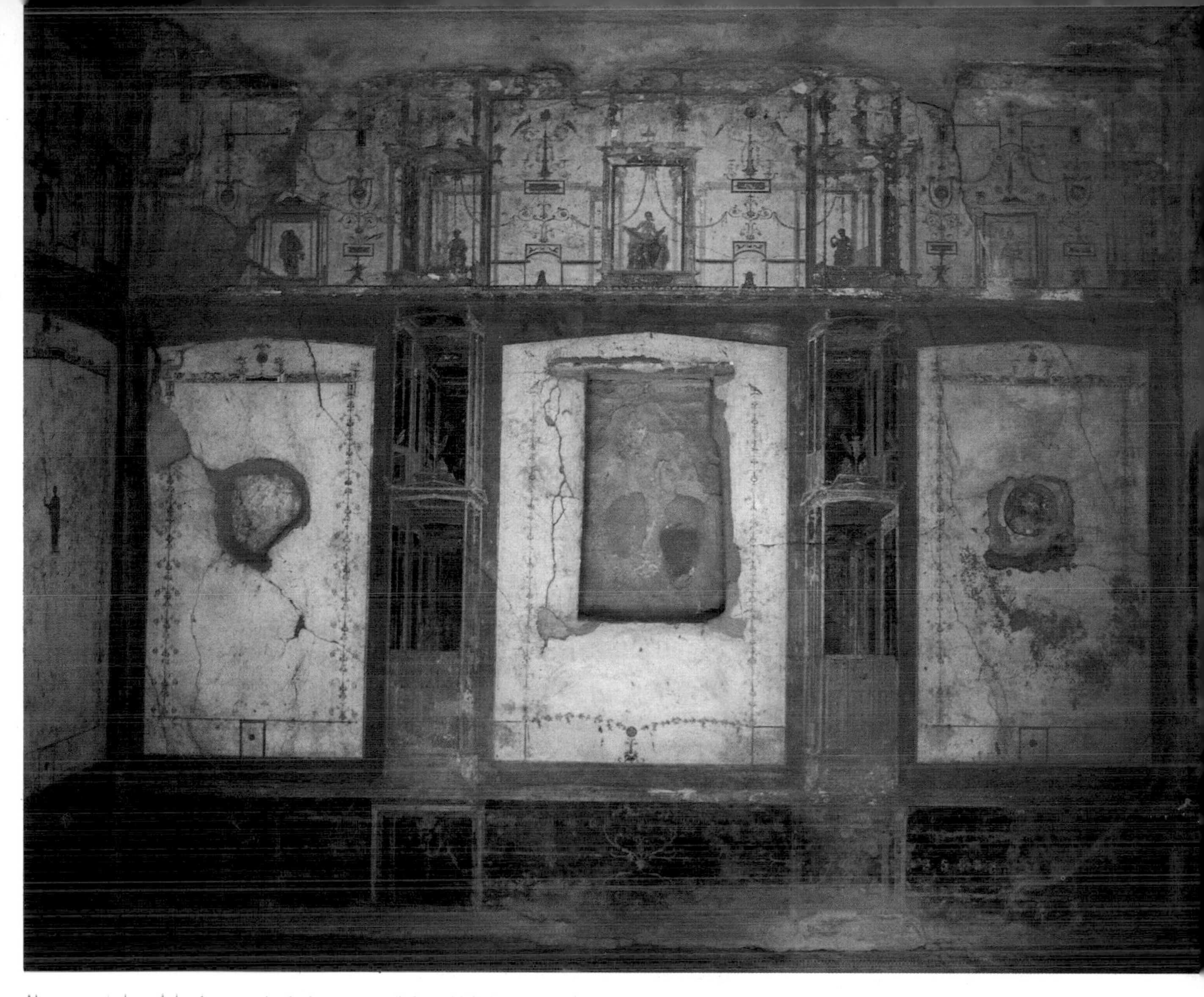

Above: a section of the frescoes in the presumed shrine of Isis in the House of Octavius Quartio, situated at the western extremity of the viridarium.

transformed into a flower bed. The arrangement of the cubicles and the *alae* is standard, even if the left *ala* had become a simple passageway to the adjacent quarter with kitchen and latrine.
The new quarter, articulated around a small *viridarium* with porticoes on three sides, is situated on the other side of the atrium. The room at the center of the west side may have been a shrine to Isis, to judge from the decoration of tendrils, trophies and figurines, a priest of Isis with cult instruments whom an inscription below identifies as Amulius Faventinus Tiburs. Two paintings on the front show Diana at the bath and Actaeon torn to pieces by his dogs. On the east side an *oecus* has the upper walls decorated with scenes from the mythical saga of Heracles against Laomedon, while the lower walls show a series of episodes involving Achilles (funeral games in honor of Patrocles, Priam asking for the body of Hector, etc.). Outside are paintings of Orpheus soothing the animals with his lyre and Venus gliding over the surface of the ocean in a shell.
The large garden which occupies over half of the *insula* (block) stretches out beyond this peristyle, crossed by two canals set in T-form (*euripi*). At the end of the crossing branch of the canal is a biclinium for meals in the open, with a fountain in the shape of an aedicule framed by two columns which present the apse lined with pumice in imitation of a grotto. On either side, two paintings of subjects in which unhappy love ends in metamorphosis: Narcissus looking at his reflection in the spring, and Thisbe killing herself on the body of her lover Pyramus who had killed himself because he thought she had been devoured by a lion. Oddly enough, the signature of the painter, a man named Lucius, has been preserved on a bench in the biclinium. Twelve statues of various subjects, some of which in Egyptian style, were found along this transverse canal, flanked by two rows of columns and piers that supported a pergola.
The principal arm of the canal, over 50 meters long and enriched by basins, was fed by a nymphaeum set under a small tetrastyle temple, at the intersection of the two canals. The holes for wooden supports show that it was flanked by avenues with pergolas. The traces of roots indidicate that the whole garden had regular rows of trees and plants.

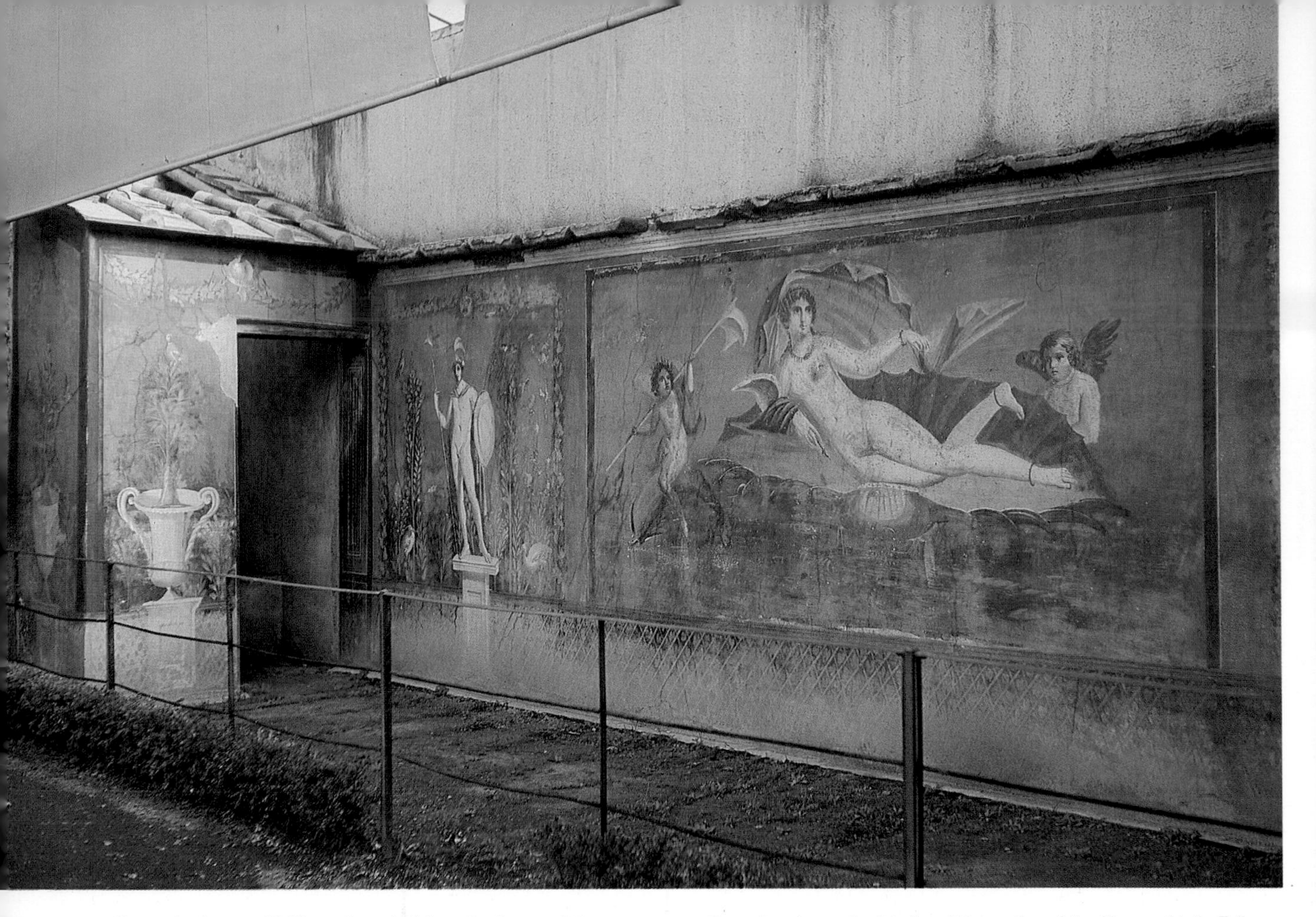

Above: the fresco with Venus in a shell from the house of the same name. Opposite, above: the interior of the portico of the House of Iulia Felix. Below: the canal in the garden of the same house.

31 - HOUSE OF VENUS IN THE SHELL

This building had been heavily damaged in the earthquake of A.D. 62 and was still under restoration when the eruption of A.D. 79 took place.
The principal nucleus of the house is on the other side of the atrium with its central impluvium. A series of rooms is articulated around a garden with a colonnaded portico on two sides. The back wall of the garden is decorated with the large fresco from which the house takes its name: Venus reclining on a shell, nude and bejeweled, her veil blown out by the wind, moves over the surface of the ocean accompanied by two cupids. Despite the fact that the figure is rather stiff and wooden and the execution is rather mediocre artistically, the painting is valid in its all-over effect.
Two large painted panels on either side of this fresco depict gardens with hedges, flowers, birds, marble basins full of water and a statue of a cloaked armed Mars on a base.

32 - HOUSE OF IULIA FELIX

It was in this house, excavated twice, once in the middle of the 18th cent. and then again between 1936 and 1953, that an inscription was found which established the norms for the rental of the shops with adjoining living quarters, apartments, a bath installation, inside the real estate (*praedia*) belonging to Iulia Felix, which, including arable land, covered a double *insula*.
The private part of the dwelling is articulated around two atriums which lead to a luxurious porticoed garden with a large canal in the center, with niches and three small bridges. A series of rooms faces on the west portico with piers, built after A.D. 62. One of these is a magnificent summer triclinium, with the couches faced in marble like the dado on the walls and a niche in the form of an aedicule with a waterfall. The walls are decorated with Nile landscapes, while the vault is lined with fragments of limestone in imitation of a grotto. The eastern portico has a series of niches with the same facing. On the back wall, in a room that no longer exists, there was a shrine to Isis with cult pictures on the walls, and from which came a bronze tripod with satyrs and a silver statuette of Harpocrates.
The bath installations were rented out and opened to the public, advantageous in view of the fact that only the Baths of the Forum were still partially functioning after the earthquake of A.D. 62 and they were therefore in great demand. The entrance opened into a vast courtyard where the clients waited their turn for the baths, as shown by the benches along the walls. From here to an uncovered swimming pool and then to the actual bath installations with the *frigidarium*, the *tepidarium*, the circular *laconicum* for sweat baths. The last two were heated by means of flooring raised on *suspensurae* and air spaces in the walls.

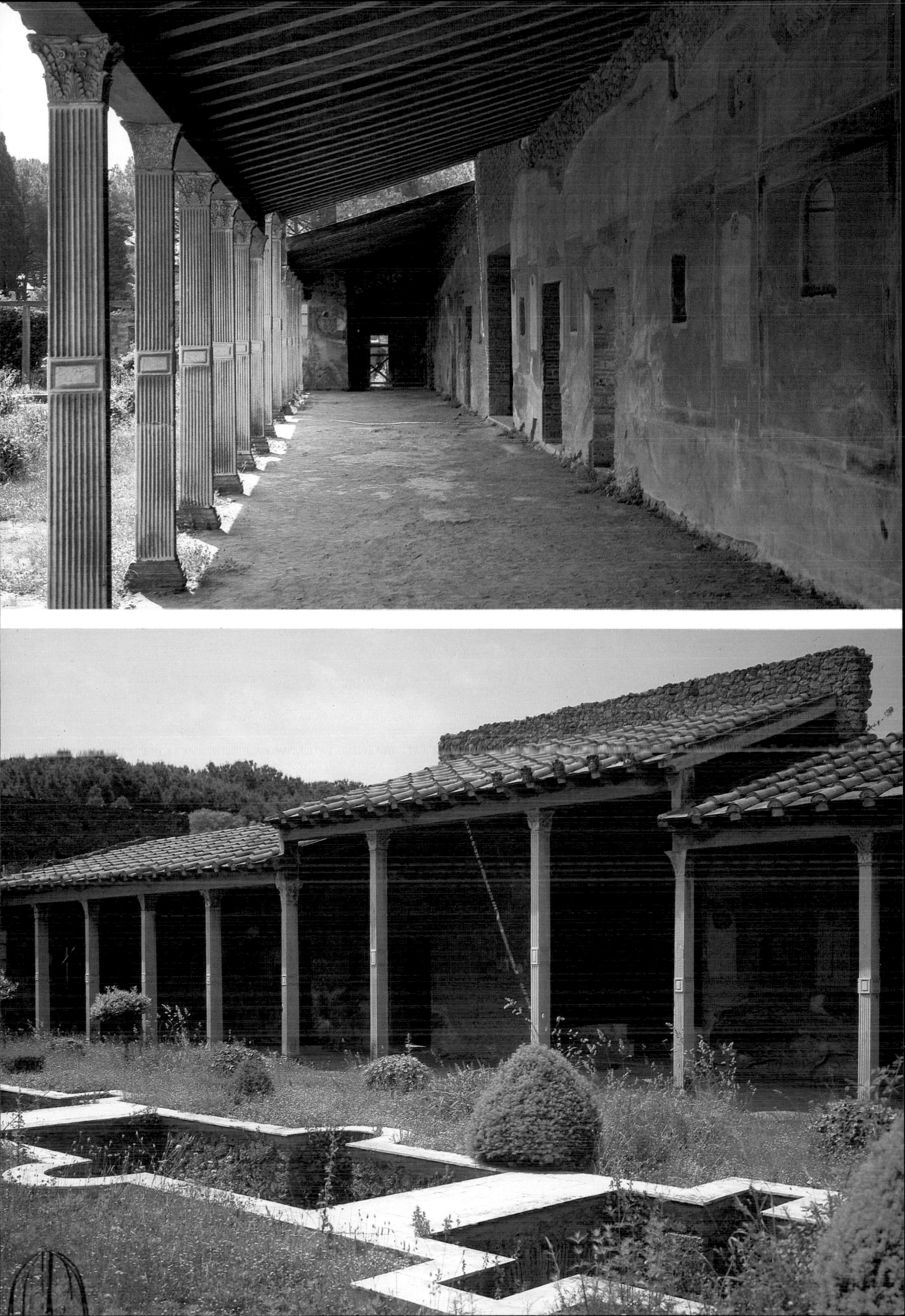

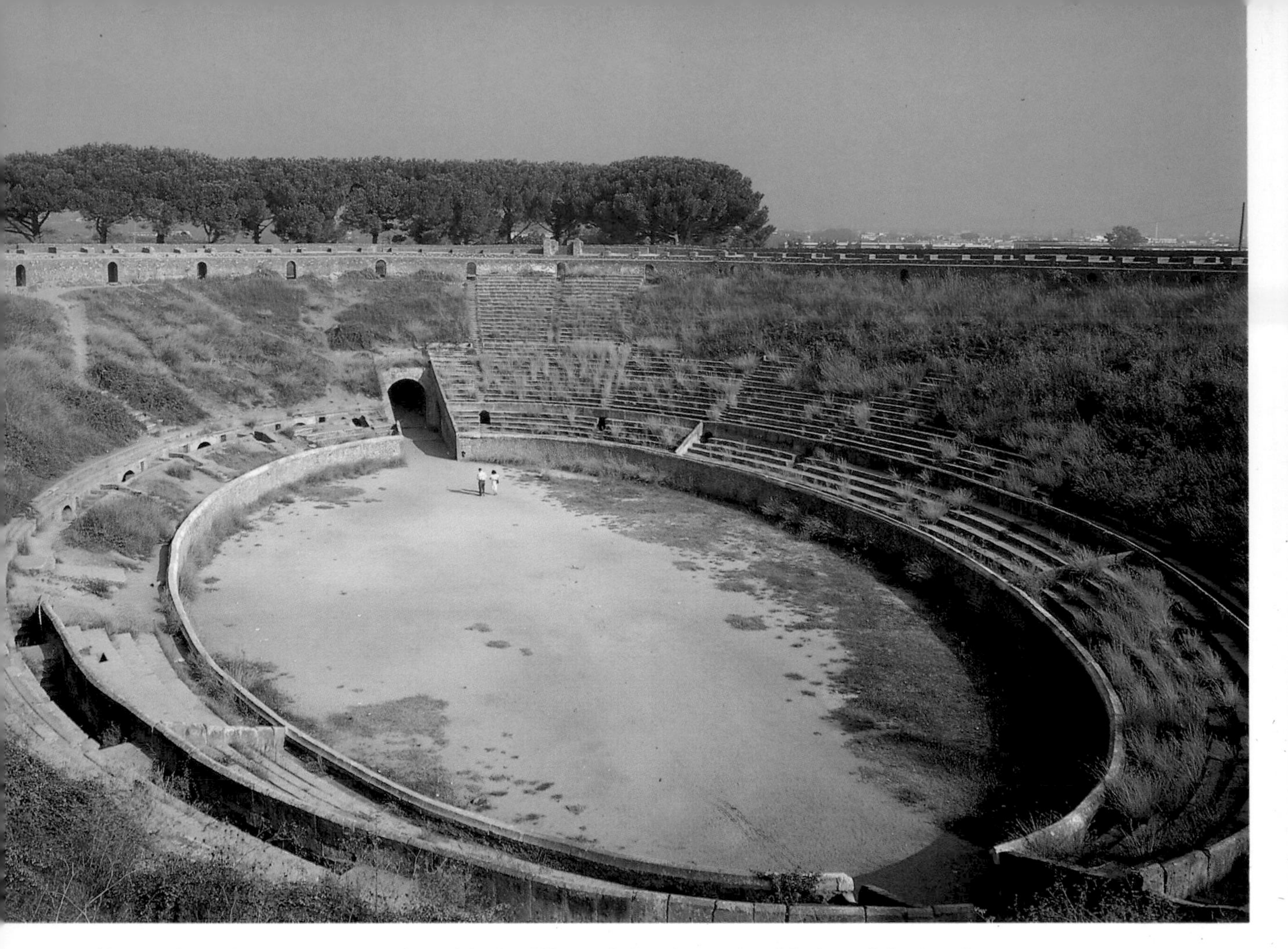

Above, and opposite page, above: two views of the Amphitheater; below: the complex of the Large Palaestra.

33 - AMPHITHEATER

Pompeii's amphitheater was built immediately following its foundation as a military colony by Sulla in 80 B.C. by the *duoviri* Quintus Valgus and Marcus Porcius, who also had the Odeion built. It is the earliest of the amphitheaters we know of (the Amphitheater of Taurus, the first one to be built in stone in Rome, dates back to no earlier than 29 B.C.) and is therefore particularly important in providing a picture of this type of typically Roman architecture. Campania moreover has been indicated as the place of origin for gladiatorial games, of which evidence exists as far back as the 4th cent. B.C.
The Amphitheater is situated in the southeastern zone of Pompeii, chosen because the area was still free of buildings at the time and because the earthfill inside the city walls could be used as a substructure for the eastern part of the *cavea*. The arena was excavated about six meters deep below the existing level of the land and the earth was then used as a landfill to support the western half of the building. A containing wall with buttresses and blind arches was erected here, constituting the principal facade of the complex. Two double stairways on the west and two simple stairways on the north and south led to an uncovered corridor which served the *summa cavea*. Access to the *media* and *ima cavea* was through four corridors which led to the *crypta*, a covered gallery, also vaulted, which runs along the lower steps of the *media cavea* and opens through arches on two orders of seats. The two main corridors also open into the entrances to the arena set at the ends of the principal axis and were paved for the use of wagons. While the north corridor regularly follows the axis of the arena, the other corridor crosses the west side of the building and then turns at a right angle, leading out at the far south of the arena, since there could obviously be no opening on the side that was backed up against the city walls. Two rooms along these corridors served as a place where the wounded gladiators were assisted or where the bodies of those who had been killed were laid.
Inscriptions inform us that the two niches set on either side of the north corridor, which was the main entrance to the arena, housed the statues of Caius Cuspius Pansa and his son of the same name. They both held important civic offices, including those of *duoviri* and were honored by the city for having restored the Amphitheater after the earthquake of A.D. 62.
The arena is elliptical and surrounded by a parapet more than two m. high, originally painted with scenes of the hunt and of matches. The *ima cavea* was for persons of rank and was divided into sectors: the central part of the first four rows consisted of four wide platforms for the *bisellia*, those on the east reserved for the decurions and those on the west for the *duoviri* and the contracters of the spectacles. The *media* and *summa cavea* were divided

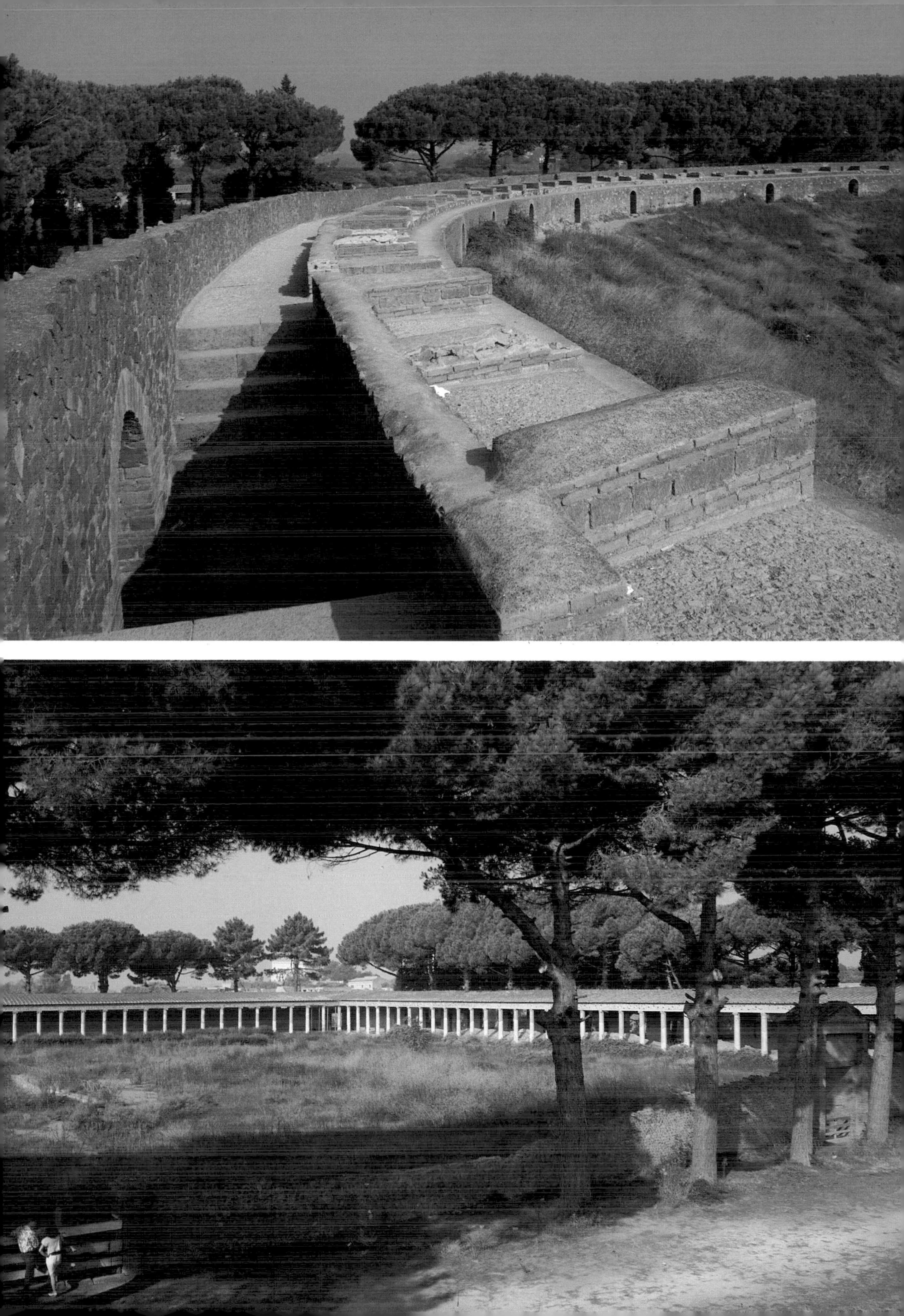

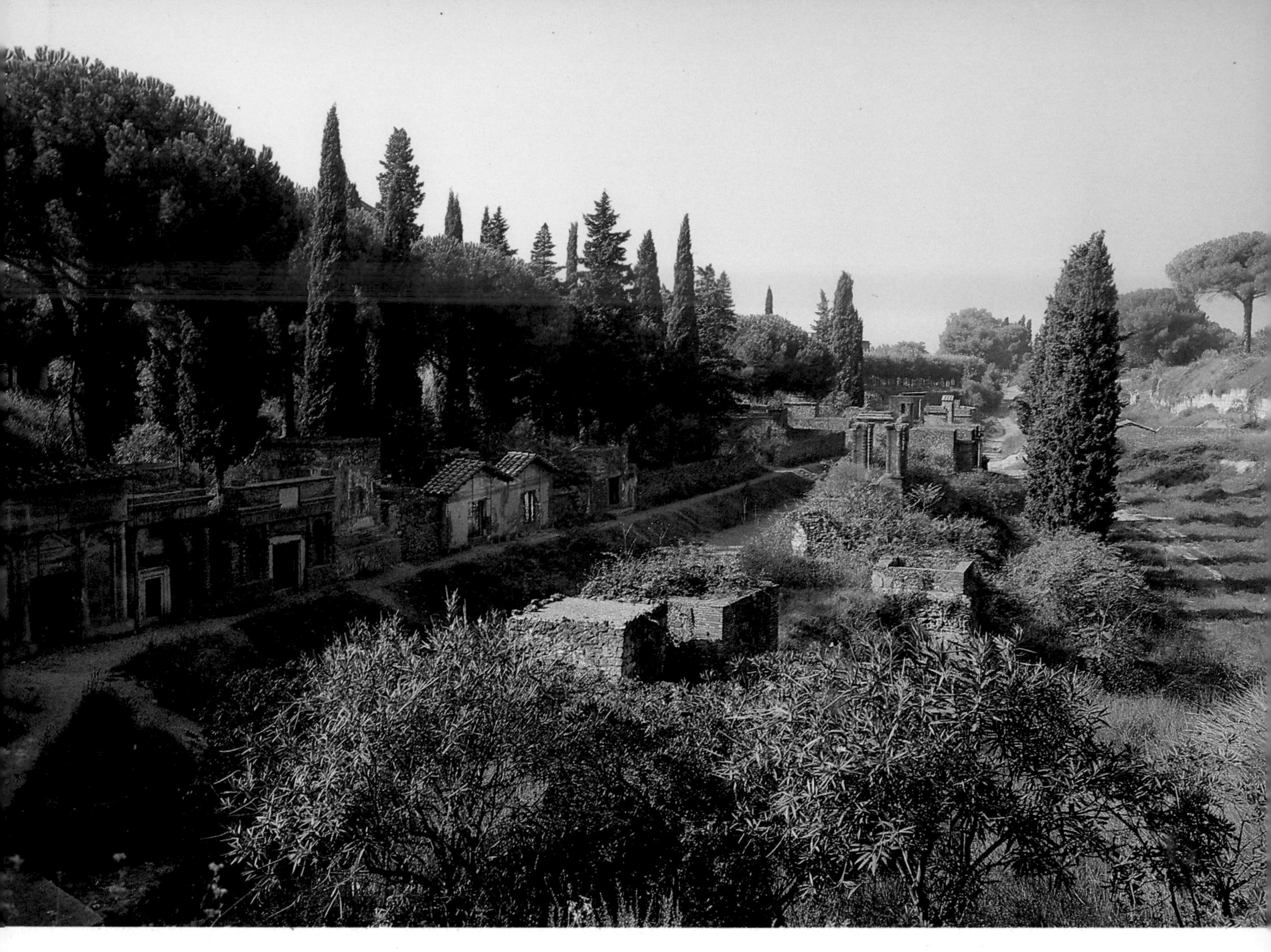

A stretch of the necropolis of Porta Nocera.

into *cunei* by flights of stairs. As can still be seen, not all the sectors here had stone seats, but there were prevalently wooden tiers. The linen *velarium* which protected the spectators from the sun was supported by poles set in two rows of stone rings that were on the outside of the upper parapet.
The Amphitheater was the scene for hunts (*venationes*) and gladiatorial games (*munera*) sponsored by the city's most eminent citizens who used this munificence as an instrument for personal propaganda. "Posters" advertising the games and illustrating the program appear frequently on the walls of Pompeii. This kind of spectacle was passionately participated in by the crowds and various gladiators became highly popular, as witnessed by the inscriptions. They were either slaves or prisoners of war who were trying to obtain their freedom, or common criminals who wanted to redeem their sentence. The colossal bloody riots with many casualties between the Pompeiians and the Nucerians were to go down in history. They took place in the Amphitheater in A.D. 59 as a result of the gladiatorial games and were mentioned by Tacitus in his *Annales*. Nero himself and the Senate intervened. The instigators of the riots were exiled and spectacles in the Amphitheater in Pompeii were prohibited for ten years, although this measure was revoked three years later after the devastating damage of the earthquake of A.D. 62.

34 - LARGE PALAESTRA

The palaestra is situated in the eastern periphery of the city, near the Amphitheater. It was created during the Augustan period, one of the projects of imperial propaganda which led to the founding of the *collegia iuvenum*, organizations of young people whose prime scope may have been that of furthering sports but whose secondary scope was that of providing an atmosphere of adhesion to the principles of the new political ideology in which the future citizens would be formed.
The palaestra of the *Iuventus Pompeiana* occupies a vast area (m 141 x 137) and consists of a central space for gymnastic exercises, surrounded by a tall perimetral wall with ten monumental entrance gateways. Inside, on three sides, runs a portico of 118 columns in brick covered with stucco. Originally there were two rows of plane trees, of which the impressions of the roots still exist. At the center of the courtyard was a large swimming pool from one m. to two m. in depth. A room preceded by two columns off the south-west side, with the base for a statue near the back wall. This was probably the space dedicated to the cult of Augustus, patron of the *collegia*. A large latrine was on the southeast side. The palaestra had been heavily damaged in the earthquake of A.D. 62 and was still being restored when the eruption of A.D. 79 took place.

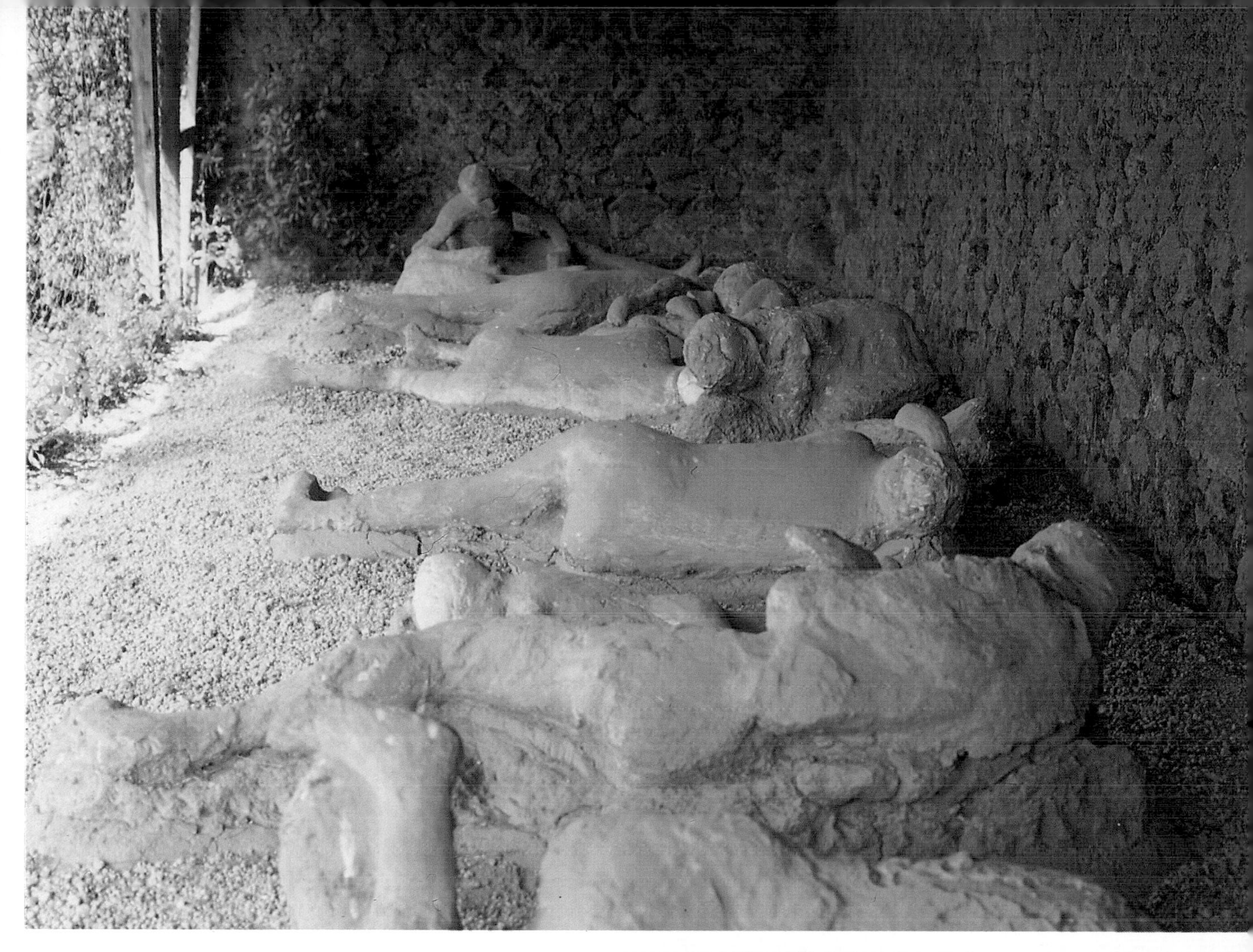

On this page, two views of the so-called « garden of fugitives ».

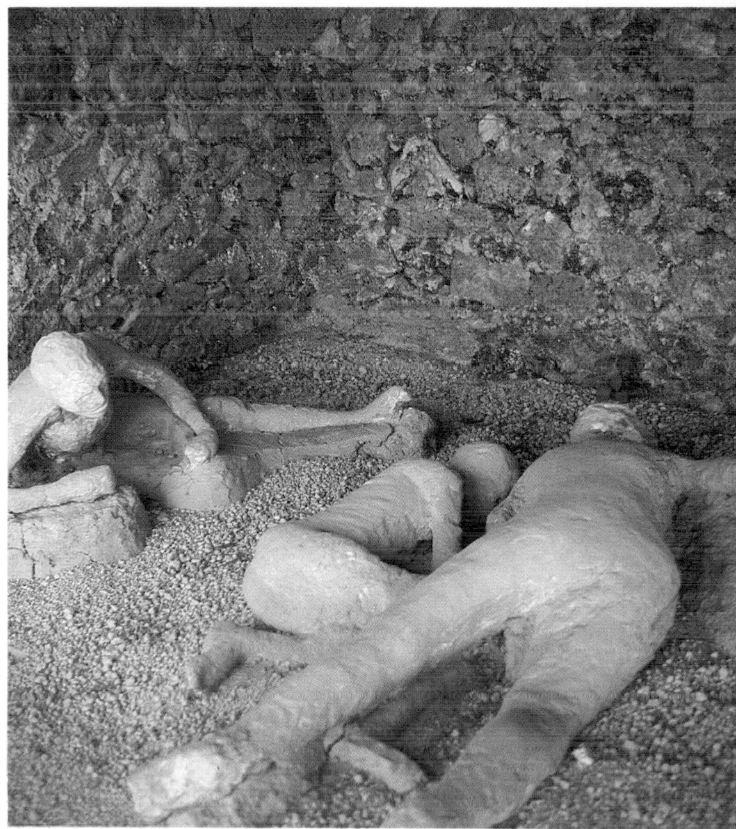

35 - NECROPOLIS OF PORTA NOCERA AND GARDEN OF THE FUGITIVES

A necropolis consisting of a series of tombs bordering the Via Nocera lies right outside the Porta Nocera. There are various types of sepulchres: chamber tombs, cube tombs (a dado), altar-shaped, aedicule tombs, hemicycle, etc. ranging chronologically from the Republican period to the last years of Pompeii.
At the point where this street intersects with the street that runs down from the Porta Nocera stands a travertine cippus which informs us that the military tribune Titus Suedius Clemens was charged, by decree of the Emperor Vespasian, with reestablishing the boundaries of the public soil.
Near the cippus is a low building, called « garden of the fugitives », in which casts of some of the victims of the eruption are kept. The thirteen bodies discovered here were those of inhabitants who died from the poisonous sulphur fumes borne by the wind. Their bodies, which were imprisoned in the ashes and pumice that solidified as time passed, left cavities in the earth which in the course of the excavations were filled with plaster, thus providing us, after centuries, with the shapes of the ancient inhabitants of Pompeii.

III PART

Stabian Baths - Via Stabiana - Lupanar - Via degli Augustali - Pistrinum of the Vicolo Torto - House of M. Lucretius - House of the Silver Wedding - House of the Centennial - House of M. Obellius Firmus

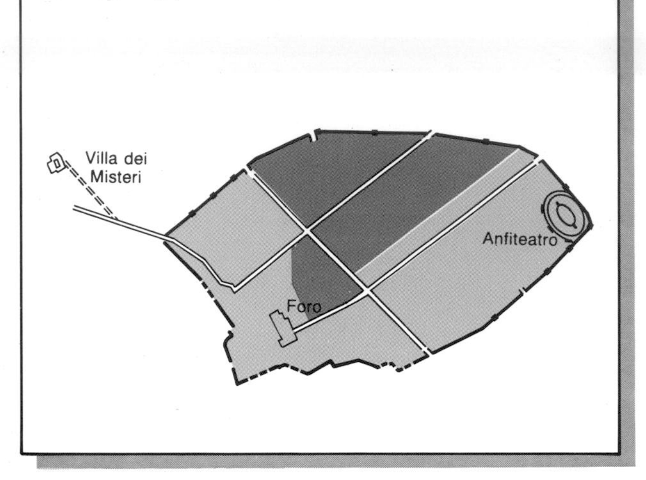

36 - STABIAN BATHS

These baths take their name from the fact that they are situated on a city block bordered by Via Stabiana and Via dell'Abbondanza. They are the oldest baths in Pompeii and four different building phases can be identified. The oldest part seems to date to the late 4th cent. B.C. and consisted of the palaestra, a series of cells with tubs along the north side and a well to furnish water. It was at this time that the palaestra was built in a trapezoidal form due to the presence of two old streets and the garden of a house that was later torn down.
The general layout of the bath however dates to the 2nd cent. B.C. as confirmed indirectly by an inscription of the *duoviri* of Sulla's colony C. Uulius and P. Aninius who state that they have reconstructed the palaestra and the porticoes and have created a *laconicum* for sweat baths and a *destrictarium* for cleansing the body. The entrance is on Via dell'Abbondanza and from here access is to the courtyard of the palaestra with colonnaded porticoes on three sides and the entrance framed by two piers, a motif also found on the portico of the opposite side. At the center of the west side is a swimming pool (*natatio*)

This page and opposite: various views of the area occupied by the palestra and the relative colonnade inside the Sabian Baths.

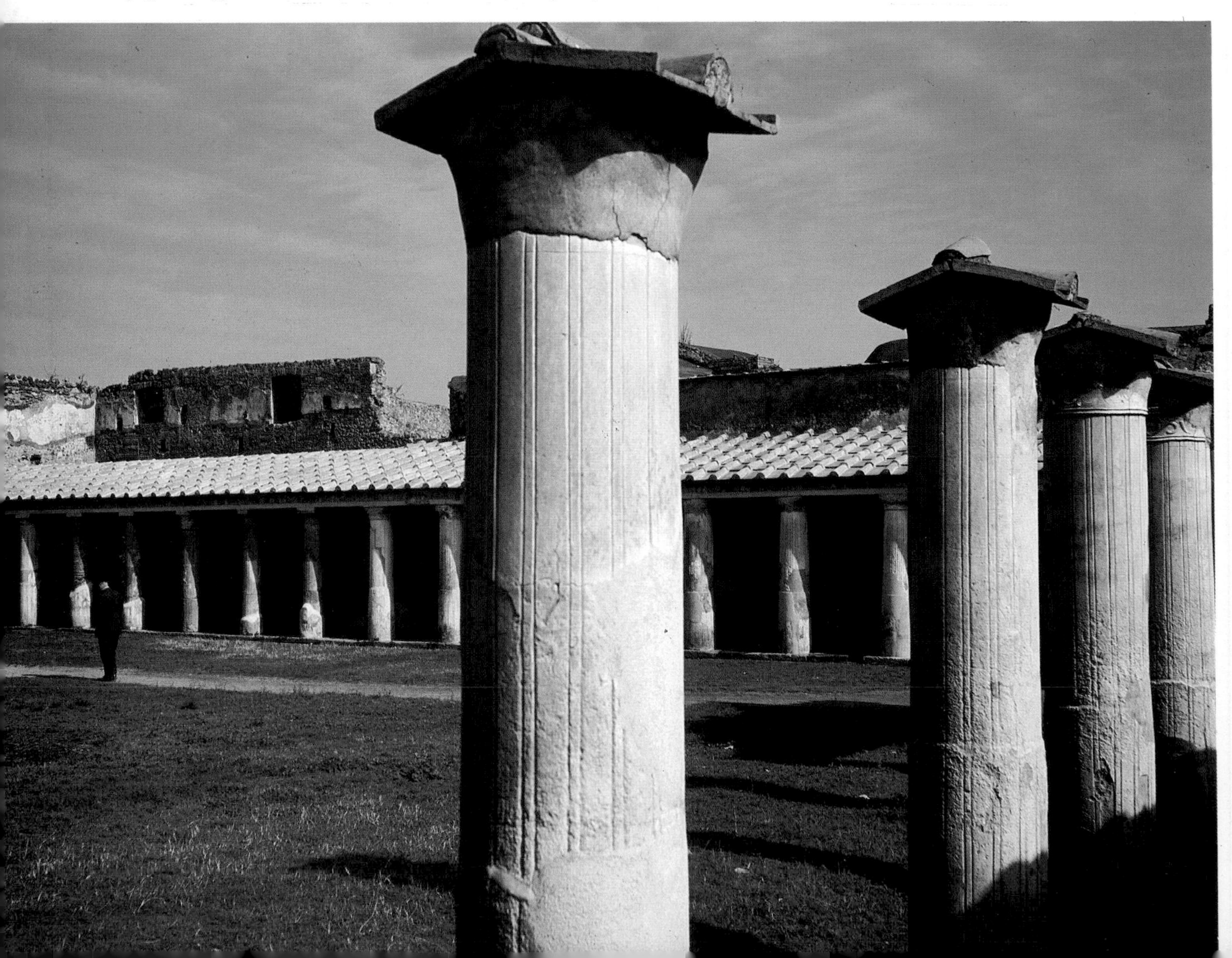

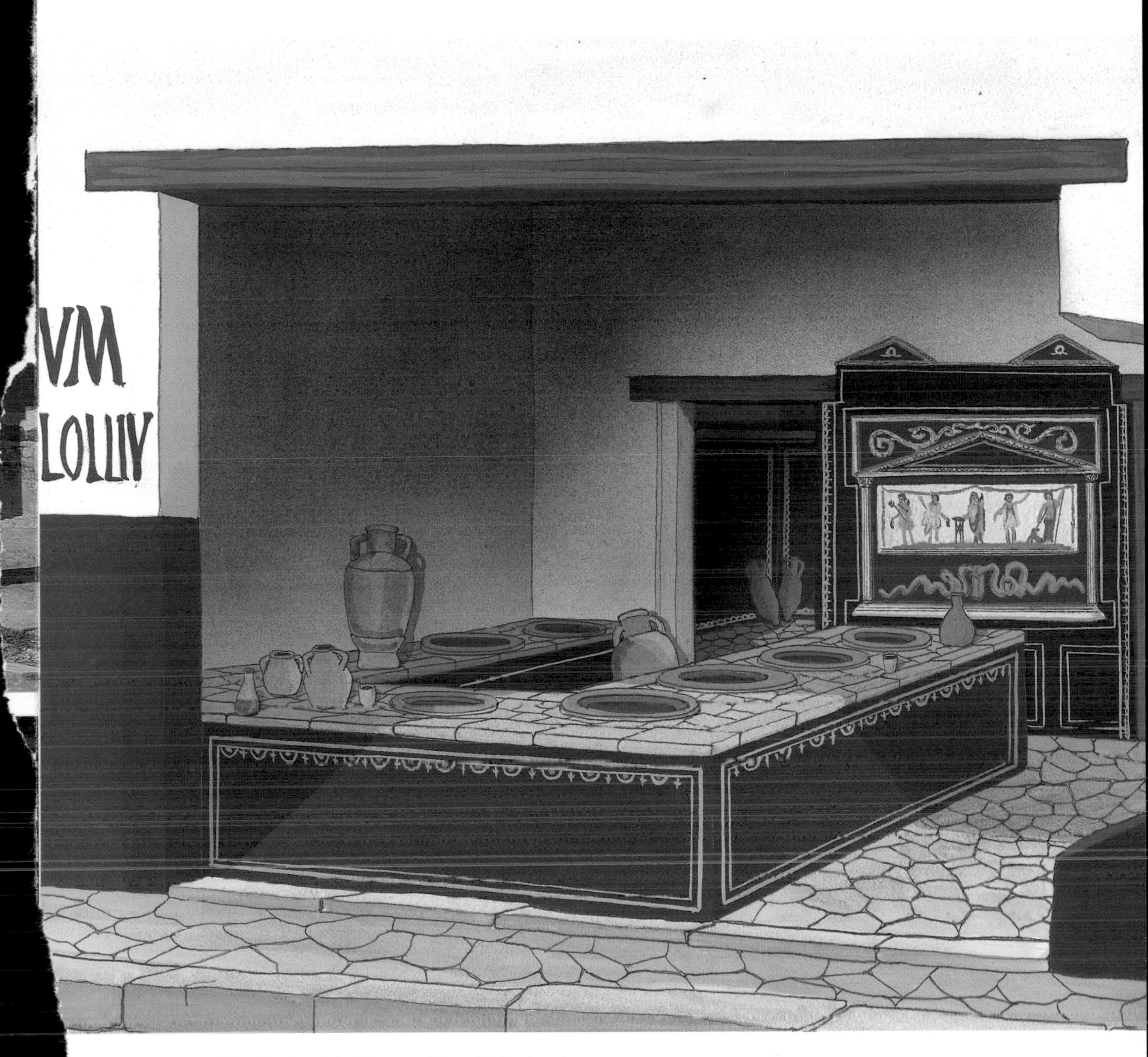

Reconstruction of the interior of the Thermopolium with the Lararium.

THERMOPOLIUM WITH LARARIUM

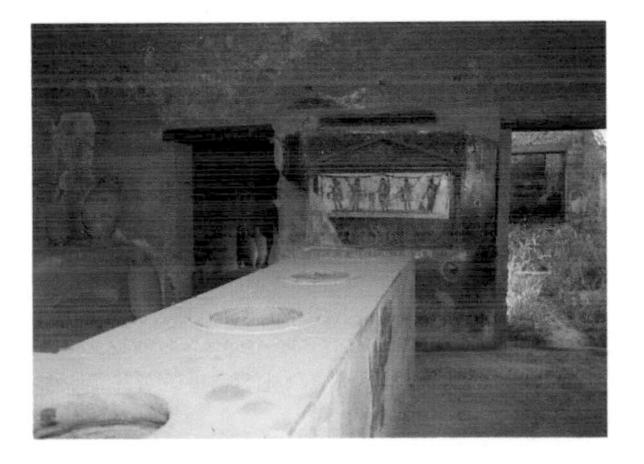

This retail shop for the sale of food and drink to the public contains the typical L-shaped counter used in stores like this, with built-in holes for the jars where food was kept hot. Various wine amphoras were found near them, as well as the supply of beverages in the storeroom behind. The numerous customers (the last day's carnings, found during the excavation, consisted of a considerable sum) could also order a special wine produced by a Hebrew (« *Ioudaikos* ») which was black as ink (« *truginon* »). The picture with the tutelary gods at the back of the shop (from whence the thermopolium takes its name) depicts Mercury, protector of commerce, and Dionysius, protector of the vine and wine.

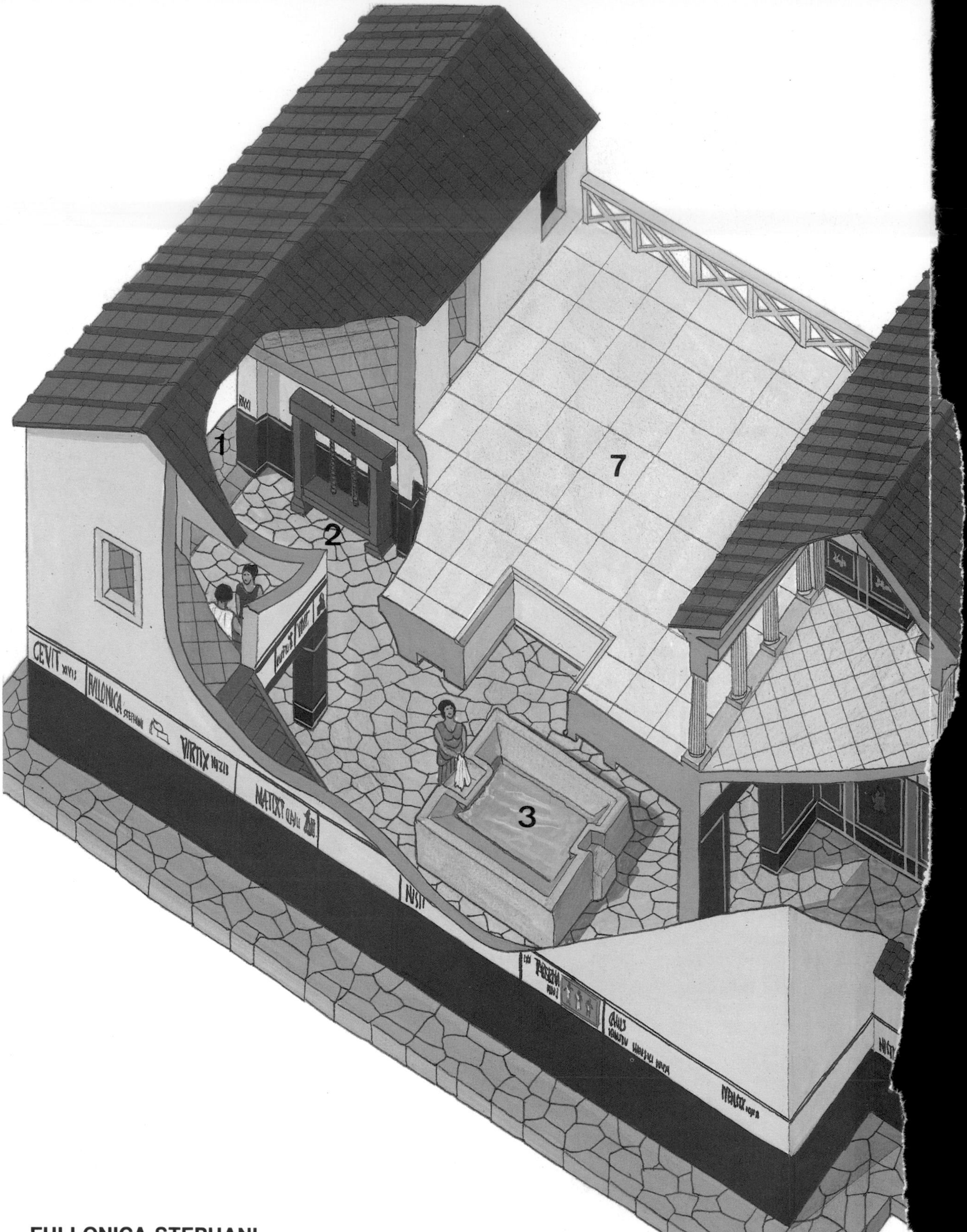

FULLONICA STEPHANI

1 - Entrance
2 - Clothes press
3 - Tub for washing
4 - Service corridor
5 - Trampling basins
6 - Intercommunicating tubs
7 - Terraces for drying clothes

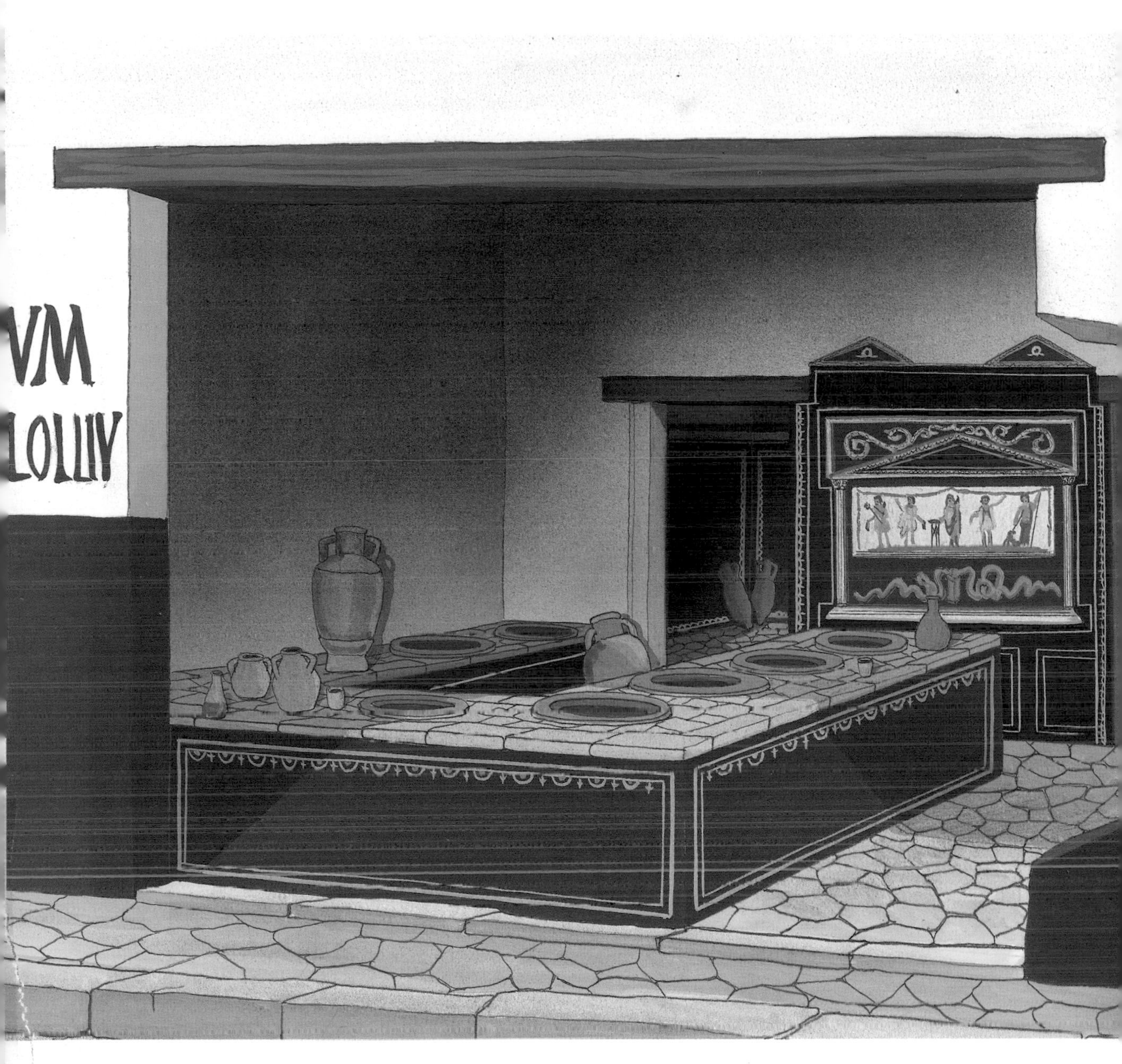

Reconstruction of the interior of the Thermopolium with the Lararium.

THERMOPOLIUM WITH LARARIUM

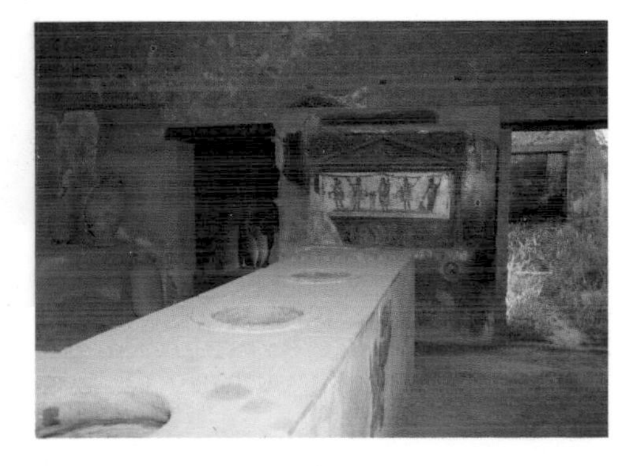

This retail shop for the sale of food and drink to the public contains the typical L-shaped counter used in stores like this, with built-in holes for the jars where food was kept hot. Various wine amphoras were found near them, as well as the supply of beverages in the storeroom behind. The numerous customers (the last day's earnings, found during the excavation, consisted of a considerable sum) could also order a special wine produced by a Hebrew (« *Ioudaikos* ») which was black as ink (« *truginon* »). The picture with the tutelary gods at the back of the shop (from whence the thermopolium takes its name) depicts Mercury, protector of commerce, and Dionysius, protector of the vine and wine.

FULLONICA STEPHANI

1 - Entrance
2 - Clothes press
3 - Tub for washing
4 - Service corridor
5 - Trampling basins
6 - Intercommunicating tubs
7 - Terraces for drying clothes

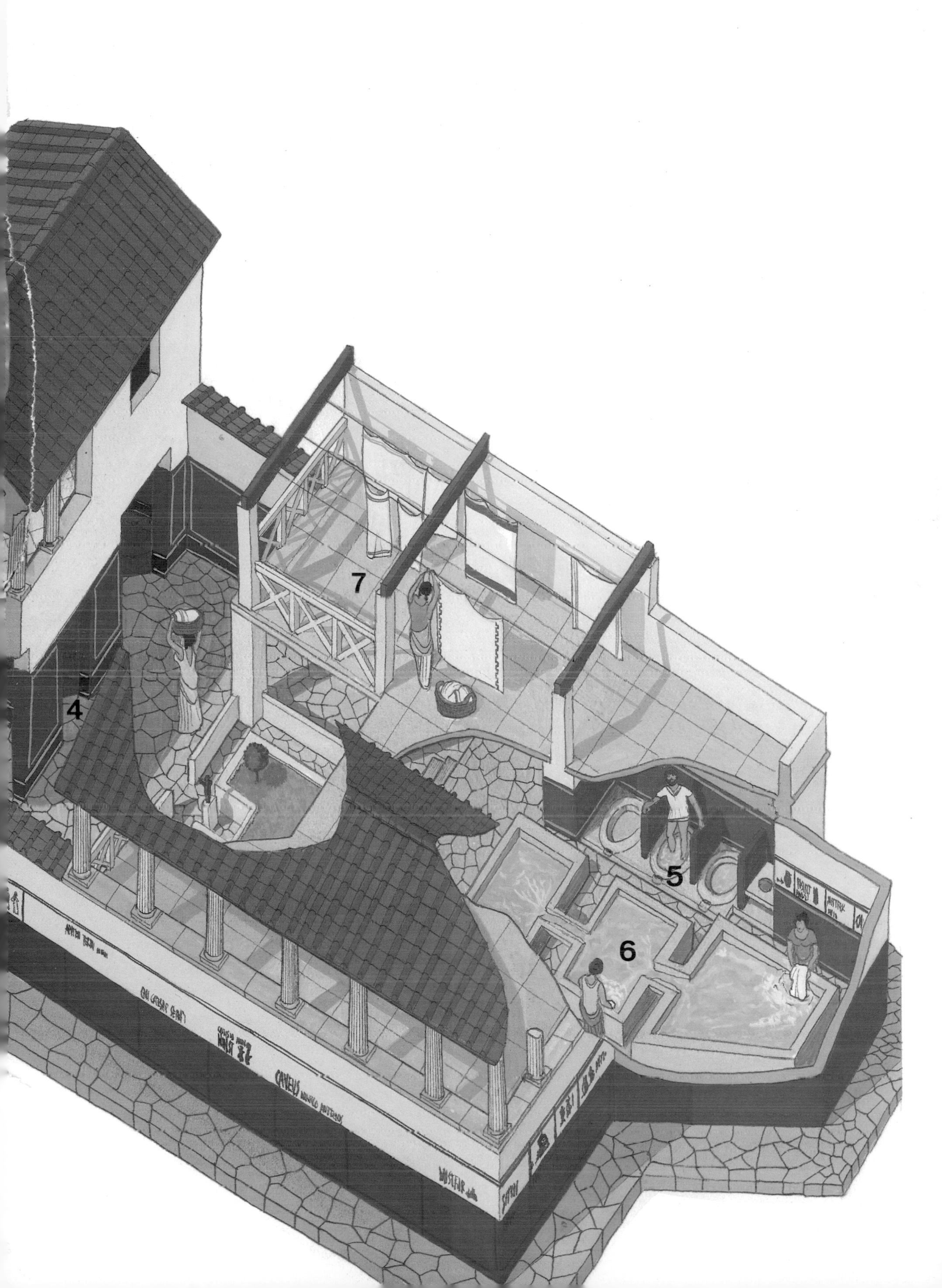

Reconstruction of the Fullonica Stephani with a cross-section of the interior (see description on p. 54).

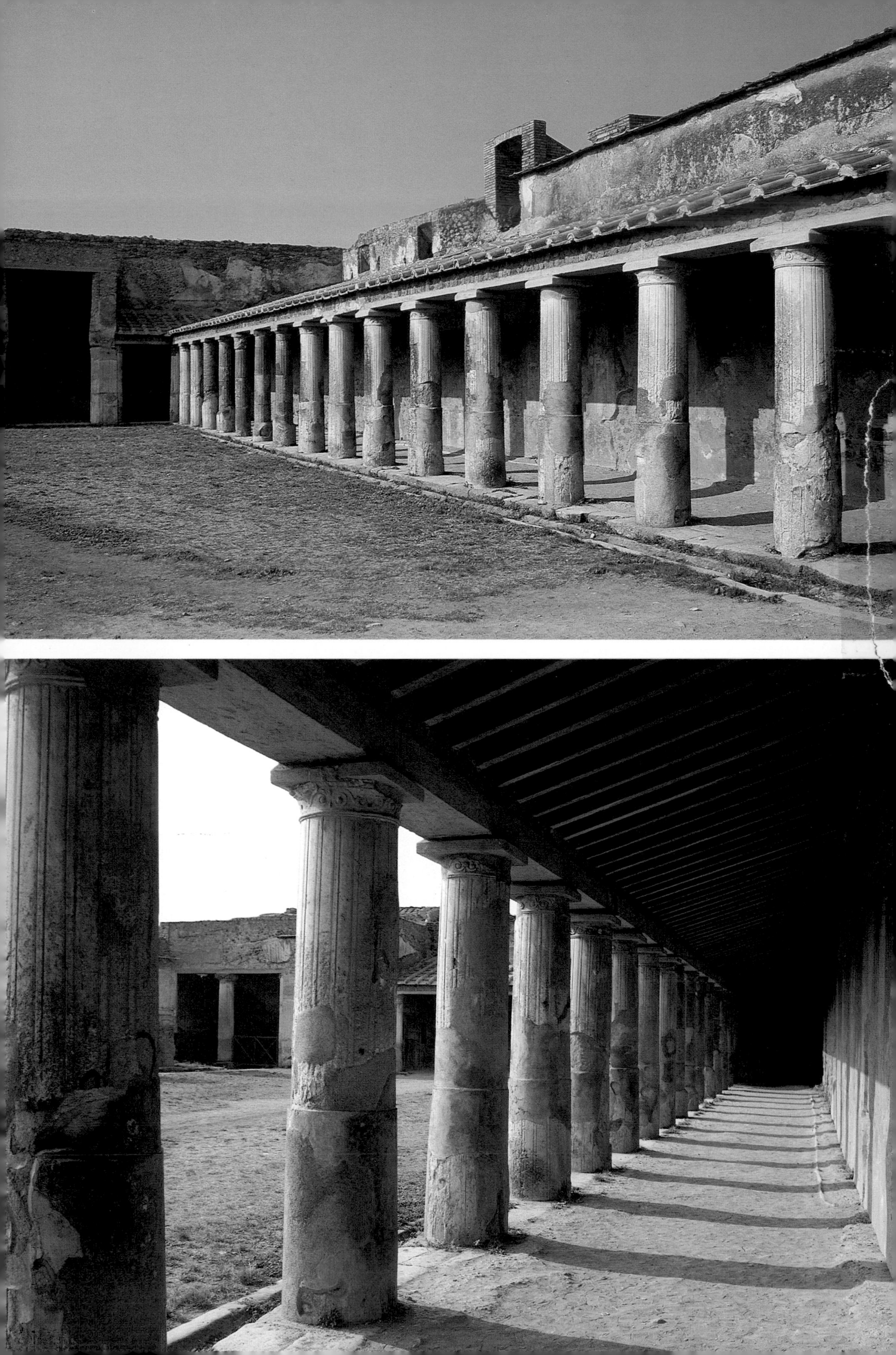

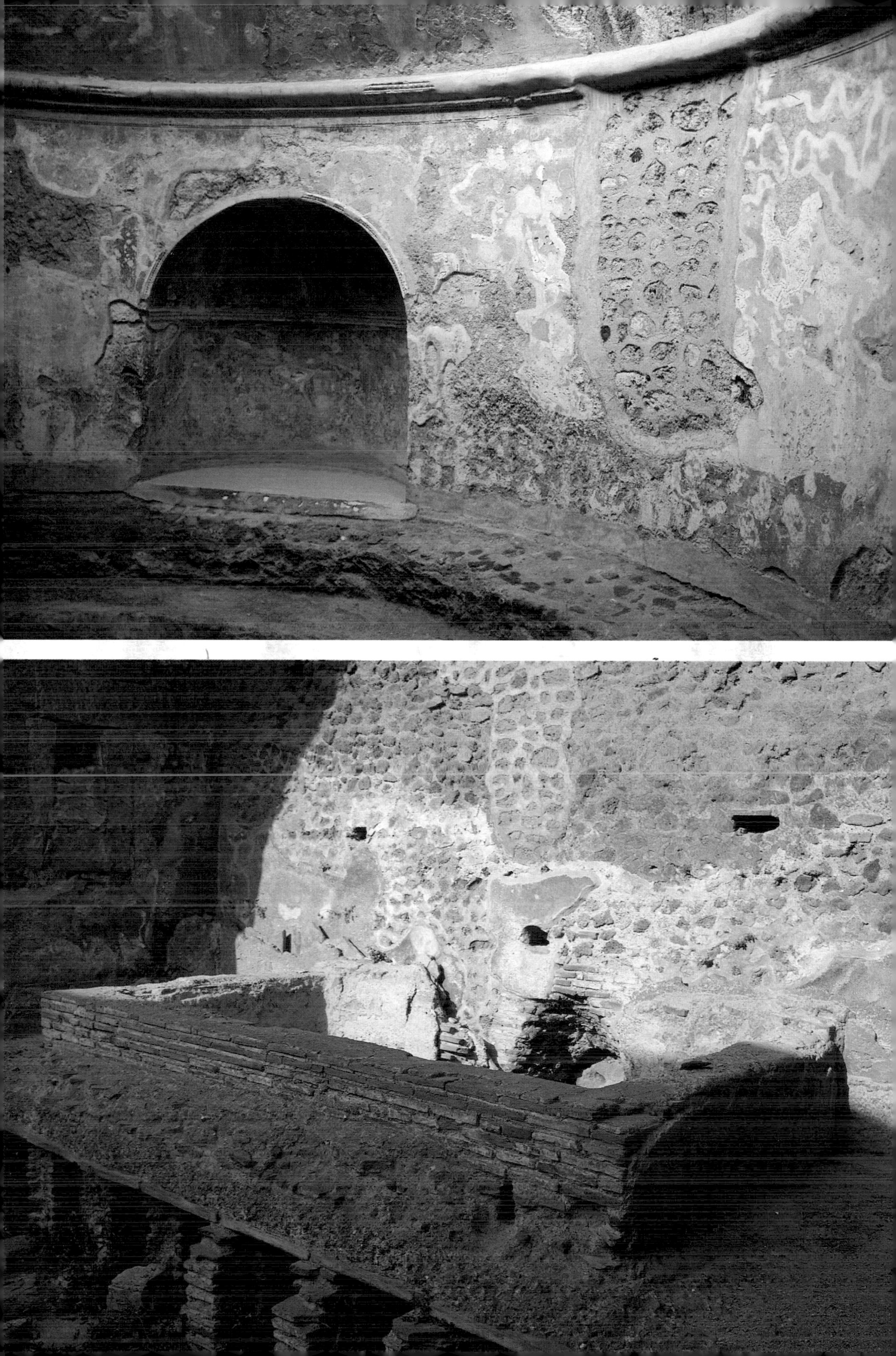

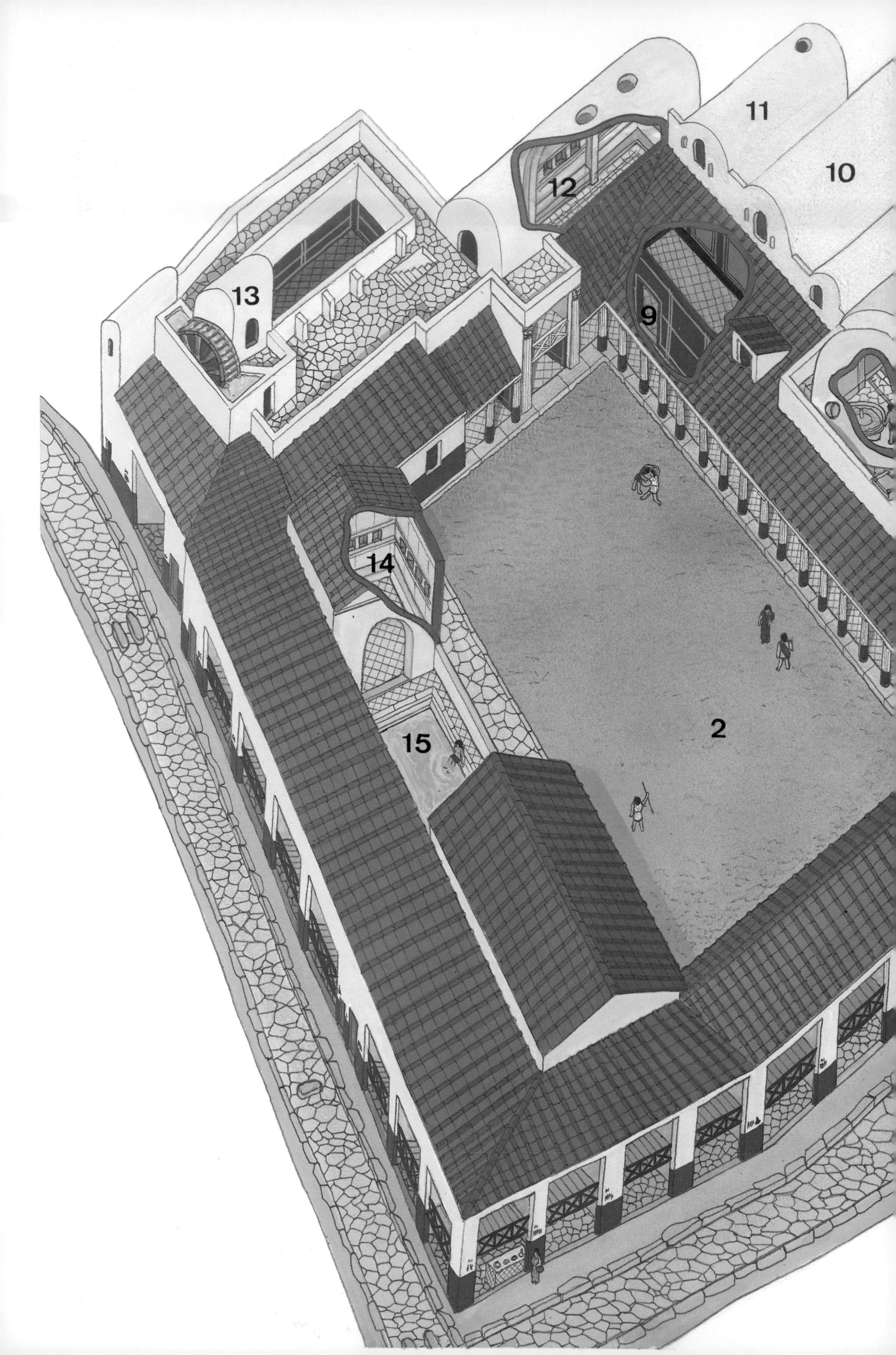

11
10
12
13
9
14
15
2

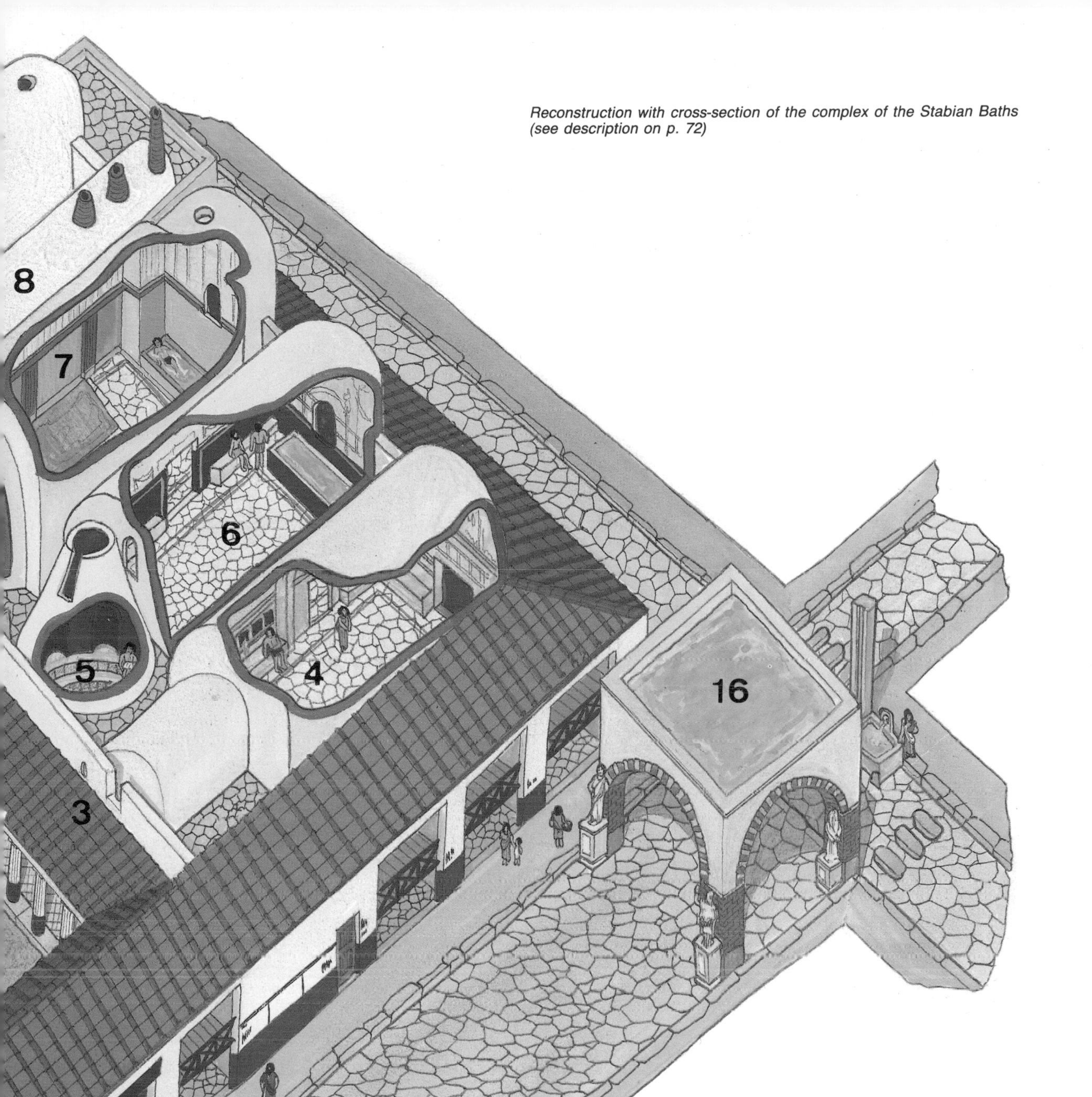

Reconstruction with cross-section of the complex of the Stabian Baths
(see description on p. 72)

STABIAN BATHS

1 - Entrance
2 - Courtyard
3 - Portico
4 - Men's apodyterium
5 - Men's frigidarium
6 - Men's tepidarium
7 - Men's calidarium
8 - Furnace
9 - Current entrance to the women's baths
10 - Women's calidarium
11 - Women's tepidarium
12 - Women's apodyterium
13 - Well with hydraulic wheel
14 - Entrance to the swimming pool
15 - Swimming pool
16 - Arch with water supply

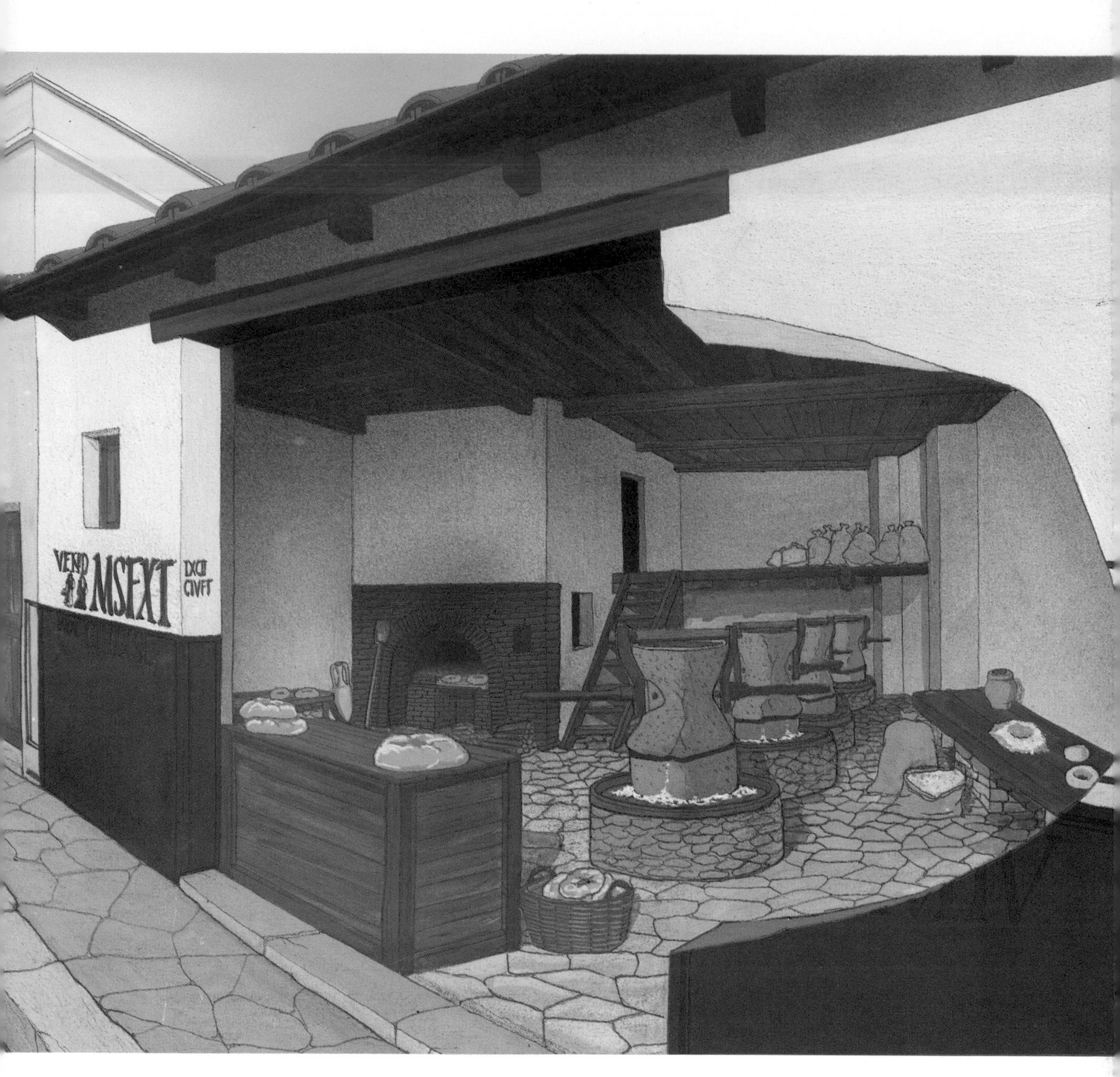

Reconstruction of the interior of the Pistrinum in the Vicolo Torto.

PISTRINUM OF THE VICOLO TORTO

In this bakery the entire process that turned wheat into bread was carried out. The grain, deposited in sacks in the storeroom, was washed in a tub and then poured into the upper cone of the mills which can still be seen. Turned by an ass or a slave, this heavy stone device, through attrition with the fixed portion, furnished a fine flour which fell on a circular container. Once kneaded into bread, the loaves were put into the oven with its arched opening (about 80 loaves could be baked at a time) and were glazed by sprinkling them with water, at least those of the best quality.
There was also a type of bread made with inferior flour which was given to the slaves.

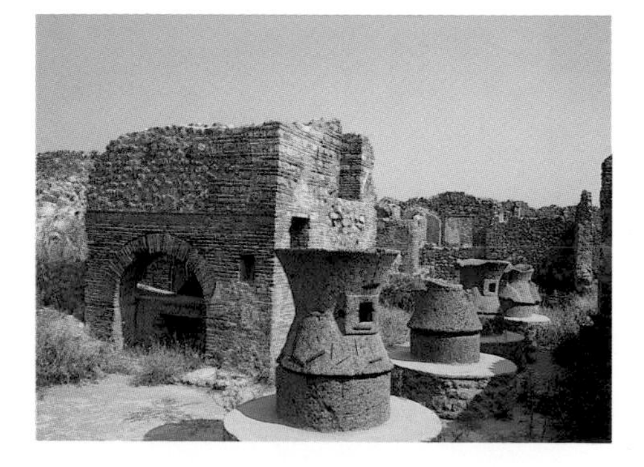

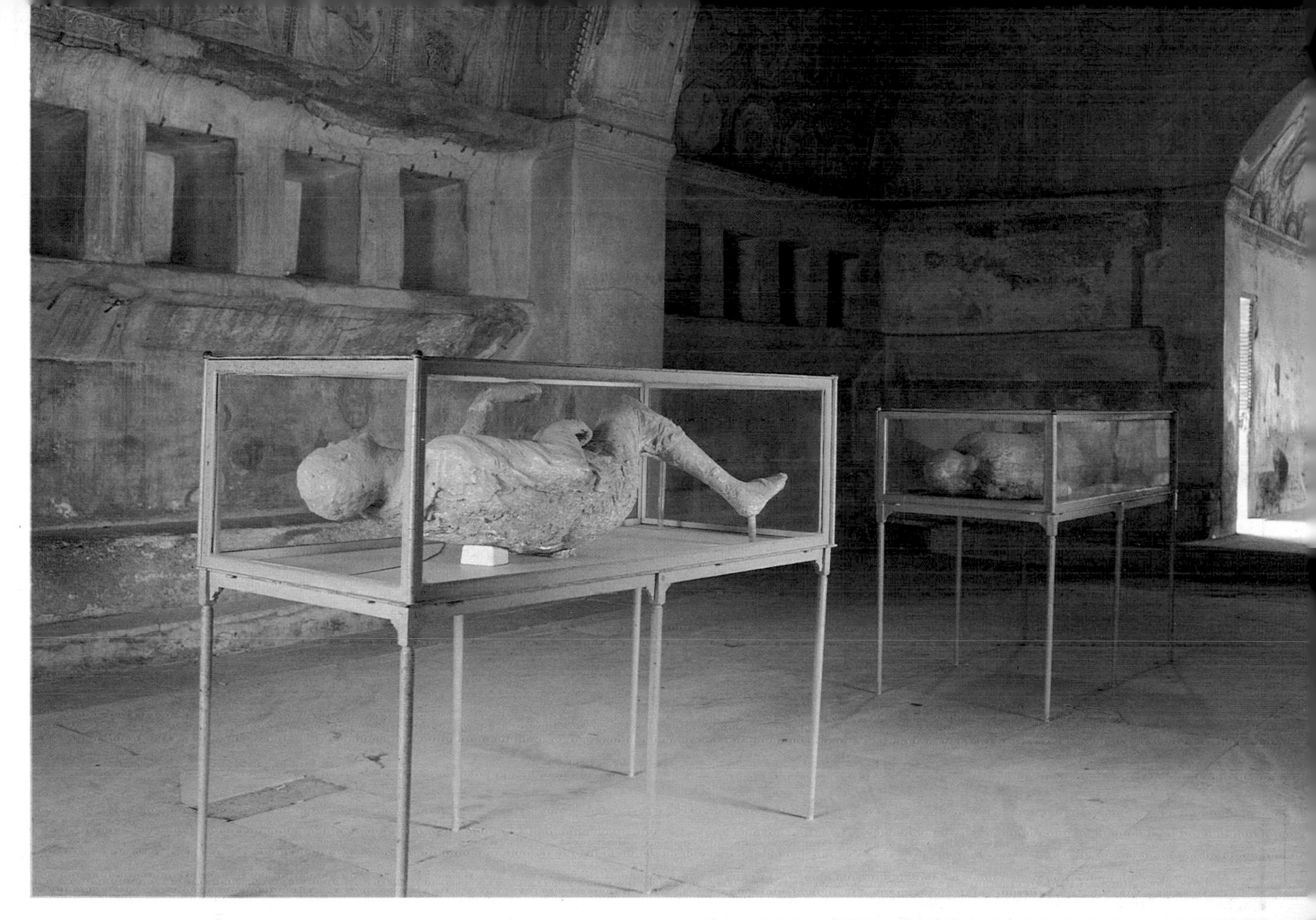

Opposite: above, the frigidarium of the baths and, below, the calidarium. This page: two sections of the apodyterium.

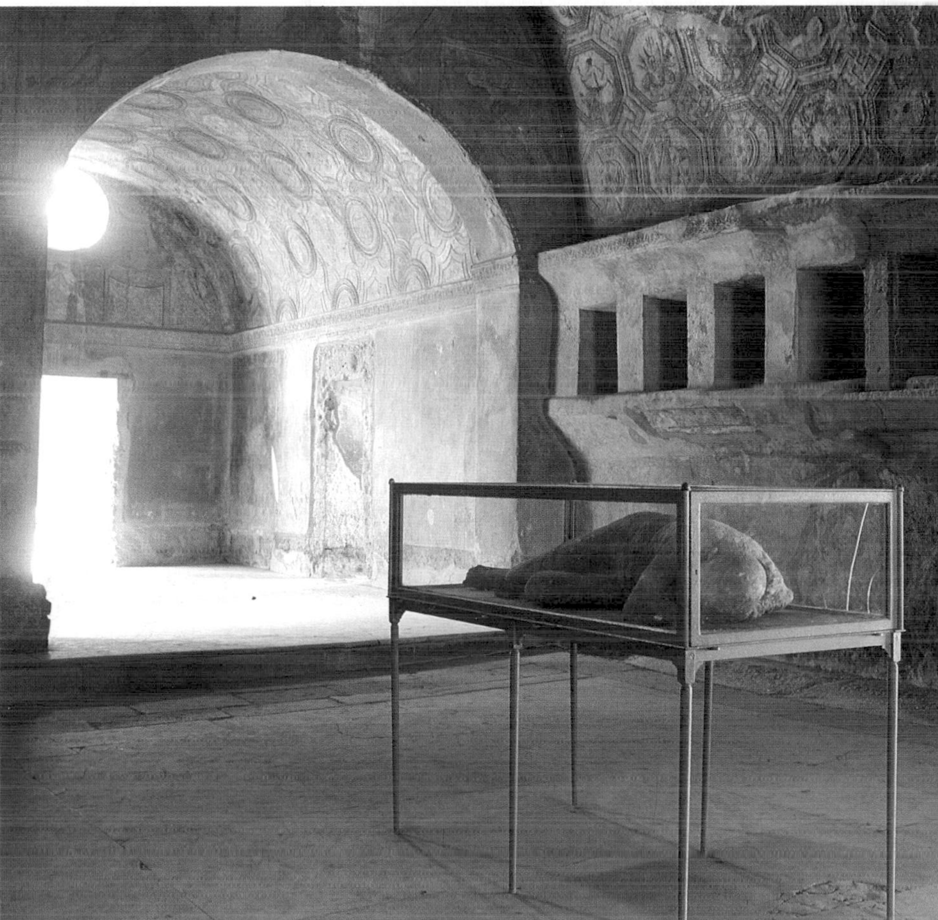

flanked by two rooms where the clients washed before entering the pool, and by a dressing room. These rooms are decorated with polychrome stuccoes that can be dated to the years after the earthquake of A.D. 62. The actual baths were on the east side and were divided into two opposing non-communicating sectors, one for men and one for women, with the *praefurnium* for heating set at the center and used by both. Entrancc to thc mcn's baths was from the southeast corner of the

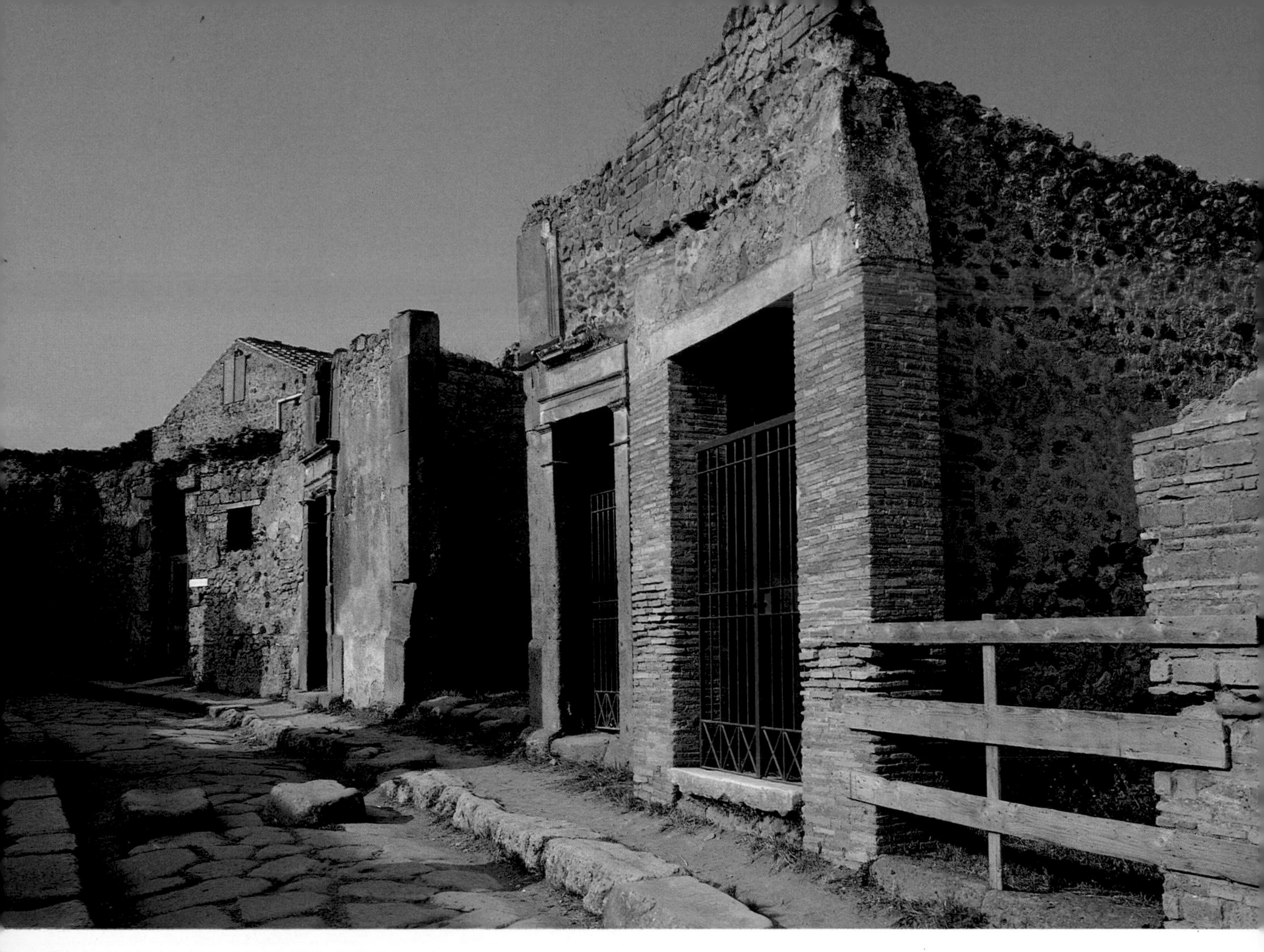

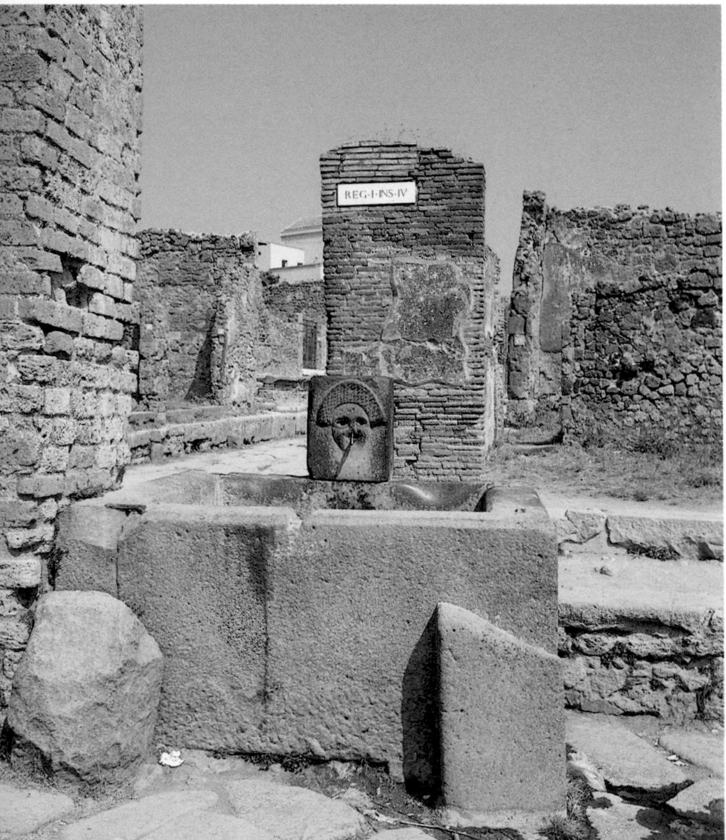

Above: a secondary entrance on the western side of the Stabian Baths.
Left: the fountain on Via Stabiana.

portico where a sundial with a dedication in Oscan was found. A passageway with a barrel vault decorated in polychrome stucco with figured medallions leads both to the *apodyterium* (dressing room), with niches in which to put the clothing and also with a stuccoed vault, and to the circular *frigidarium*. The latter, with a domed ceiling painted blue to represent the starry skies, was orginally the *laconicum* built in Sulla's time, and only later turned into the cold baths. Next comes the *tepidarium* for lukewarm baths, with a pool on the short side, and then the *calidarium*, which, like the preceding room, has the pavement raised up on *suspensurae*, and walls with airspaces for the passage of hot air; a pool for hot baths is on the short side, while across from it is the *labrum*, a circular pool for cold baths.

37 - VIA STABIANA

This street is one of the three *cardines* of Pompeii (the others are Via di Mercurio - Via del Foro - Via delle Scuole and Via di Nocera), the streets that cross the city on a north - south axis. The route followed by Via Stabiana, which lies in the valley between the two lava ridges on

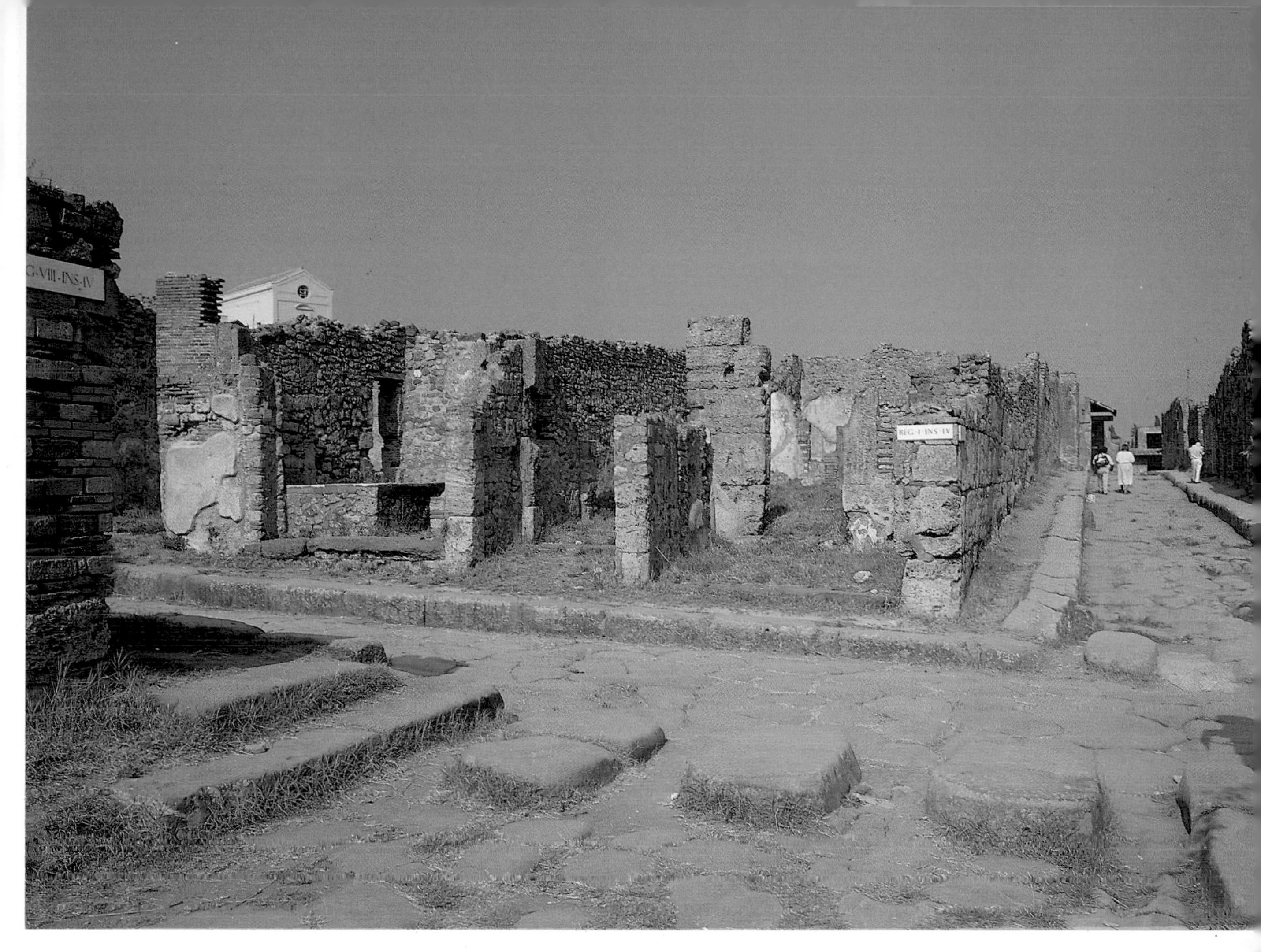

Above: the intersection between Via Stabiana and Via del Tempio d'Iside. Below: a stretch of the Via Stabiana.

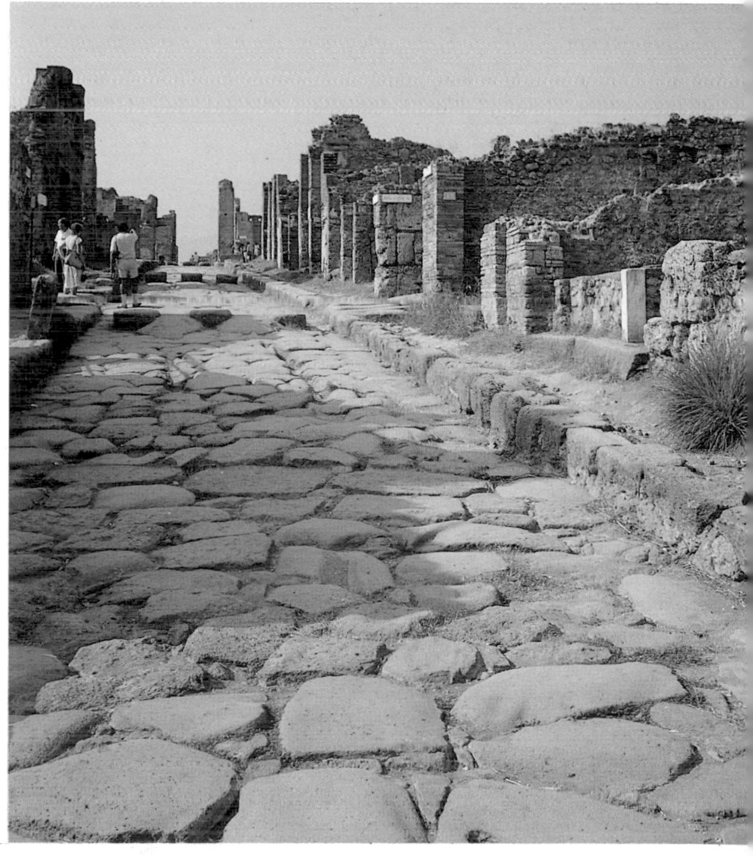

which Pompeii is situated, has been used since oldest times, since it joined the city to Stabia and Sorrento and the coastal route that joined Naples to Stabia also passed along it for a stretch. It then joined Pompeii to its river port on the Sarno, an important trade route; traces of a suburb with mercantile installations and warehouses were found on this line about one kilometer from Pompeii in the hamlet of Bottaro.

As part of the town plan of Pompeii, it was used as the north - south artery and lengthened so that it joined the Porta di Stabia with the Porta Vesuvio and the two eastern *decumani* running east - west, the Via Nolana and the Via dell'Abbondanza, crossed it so as to create a regular grid plan which was to condition all future development of the city. The Via Stabiana was the means of communication between the areas where large numbers of persons congregated, such as the Stabian Baths and the Central Baths, situated along the street, and the zone of theaters and the Temple of Isis. It was also extremely important as a thoroughfare for trade, confirmed by the wear the basalt pavement shows near the gates. After A.D. 62 the area around the intersection with Via dell'Abbondanza became the principal center of trade and economic life in the city.

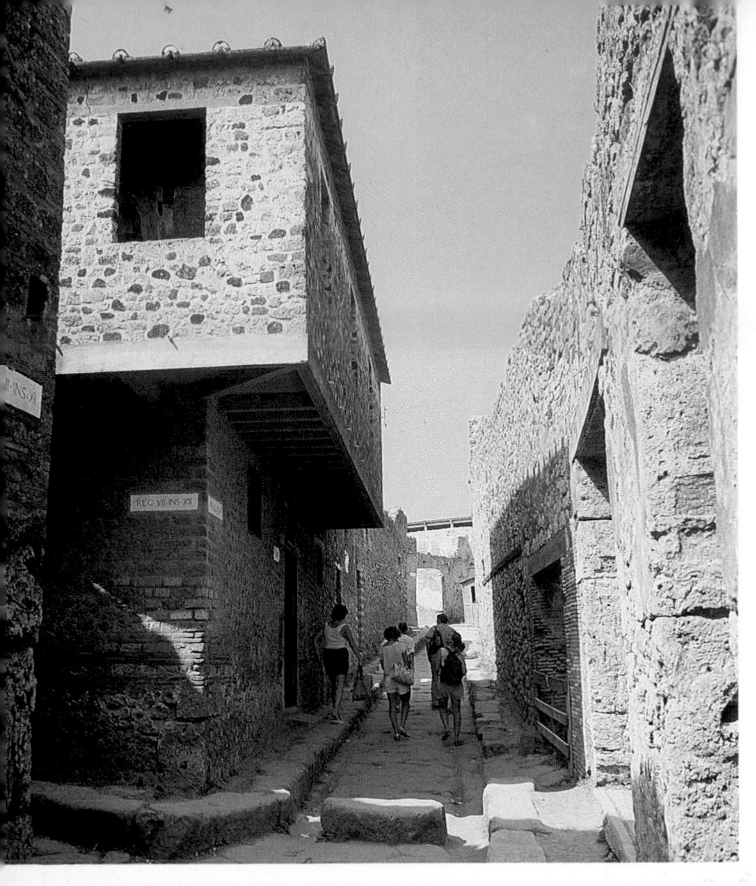

38 - LUPANAR

The *lupanar* on Insula VII is the only one of the twenty-five houses of prostitution known in Pompeii which was built specifically as such. The others are to be found on the first floors of the inns or taverns or even in private homes, or consisted simply of a room with a bed, accessible directly from the street. As customary this brothel was situated at the intersection of secondary streets.
This brothel has ten rooms, five on the lower floor and five larger ones on the upper floor, with a balcony in front that acted as a passageway and which could be reached by an independent flight of wooden stairs. A Priapus with two phalluses was painted next to the entrance on the ground floor, shown beside a fig tree, holding his two male members. The rooms have masonry beds on which mattresses were spread. Erotic scenes which probably indicated the "specializations" offered to their clients were painted above each door. The interior of the brothel must have been redecorated shortly before the eruption, for there is the impression of a coin dating to later than A.D. 72 in the intonaco of one of the rooms. On the other side of a wall on the ground floor there is a latrine. A large number of inscriptions, over 120 of which are still legible, were scratched into the walls both by the client and by the girls who worked there as prostitutes. We can

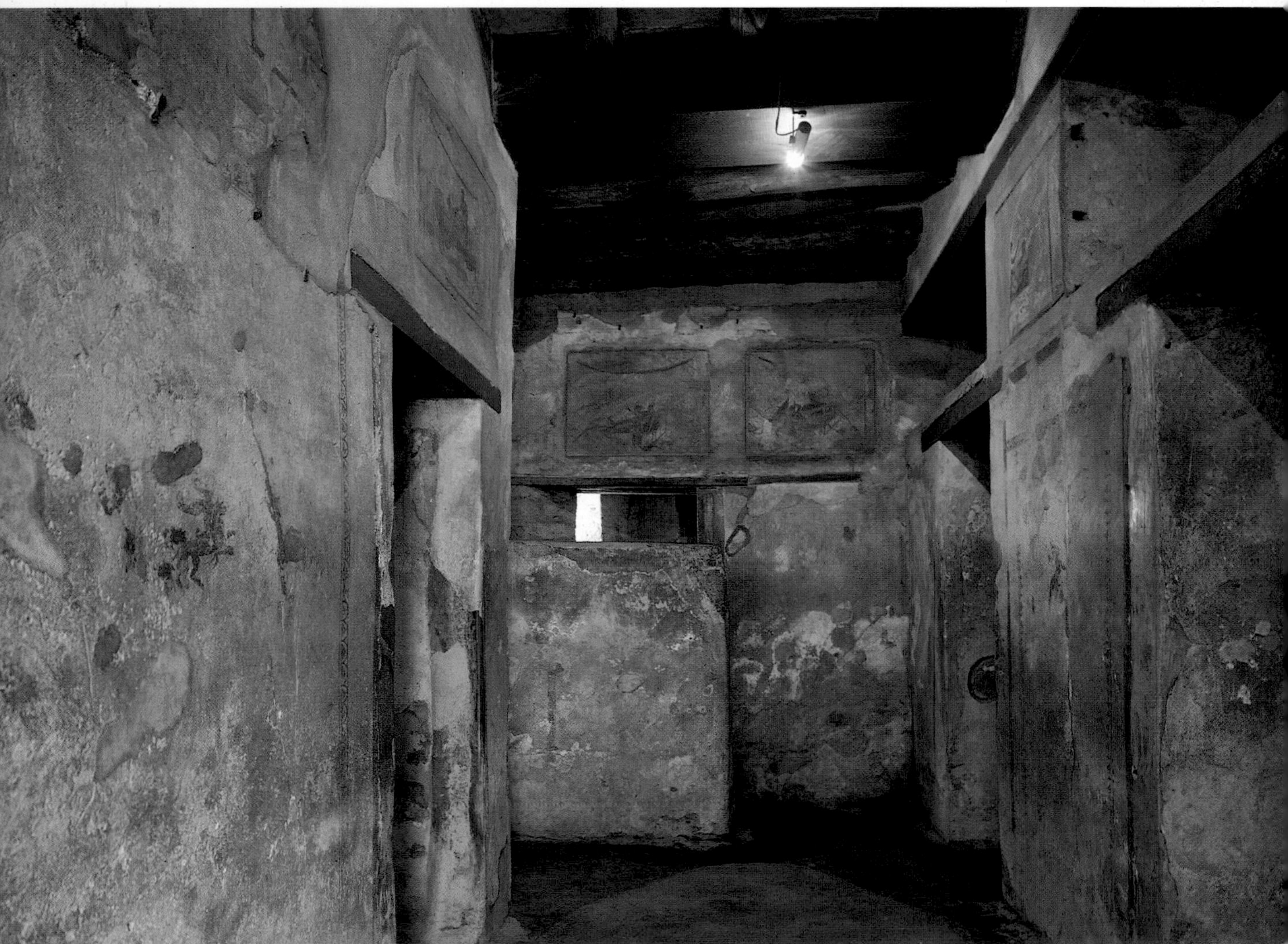

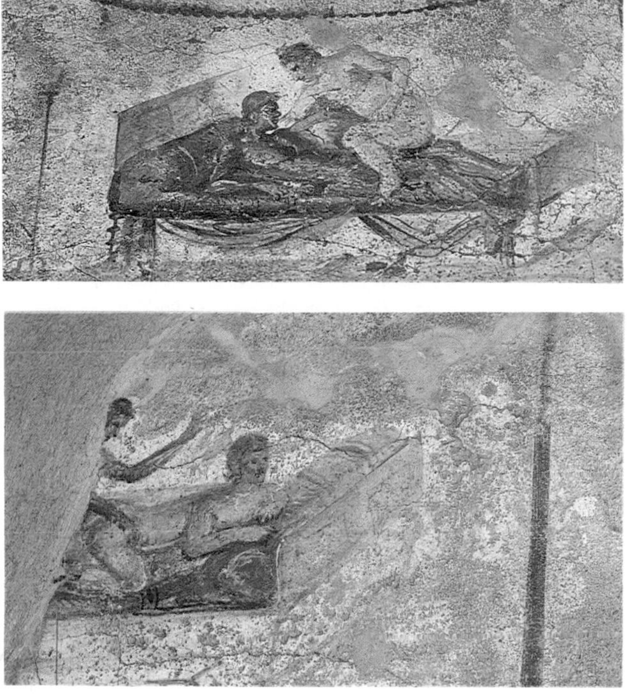

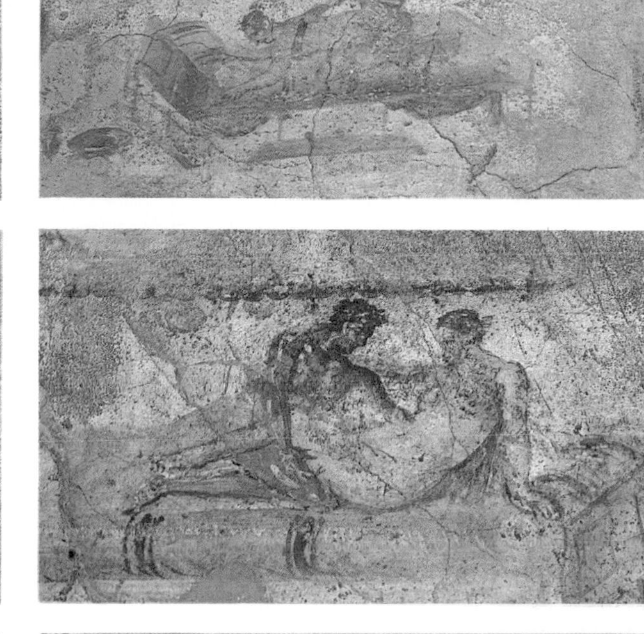

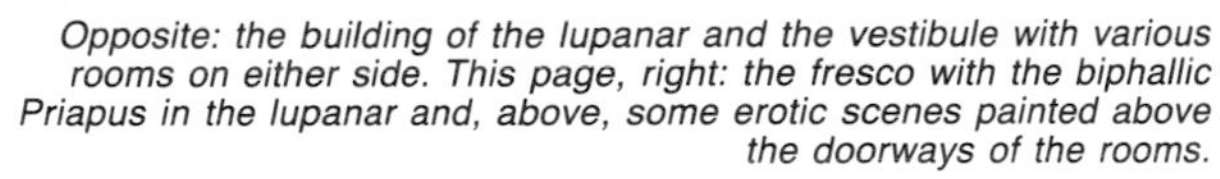

Opposite: the building of the lupanar and the vestibule with various rooms on either side. This page, right: the fresco with the biphallic Priapus in the lupanar and, above, some erotic scenes painted above the doorways of the rooms.

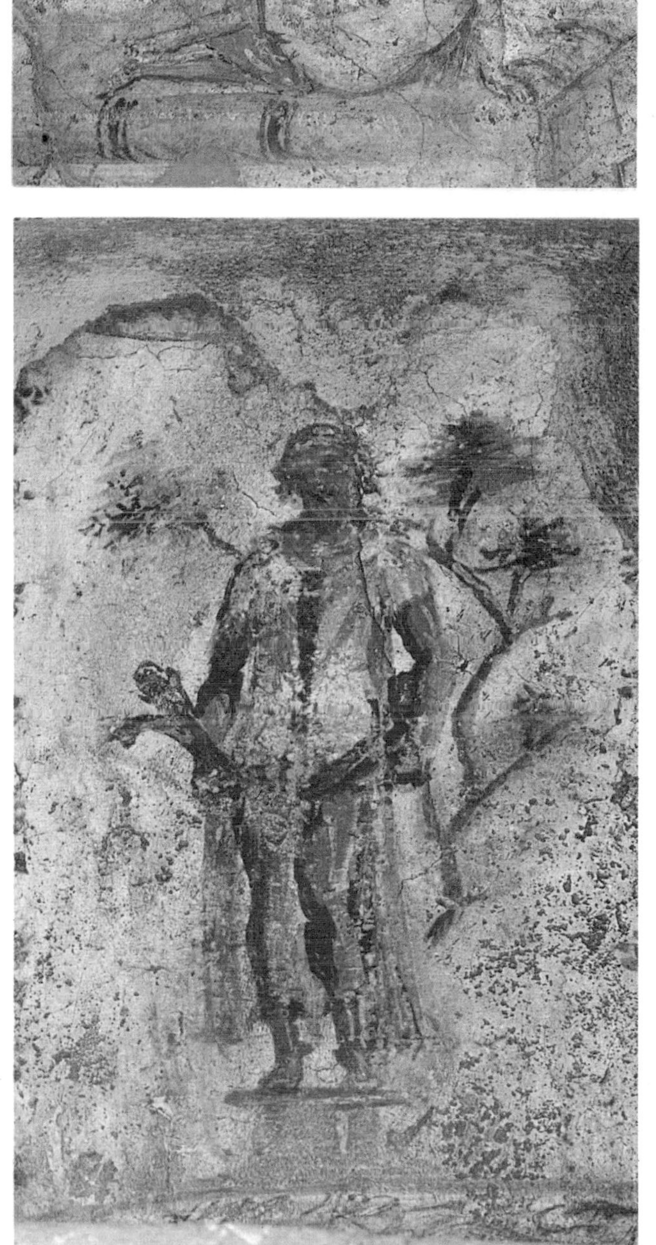

still read the boasts of faithful clients, exclamations of satisfaction, complaints because of having contracted venereal diseases, expressions of specific desires, coarse word-plays, etc. We find that many of the girls had foreign Greek or Oriental names, a sign of the fame enjoyed by "exotic" prostitutes. The client could also have boys. The prices were very low, one of the reasons being that these brothels were frequented by the lowest levels of society and by slaves. On the average the cost of a sexual service was two *asses*, the equivalent of the cost of two cups of wine.

Caligula had ordained a tax on prostitution, which corresponded to the price charged one client per day. Prostitutes could not testify in court, nor, after legislature passed by Domition be the recipient of an inheritance, even if they had stopped practicing this profession. Only marriage might make it possible for them to acquire the rank of *matrona*.

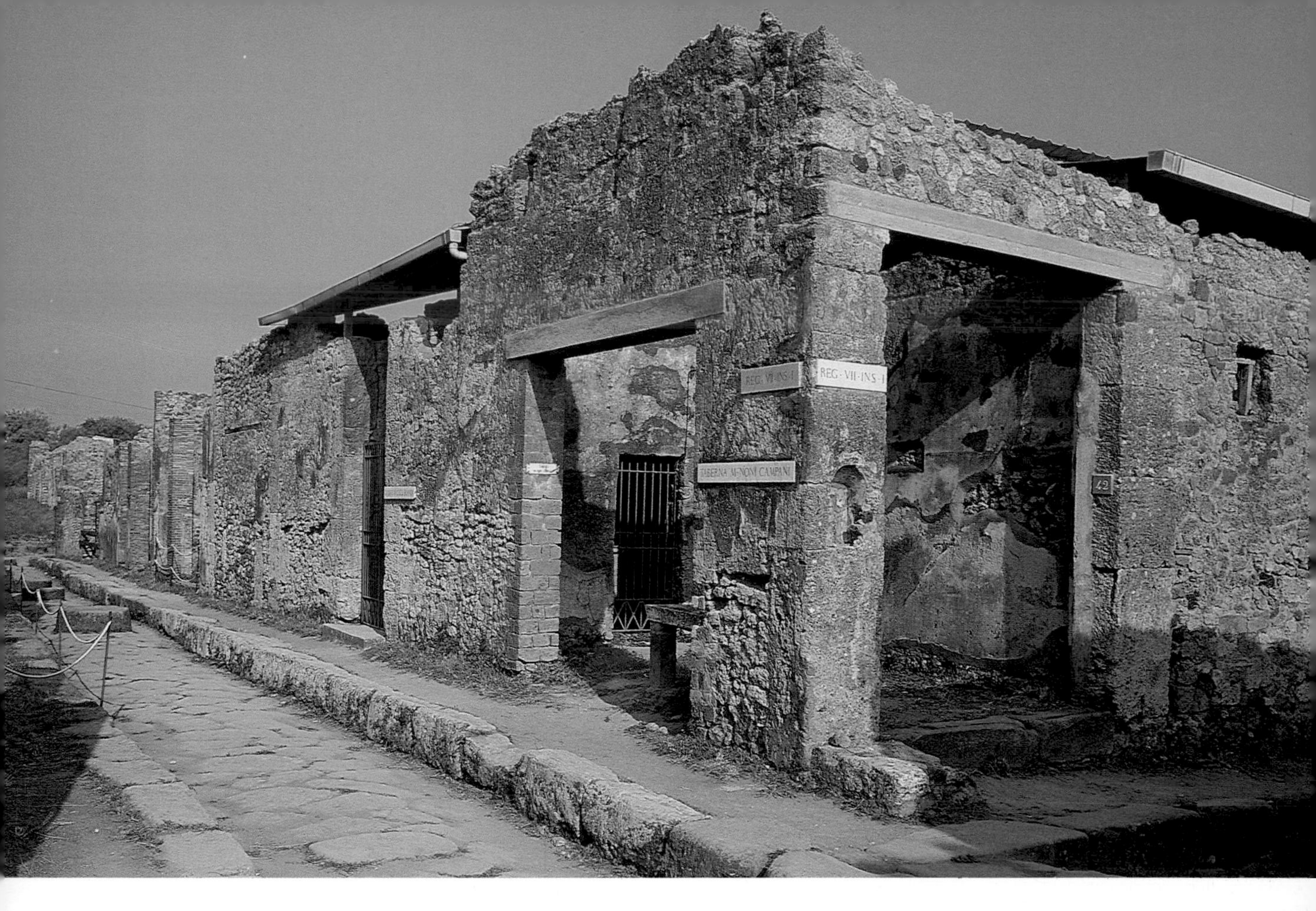

Above: the Taberna of Nonio Campanio on the Via degli Augustali.
Right: the stretch of the Via degli Augustali near the area of the forum.

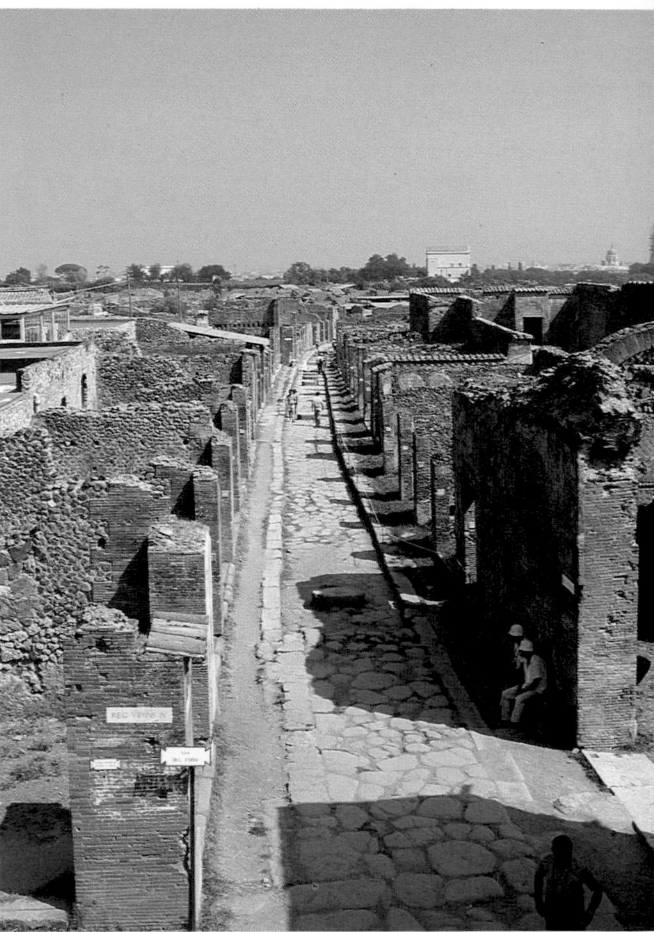

39 - VIA DEGLI AUGUSTALI

The route followed by this street joined the Via Stabiana to the Via del Foro, to which it is not at right angles. It runs along a straight line only in the stretch leading to the Forum, where the row of shops situated on the north side of the Macellum are to be found.
Together with the Vicolo dei Soprastanti, into which it turns on the other side of the Via del Foro, it is commonly accepted as comprising the northern boundary of the first real urban core of Pompeii which developed around what is now the Civil Forum and which was bordered on the east by the Vicolo del Lupanare and the Via dei Teatri. This settlement seems to date back to the second half of the 6th cent. B.C. This street leads to one of the most popular quarters of Pompeii, with various inns and taverns.

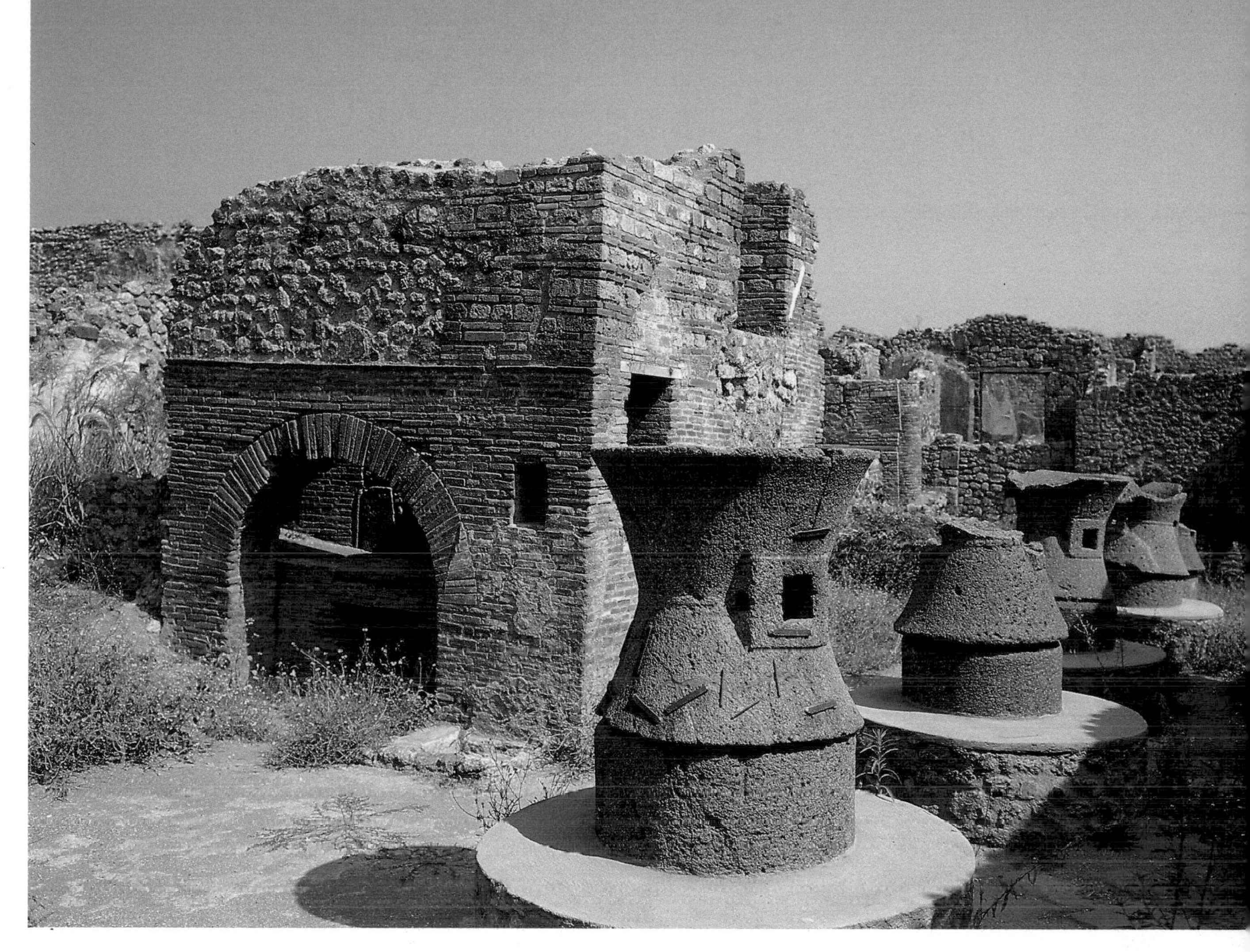

Above: the Pistrinum of Vicolo Torto as it is now.

40 - PISTRINUM OF THE VICOLO TORTO

This bakery belonged to N. Popidius Priscus for it is connected to his house by a door set at the back of the complex. The machinery for the production of bread consists of four millstones in porous lava, very compact resistent stone so there were no risks of its losing tiny fragments in the grinding process which might be mixed with the flour. The form of these mills resembles an hourglass with a biconical or hollow *catullus* which rotates above on a cone-shaped pivot (*meta*), set on a base in masonry and surrounded by a paved floor on which the animals yoked to the beams inserted in the *catullus* walked.
The wood-burning oven is next to the grindstones. It is in concrete and set into a square chamber with a vent at the top so the air needed for combustion could circulate inside and it had a chimney. On the front the loaves were put in through an arched opening in brick. A masonry tub was used for washing the grain. Two rooms next to the oven were destined for the storage of the bread after it was baked and as granary.
This bakery served only for the production and wholesale distribution of bread which may also have been sold by itinerant venders since it had no actual shop open to the public.

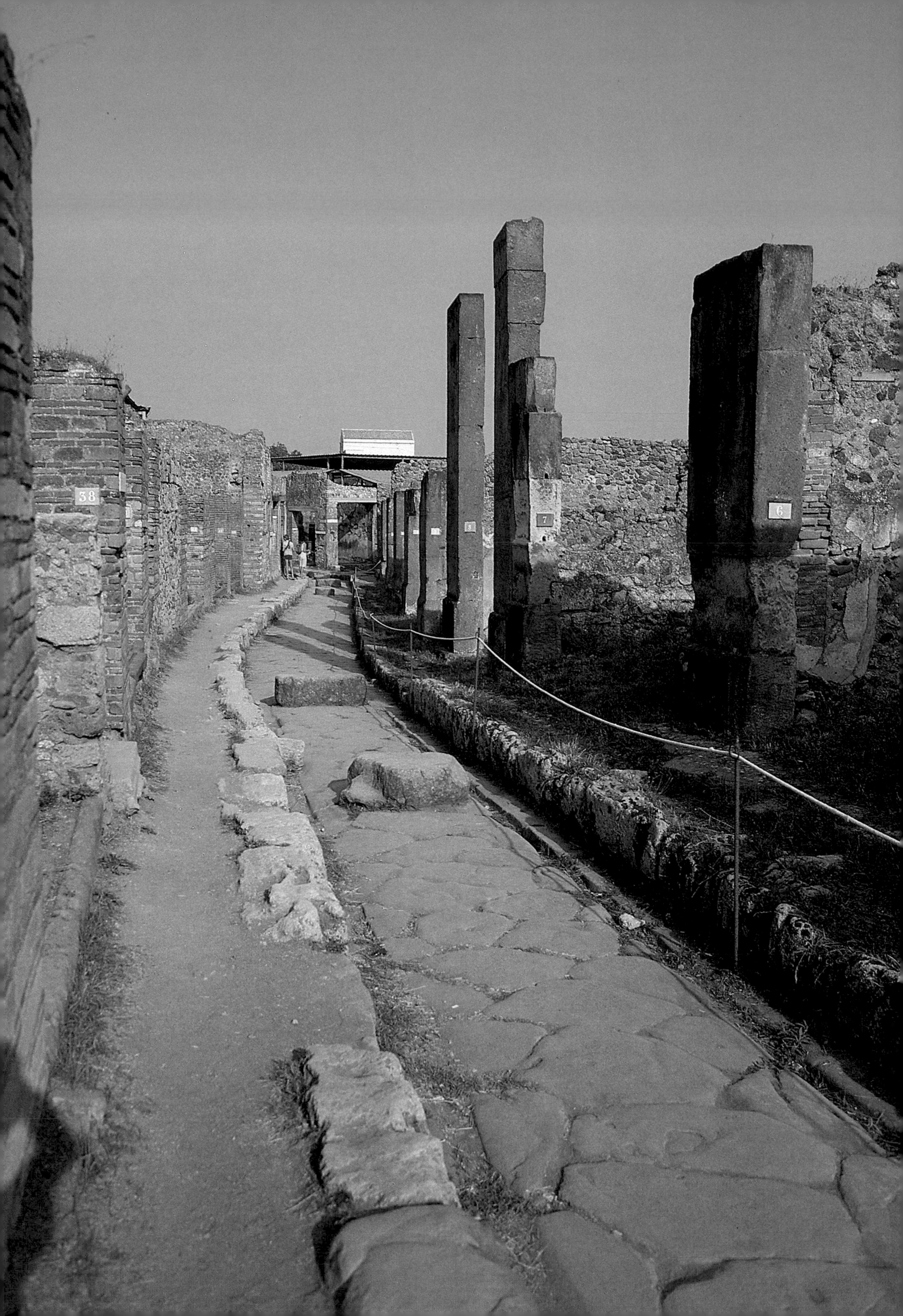
38
7
6

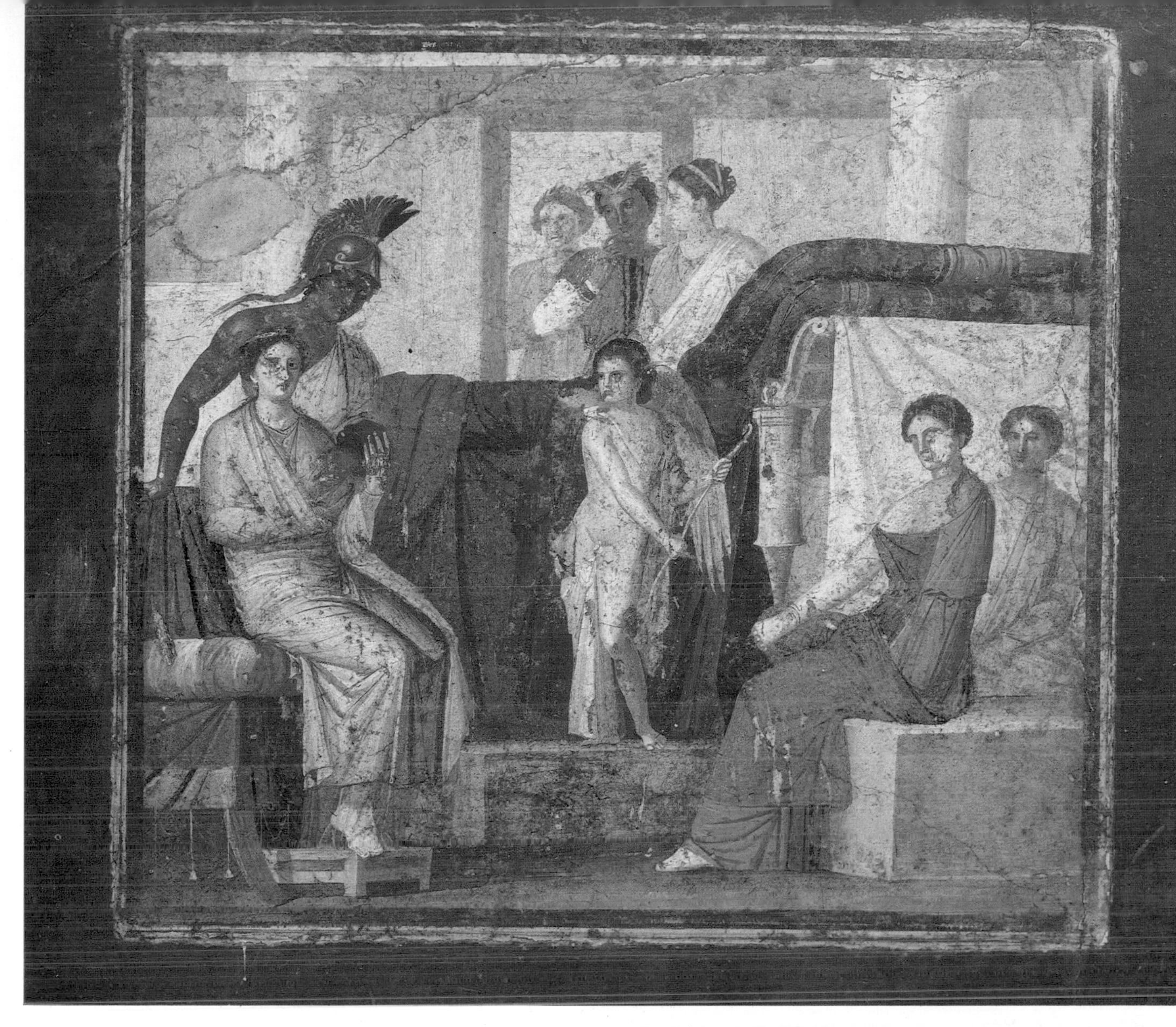

Opposite: a stretch of the Via degli Augustali. Above: the fresco of the wedding of Mars and Venus in the House of M. Lucretius and, alongside, a medallion of Mercury in the same house.

41 - HOUSE OF M. LUCRETIUS

This house is attributed to M. Lucretius because his name appears as addressee on a letter depicted, with a kit for writing letters, in a wall painting in a room near the garden. He was an important figure who held the office of *decurion* in the city and was a priest of Mars.
This patrician house had fine wall paintings, now mostly in the Museo Nazionale in Naples. In the atrium there are still some frescoes in Style IV with imaginary architecture, and in the tablinum the Triumphs of Bacchus with a satyr and a Victory. There must also have been various panel paintings in the tablinum which unfortunately have been lost.
The atrium lacks a central impluvium and it is therefore to be supposed that it was not covered with the customary shed roofs that sloped down towards the interior, but was covered by a roof that completely covered the house with a watershed towards the exterior (*atrio testudinato*). The lararium is in the atrium and the large tablinum opens in

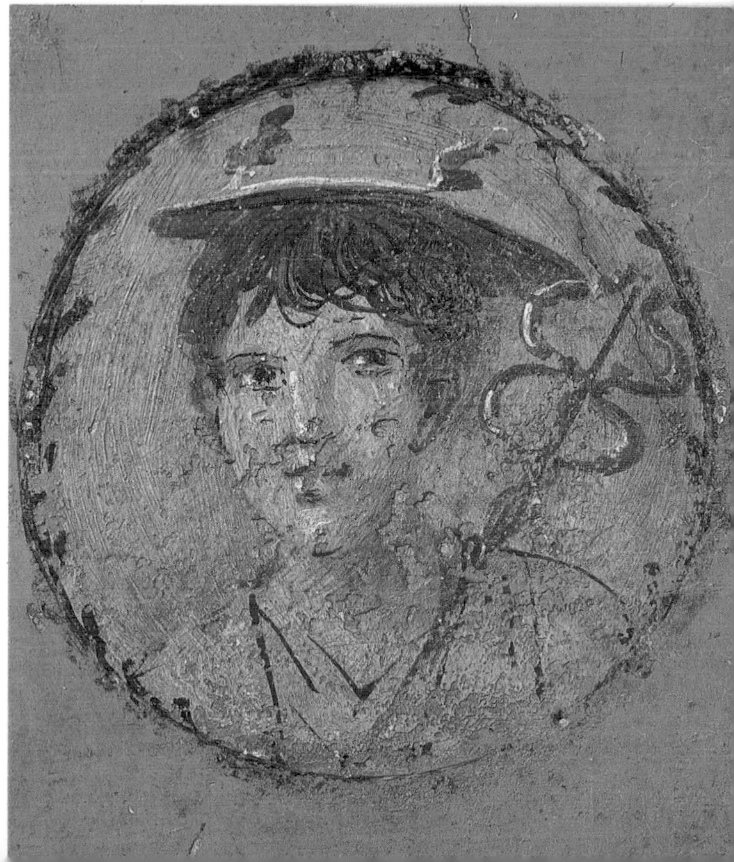

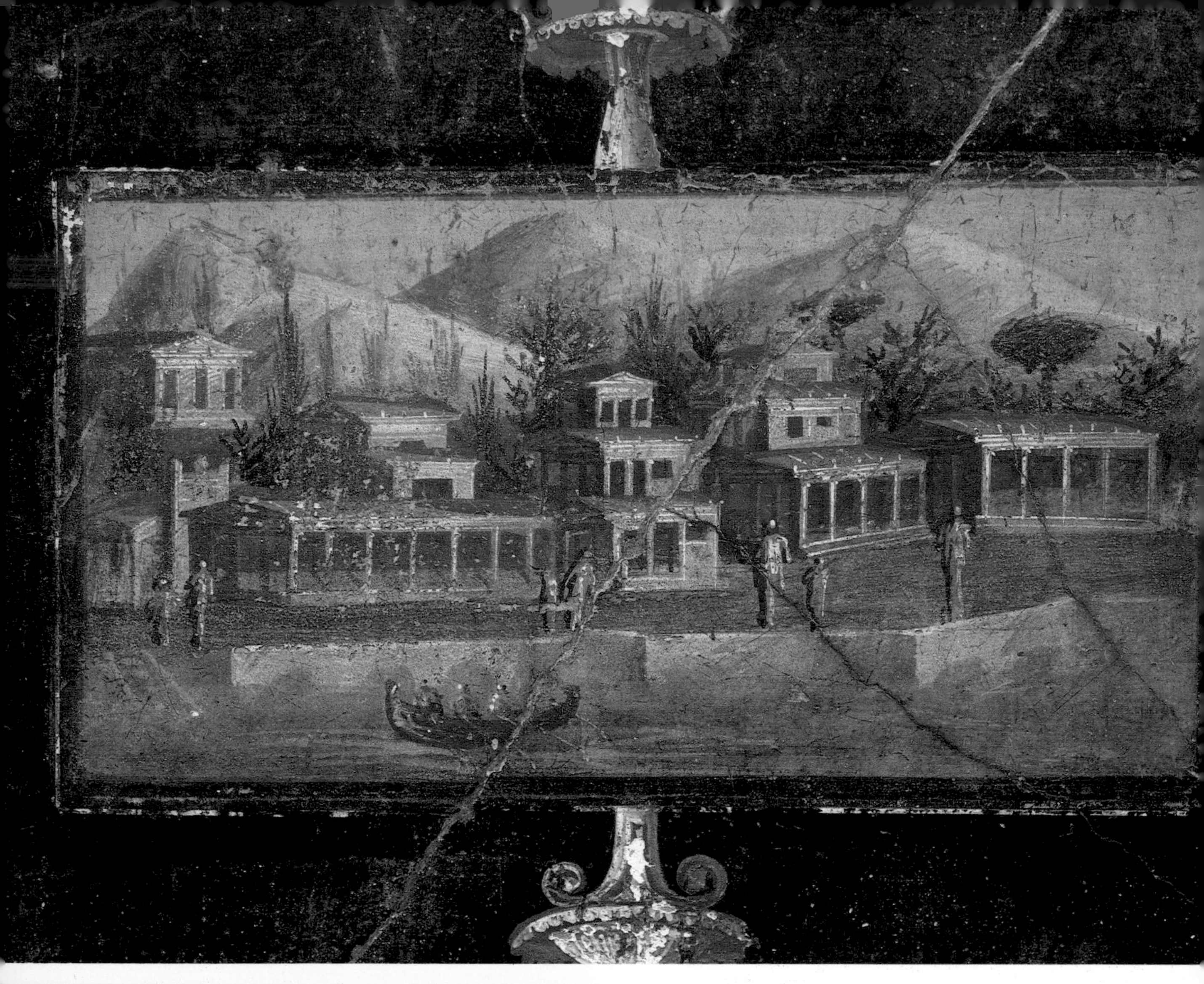

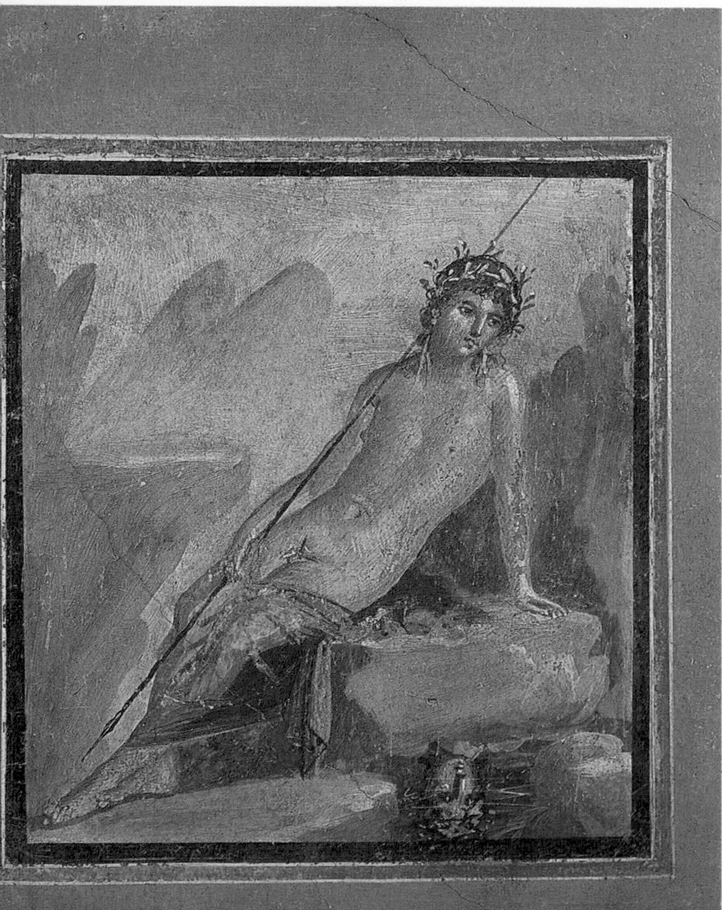

Above: a fresco landscape inside the House of M. Lucretius and, on the left, the fresco with Narcissus at the spring.

the back wall, beyond which a lovely garden stretches out in scenic perspective on a higher level. With herms and statues of satyrs, cupids, and various animals set among the beds, at the back was a fountain with mosaic decoration, where the water poured out of a goatskin held by a marble silenus.

42 - HOUSE OF THE SILVER WEDDING

The name derives from the fact that the house was excavated in 1893, the year in which the monarchs of Italy celebrated their silver wedding anniversary. The house was built in the Samnite period in the second cent. B.C., and its last owner was L. Albucius Celsus.
The vestibule leads into an imposing austere tetrastyle atrium, with an impluvium in the center and a marble

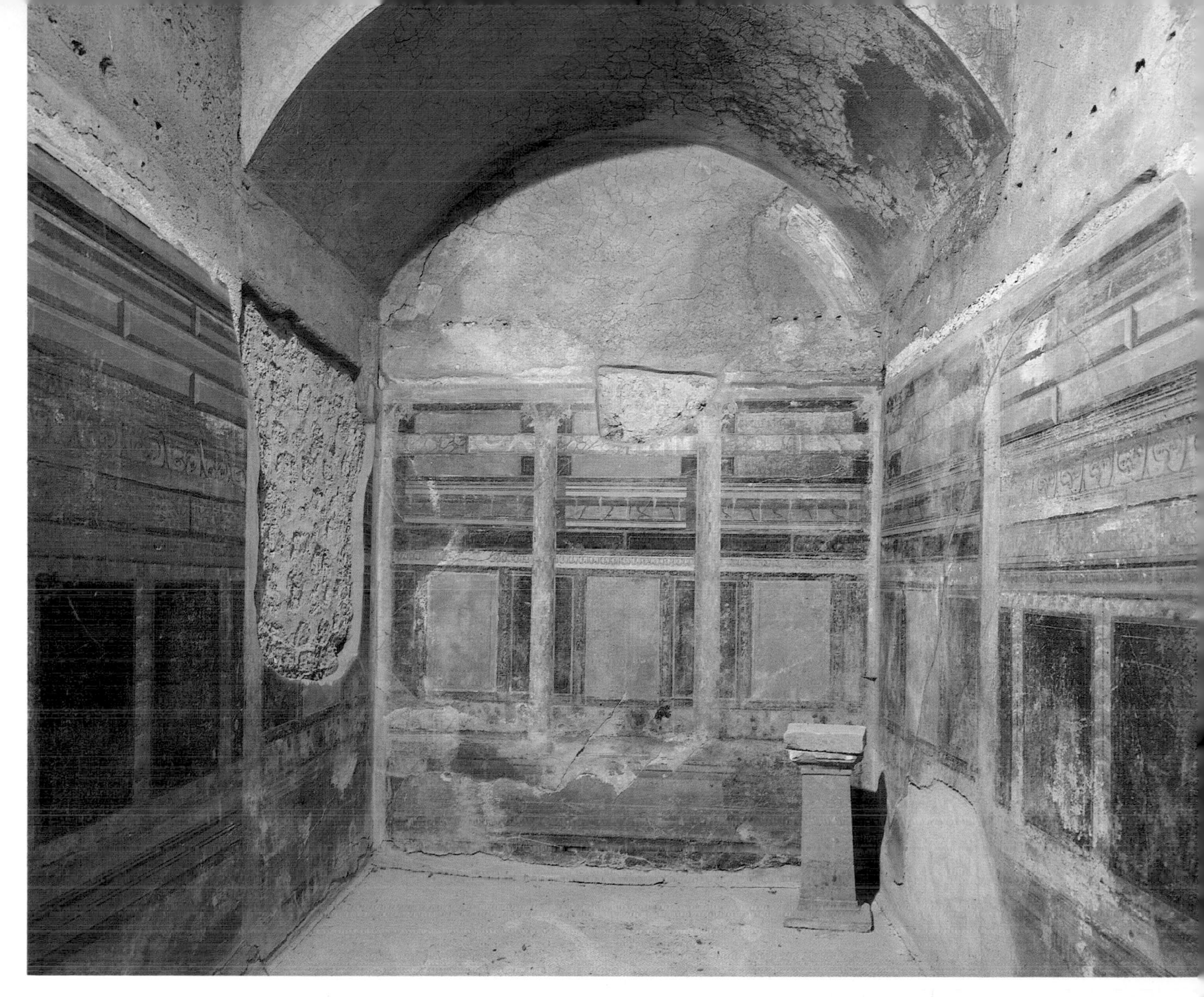

Above and right: two rooms with frescoes in the House of the Silver Wedding.

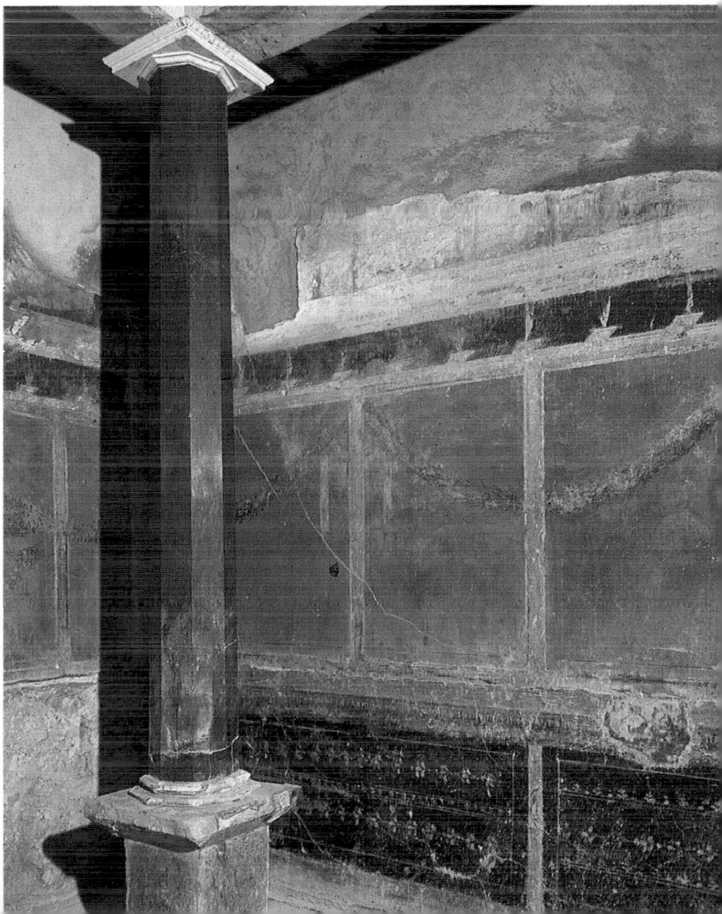

pedestal which served as a fountain. The compluvium roof has palmette antefixes and lion-head gutter spouts. At the back are the tablinum and two other rooms, beyond which is the peristyle of Rhodian type, with a higher ceiling on one side, making it sunnier, supported by large Doric columns unlike those on the other sides. The garden is in the center and glazed Egyptian-type statuettes of animals were found here.

A kitchen and a bath consisting of an *apodyterium*, *tepidarium* and *calidarium* open off the west arm of the peristyle, while a pool in a garden behind served as a *frigidarium*. A summer triclinium is next to the baths. At the back an exedra with yellow walls decorated with garlands and wreaths is flanked by two cubicles, also decorated in Style III painting. The west side houses an *oecus* with a vaulted ceiling supported by four columns, with wall paintings in Style II and a mosaic pavement. On this side there is an entrance to another larger garden with a pool in the center and the remains of an open-air triclinium.

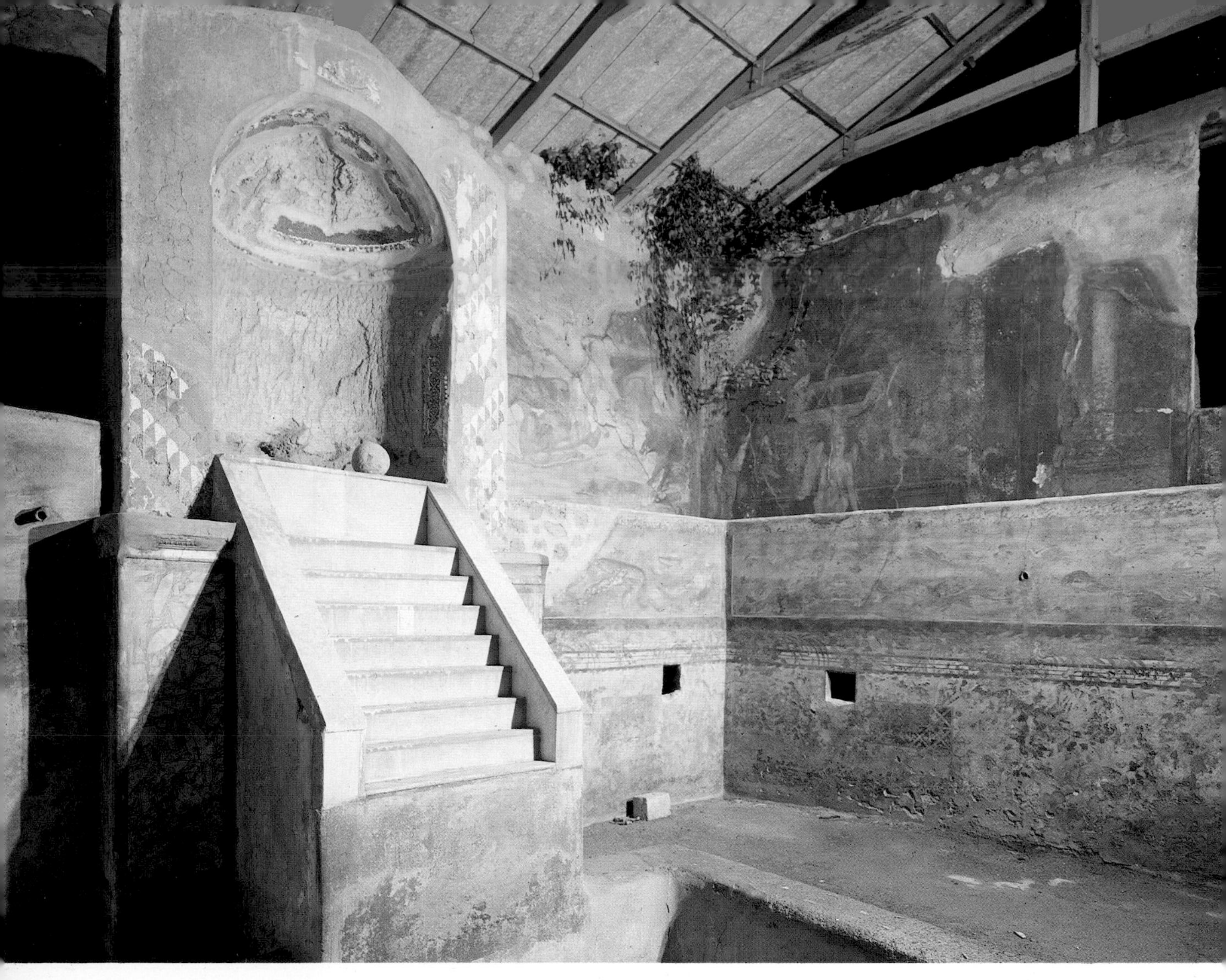

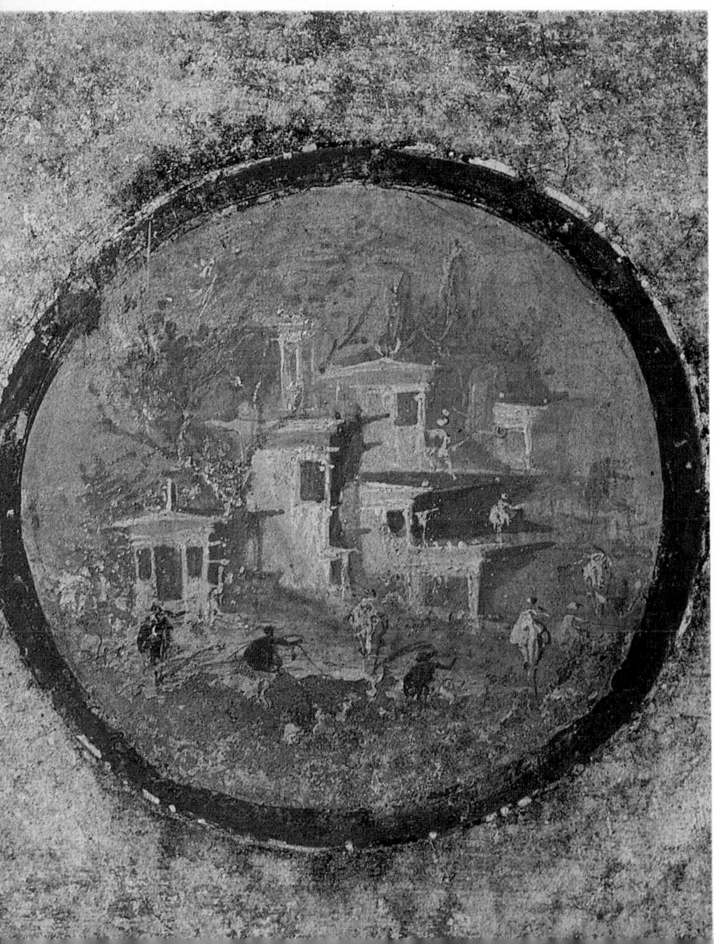

Above: the niche nympheum with the waterfall in the House of the Centennial and, on the left, a medallion in the same house with a fresco landscape.

43 - HOUSE OF THE CENTENNIAL

This vast house owes its name to the fact that it was excavated in 1879, the 18th centennial of the eruption which buried Pompeii. It was built in the 2nd cent. B.C. and its history includes phases of restructuring and renovating in the Imperial period. It is comprised of two dwellings articulated around two Tuscan atriums with impluvium at the center.
The large main atrium with its mosaic pavement has walls decorated with pictures in Style IV painting of theater subjects. At the back wall is the tablinum flanked by two rooms, one with white-ground walls and one with black-ground walls. The garden surrounded by a peristyle is situated behind the tablinum. The famous bronze of the Satyr, with a goatskin, which decorated the edge of the swimming pool was found here. At the back of the peristyle is a nymphaeum with a niche decorated with mosaics, from which a waterfall cascaded into a basin set at a lower level. The small cryptoporticus which supports the niche has paintings of naturalistic subjects while the upper parts of the walls in the courtyard are frescoed with hunts of wild beasts.

Right, above: a picture with erotic subject in a cubicle in the House of the Centennial. Below: the tetrastyle atrium in the House of M. Obellius Firmus.

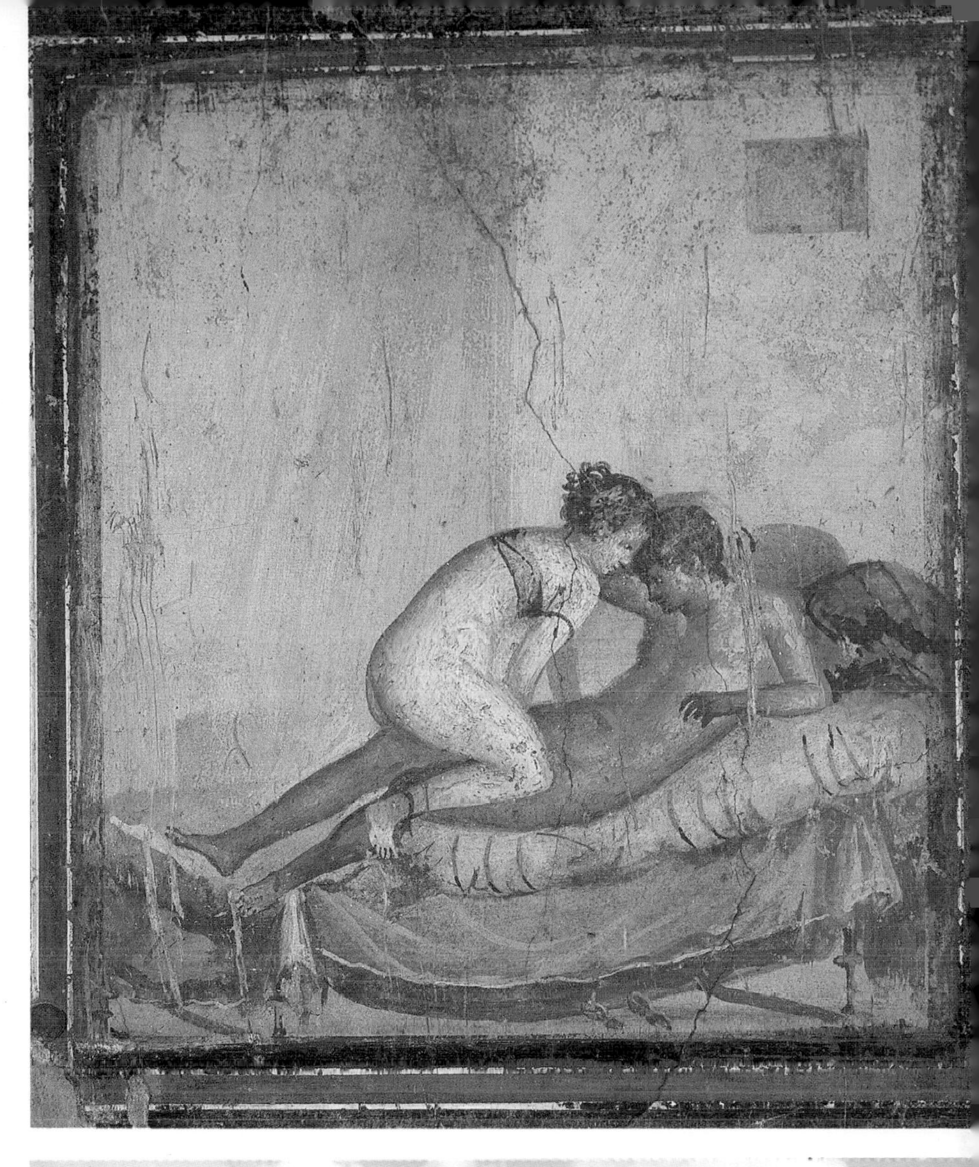

Various rooms decorated with paintings of a mythological nature, an isolated cubicle with erotic pictures, a bath, belong to the southwest quarter, access to which is through a secondary entrance. The painting with Bacchus and Vesuvius covered with forests, now in the Museo Nazionale in Naples, comes from the lararium in the atrium.

44 - HOUSE OF M. OBELLIUS FIRMUS

The house belonged to M. Obellius Firmus, whose name appears several times in the election inscriptions found on the walls of the neighboring buildings and even inside the house itself. The building technique and the ground plan date the building to the Samnite period.

At the front it consists of two entrances and two atriums. The main one is tetrastyle with columns in tufa and a centralized plan and with a traditional layout of rooms - a series of cubicles at the sides, the *alae* and the tablinum at the back. The temple-like lararium is in the southwest corner, while there is a safe near the south wing. The secondary atrium is of the Tuscan type and also follows the canonic plan as much as the restricted space permits.

The back half of the house consists of a peristyle with columns on three sides and a large garden. A series of rooms is set along the southwest side. These include a kitchen, a small bath, a cubicle with an alcove decorated with pastoral scenes, an *oecus*. Adjacent to the garden are a cubicle and a communicating *oecus* with wall decoration of particularly fine quality: a swamp landscape and two *pinakes* (pictures) with an offerer and Cybele in the cubicle and imaginary Style II architecture in the *oecus*.

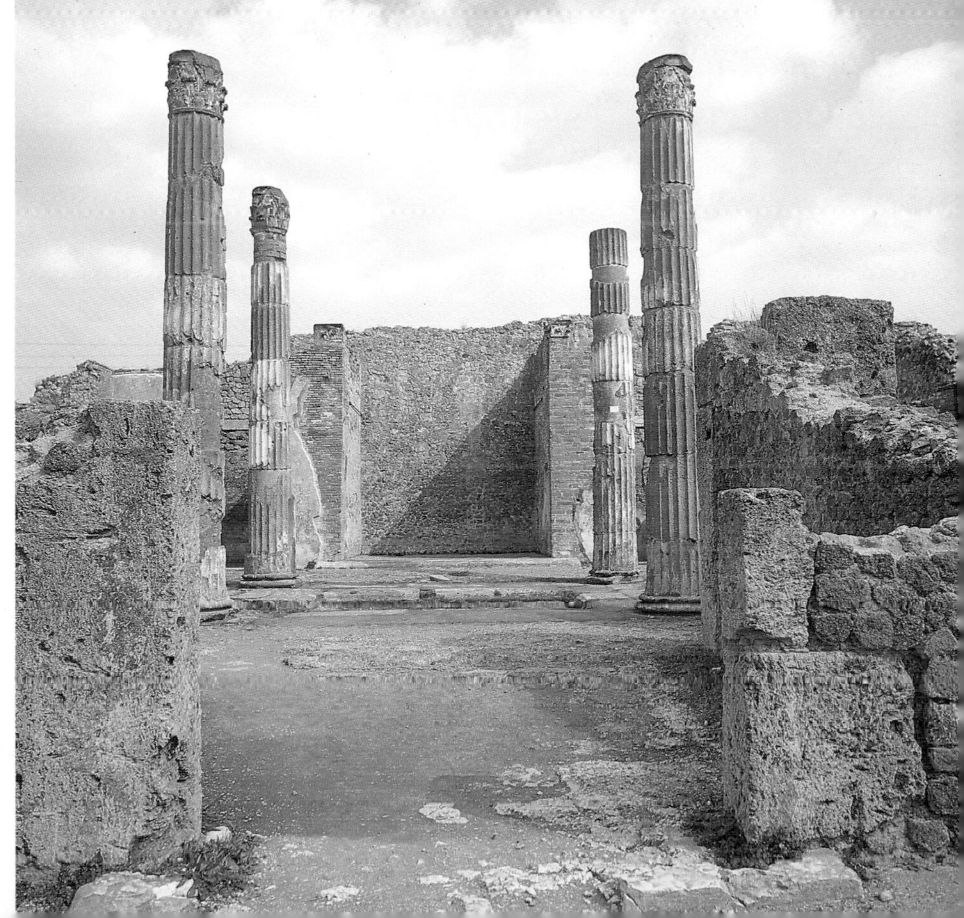

IV PART

House of the Golden Cupids - House of the Great Fountain - House of the Dioscuri - House of the Vettii - House of the Faun - Temple of Fortuna Augusta - Arch of Caligula - Forum Baths - House of the Tragic Poet - Bakery of Modestus - Via Consolare - House of Sallust - Porta Ercolano - Via dei Sepolcri - Villa of Diomedes - Villa of Mysteries

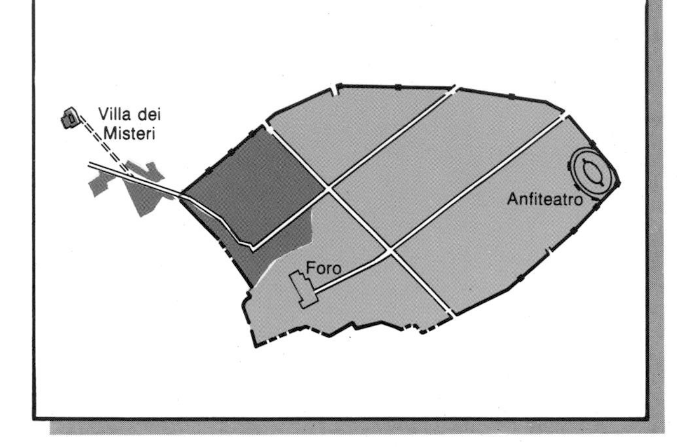

45 - HOUSE OF THE GOLDEN CUPIDS

The house belonged to Gneo Poppaeo Abito, perhaps related to Poppaea, Nero's wife, and it is without doubt one of the most interesting in Pompeii as regards the elegance and refinement of the architectural and decorative aspects typical of the spirit and artistic taste of Nero's time. It is not large and has a rather irregular ground plan, dictated by the space available and the lay of the land.

In the front the house has a vestibule and an atrium with a central rather small impluvium. Only three rooms face onto the atrium, two cubicles on either side of the vestibule and a tablinum at the back with paintings that represent the meeting between Paris and Helen in the presence of Eros.

But the real heart of the dwelling is the peristyle: the garden has a pool at the center surrounded by flower beds and, originally, statuettes of animals, herms, reliefs. The back wall is raised to increase the scenographic effect and at the center has a pediment on fluted piers with an *oscillum* (marble disk against the evil eye) hanging from the architrave. Theater masks are also hung in the intercolumniations of the portico as a finishing touch to the

Below: the peristyle of the House of the Gilded Cupids. Opposite, above: the matrimonial cubicle and, below, the fresco with Pelias and Jason.

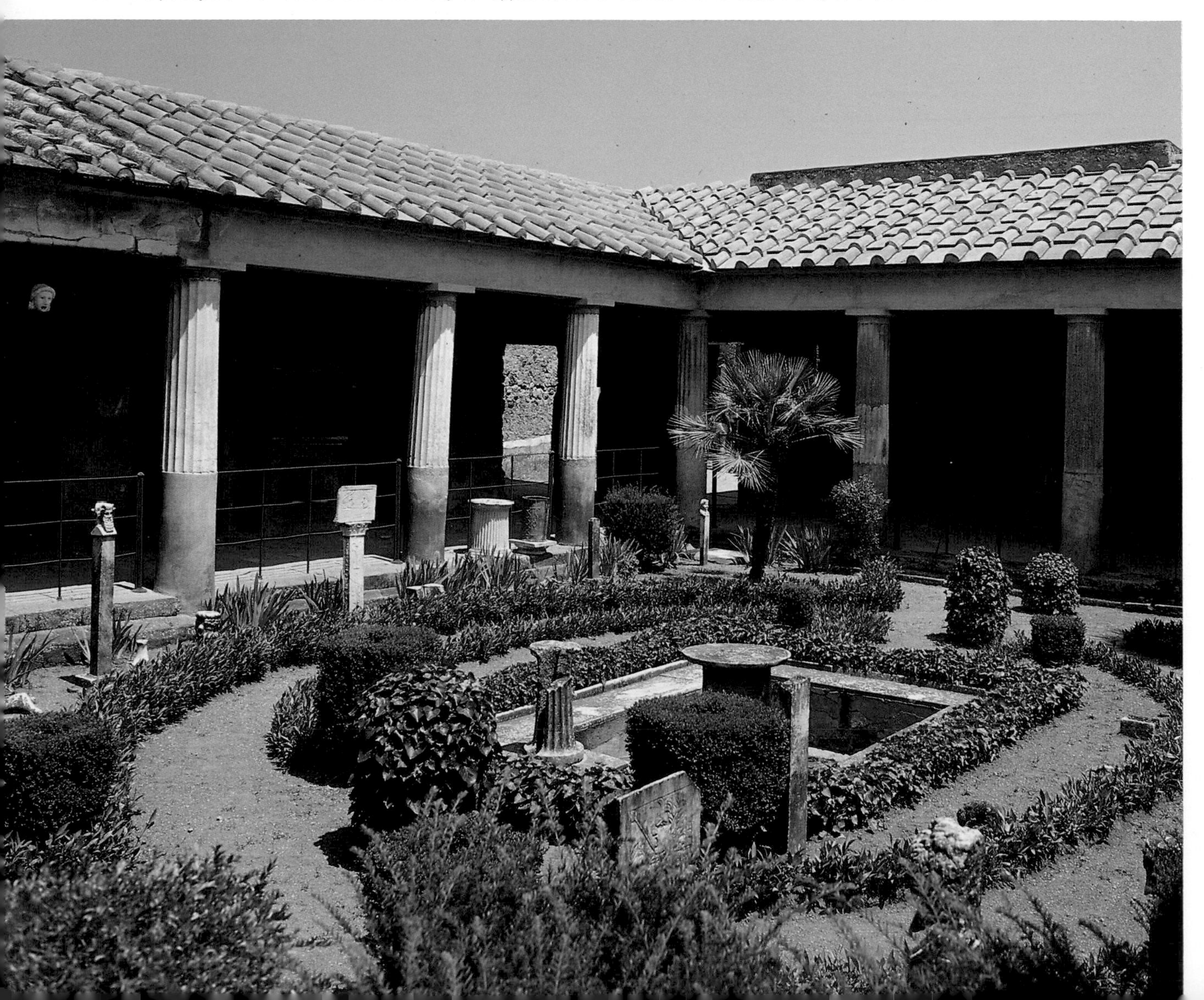

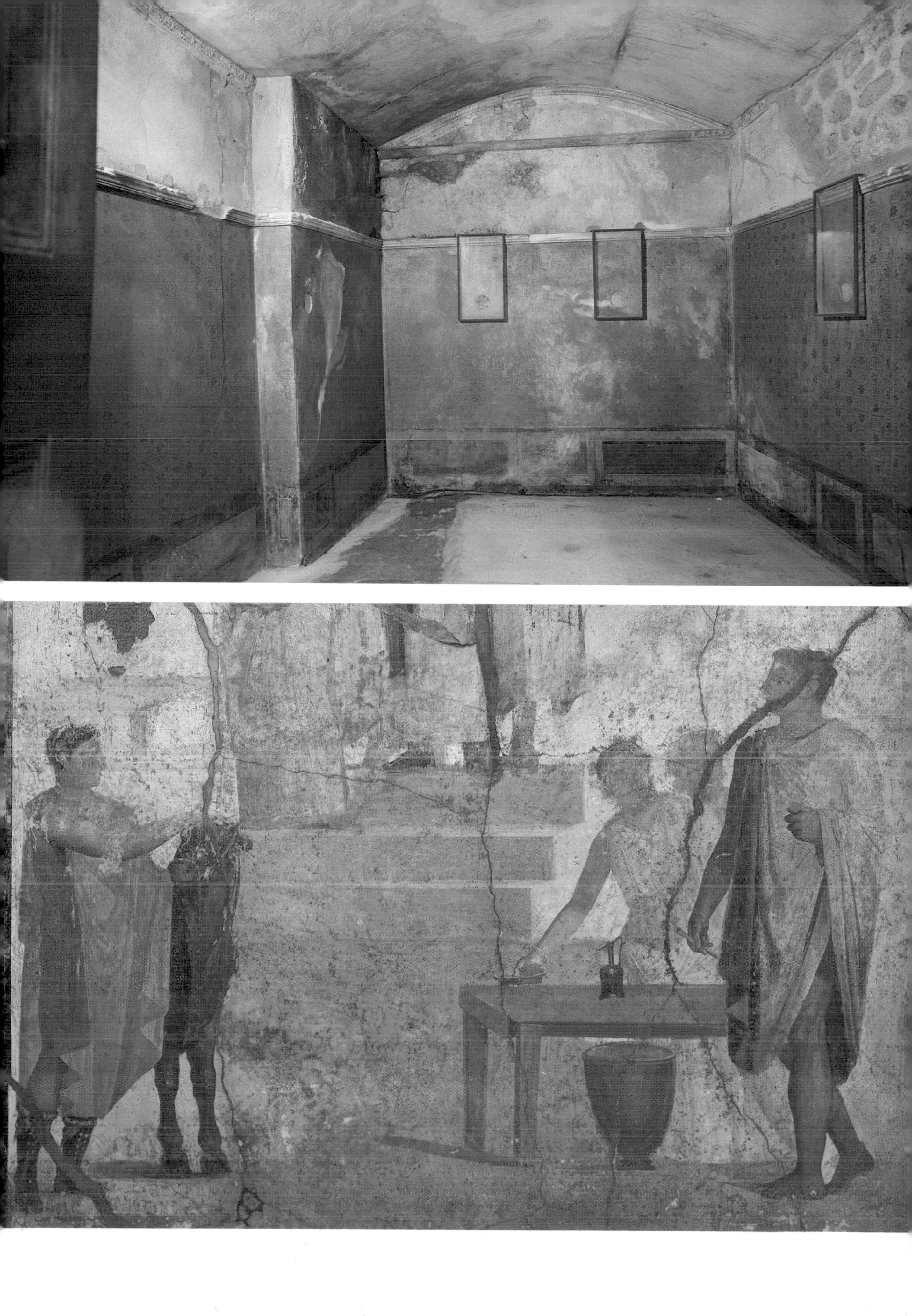

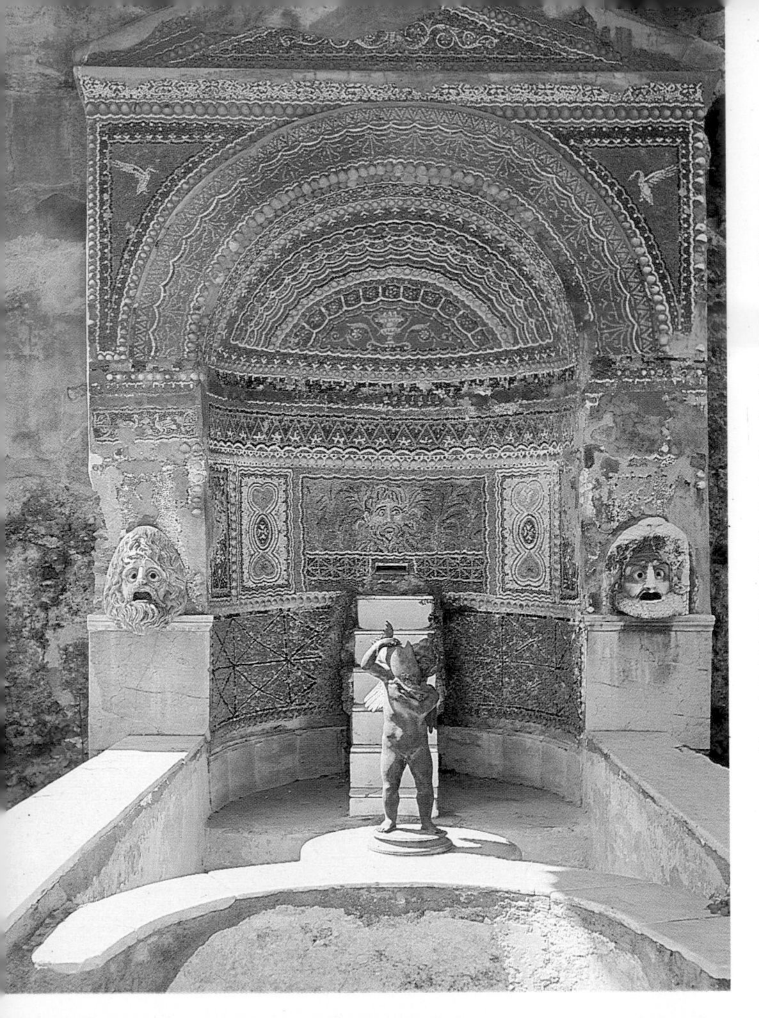

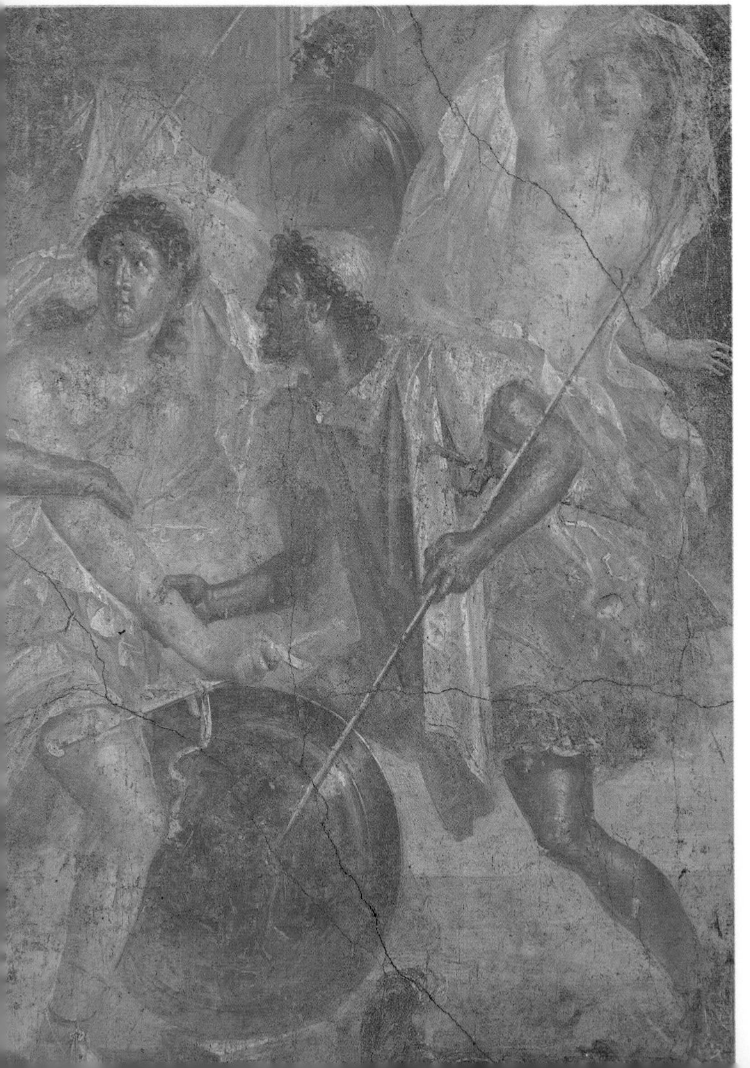

refined decoration of the ensemble.
A triclinium on the east side of the peristyle enjoys a view of the garden and is decorated with Style III paintings of mythological subjects: Thetis in Vulcan's workshop acquiring weapons for her son Achilles; Achilles in his tent with Briseis and Patrocles; Jason before Pelias. A series of marble reliefs is set into the south wall of the peristyle: depictions include theater masks and a dancing satyr of neo-attic inspiration. The same side also has a room with wall painting of pictures of various subjects.
The back wing of the peristyle has a triclinium at the center which still shows the damage inflicted by the earthquake of A.D. 62. On either side are two cubicles: the one on the left, perhaps used as a *gynaeceum*, opens onto a small garden and is frescoed with representations of the Seasons; the one on the right is decorated with pictures of amorous subjects, (Diana and Actaeon, Venus Fishing, Leda and the Swan) and portraits of women. Service rooms are situated in the corner across the way. And lastly, on the north side is the double bedroom decorated with cupids in gold leaf and applied on glass disks which give the house its name.
The eclecticism of the owner in the field of religion is witnessed by the presence in the house of a shrine to Isis in the eastern corner of the peristyle and a traditional lararium with figures of the Capitoline triad near the cubicle of the Gilded Cupids.

46 - HOUSE OF THE GREAT FOUNTAIN

This house takes its name from the monumental fountain in a nymphaeum near the back wall of the small garden situated beyond the atrium. The fountain, with a pediment set over a niche, completely faced with mosaic in polychrome glass tesserae, has an opening from which the water gushed and cascaded down steps into a basin below. The rest of the decoration consists of three tragic masks projecting from the jambs of the niche and a bronze statue of a putto with a dolphin set on a base inside the basin, now replaced by a copy.
The facade of the house in rusticated tufa ashlars should also be noted.

47 - HOUSE OF THE DIOSCURI

A painting in the entrance, now in the Museo Nazionale in Naples, of the Dioscuri, Castor and Pollux, sons of Jupiter and Leda, gives the house its name.
This is one of the rare examples in Pompeii of a house with a Corinthian atrium, where the atrium with a central impluvium is surrounded by columns, in this case twelve columns in tufa (the other two alternatives were the Tuscan atrium without columns and the tetrastyle atrium with four columns at the corners of the impluvium). Wall paintings with pictures of mythological subjects were frescoed on the walls of the rooms on either side of the tablinum. Most of them have been detached and are now in the Museo Nazionale in Naples and the British Museum in London.
An initial porticoed courtyard with Doric columns is situated beyond the tablinum and has a temple lararium on

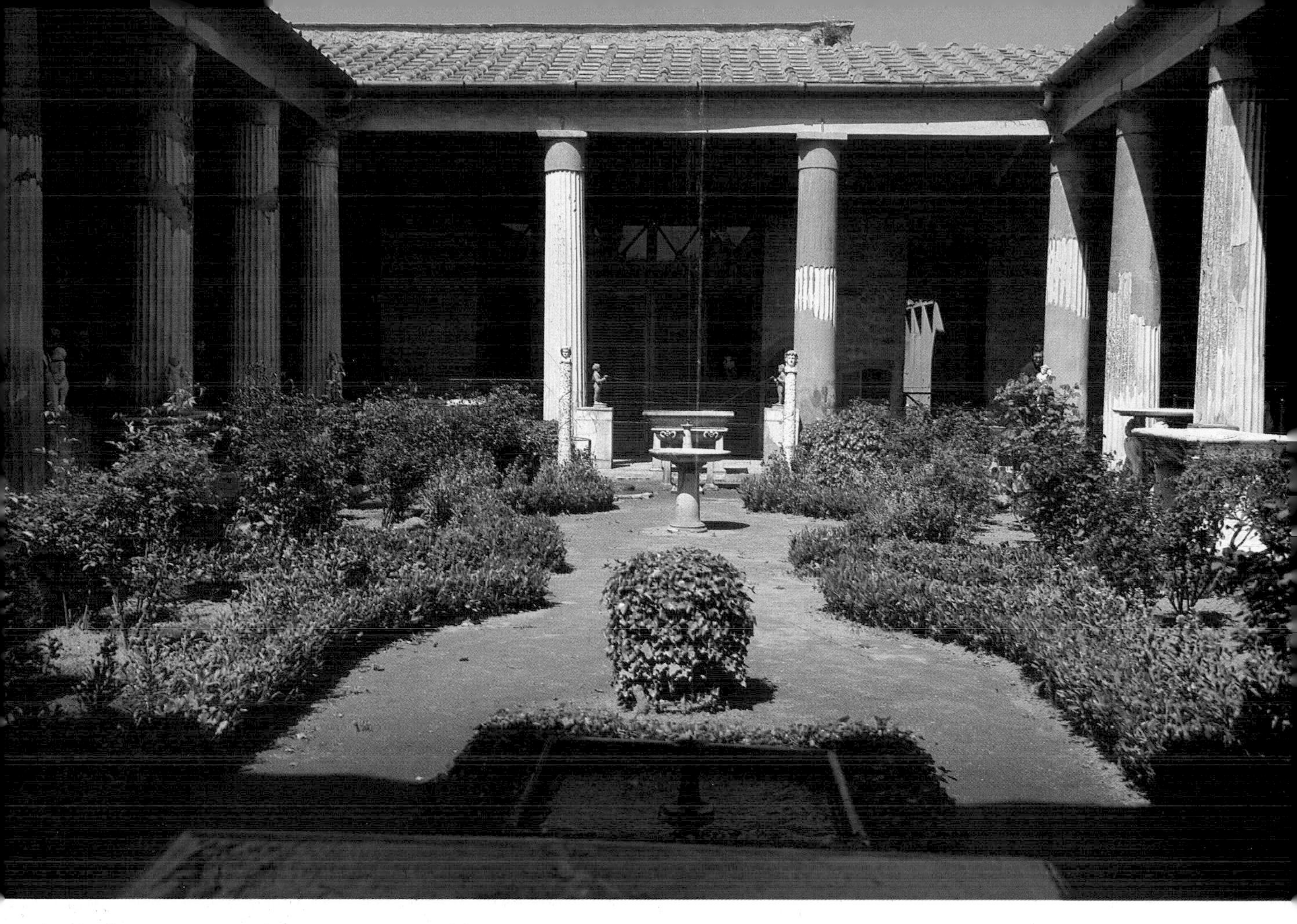

Opposite, above: the mosaic fountain in the House of the Large Fountain; below, the fresco with Achilles recognized from the House of the Dioscuri, now in the Museo Nazionale in Naples. Above: the peristyle of the House of the Vettii

the back wall. The second peristyle with a large basin at the center was added later and is reached from the right side of the atrium. Most of the Style IV wall painting is still in place and depicts carpets hung in imaginary architectural surrounds, alternating with panels of still lifes.

48 - HOUSE OF THE VETTII

This luxurious patrician dwelling furnishes us with an important example of what the taste in architecture and decoration was like in the last years of Pompeii, and bears witness to the importance acquired by the merchant classes of *homines novi* who disposed of considerable fortunes. The owners of this house were the affluent freedmen Aulus Vettius Restitutus and Aulus Vettius Conviva, as we know from their bronze seals found in the atrium and the election slogans on the walls outside. The latter figure was *augustale*, that is he belonged to an order nominated by the emperor to qualify for which it was necessary to contribute to costly public works.
The present ground plan is the result of the restructuration of an older house that was effected in the middle of the first cent. A.D. with restoration after A.D. 62.
The entrance portal leads into the vestibule with walls decorated with a cock fight, a sheep with Dionysiac at-

1 Atrium
2 Alae
3 Oeci
4 Peristilium
5 Viridarium
6 Triclinium
7 Triclinium

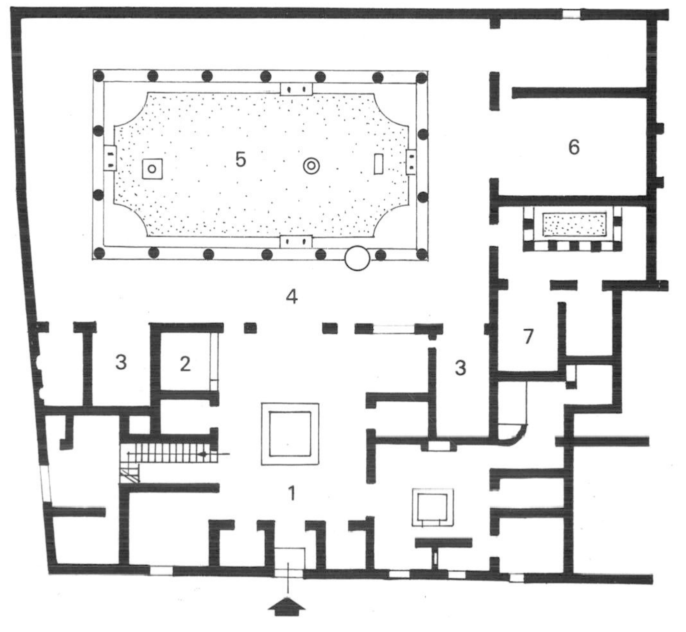

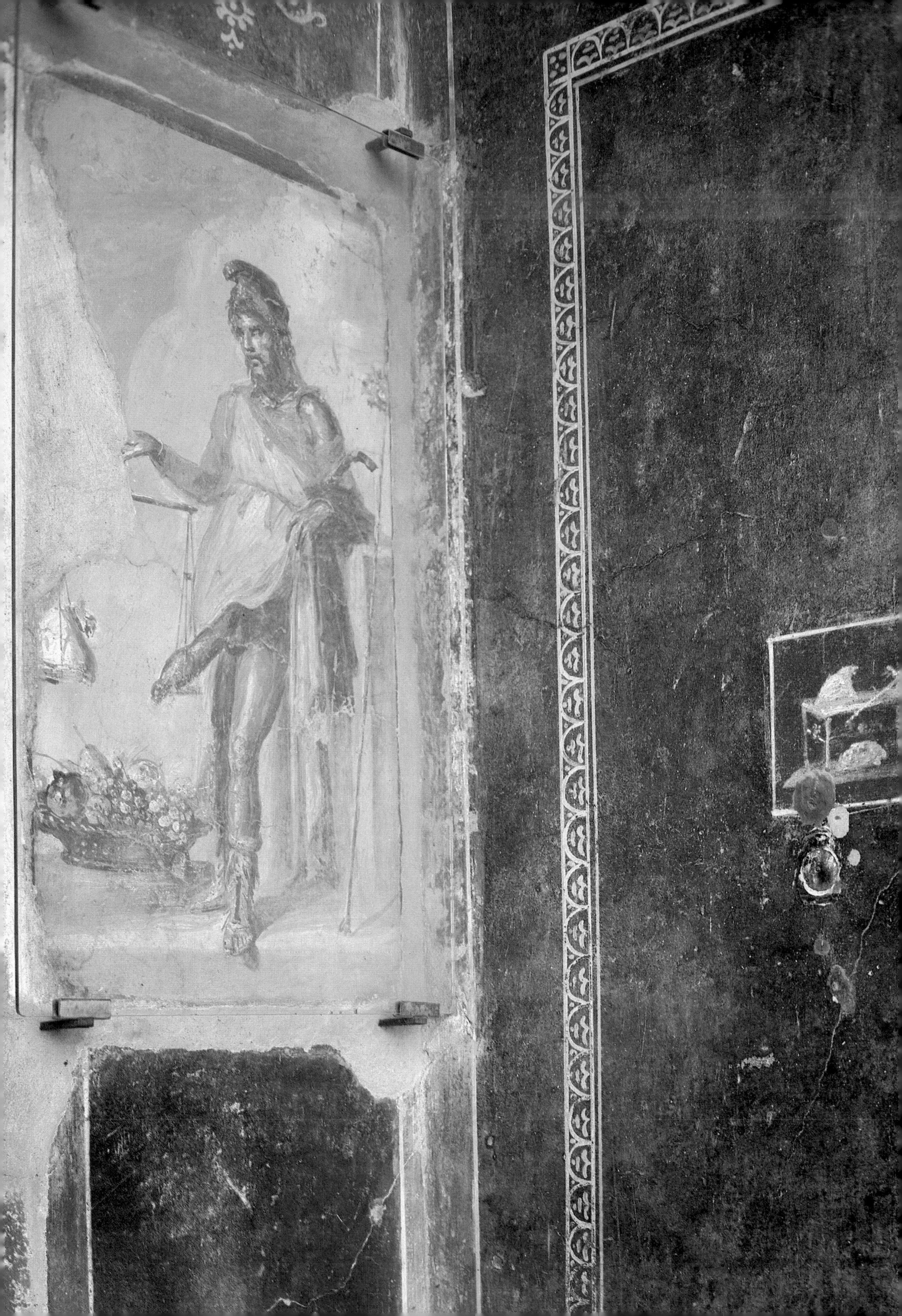

Opposite: Priapus weighing his phallus, on the wall next to the entrance to the House of the Vettii. Right, above: the lararium of the same house and, below, the cubicle with erotic pictures and a fountain statue.

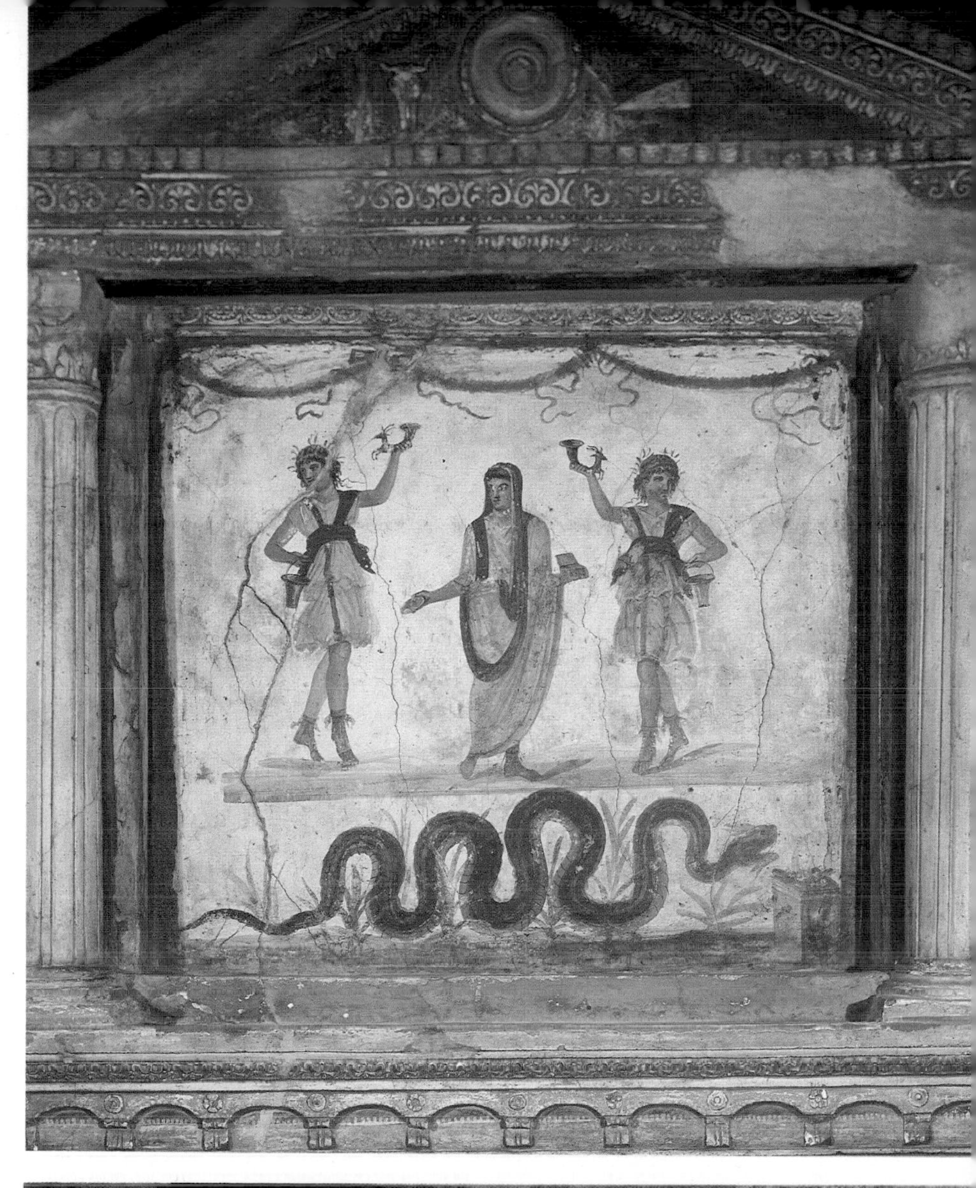

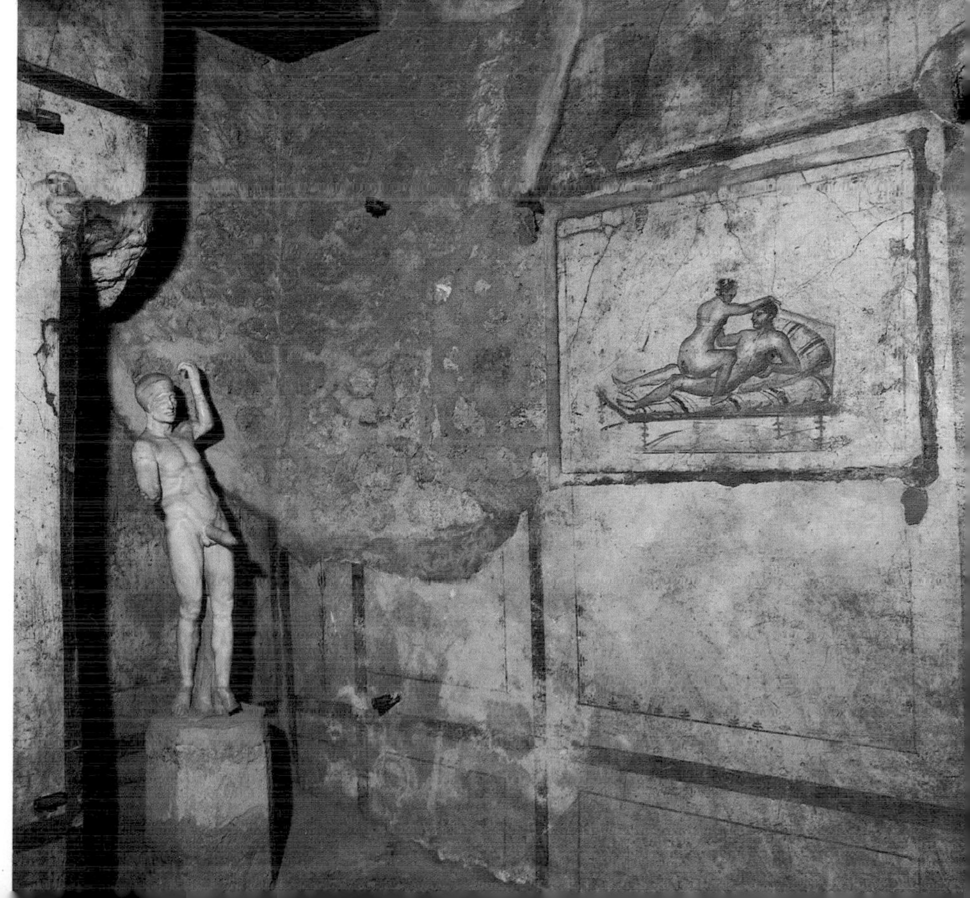

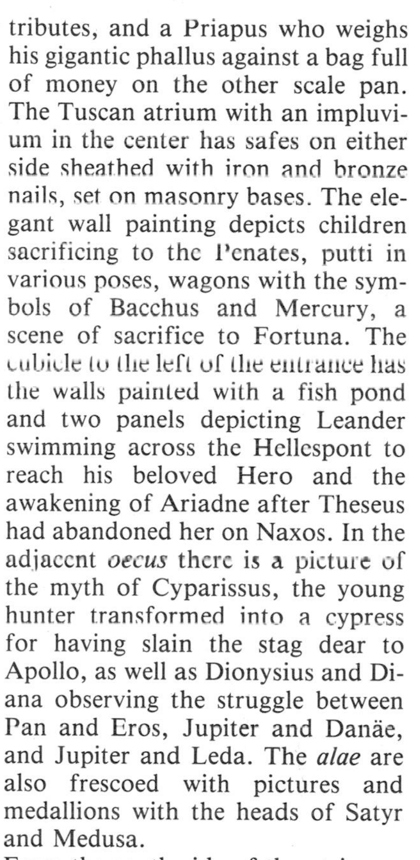

tributes, and a Priapus who weighs his gigantic phallus against a bag full of money on the other scale pan. The Tuscan atrium with an impluvium in the center has safes on either side sheathed with iron and bronze nails, set on masonry bases. The elegant wall painting depicts children sacrificing to the Penates, putti in various poses, wagons with the symbols of Bacchus and Mercury, a scene of sacrifice to Fortuna. The cubicle to the left of the entrance has the walls painted with a fish pond and two panels depicting Leander swimming across the Hellespont to reach his beloved Hero and the awakening of Ariadne after Theseus had abandoned her on Naxos. In the adjacent *oecus* there is a picture of the myth of Cyparissus, the young hunter transformed into a cypress for having slain the stag dear to Apollo, as well as Dionysius and Diana observing the struggle between Pan and Eros, Jupiter and Danäe, and Jupiter and Leda. The *alae* are also frescoed with pictures and medallions with the heads of Satyr and Medusa.

From the south side of the atrium a corridor with steps going to an upper floor leads to a spacious service entrance on the sides of which are a stable and a latrine. The north side opens onto the servants' quarters, articulated around a secondary atrium with an impluvium in tufa and a fine aedicule lararium with Corinthian half columns supporting a tri-

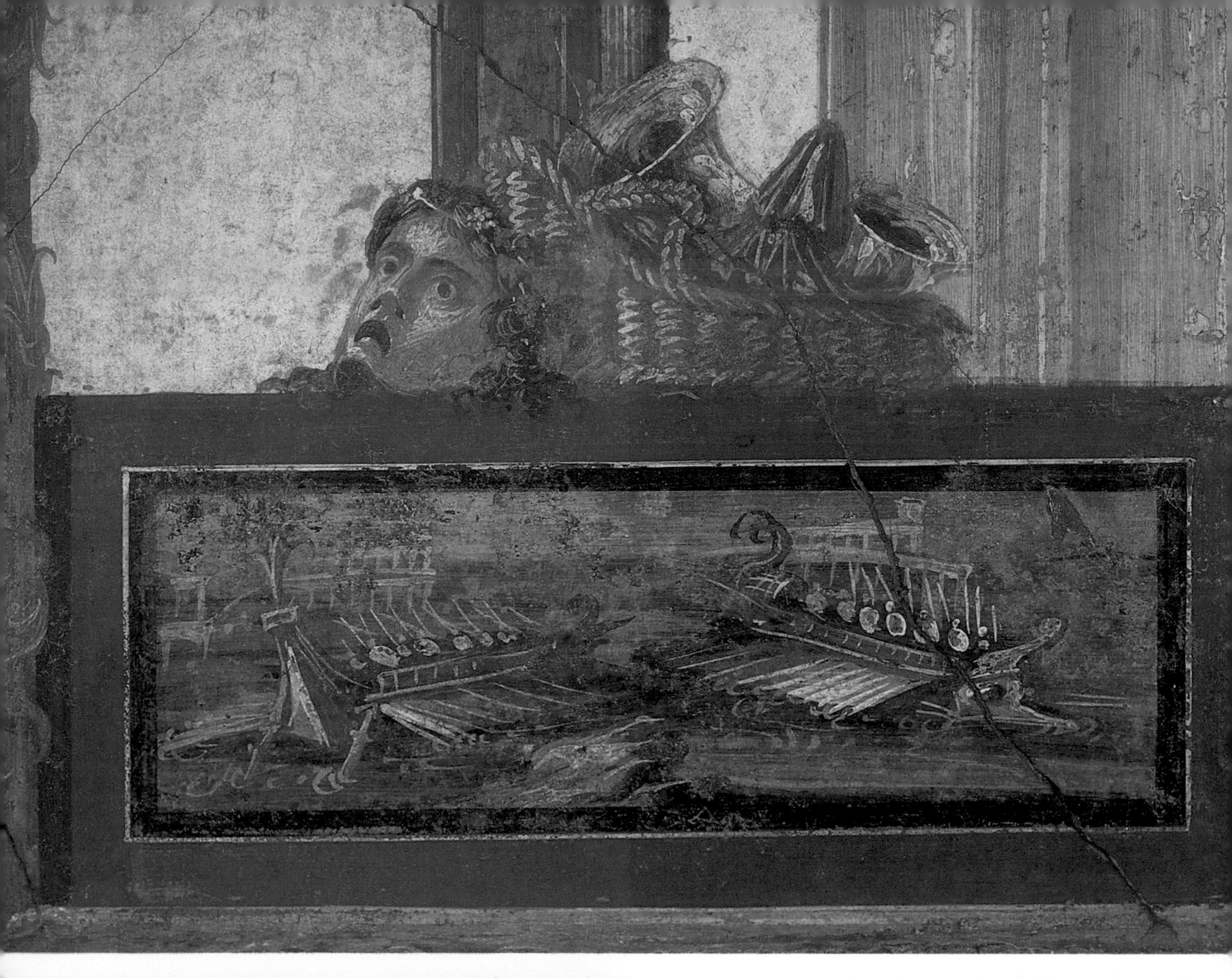

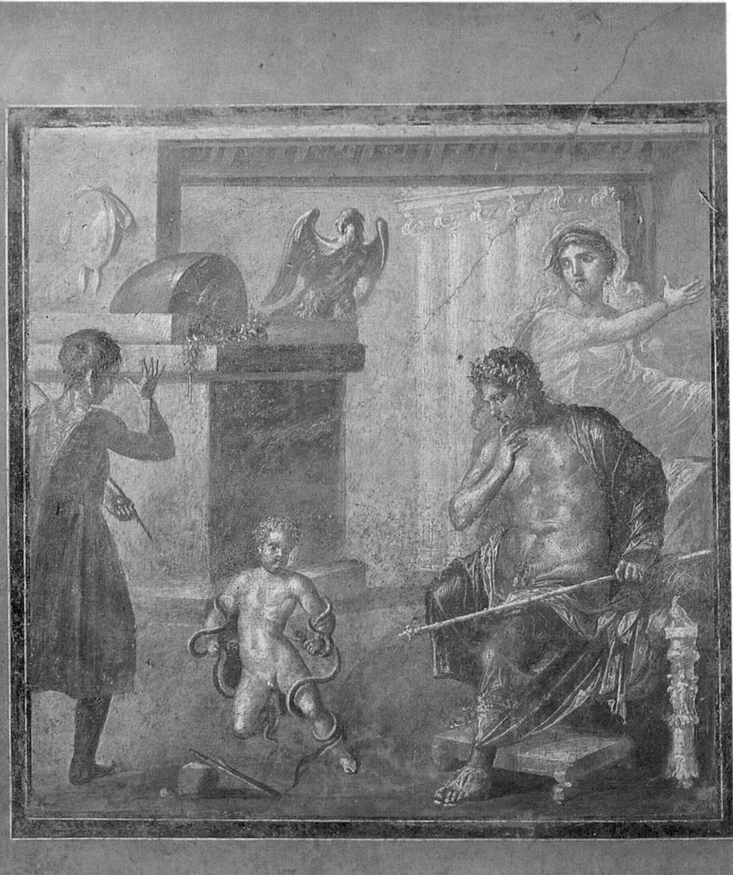

Above: a naval battle below a theater mask and objects for the cult of Dionysius in the triclinium of the House of the Vettii. Left: the picture with Hercules strangling the serpents, in an oecus in the house.

angular pediment with cult objects in stucco: the Genius in a *toga praetexta* is shown executing a libation between two dancing lares holding the drinking horn while below a crested serpent (a common monster in the lararium) moves towards an altar which holds offerings of food. The kitchen is reached from the west corner where bronze equipment is still in the hearth: a grill, tripods and various utensils. The cubicle behind is decorated with erotic paintings.

In the absence of a tablinum, the back wall of the atrium opens on a large peristyle where numerous marble and bronze fountain statues, circular and rectangular basins, marble tables, two bifrontal herms on columns, are set up as they originally were. The garden beds have also been restored to what they once looked like. At the center of its yellow-ground walls the *oecus* to the left of the entrance to the peristyle has pictures with subjects taken from the Theban myths: Amphion and Zethus bind Dirce to a bull to avenge their mother Antiope, who had been her slave; Pentheus king of Thebes is assaulted and killed by the Bacchantes for not having permitted the introduction of the cult of Dionysius into the city; the infant Hercules strangles the serpents sent by Hera. The panels at the sides are decorated with elegant architectural perspectives.

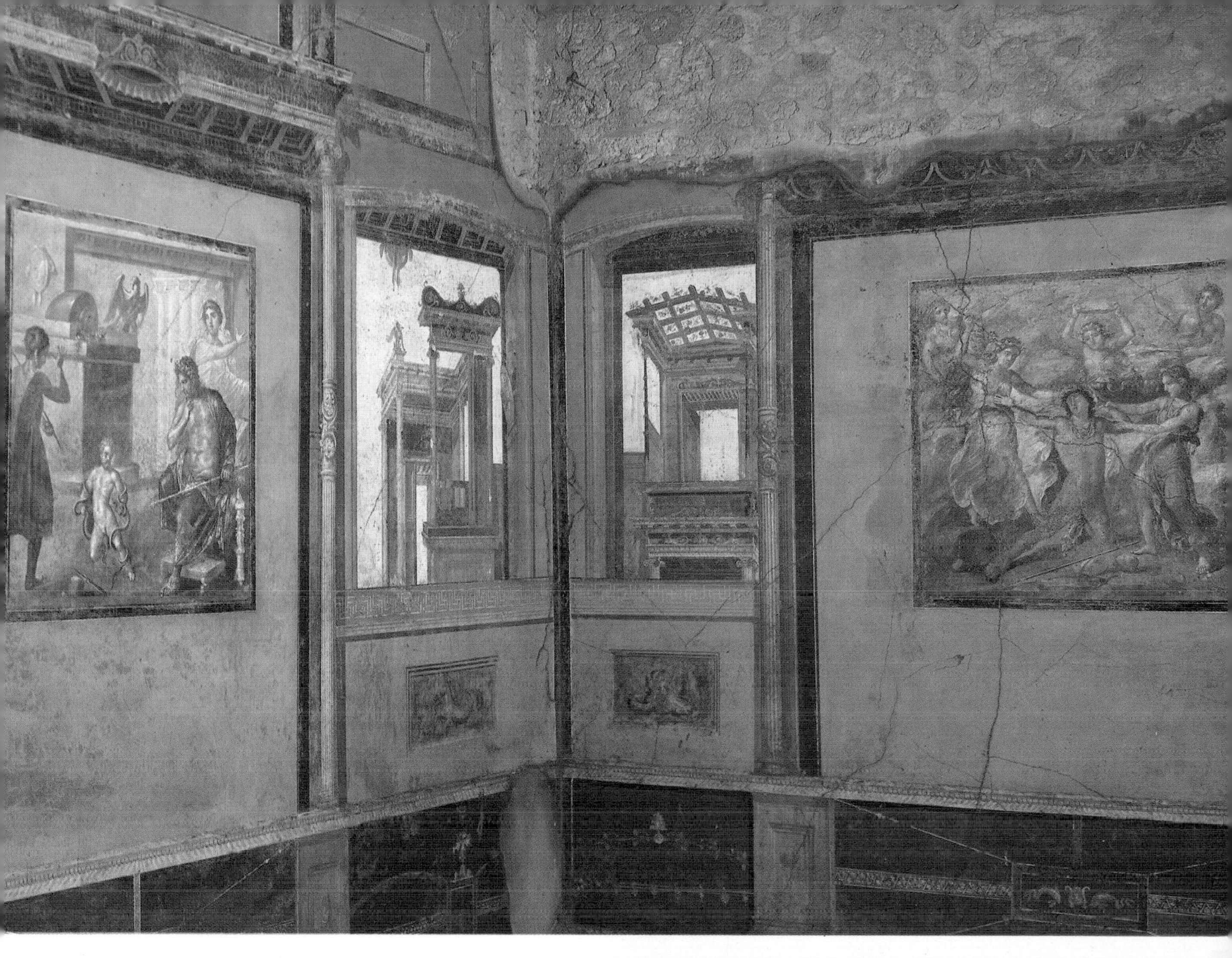

Above: an oecus in the House of the Vettii with, in the background, the fresco with Pentheus killed by the Bacchantes. Right: Daedalus and Pasiphaë in a picture in the triclinium.

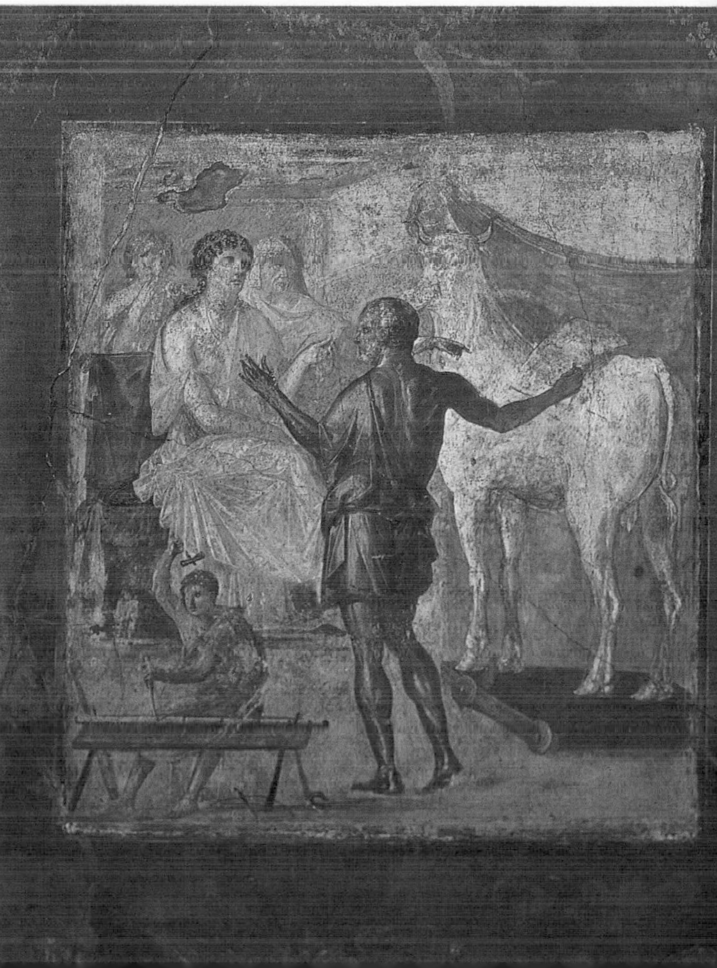

The triclinium opens off the northern corner of the peristyle. The walls are frescoed with pictures inserted into an elegant Style IV decoration, with Seasons in frames and perspective architecture, ornamental elements which turn into delicate figurines, small pictures of naval battles set under theater masks and Dionysiac cult objects. Above is a frieze of imaginary architecture and figures of gods, while the dado below is in faux marble. The pictures depict love between the gods and human beings: on the left wall Daedalus shows Pasiphae, the wife of Minos, whom Zeus out of revenge had caused to fall in love with a bull, the model of the wooden cow he had made. The result of the union between Pasiphae and the bull was to be the Minotaur. The myth of Ixion is depicted on the back wall. Zeus had condemned him to be bound with snakes to a wheel made by Hephaestos because he had tried to make love to Hera, whose place was taken at the last minute by a cloud in her form (Nephele) and who was to generate the Centaurs. Hermes, Hera enthroned, and Isis are present while the cloaked woman can be identified as the imploring Nephele. The scene on the right wall shows Ariadne in Naxos, awakened by Dionysius, while Theseus flees with his ship.

A gynaeceum lies on the northwest side of the peristyle, set on a large colonnaded court with cubicle and a triclini-

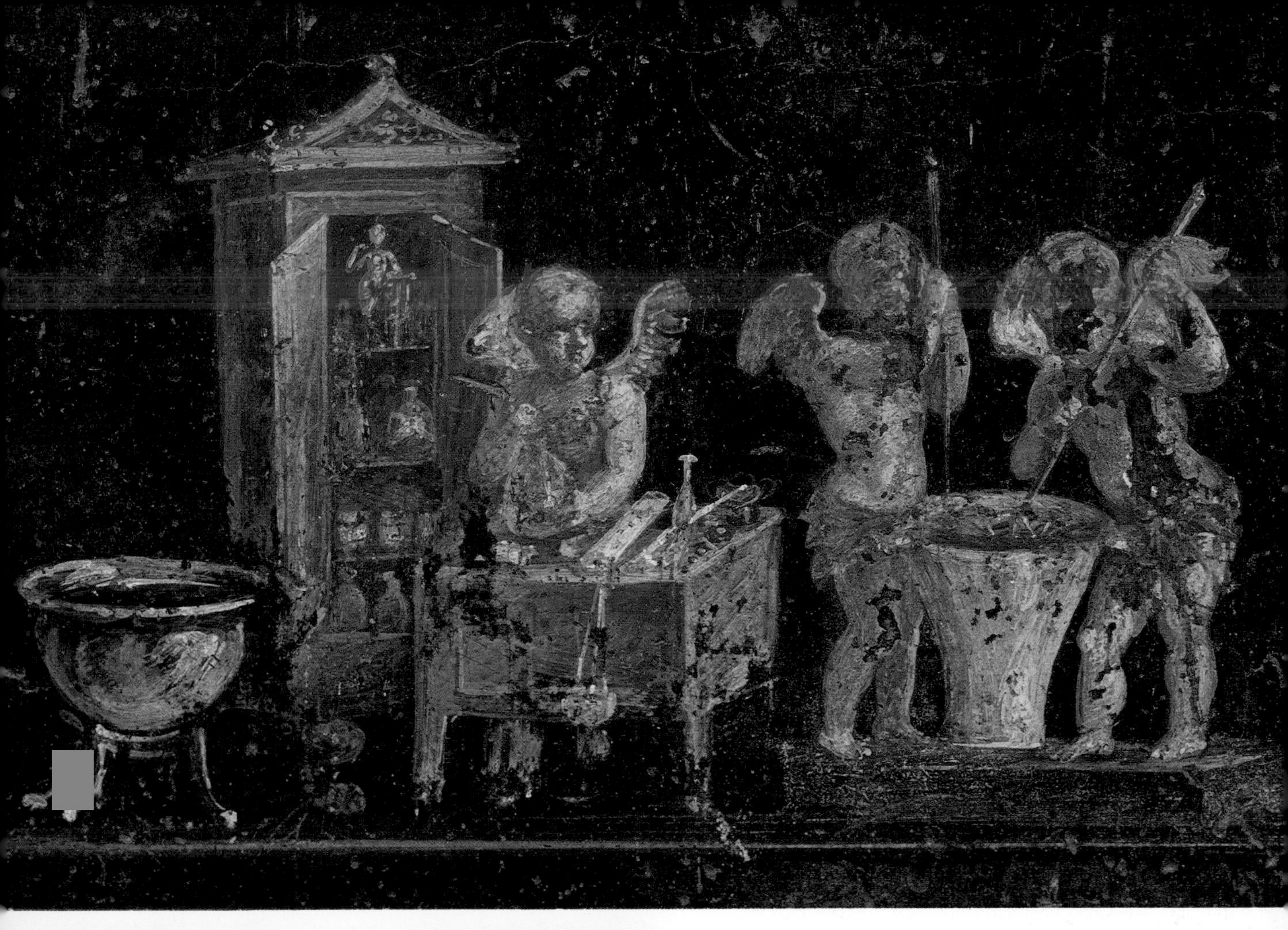

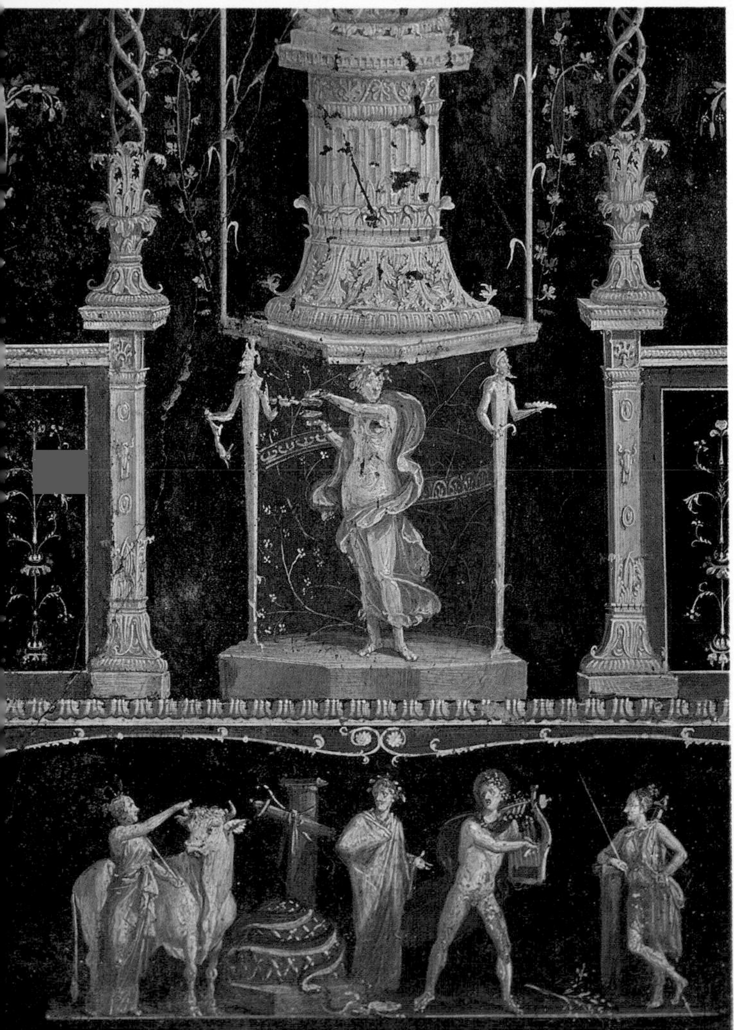

On both pages, various views of the main triclinium of the House of the Vettii. Above: cupids preparing perfumes. Below: Apollo overcoming Python below a candelabrum. Opposite, above: cupids with wine amphoras and, below, other goldsmith cupids.

um. The pictures in the decoration depict Achilles on the island of Scyros and the drunken Hercules about to seduce Auge who is washing her peplos. The result of their love will be Telephus. The large *oecus* which opens onto the peristyle next to the gynaeceum contains some of the most famous and striking pictorial decoration in Pompeii. Black bands articulate the red walls. The pictures from the central sectors, probably on panels and therefore portable, are no longer extant, while flying mythical couples and ithyphallic Hermaphrodite with Silenus is depicted in the lateral sections. A frieze that runs along over the dado shows cupids and *psychai* busy at work, taking part in sports, or in religious activities. Beginning to the right of the entrance there is first a competition in target shooting, the cupid flower venders transport flowers on a goat and sell garlands. Next comes the preparation and the sale of perfumed oils, a race with chariots drawn by antilopes, and cupid-goldsmiths making and selling precious objects. Next come the activities of the *fullones* cupids, bakers and vintners. The frieze terminates with the triumphal procession of Dionysius on a wagon drawn by goats and followed by an ithyphallic Pan playing the double flute. Some of the friezes on the pilasters below the candelabra depict Agamemnon about to kill the deer sacred to Artemis, Apollo who has defeated the serpent Python, Orestes and Pylades before Iphigenia and the Tauri.

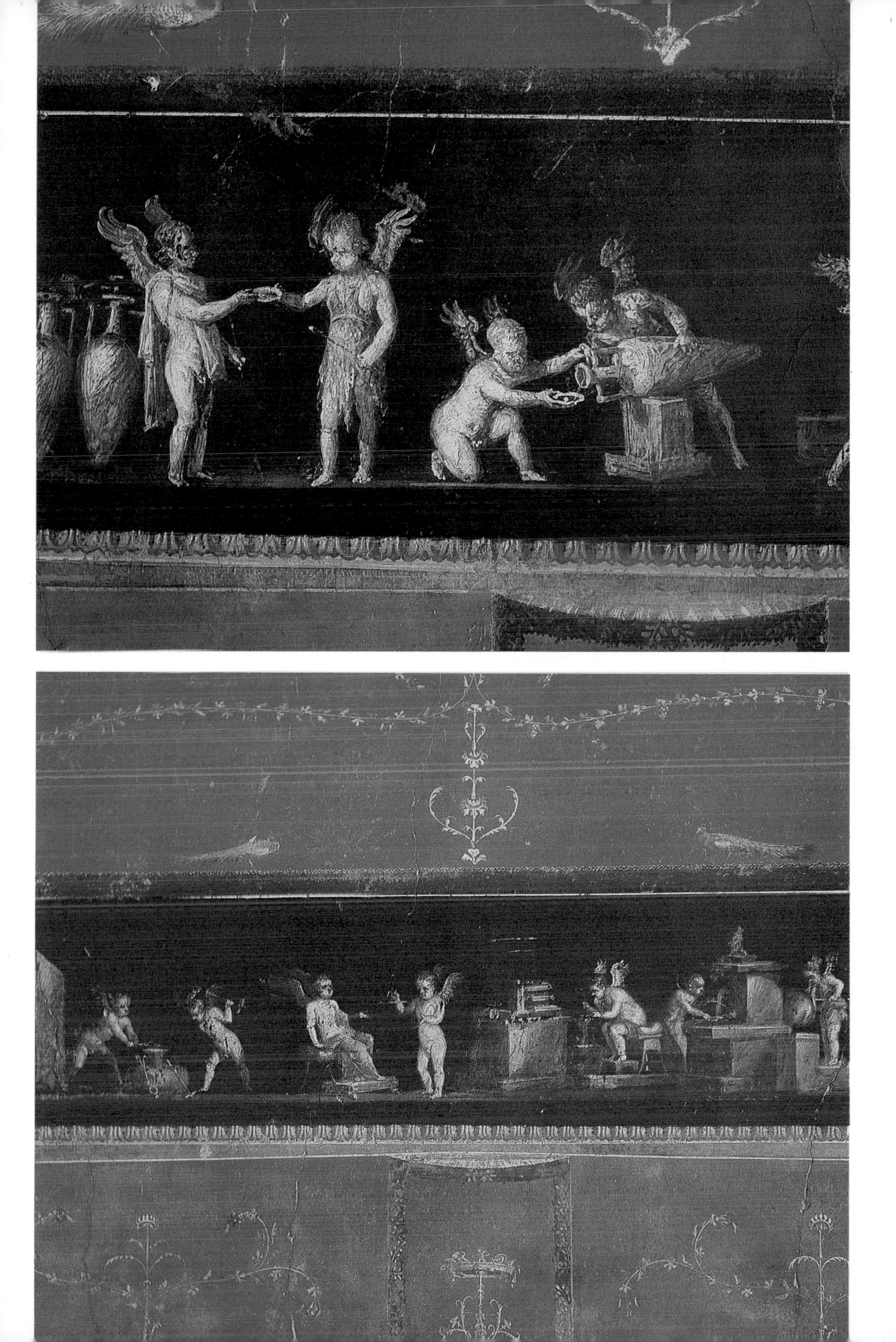

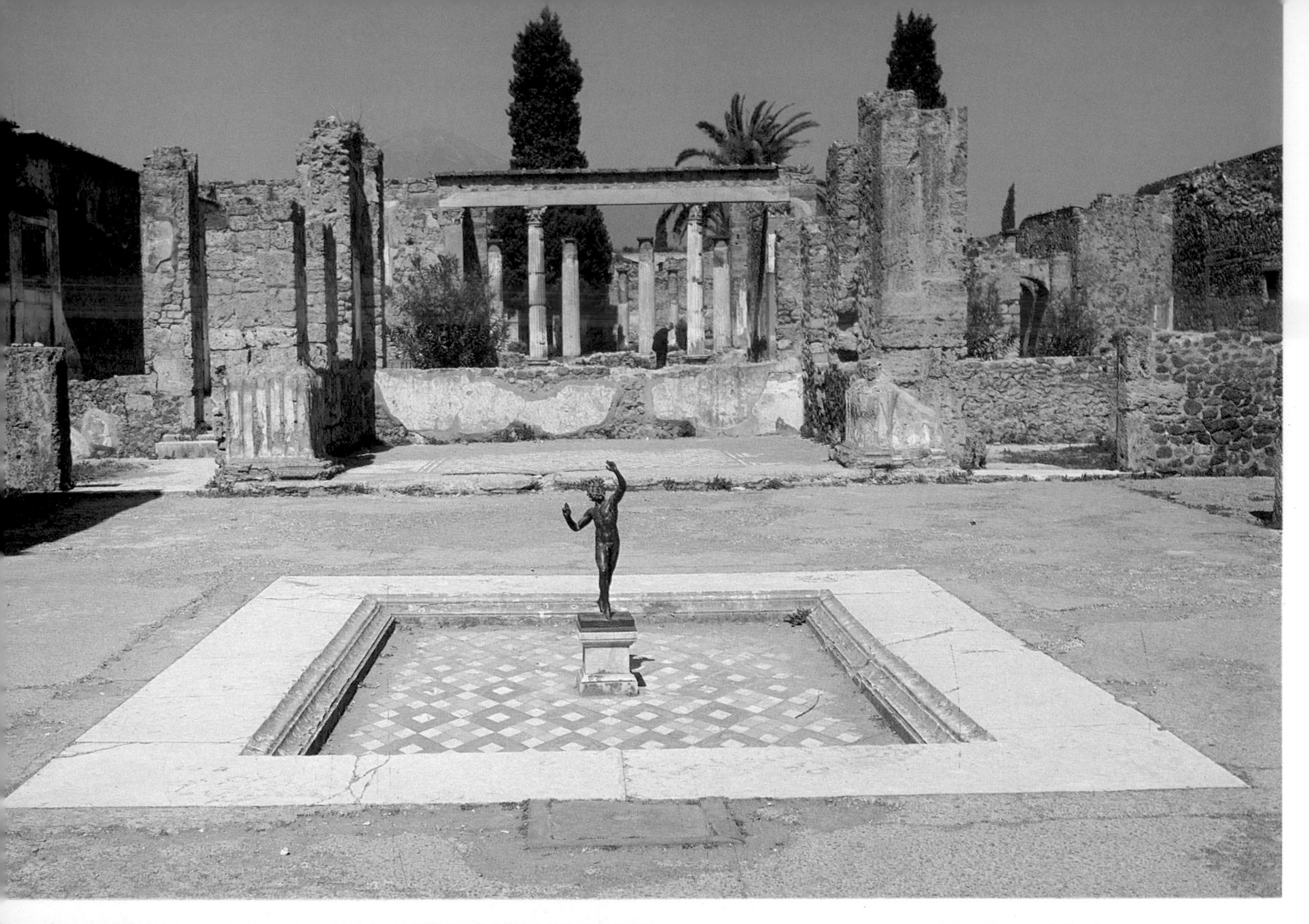

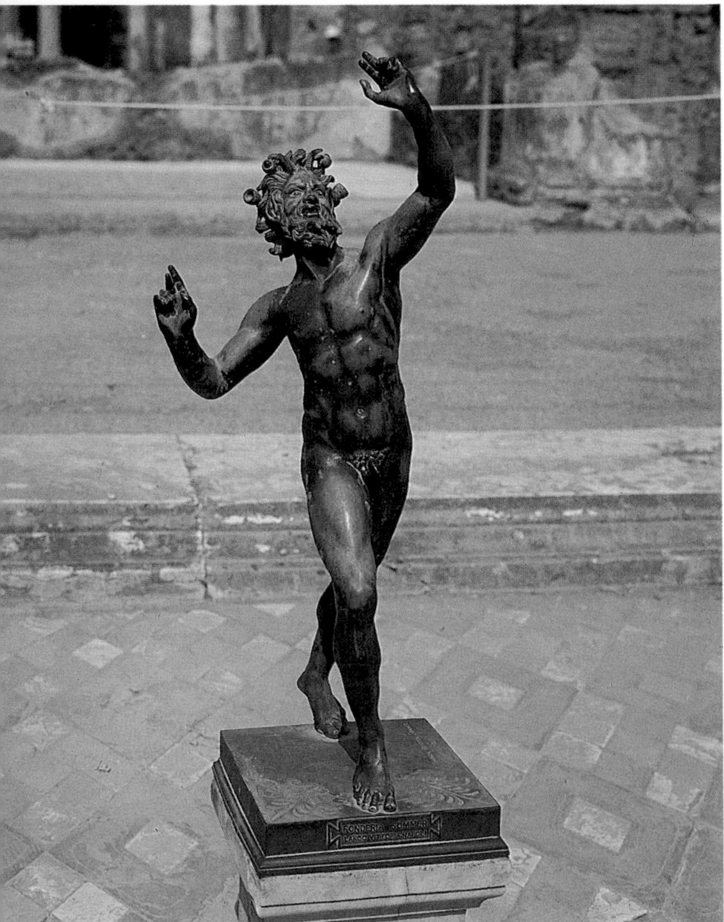

Above. the principal atrium of the House of the Faun as it is now and. below, the copy of the bronze figurine which gave its name to the house. On the facing page: the principal atrium in all its original splendor.

49 - HOUSE OF THE FAUN

This imposing private house which belonged to an unknown aristocratic Pompeian family is a fine example of the result of the fusion of the architectural models of the Italic house centered around the atrium and the Hellenistic peristyle dwelling.
The extraordinarily large size of the house is an indication of the wealth accumulated by the Roman-Italic upper classes after the conquests in the east. It occupies an entire *insula* superimposed on an earlier 3rd cent. B.C. dwelling which with its *hortus* was on the site of what is now the first peristyle.
The House of the Faun, discovered and excavated around 1830, was built in two phases, the first dating to the early 2nd cent. B.C. and including the first peristyle, and the second of the late 2nd cent. B.C. in which the second peristyle was added and the final size was established.
The house consists of two quarters which communicate but have independent entrances set in a row of shops. The main quarter, to the west, is reached through a vestibule with a lararium that consists of a temple facade with small Corinthian columns. From here one passes into a large Tuscan atrium with an impluvium paved in a pat-

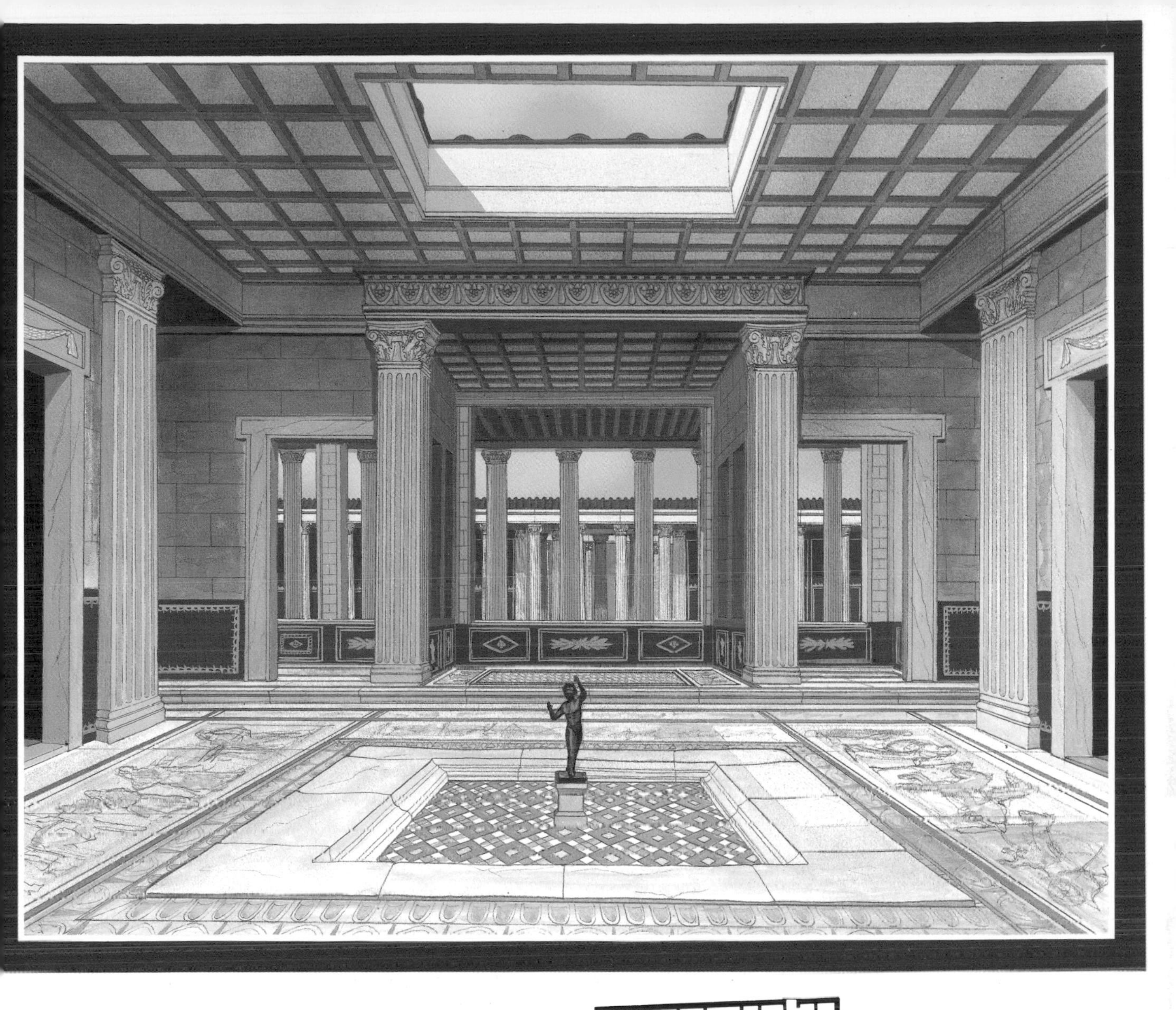

tern of polychrome rhombs. At the center was a bronze statuette of a dancing faun (now replaced by a copy) after which the house is called. Two series of cubicles and two *alae* are arranged around the long sides, in line with the typical Etrusco-Italic scheme. The one on the right has an *emblema* with a cat attacking a partridge while the one on the left has an *emblema* with three doves taking a jewel from a casket. The back of the atrium consists of a tablinum in the center flanked by two tricliniums. The skeleton of a woman was found in the tablinum, caught as she was trying to flee with her jewels and belongings. The pavement is in *opus sectile*.
The tricliniums had *emblemata* depicting fishes and a woman on a panther. The eastern apartment is articulated around a tetrastyle atrium on which various service rooms open. A corridor on the east side of the first peristyle communicated with a stable, a latrine, a bath with *tepidarium* and *calidarium*, a kitchen and a triclinium.
The first peristyle had Ionic columns in tufa that were stuccoed and was also accessible from one of the tricliniums of the western quarter. An exedra preceded by two columns and two antae piers with stuccoed Corinthian capitals faces onto the north side; on the threshold there is a Nilotic mosaic while on the pavement inside was the

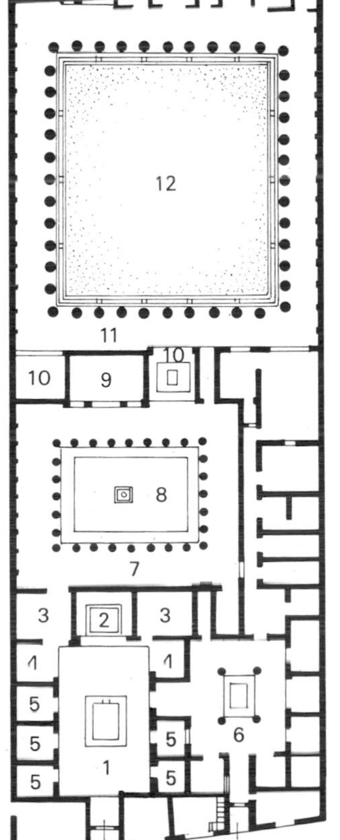

1 Atrium Tuscanicum
2 Tablinum
3 Triclinia
4 Alae
5 Cubicula
6 Atrium Tetrastilum
7 Peristilium
8 Viridarium
9 Exedra
10 Triclinia
11 Peristilium
12 Viridarium

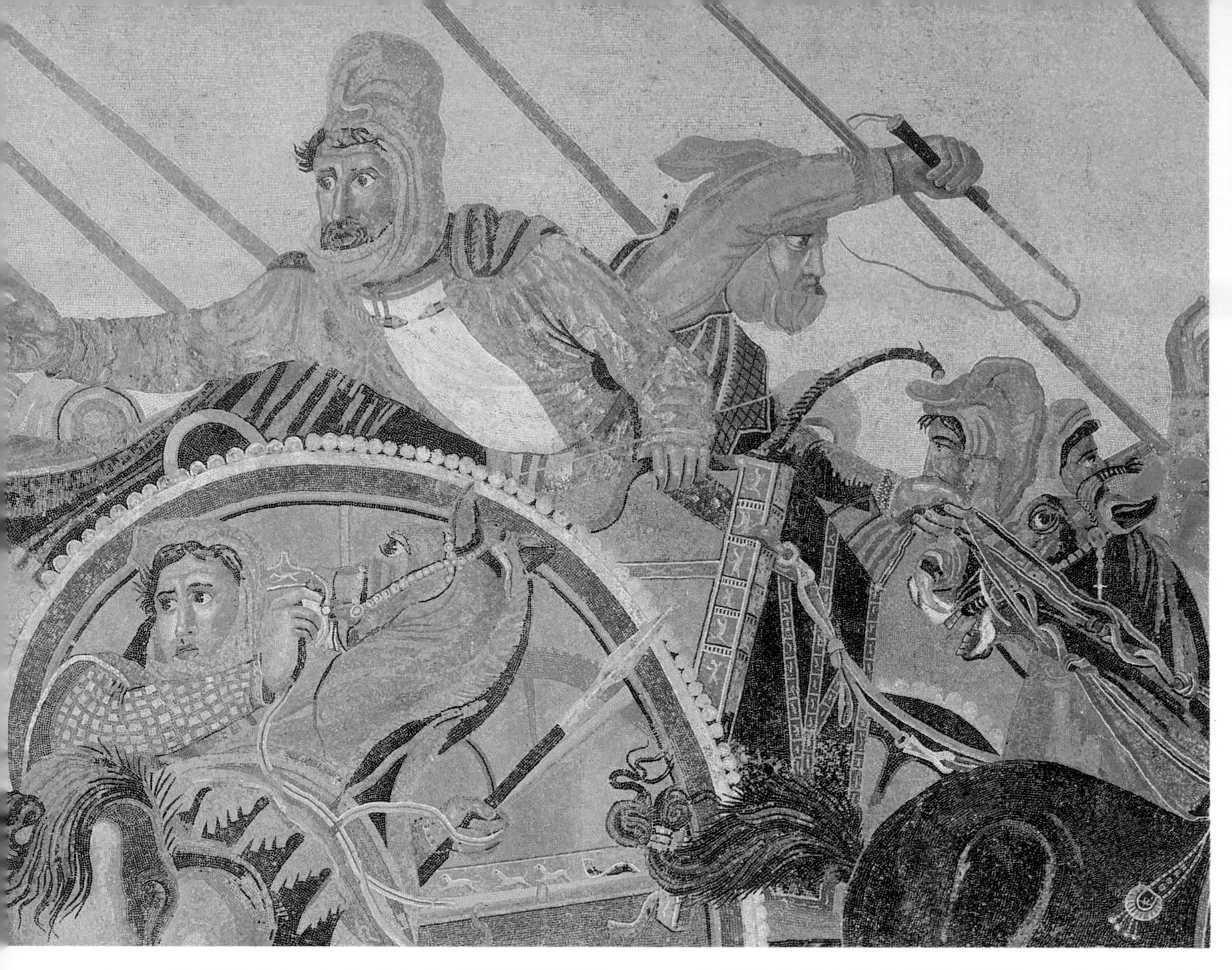

Above a detail of the large mosaic, now in the Museo Nazionale in Naples, of the battle between Alexander and Darius who can be identified as the figure on the chariot.

Opposite, above: the first peristyle of the House of the Faun with the garden at the center, seen from he northern exedra. Below: the second large peristyle of the house, set on the north side.

famous mosaic of the battle between Alexander the Great and Darius, now in the Museum of Naples.
Various rooms, including an *oecus* decorated in Style II painting, face onto the second peristyle, which is much larger than the first (45 x 40 m.) and with forty-four Doric columns covered with stucco. At the back are other small service rooms and the secondary entrance to the house. The niches of a lararium are at the northwest end and various cult objects and a bronze statuette representing the Genius of the house were found nearby.
Special mention must be made of the large Alexander mosaic referred to previously. It consists of over a million tiny tesserae and had already been damaged in antiquity, especially in the earthquake of A.D. 62 as shown by restorations in larger tesserae and integrations in stucco. This work is particularly important for it is the copy of an early Hellenistic painting, probably (according to Pliny) by Philoxenos of Eretria. Particular attention has been paid to the innovative feeling for light and chiaroscuro, a basic conquest of Hellenistic painting which the mosaic artist has faithfully reproduced in his sweeping composition. The figures overlap and are superposed in the impetus of the battle that arrives from various directions up to the point where the horse at the center is shown from behind as it moves illusionistically into the depth of the picture. Alexander bursts in from the left, his head uncovered, leading the Macedonian cavalry, and spearing a Persian nobleman, while Darius, at the center of the composition, flees in his chariot.
Many of the details reproduced here which we know from written sources seem to indicate that this is the battle of Gaugamela, the last decisive encounter between the two. The original painting may have reached Rome from Greece after the conquests and the systematic plundering of works of art in the 2nd cent. B.C.
These same cultural streams, in which the architectural and artistic values of Hellenism are reproposed and flourish in the Roman-Italic ambience, also dictated the forms of this house, which can be compared with the Palace of the Columns in Ptolemais which belonged to a Ptolemaic governor, and the Royal Palace of Pergamon, where one of the Diadochi lived.

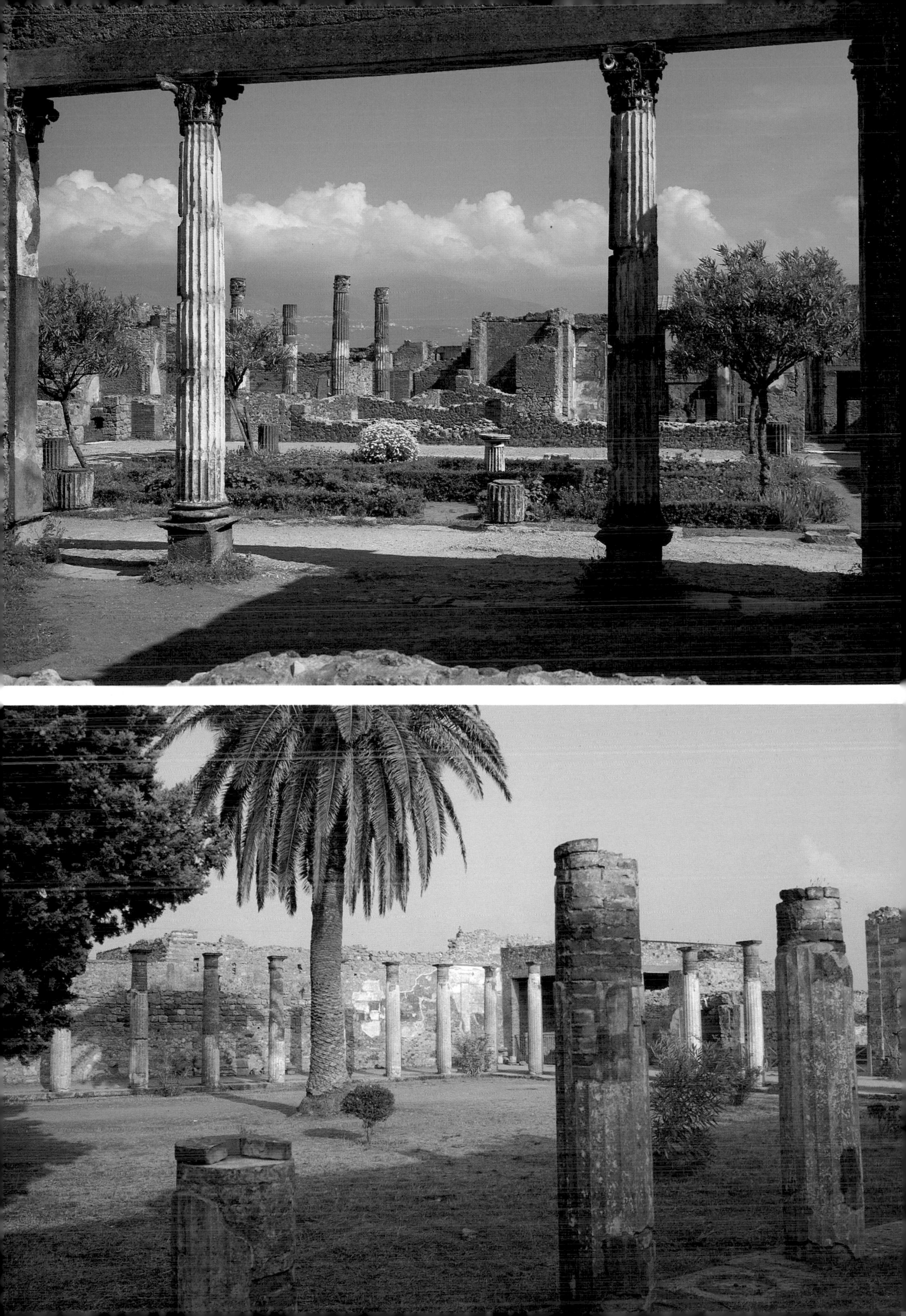

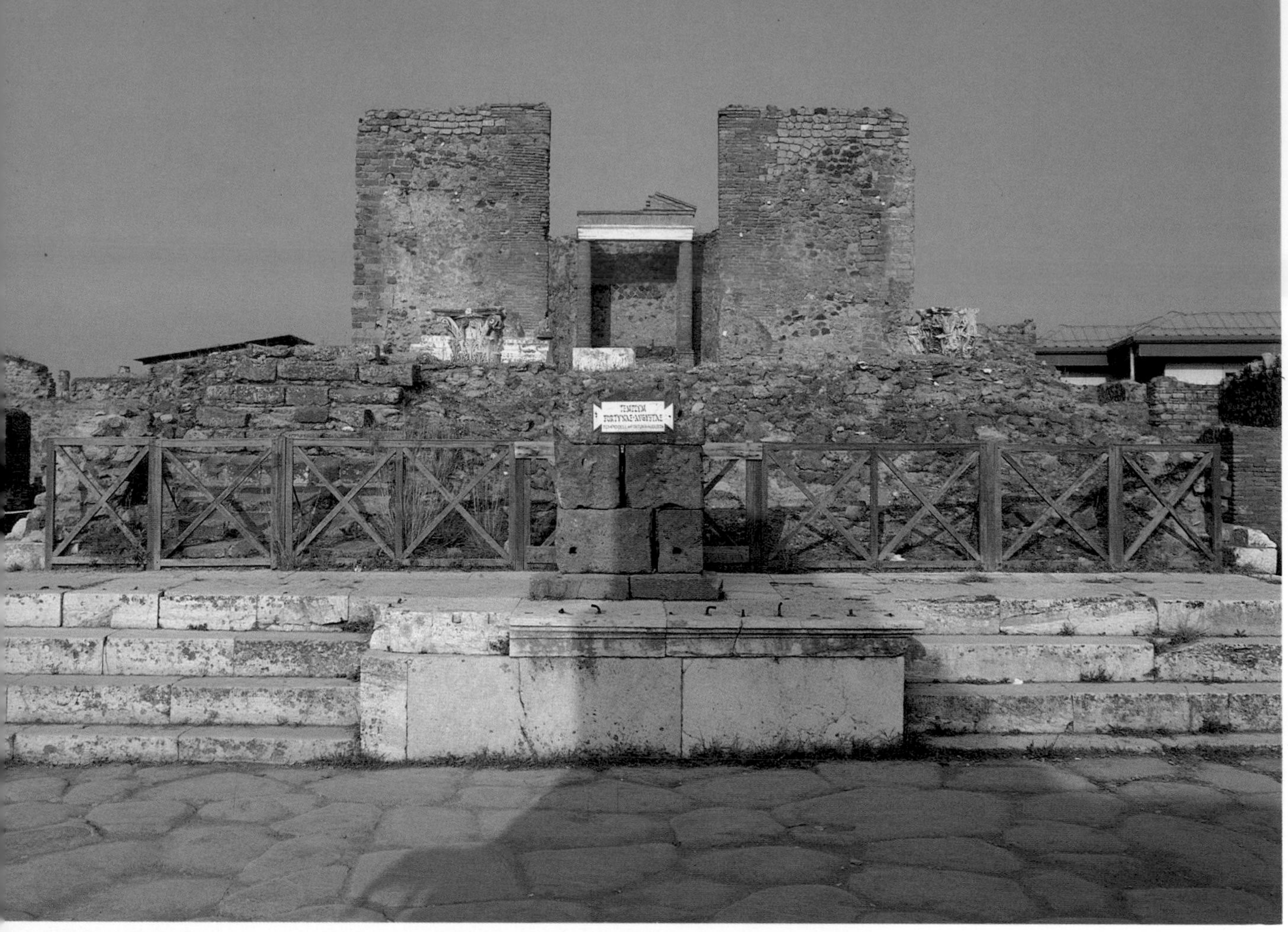

Above: the facade of the Temple of Fortuna Augusta. Below: the side of the building facing the stretch of Via di Nola which has taken its name of Via della Fortuna from the temple. Opposite: the reconstruction of the temple.

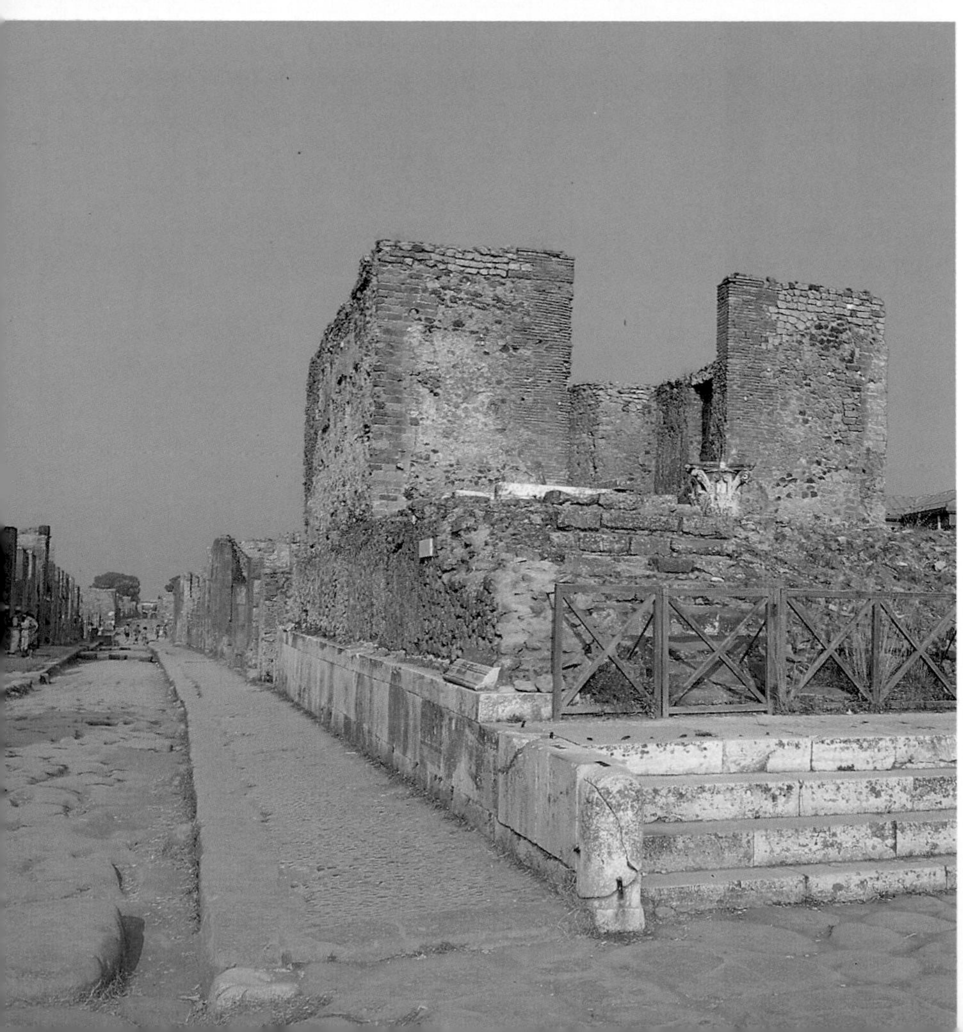

50 - TEMPLE OF FORTUNA AUGUSTA

It is situated at the intersection between Via di Nola and Via del Foro. The inscription, originally on the front of the building but found inside the cella, informs us that the temple was built by a private citizen Marcus Tullius on his own property and at his own cost. Under Augustus he held the most important offices in the city (he was *duovir*, augur, military tribune) and obviously the erection of a temple dedicated to Fortuna Augusta was an act of propaganda and political support of his benefactor.

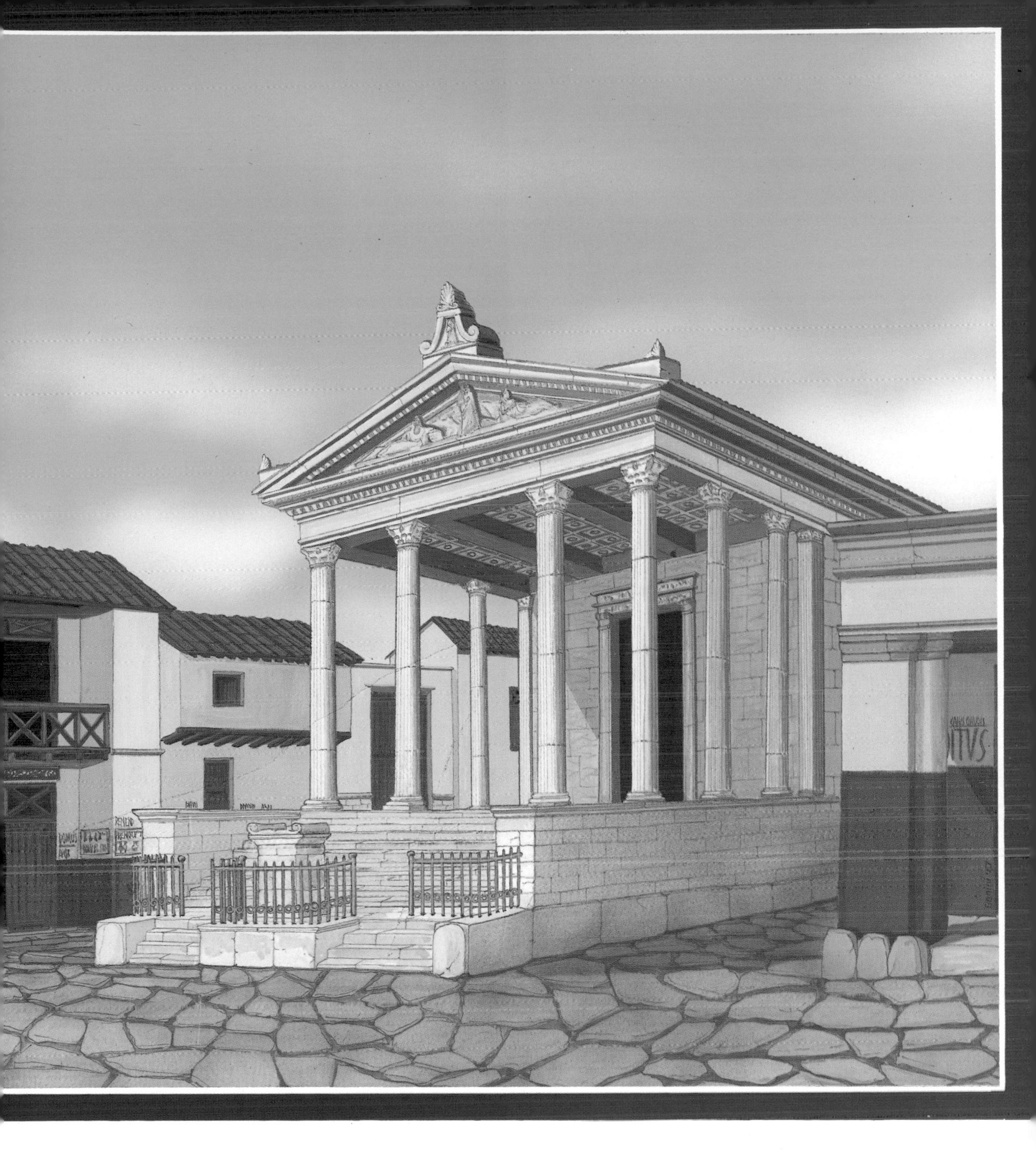

The building, which is not very large, had suffered severe damage in the earthquake of A.D. 62 and at the time of the eruption in A.D. 79 restoration was still limited to the cella, which was built in *opus incertum*, originally faced in marble, while the restoration is in brick. The all-over layout is reminiscent of that of the Temple of Jupiter in the Forum: the high podium on which the cella stands, preceded by a pronaos of four columns on the front and two at the sides, was reached by stairs set on the facade, interrupted by a platform where the altar is placed. At the back of the cella a shrine framed by two columns was meant to house the cult statue of the goddess Fortuna.

The side walls have four niches for statues, two of which were found when the excavations were in progress. An inscription found in the alley to the south of the building tells us that this area still belonged to Marcus Tullius. At the back are the dwelling quarters for the temple guardian.

The college of the ministers of the cult was founded by Marcus Tullius himself. Four of their dedicatory inscriptions (plus that of a private individual) refer that they had consecrated in the temple statues of Fortuna or the reigning emperors in a period that ranged from Augustus to Nero.

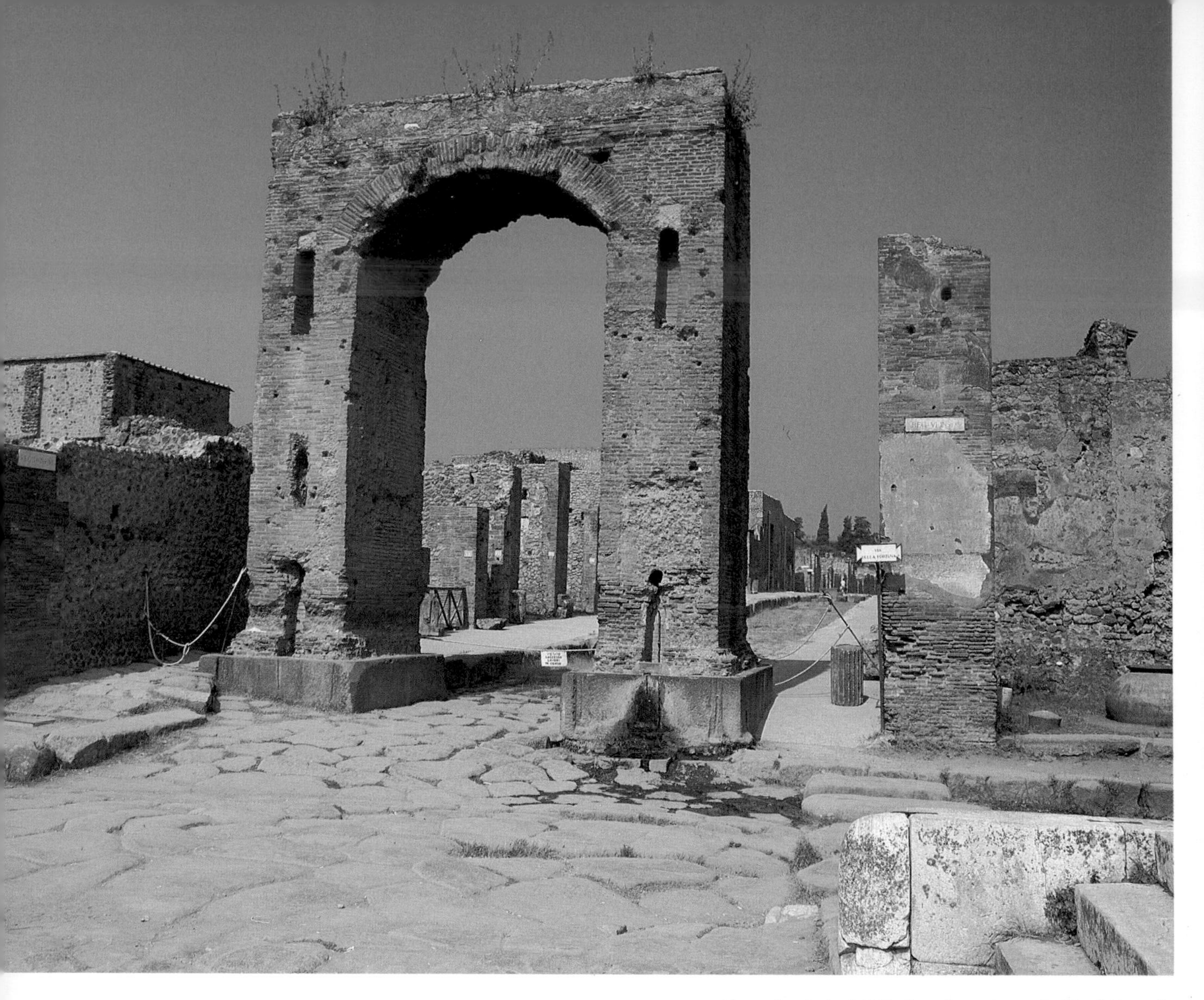

Above: the Arch of Caligula at the entrance to Via di Mercurio, as it is now. Opposite: the reconstruction of the arch.

51 - ARCH OF CALIGULA

This arch is set astride Via di Mercurio, of which it marks the beginning, in front of the Forum Baths and the Temple of Fortuna Augusta, near the intersection where Via delle Terme, Via della Fortuna, Via del Foro and Via di Mercurio cross.
This is an honorary arch in brick with a single passageway and its attribution to Caligula is based on an equestrian statue in bronze, found in fragments, which must have originally been set on the attic and which has been identified as Caligula. The arch was built on the same axis as the arch attributed to Tiberius or Germanicus, which constitutes a monumental entrance to the Civil Forum, and which was also topped by an equestrian statue.

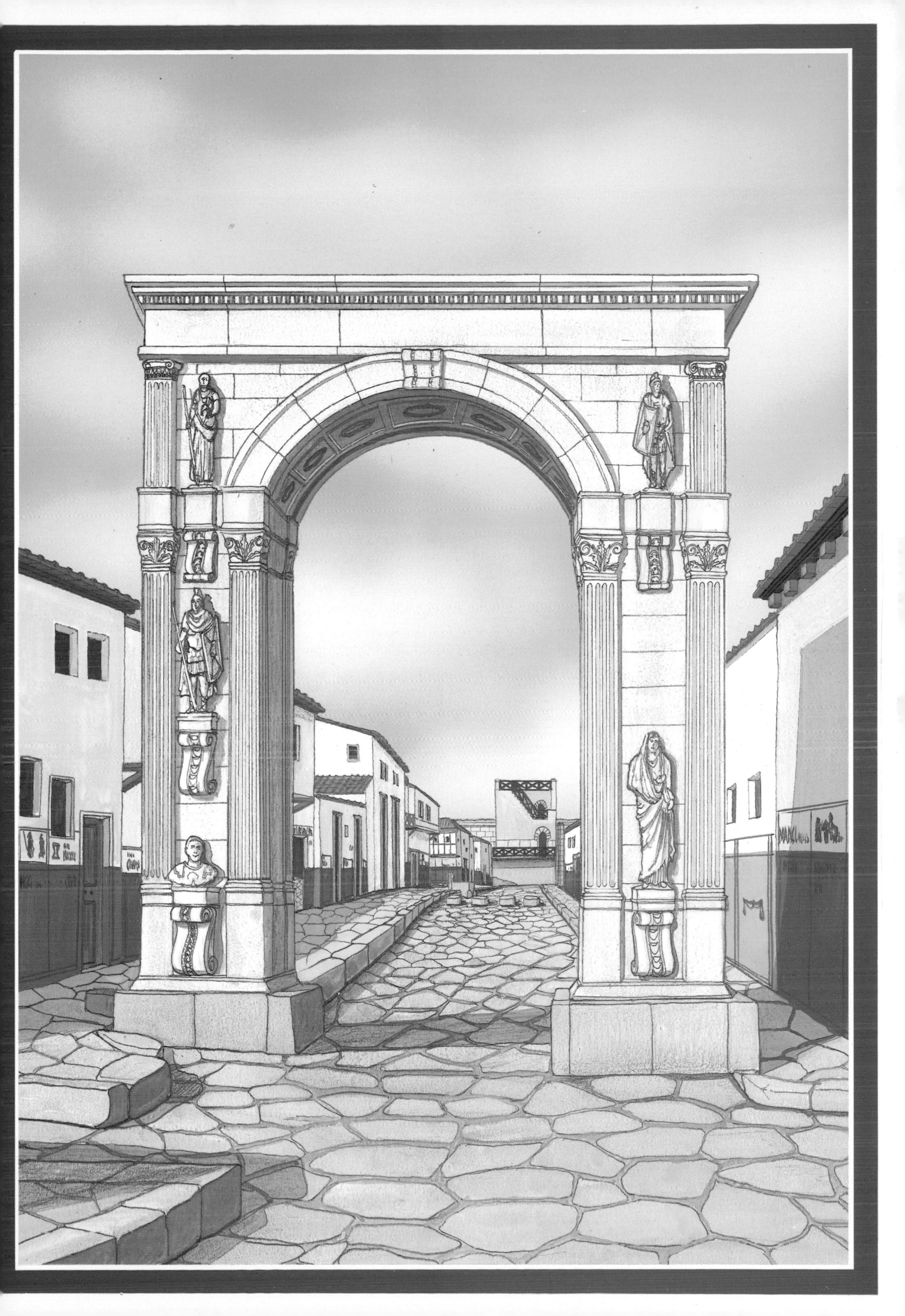

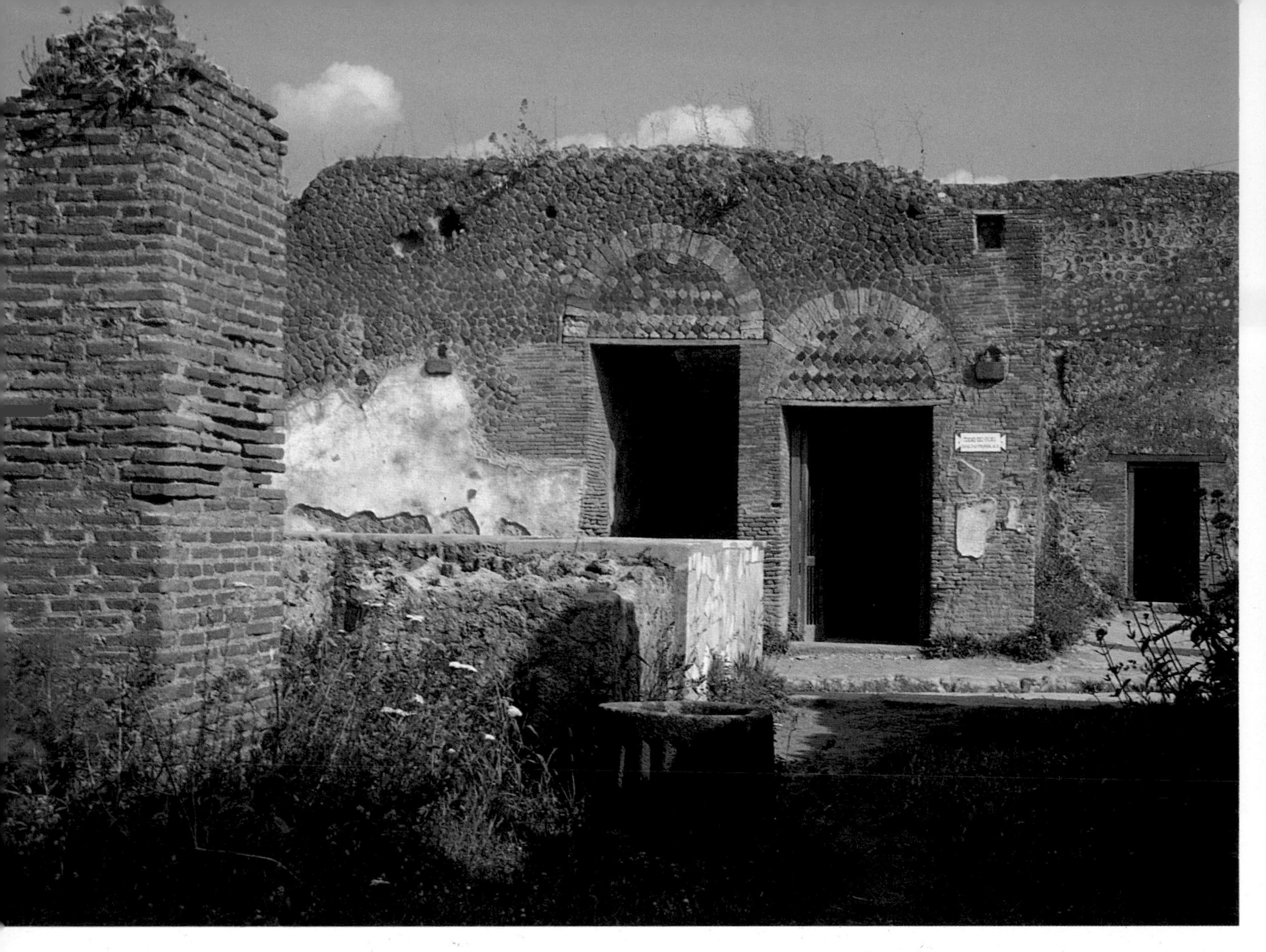

Above: the entrance to the Forum Baths. Opposite, above: the apodyterium of the baths with casts of two of the victims of the eruption. Below: the tepidarium.

52 - FORUM BATHS

This bath establishment stands in a block at the crossing of Via delle Terme and Via del Foro. These were the only baths still functioning in Pompeii after the earthquake of A.D. 62, which had not damaged them seriously, and since the establishment was not particularly large, it must certainly have been overcrowded, particularly in view of the fact that the baths had become a habitual meeting place where the Roman citizens of all social classes spent their free time.
The Forum Baths were built shortly after the establishment of Sulla's colony (80 B.C.) by the *duovir* Lucius Caesius and the *aediles* Caius Occius and Lucius Niraemius, as an inscription found in two copies tells us. The layout seems to be based on the older Stabian Baths. It was divided into two separate, non-communicating sectors, for men and for women, and the *praefurnium* in between provided hot water and steam to both. The men's section had three entrances, in Via delle Terme, Via del Foro and in Vicolo delle Terme. The last two lead into a courtyard with colonnaded porticoes on three sides and arches on piers on the fourth. A latrine installed after the earthquake of A.D. 62 is to be found near the entrance in Vicolo delle Terme. A narrow corridor, in which five hundred oil lamps were found (the baths were open afternoons and evenings) leads from the courtyard to the *apodyterium* (dressing room) to which the third entrance of Via delle Terme leads directly. The *apodyterium* has a pavement of white mosaic with a black band around it and a vault decorated with stuccoes, of which very little remains. No niches were found in which the clothing could be kept but nail holes in the wall seem to indicate that wooden compartments for this scope were hung there.
The *frigidarium* is a round room with four semicircular niches covered by a dome with a skylight for illumination. A stepped marble tub was used for cold baths after the room had lost its original function of *laconicum* for sweat baths. The walls are decorated with paintings of gardens and a stucco frieze with cupids (*erotes*). The rectangular *tepidarium* has a barrel vault decorated with coffering and medallions with subjects relating to the gods and mythology. A series of niches on the middle part of the walls is framed by atlantes figures in clay covered with stucco that were part of the original decoration of the baths shortly after 80 B.C. which closely recall those in the Odeion of the same period. A band of tendrils in stucco that runs along over the niches and the decoration of the vault belong to the restoration after A.D. 62. The *tepidarium* was still heated by the old system of braziers: inside one can still see three benches and

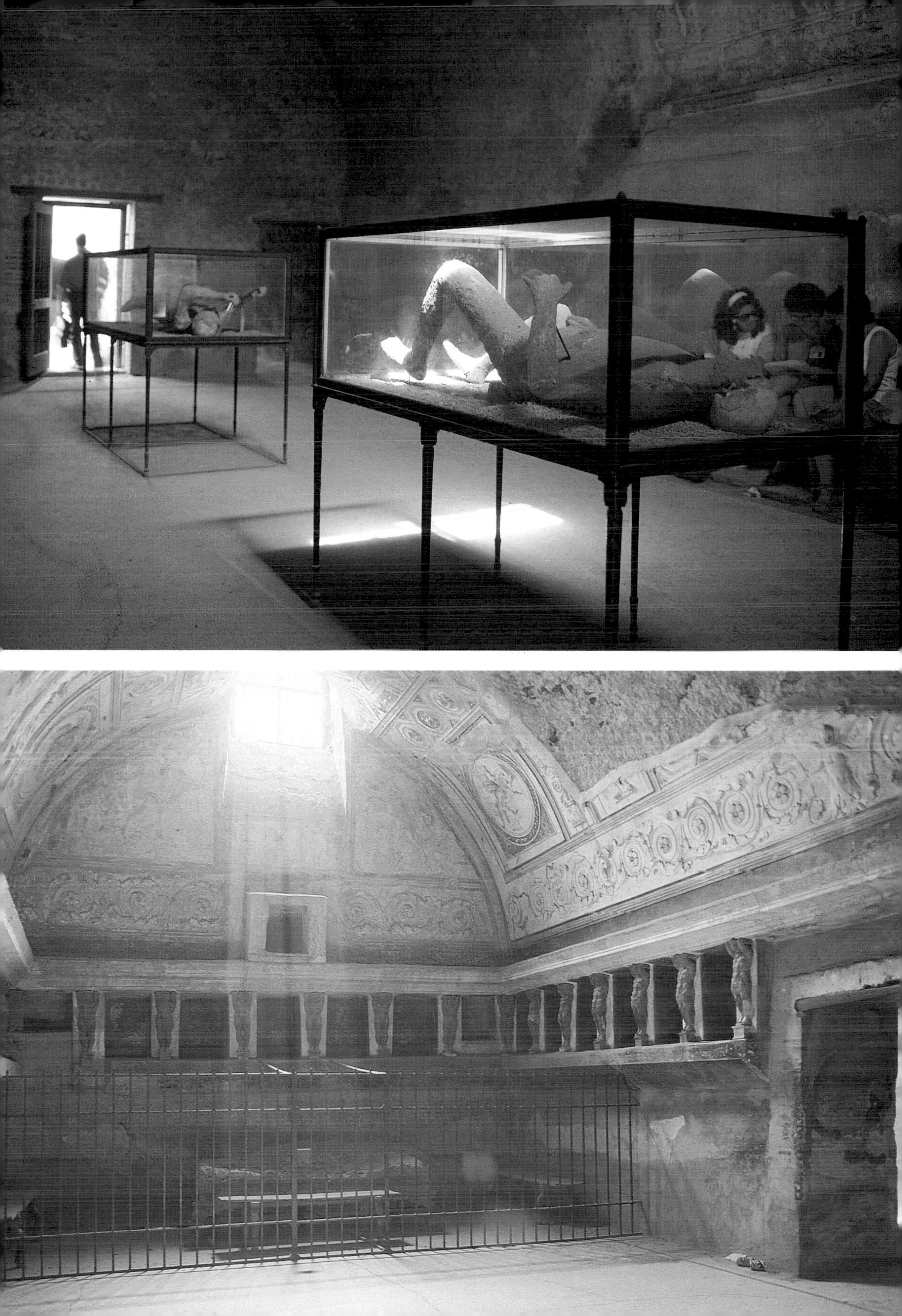

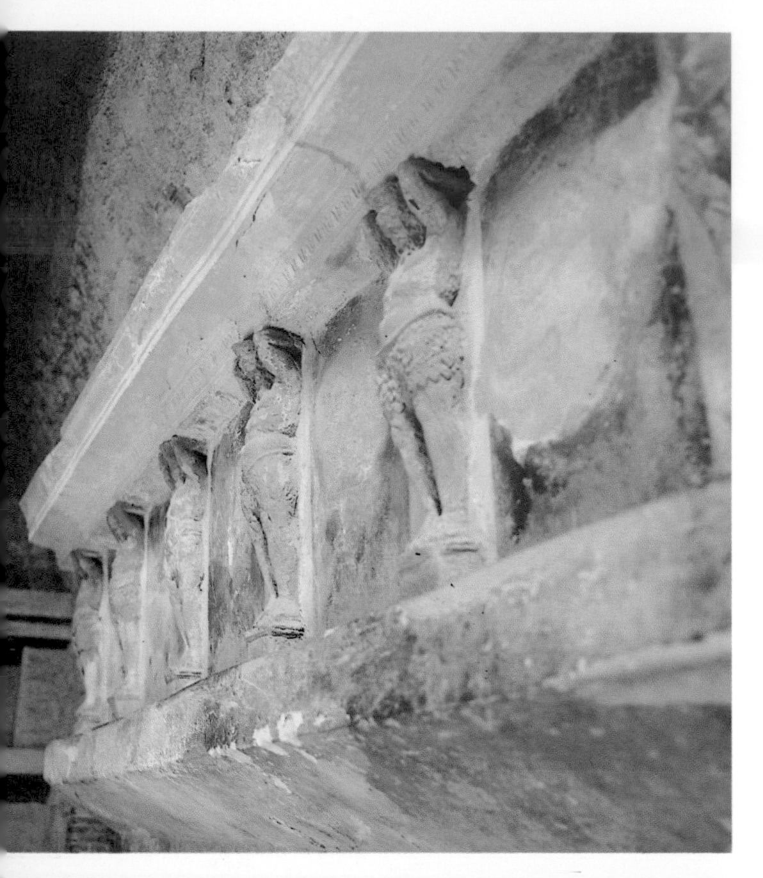

a brazier in bronze, all decorated with the heads of cows, which allude to the name of the donor, the wealthy Capuan M. Nigilius Vaccula.
The *calidarium* with its apse however is equipped with a modern heating system with the pavement raised up on *suspensurae* (brick piers) and the walls with air spaces created by tiles with accentuated fins (*tegulae mammatae*) to permit the passage of hot air. The vaulted ceiling is decorated with a strigil design in stucco. The marble basin for cold water (*labrum*) in the apse was provided in 3-4 A.D. by the *duoviri* Cn. Melissaeius Aper and M. Staius Rufus. The tub for hot baths, the *alveus*, is on the opposite side, raised on two steps. Entrance to the women's baths is on the Via delle Terme, which leads directly to the *apodyterium*, which must have been furnished with wooden shelves for clothing, as was the case in the men's sector. This is where the pool of the *frigidarium* is. Both the *tepidarium* and the *calidarium* were heated by the *suspensurae* system and walls with air spaces.

This page: the tepidarium of the Forum Baths with above a detail of the atlantes figures on the band with niches. Opposite, above: the apsed calidarium and, below, the circular frigidarium.

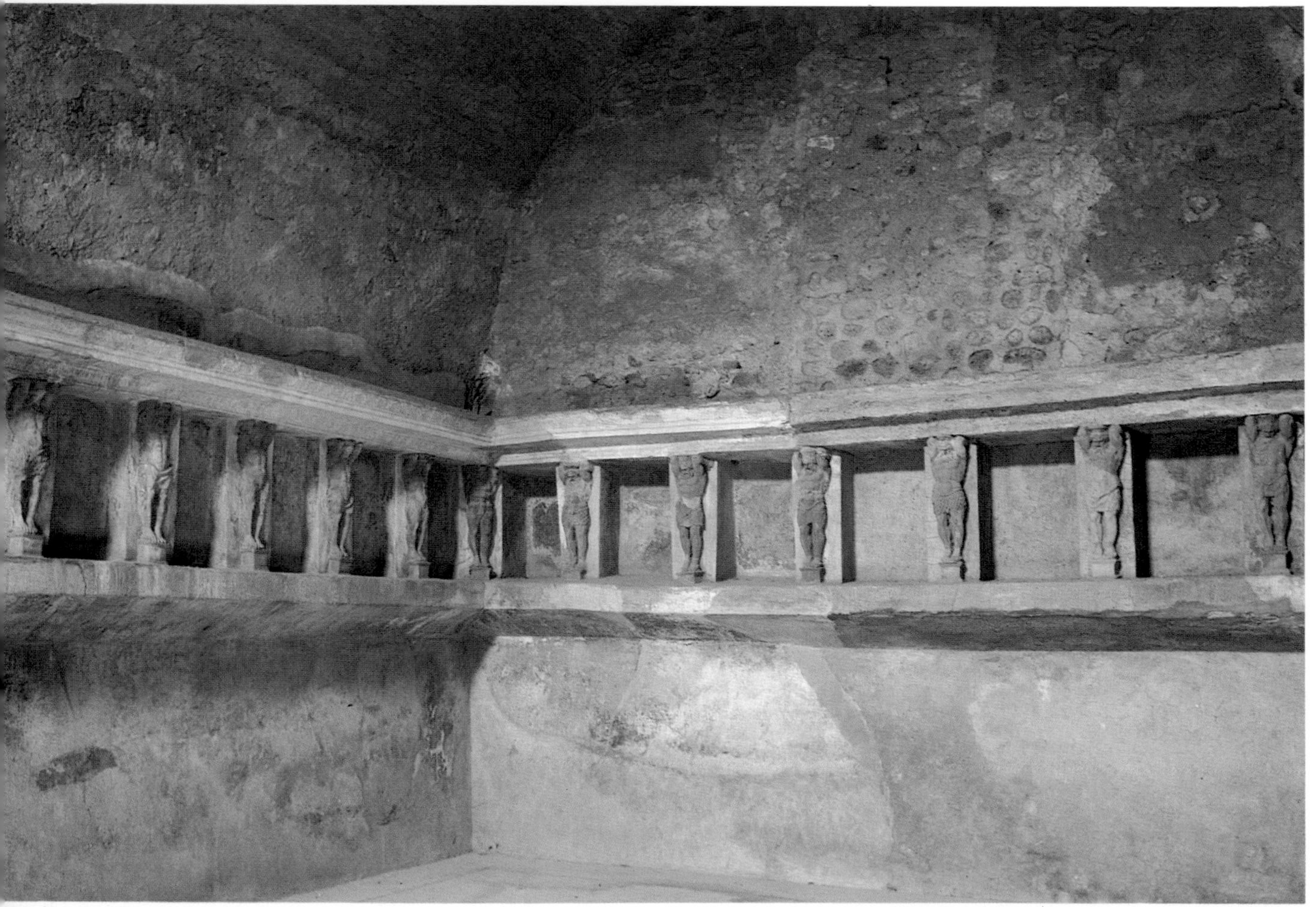

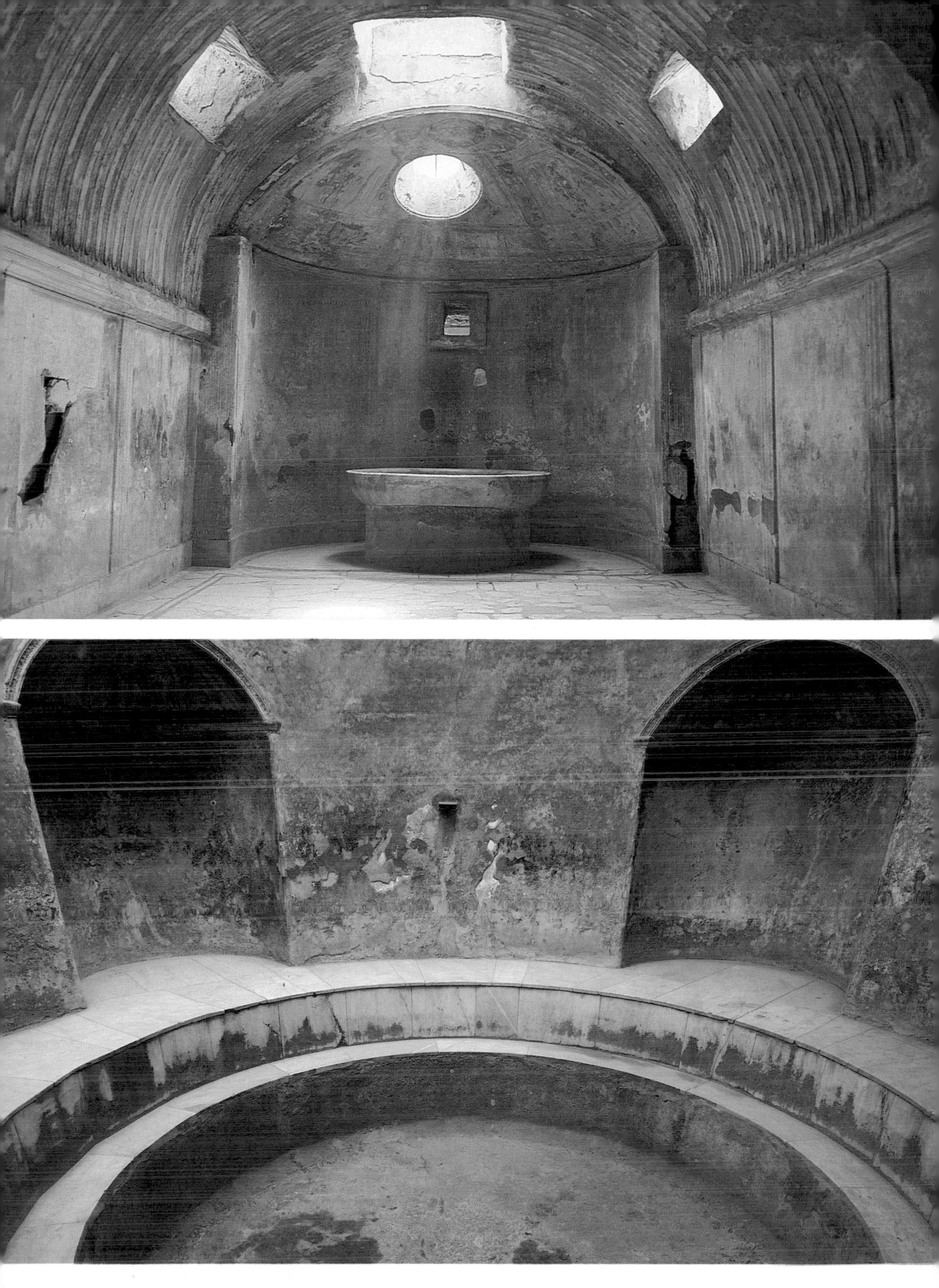

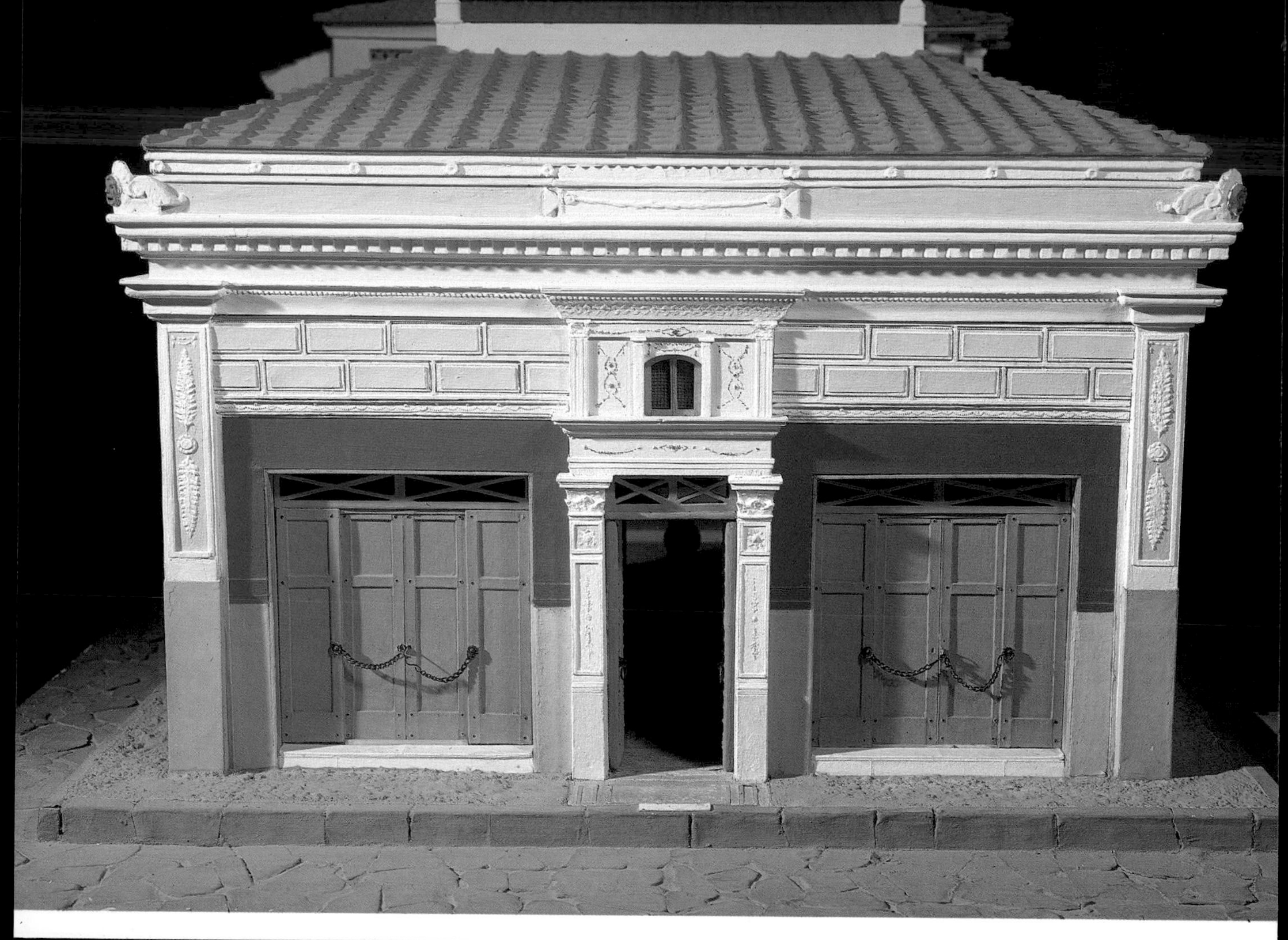

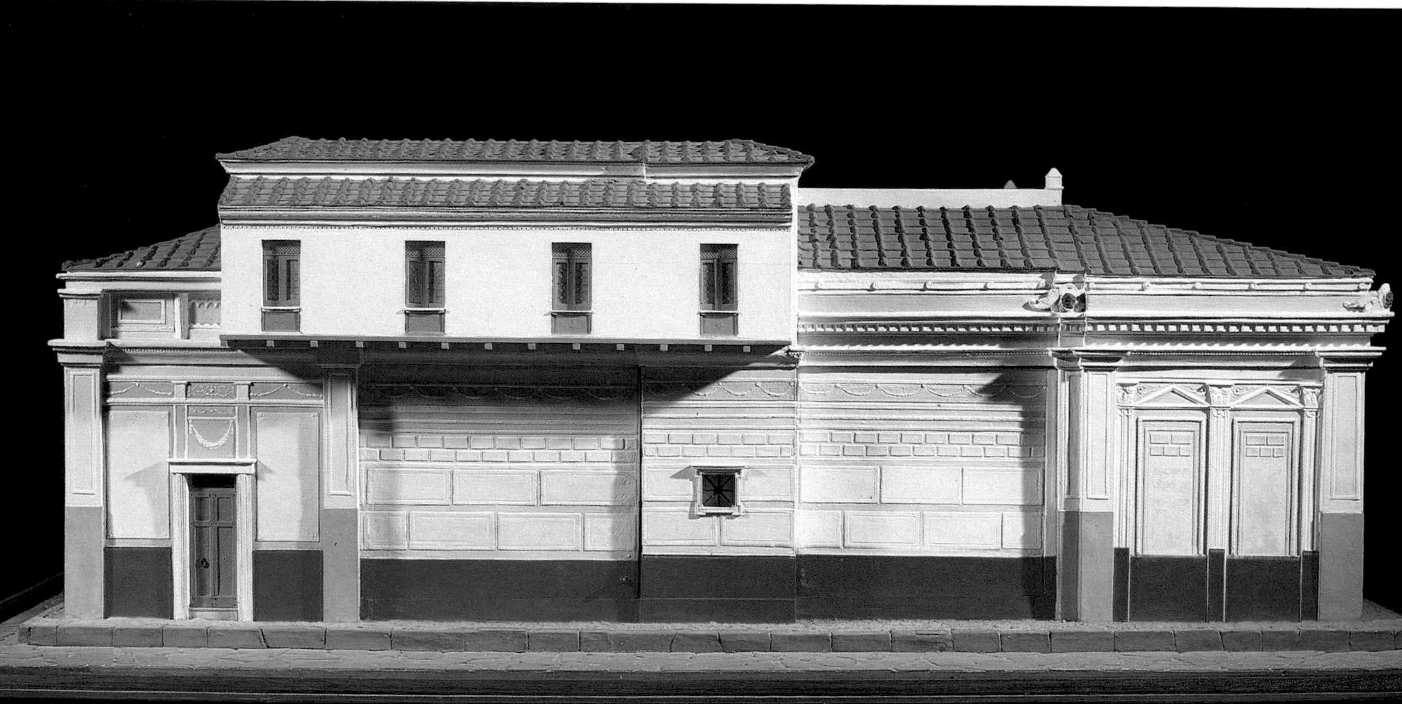

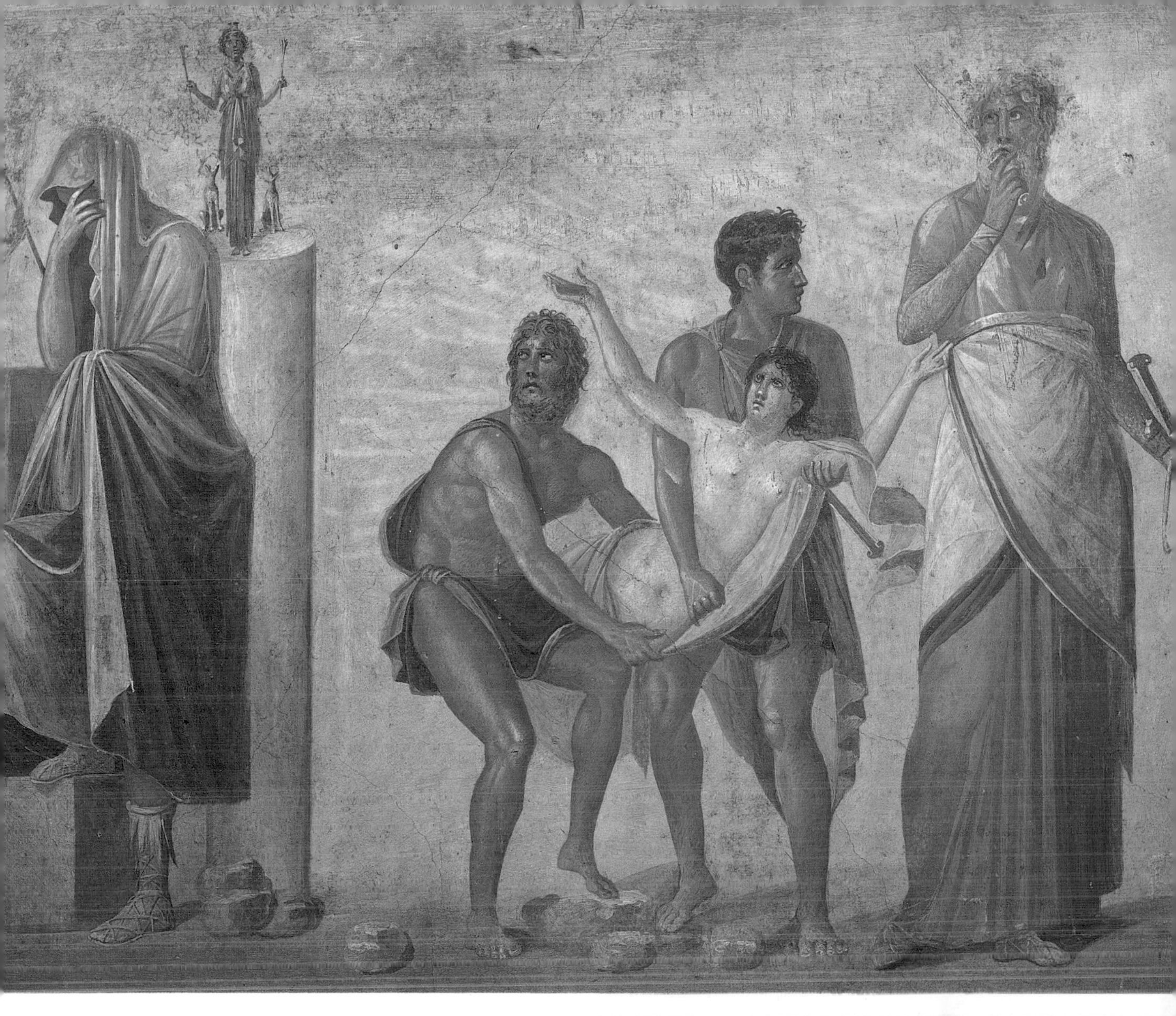

Opposite: two views of the reconstructed model of the House of the Tragic Poet. Above: the fresco of the same house, now in the Museo Nazionale in Naples, with the sacrifice of Iphigenia. Below: the entrance mosaic with the words « beware the dog ».

53 - HOUSE OF THE TRAGIC POET

This house is a good example of the Pompeian house in the Imperial age, not overly large, with an underlying architectural concept aimed at a feeling of intimacy, in a climate that was radically opposed to the one in which the large Hellenistic town houses had been created. The same scheme centered around the atrium of Etruscan Italic tradition was maintained in the front part of the building. The entrance is set between two *tabernae* which communicate with the vestibule, a sign of the merchant origins of the owner of the house. A floor mosaic in the entrance depicts a dog with a chain, as if he were a watchdog, together with the warning *cave canem* (beware of the dog). Entrance to the atrium follows, the walls of which are decorated with heroic and mythical scenes inspired by the Iliad. The cubicles and the *alae* face out on the atrium and two staircases originally led to the living quarters on the floor above. At the center is the marble impluvium basin.

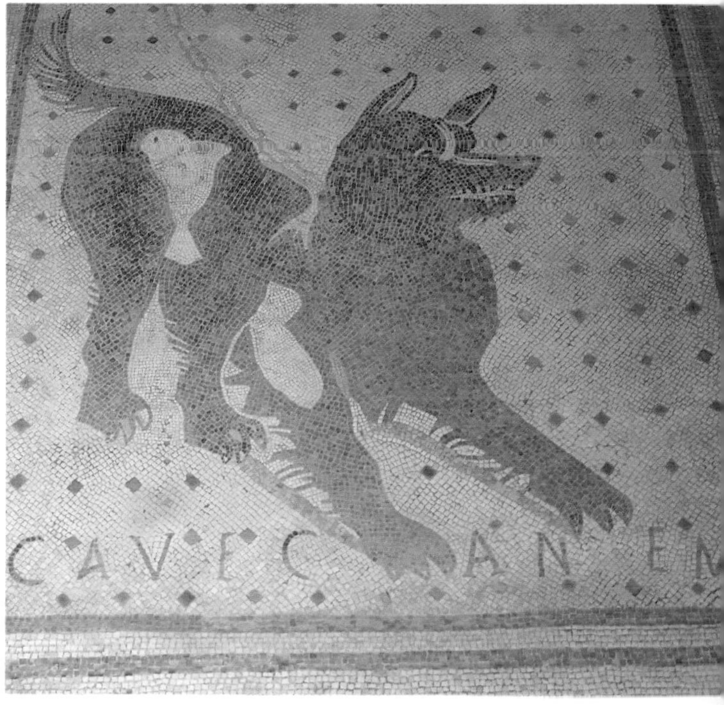

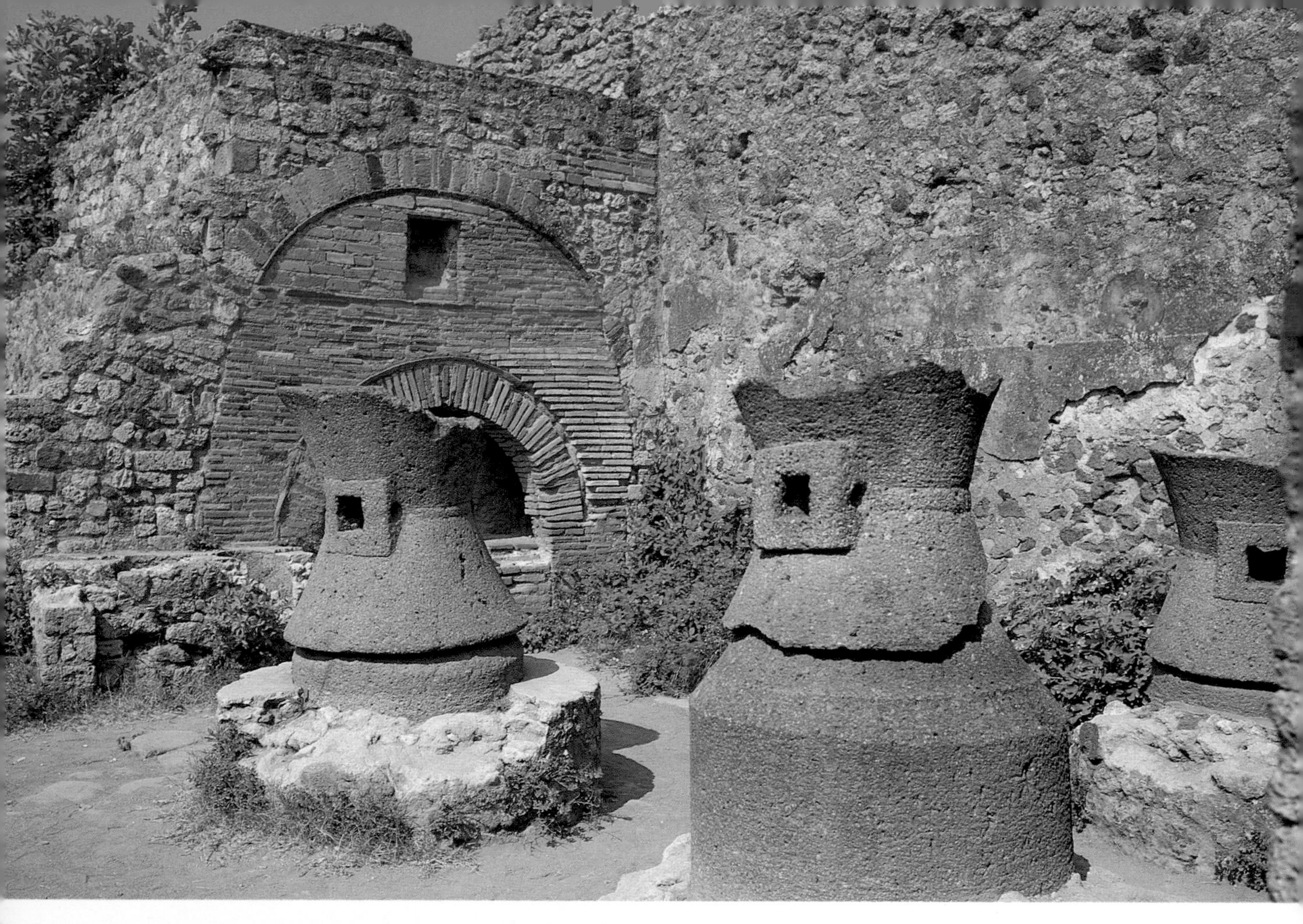

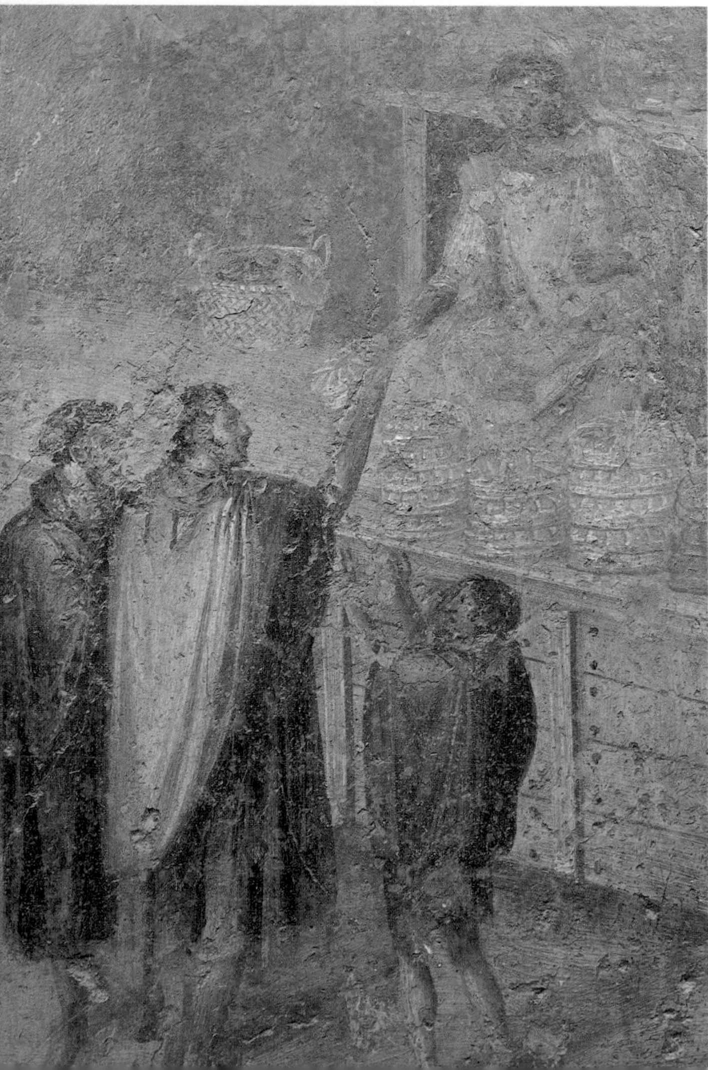

Above: the interior of the Bakery of Modestus; Below: a fresco from Pompeii in the Museum of Naples which depicts a bakery.

As usual, the back wall of the atrium is occupied by the tablinum which had a floor mosaic depicting a theater rehearsal under the direction of a *corrego*, which gave the house its name. One wall was frescoed with a picture of Admetus and Alcestis, later detached and taken to the Museo Nazionale in Naples, as were the mosaic and the wall paintings of the atrium.
Beyond the tablinum lies the small garden adjacent to the back wall of the house and surrounded on the other three sides by a columned portico. An *oecus* opens on the northeast side. It still contains two of the three pictures originally frescoed on the walls, depicting Ariadne abandoned by Theseus, and Venus contemplating a nest of cupids. The kitchen is next to the *oecus*. On the other side of the portico are two cubicles which also have their walls decorated with pictures of mythical subjects. The service entrance to the house (*posticum*) is in the extreme northwest corner.

54 - BAKERY OF MODESTUS

This shop belonged to the baker Modestus. A long entrance corridor leads to an atrium with a large tub in the center for washing grain. The area where the grain was ground and the bread was baked is reached from the back

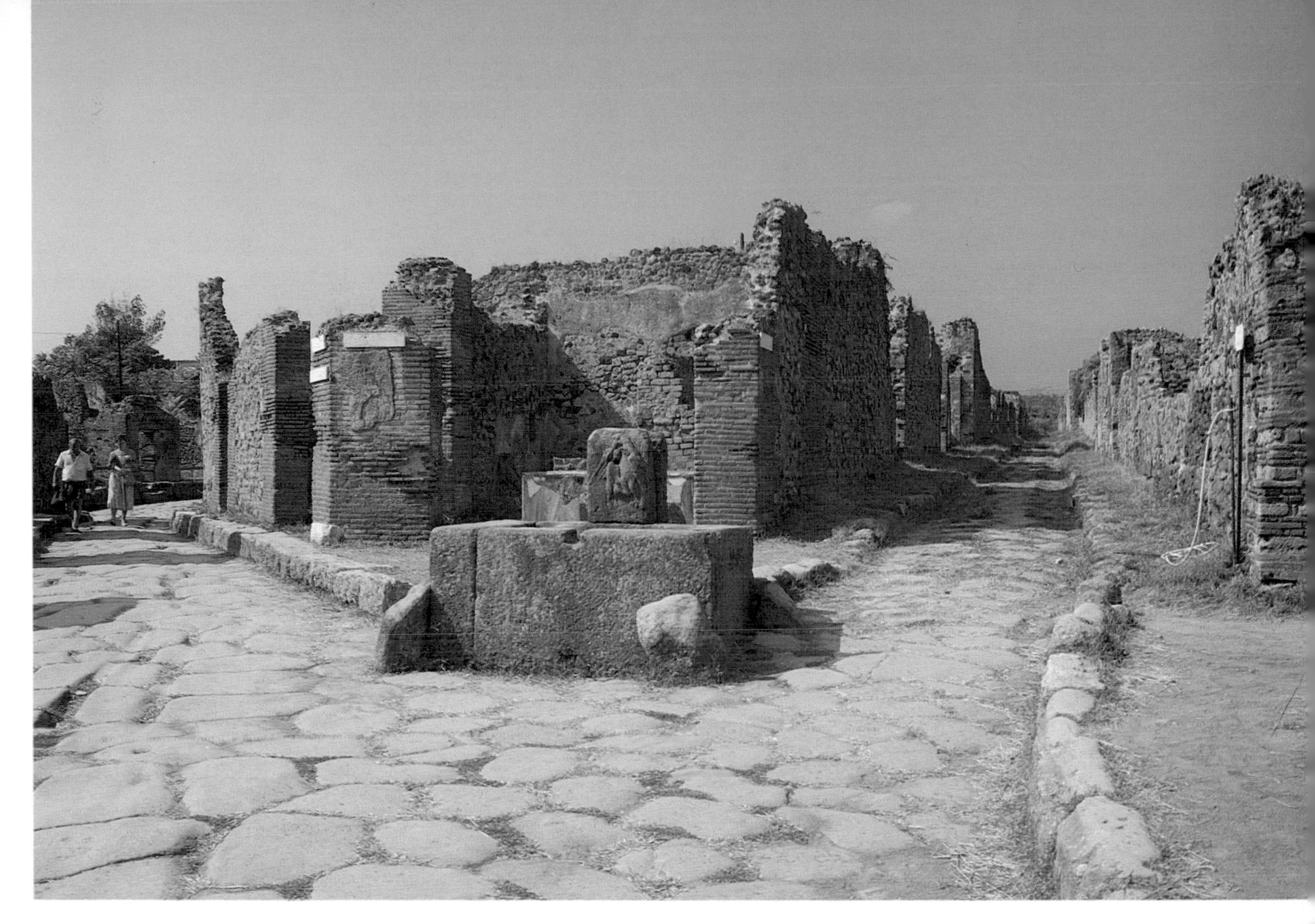

Above: the fork with the Via Consolare on the left. Below: a detail of the taberna situated at the fork.

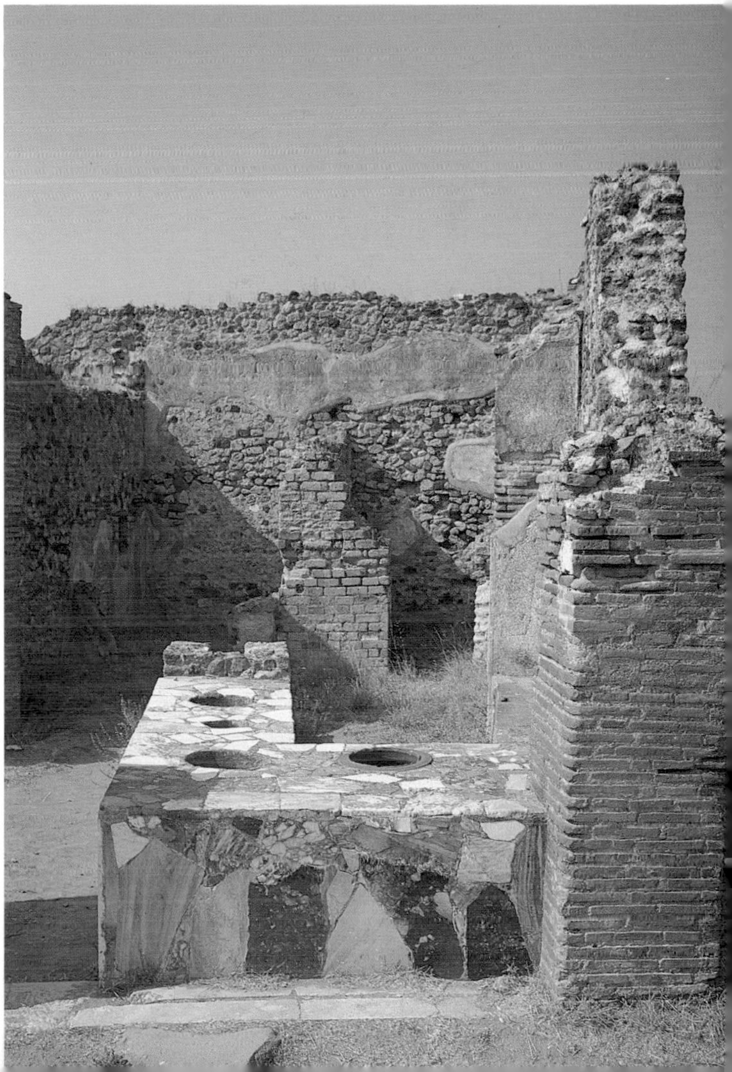

of the atrium. The grindstones in lava still here consist of two parts - an immobile conical element called *meta* which was inserted into a biconical hollow called *catillus*, which rotated around it, drawn by mules yoked to it by wooden beams. The grain was poured into the top of the *catillus* and the flour was collected in lead sheeting situated at the masonry base on which the *meta* stood.
Next to it was the actual oven, which was found with the iron shutter still closed: inside were 81 carbonized round loaves of bread, evidently put in the oven just before the eruption.

55 - VIA CONSOLARE

The Via Consolare is the northwest boundary of the network of city streets and runs parallel to a stretch of the city wall. This was one of the protohistoric roads which dictated the original layout of the city of Pompeii. What we see today is the route dating to historical times which led towards Cumae. Its obvious cultural and commercial importance was augmented by the fact that it connected Pompeii with the *Salinae Hercules* which lay on the coast near Torre Annunziata.
Around the middle of the 2nd cent. B.C. the Via Consolare, like the other city streets, was paved with poly-

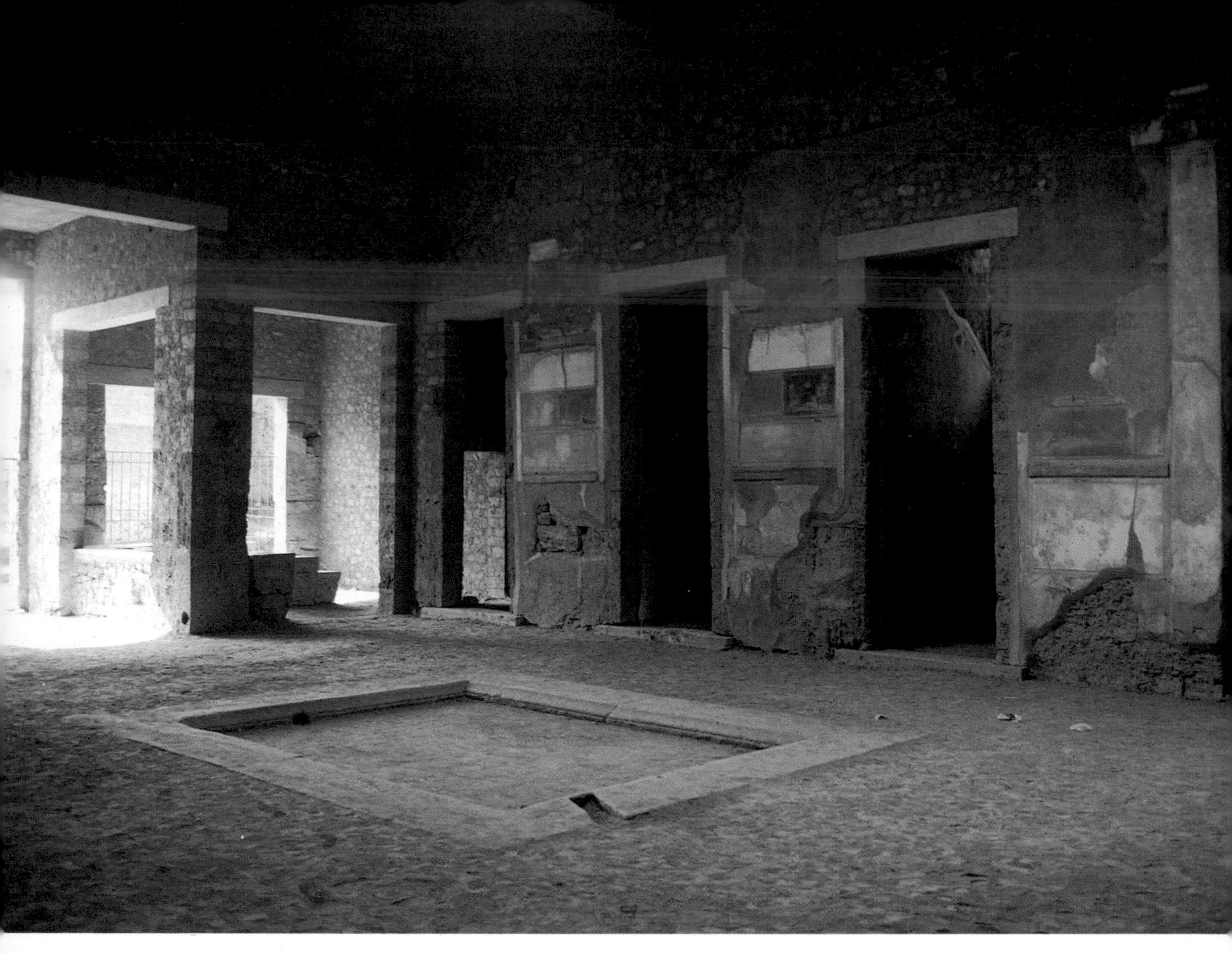

Above: the large atrium of the House of Sallust with the remains of Style I pictorial decoration.

gonal basalt stones, as evidenced by road cippi inscribed in Oscan with the names of the *aedili* of the Samnite period who had promoted the undertaking; we are informed that this street, which ran from the area of the Forum to Porta di Ercolano, was known as *Via Sarina*, or salt road, for the reasons mentioned above (just as the Porta di Ercolano was called *Veru Sarinu*, or Salt Gate). With relationship to the grid town plan of Pompeii, the Via Consolare follows an irregular route and, after being joined by one of the principal *decumani* of the city, the one comprised of Via di Nola - Via della Fortuna - Via delle Terme, it bends northwest and leads out the Porta di Ercolano. Along it lies the House of the Surgeon, one of the oldest houses in Pompeii (4th cent. B.C.)

56 - HOUSE OF SALLUST

This house is erroneously attributed to Sallust on account of the election propaganda on his behalf found on the facade. The real owner was A. Cossus Libanus, as can be read in a seal of his found inside the house. The core of the house belongs to the Samnite period and is built in the typical blocks of tufa (3rd cent. B.C.). A series of shops opens, on the facade, with a *pistrinum* (bakery) at the western corner, which still contains grindstones, and a *caupona* (tavern) with a counter for serving wine next to the entrance vestibule and communicating with the interior of the dwelling. The vestibule leads to a large Tuscan atrium with a central basin in tufa for collecting water. Part of the wall painting in Style I, stuccoed and painted in imitation of a facing of polychrome marble, is still extant. Various rooms are set around the atrium. They have tall doorways, that narrow towards the top, in a style typical of this period. Style I decorations still exist in some of these rooms.

A porticoed *hortus* with a summer triclinium covered with a pergola in the north corner stretches out beyond the tablinum.

The eastern sector of the house seems to belong to a second phase dating to the 1st cent. B.C. Reached from the atrium through a corridor, it consists of a garden with a peristyle surrounded by cubicles, a dining room, a kitchen. The back wall of the garden has a large fresco depicting the myth of Actaeon attacked by his dogs for having watched Diana at her bath.

Presumably the original Samnite house was transformed into an inn in the 1st cent. B.C., as the *caupona* which communicates with the interior and the considerable number of bedrooms, some of which are on a second floor that was built at the time, would seem to indicate. The eastern sector, also built then, must have been

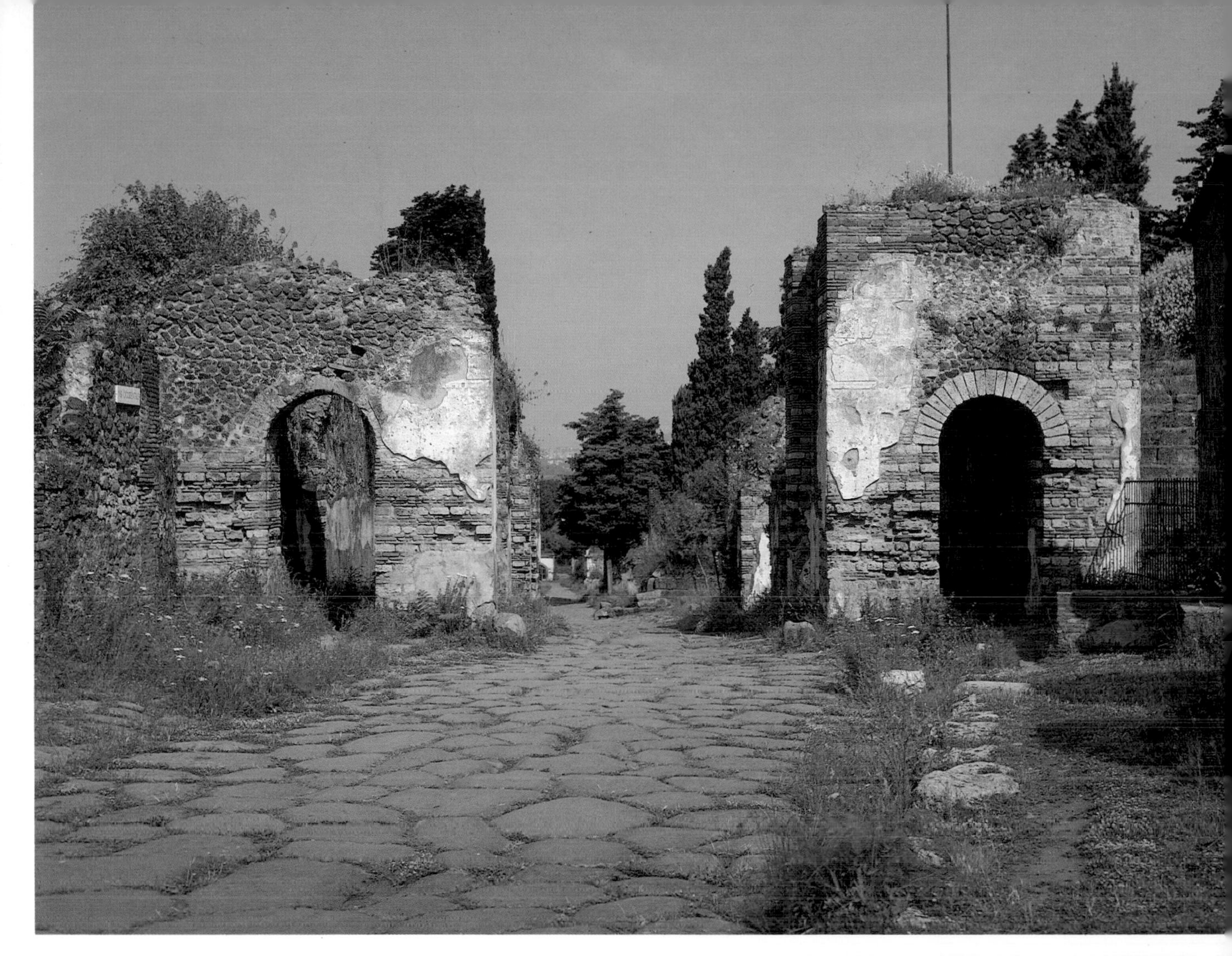

Above: the Porta Ercolano in the northwest corner of the city. Below: a detail of a smaller pedestrian passageway.

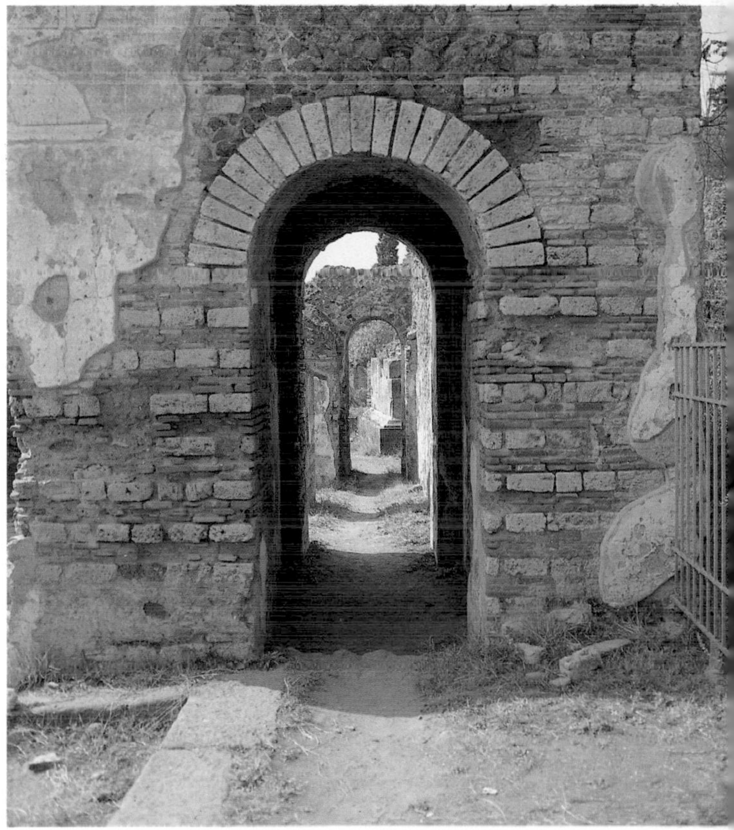

reserved for the private quarters of the owners and operators of the inn.

57 - PORTA ERCOLANO AND VIA SEPOLCRI

This gate is situated in the northwest corner of the city walls of Pompeii. Of the three passageways, the one in the center is larger to allow for the passage of vehicles, and the ones at the sides for pedestrians are smaller. It is built in a mixture of *opus listatum* with brick and tufa and *opus incertum* with lava stone.
In this last phase the gate dates to the years when Pompeii was transformed into a colony by Sulla and is later than the adjacent stretches of Samnite wall with the *agger* behind, in which even earlier stages have been identified. This gate is the starting point for the Via dei Sepolcri, the first stretch of the road that led to Herculaneum and Naples. It is customary for the cemeteries to extend along both sides of the roads outside the city gates. In this case monumental tombs alternate with *tabernai* and the villa of Cicero, that of the Mosaic Columns and that of Diomedes. These tombs range in date from Sulla's colony (80 B.C.) to the eruption of A.D. 79, except for a few groups

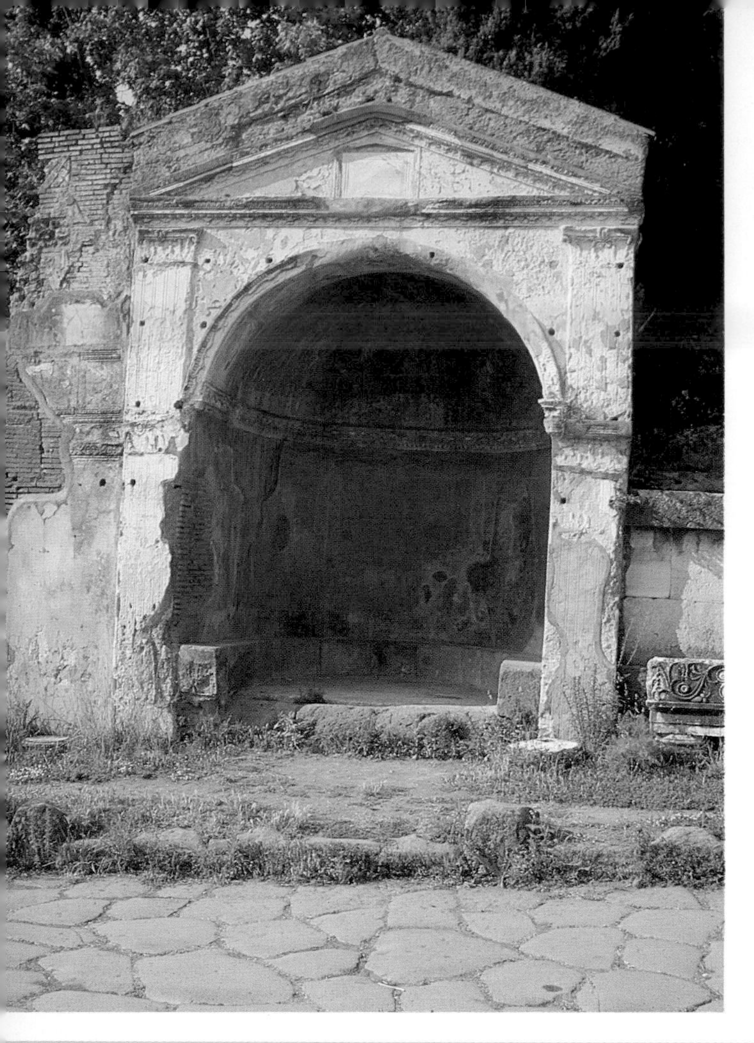

of Samnite *fossa* tombs, of the 4th-3rd cent. B.C. There are a variety of architectural types with aedicule tombs on a podium, altars that are elevated, fenced in or the *schola* type with a semicircular exedra.

58 - VILLA OF DIOMEDES

This large suburban villa lies along the Via dei Sepolcri and has erroneously been attributed to Marcus Arrius Diomedes, whose tomb faces the entrance. The house was excavated in 1771-1774, causing a great furor. Unfortunately most of the rich decoration it undoubtedly had no longer exists.
The villa, in a marvelous panoramic site, was certainly one of the largest houses in the city and its grandeur testifies to the considerable wealth some of the families in Pompeii had acquired.

Above: a semicircular exedra tomb. Below: the entrance portico to the Villa of Diomede.

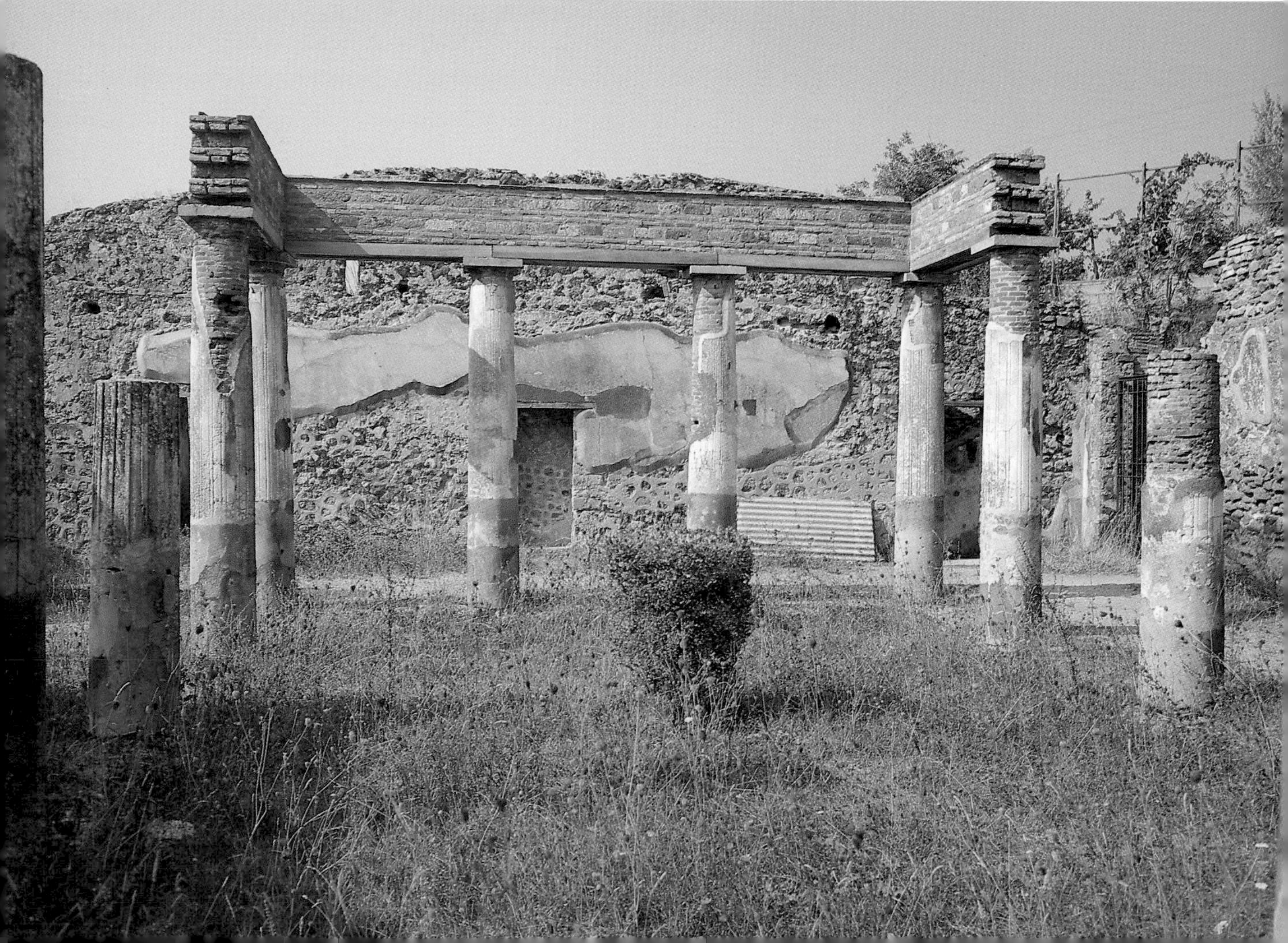

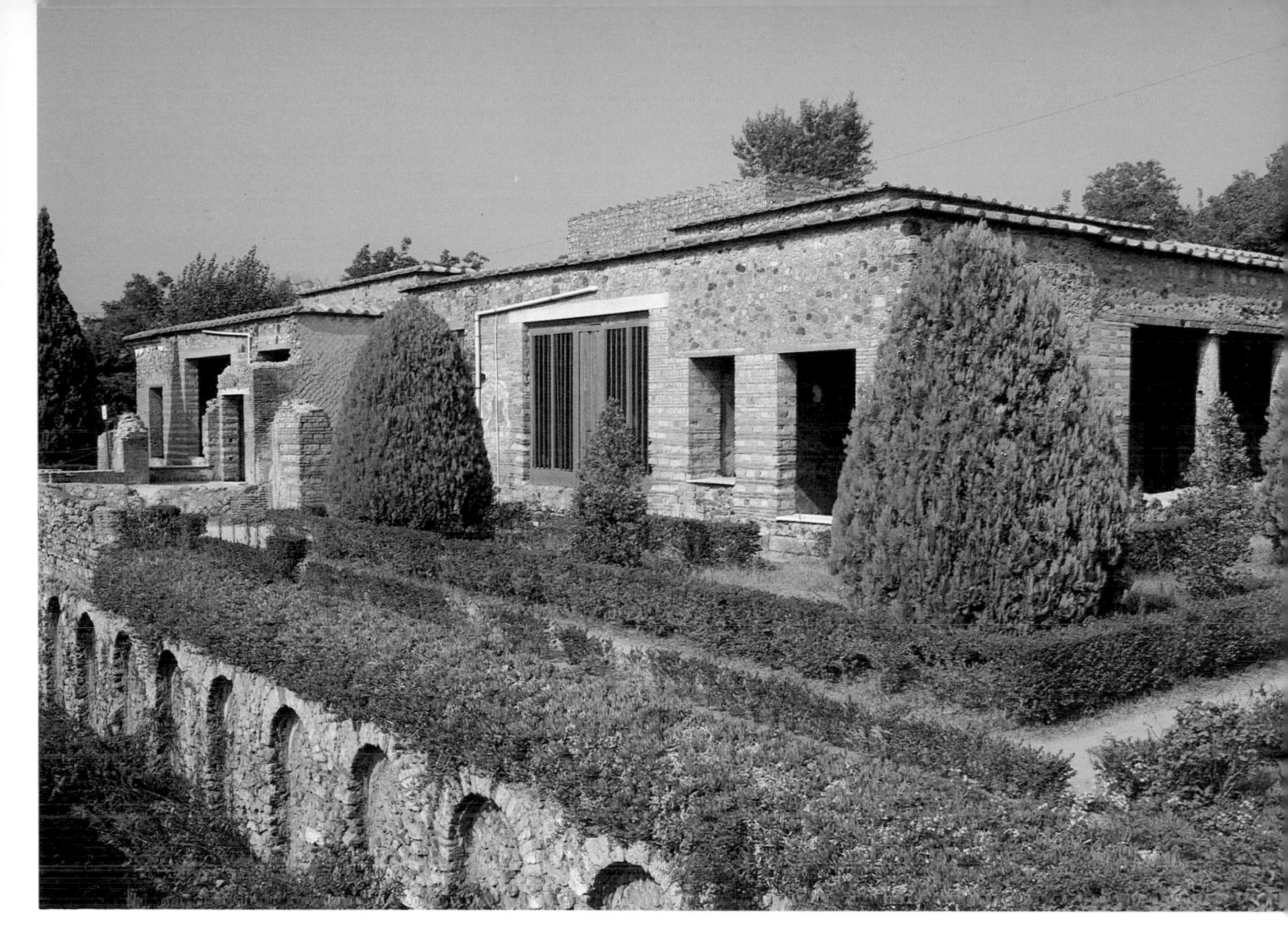

Above, the Villa of Mysteries.

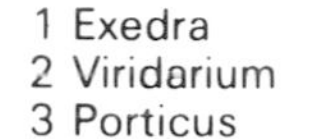

1 Exedra
2 Viridarium
3 Porticus
4 Atrium tuscanicum
5 Cubicula
6 Peristilium
7 Porticus

59 - VILLA OF MYSTERIES

The large complex of the Villa of Mysteries represents one of the most outstanding examples of suburban patrician villas in antiquity. The square ground plan is laid out on a plot of sloping land so that the western part was realized on an artificial earth fill and supported by a cryptoporticus. In its first phase the villa dates to the first half of the 2nd cent. B.C. but the layout as we know it is the result of remodelling between 70 and 60 B.C., at which time most of the wall painting was also executed. After the earthquake of A.D. 62 the villa underwent a radical transformation from the patrician dwelling it had been to a rustic villa, probably the result of a change in owners. The original entrance of the villa was on Via Superiore, a branch of Via dei Sepolcri, on the opposite side of its current entrance; it leads directly into the area of the peristyle with its sixteen Doric columns. This sector was transformed into servants' quarters with the addition of a series of lodgings on two floors in the space between the original facade of the villa and the Via Superiore. The kitchen courtyard with two ovens is on the south side of the peristyle. Next to it is the small bathing installation comprised of three rooms, including a circular *laconicum* which was no longer used and had been turned into a pantry. A cubicle with two alcoves and an *oecus* decorated in Style II look out on the small tetrastyle atrium

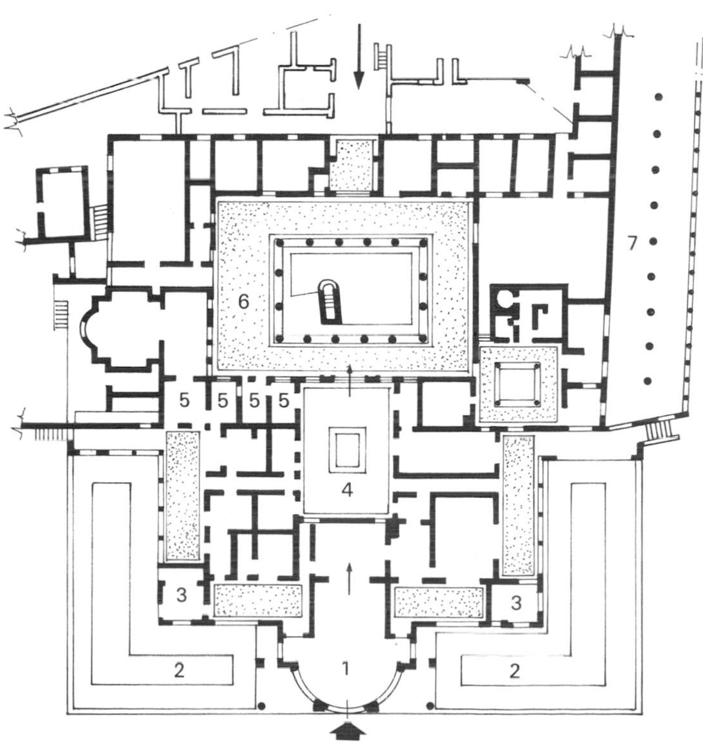

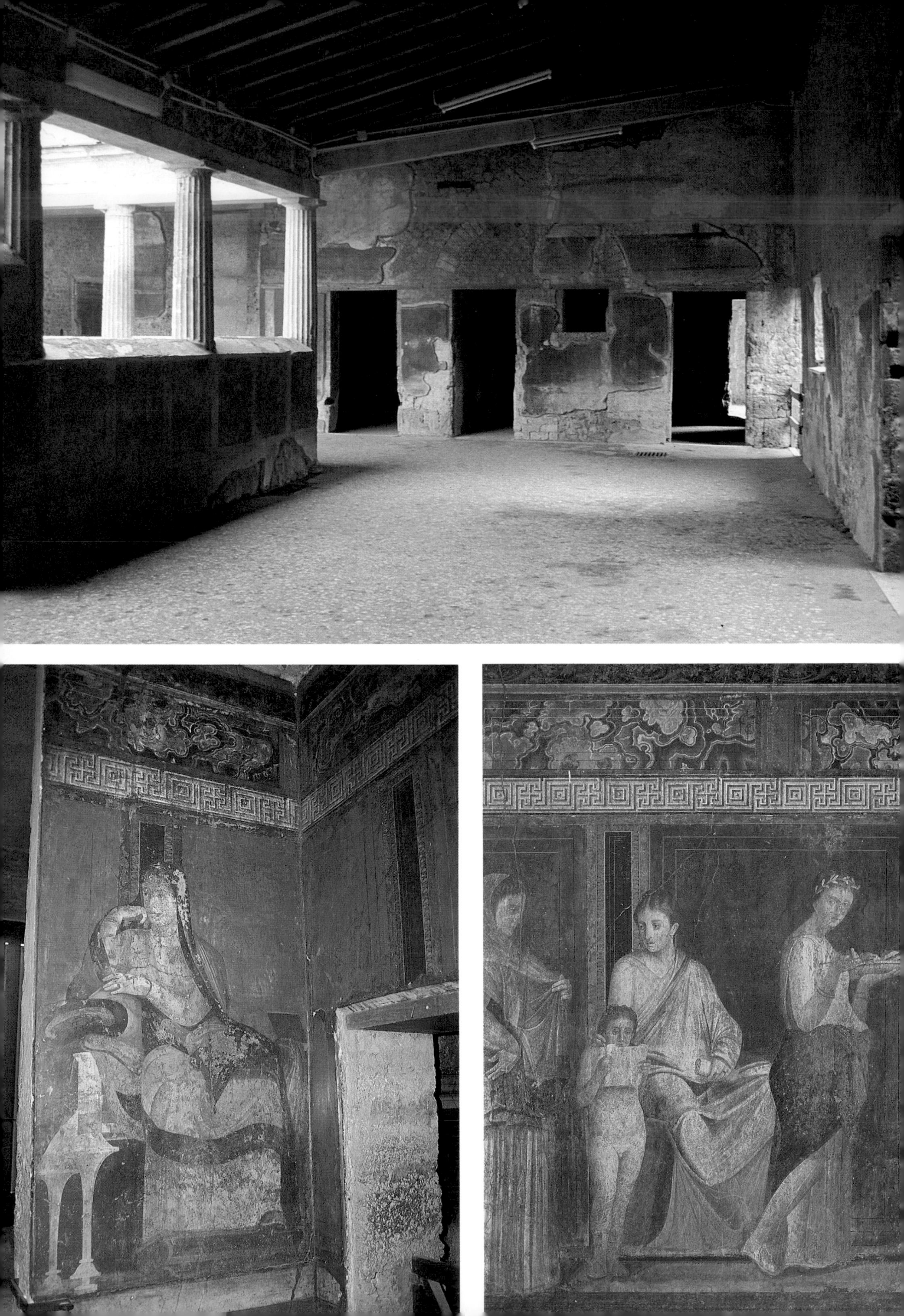

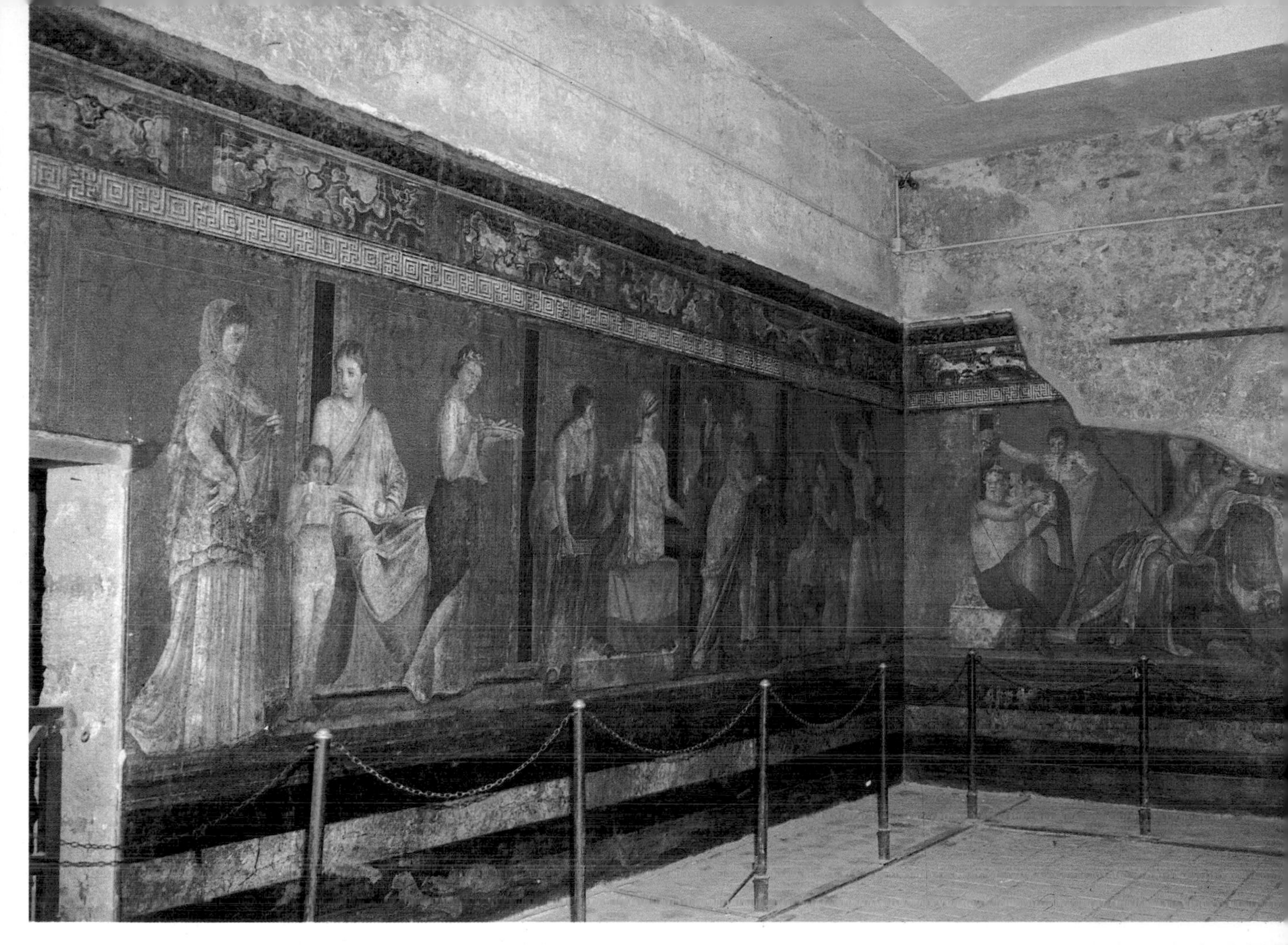

Opposite, above: the interior peristyle. Below, left: the mistress of the house and, on the right, the reading of the ritual. On this page above: the room with the Fresco of the Dionysiac mysteries; below: a satyr and a maenad with a fleeing figure.

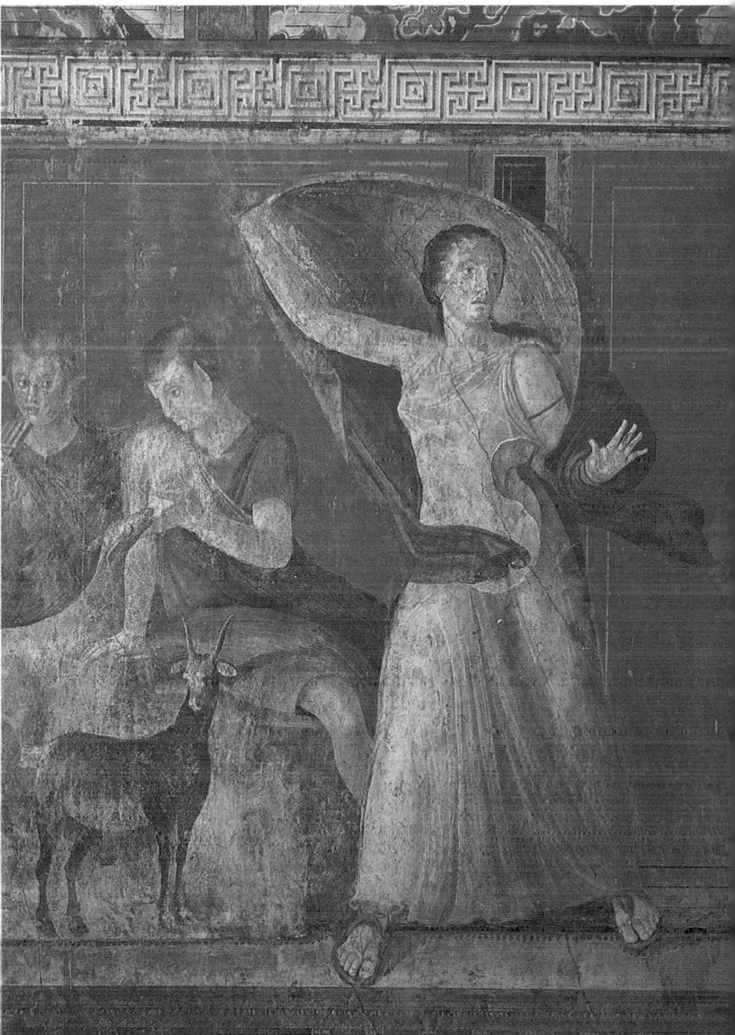

across the way. Near the northeast corner of the peristyle, two large rooms had been given over to the making of wine and a *torcularium* with two grape presses had been set up, confirming the fact that the villa had at this point been turned into a farm. Next to this is the lararium with an apse, probably where the statue of Livia found in the peristyle was originally located. The owner's living quarters are articulated around a large Tuscan atrium decorated with Nile landscapes. Originally there were also pictures on wooden panels. The cubicle with a double alcove in the north side of the atrium contains one of the most striking examples of Style II wall painting with bold and complex architectural prospects which are illusionistically articulated on various levels until they seem to break through the wall. The tablinum, on the back wall, has an elegant Style III pictorial dècor: Egyptian-style figurines and Dionysiac symbols are painted in miniature on the black-ground walls. Beyond the tablinum is an exedra-like veranda with windows, flanked by hanging gardens and two porticoed wings.
A cubicle with two alcoves situated to the south of the tablinum leads to the salon frescoed with the *megalographia* after which the villa is named, and which can also be reached from the southern portico. This may be the most famous painting of antiquity as a result of the unusual life-size dimensions of the figures and the imposing composition. Traditionally this cycle is interpreted as depicting the rites of initiation into Dionysiac mysteries.

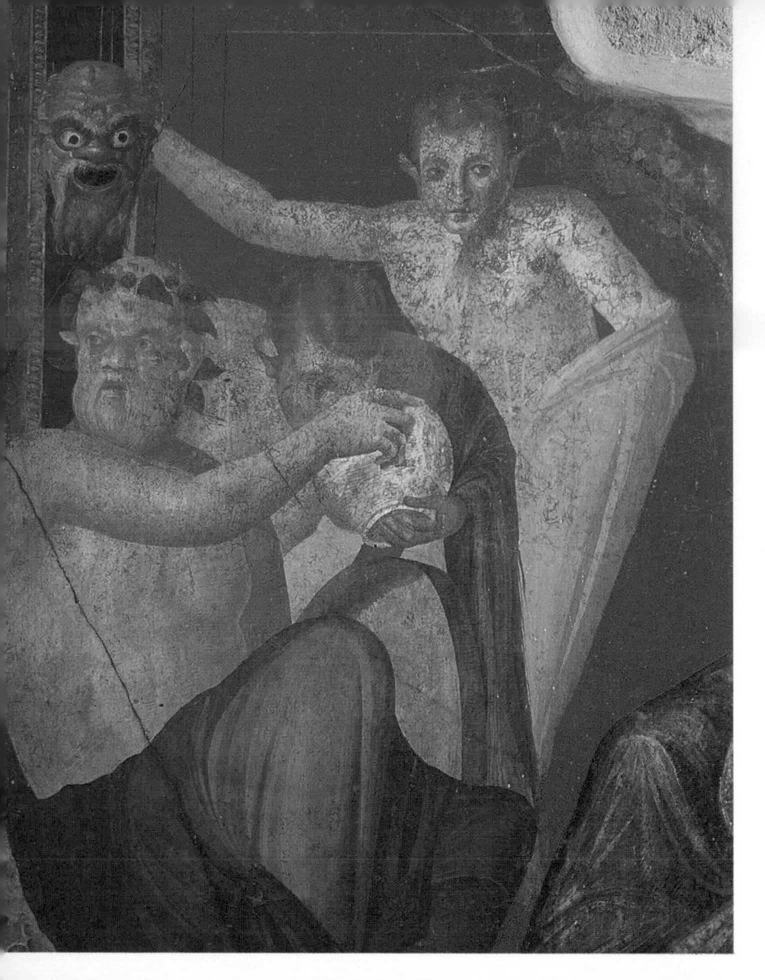

Beginning with the left wall the ritual is read by a nude boy between two matrons; a girl with a tray of offerings moves towards a seated sacrificing figure seen from the back, and assisted by two attendants; next come an old Silenus playing the lyre, a young satyr and a nymph (*panisca*) nursing a kid, a terrorized woman shown shrinking back and about to flee at the sight of the flagellation of one of her companions that is taking place in the opposite corner. The back wall begins with an old Silenus offering a young satire drink, while another satire raises a theater mask over his head; the center of the wall is occupied by Dionysius leaning back on the lap of Ariadne who is seated on a throne, followed by the unveiling of a phallus, symbol of fertility, by a kneeling woman, and a winged female flagellant about to strike. Ideally this is part of the scene on the right wall showing the flagellated woman, perturbed and kneeling with her head in a companion's lap, while a nude maenad dances in an orgy of ecstasy; then comes the preparation of a young bride, as she waits for the initiation rite, assisted by two cupids and a matron, and finally, a seated matron with her head covered, probably the owner of the house, who observes the entire scene.
The fresco must be attributed to a Campanian painter who worked in the villa around 70-60 B.C. and who was inspired by Hellenistic models of the 4th-3rd cent. B.C.

Left: a silenus offering a satyr drink. Below: the unveiling of the Dionysiac phallus. Opposite, above, the weeping scourged figure (on the left) and a dancer (on the right); below: woman sacrificing with servants and a silenus.

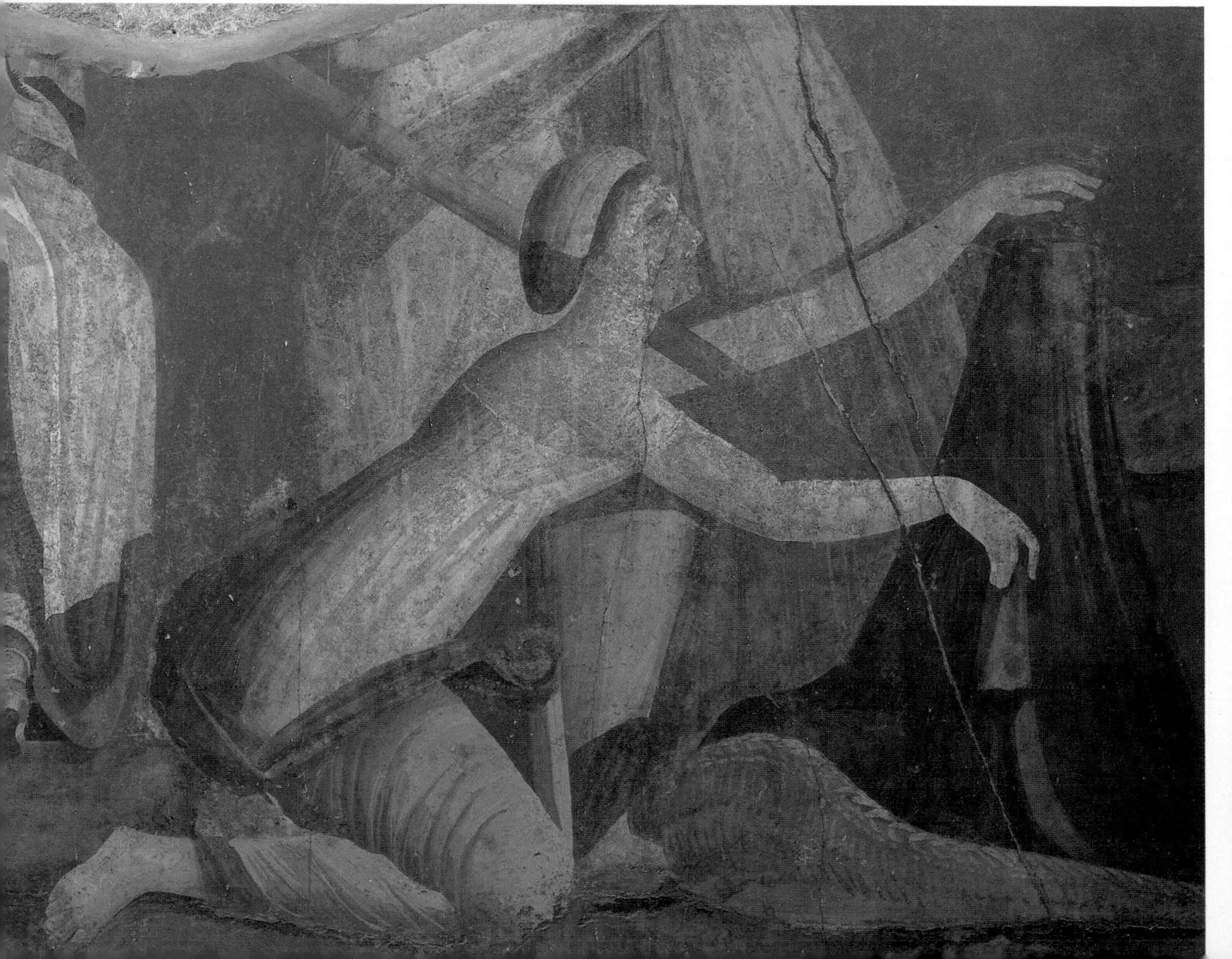

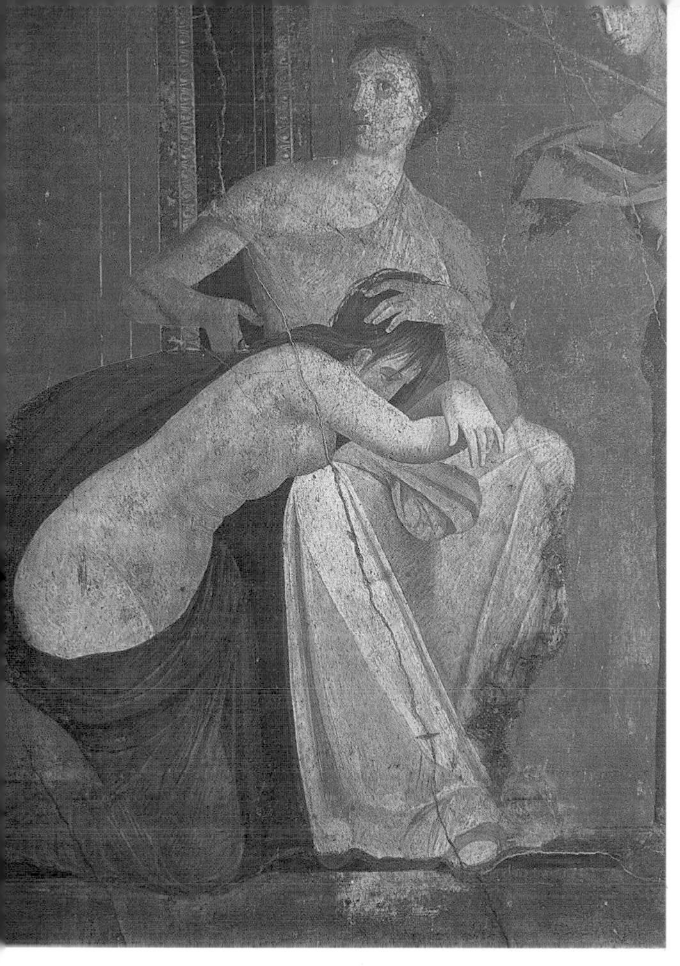
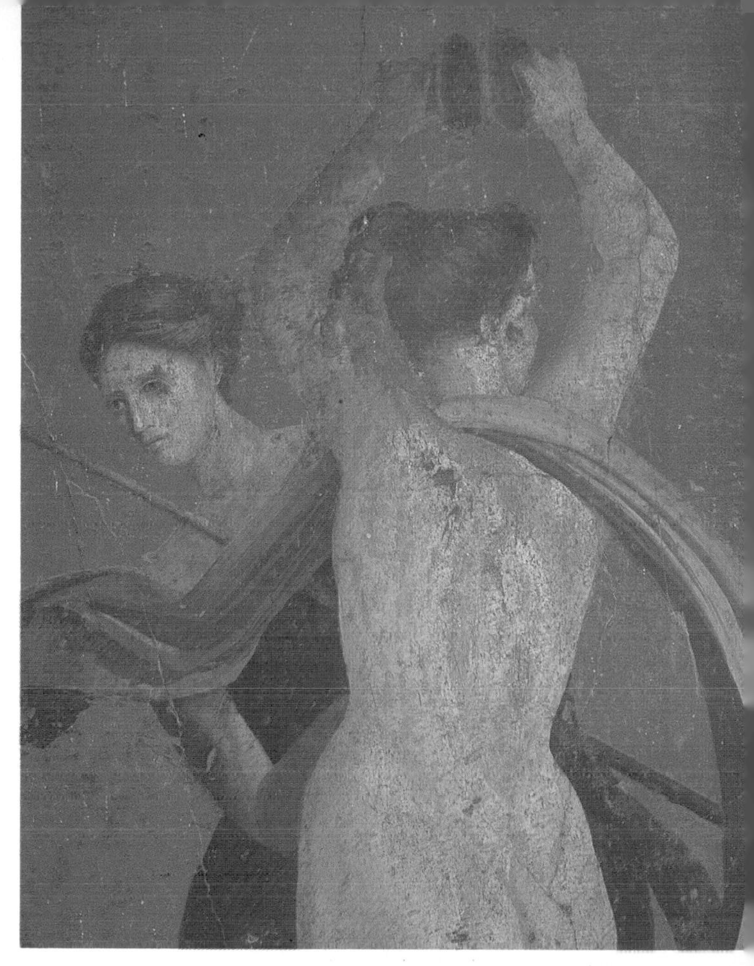
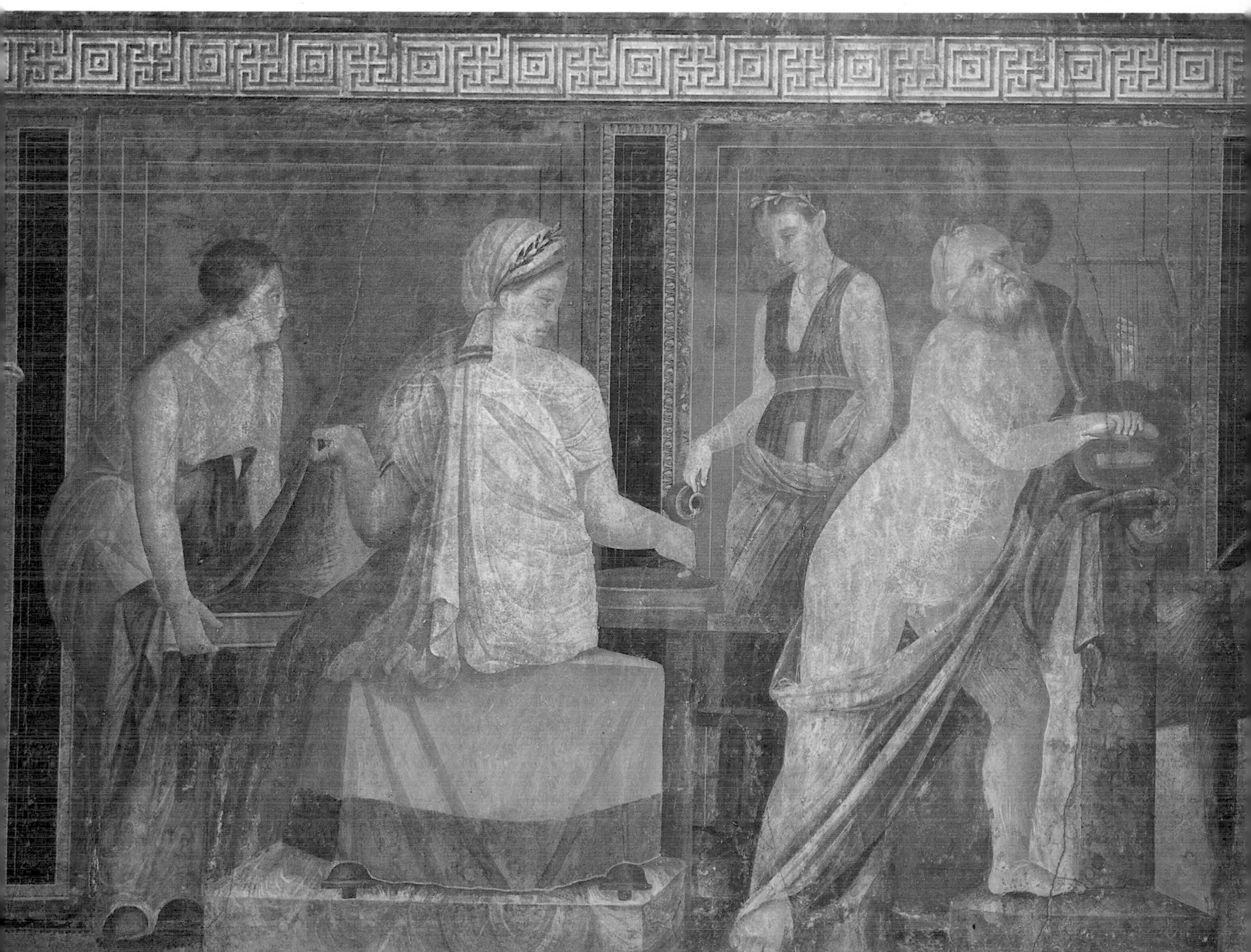

TABLE OF CONTENTS